MW01231455

FULLER GENEALOGIES

COMPILED, PUBLISHED AND FOR SALE BY

WILLIAM H FULLER

23 School St., Palmer, Mass.

[1914]

VOLUME I.

Genealogy of some descendants of Edward Fuller of the Mayflower.
I volume 8 vo., cloth, 25 illustrations, 306 pp.
Price, Postpaid, $5 00

VOLUME II.

Genealogy of some descendants of Dr. Samuel Fuller of the Mayflower
I volume, 8 vo , cloth 31 illustrations, 263 pp.
Price, Postpaid, $5.00

VOLUME III

Genealogy of some descendants of Captain Matthew Fuller, John Fuller
of Newton, John Fuller of Lynn, John Fuller of Ipswich, and Robert
Fuller of Dorchester and Dedham, with supplements to Vols. I and II.
8 vo., cloth, 14 Plates of illustrations, 325 pp.

Price, Postpaid, $5.00

LIST OF CONTENTS

———— - - -

PREFACE

This third volume of American Fuller Genealogy contains genealogical data concerning descendants of Captain Matthew Fuller, John Fuller of Newton, John Fuller of Lynn, John Fuller of Ipswich, and Robert Fuller of Dorchester and Dedham, immigrants who came to America before 1650

By correspondence with descendants, from items found in published family genealogies; and from examination of unpublished records, these genealogical lines have been extended from certain sources of information used as a basis, to the extent shown in the following pages.

These sources were, in general, the manuscripts of Prof H W Brainard of Hartford, Ct, Jackson's History, and the published and unpublished vital records of Newton, the vital records of Lynn, of Ipswich, and those of Dorchester and Dedham

The compiler feels quite sure that in a work of so much detail, there must be many errors, but hopes by careful attention given to have reduced them to the least that could be expected

The writer takes this opportunity to thank all those who have helped in any way the preparation of this volume

Supplements to Vols I and II contain much additional information, and research workers should not fail to examine them

WILLIAM HYSLOP FULLER

Palmer, Mass , Sept 1914

LIST OF ILLUSTRATIONS

ABBREVIATIONS

---

b, m, and d, for born, married, and died

bapt, for baptized

dau, for daughter.

Rec, for record

V R, for vital records

M Int Pub, for marriage intentions published

Gene, Genealogy

J P, Justice of the Peace

P M, Postmaster

G S, Gravestone.

Names of sons printed in heavy type indicate that they married and genealogies are to be found further on. State not given after name of town indicates town in Massachusetts.

AMERICAN FULLER GENEALOGY.

CAPTAIN MATTHEW FULLER LINE.

MATTHEW[1] FULLER, b. —— in England; d. in Barnstable, Aug., 1678; m. ——, Frances ——; b.——, in England; d.—— in Barnstable.

MATTHEW[1] FULLER probably b. 1603 in Redenhall Parish, in Harleston, Norfolk Co., England, came to America and settled in Plymouth, in 1640.

At this time he was married, and a parent. Of his early history, little is known, but he was doubtless acquiring the knowledge of surgery and military affairs which he afterwards put to good use. In April, 1642, ten acres of land were granted him in Plymouth, and in the same year he was juryman and propounded freeman of the Colony, but was not sworn and admitted until June 7, 1653. In 1643, he was appointed sergeant in the military company of the Colony, of which Miles Standish was captain. About 1650, he removed to Barnstable. In 1653, he represented that town in the Colony Court, and was already lieutenant of the militia there. June 20, 1654, he was appointed lieutenant under Capt. Standish of the Company of fifty men, the quota of Plymouth Colony, in the proposed expedition against the Dutch at Manhattan. All preparations had been made, when news of peace arrived and further service became unnecessary. Oct. 2, 1658, he was elected one of the Council of War, and in 1671 its chairman, and one of the magistrates of the Colony, and in the same year lieutenant of the forces to be sent against the Saconet Indians. Dec. 17, 1673, he was appointed Surgeon-General of the Colony troops, and also of those of Massachusetts, if that Colony approved. For this service he was allowed 4 shillings a day. In King Phillip's War he was captain of the Plymouth forces. In the Quaker controversy, Capt. Fuller took a noble stand in favor of religious toleration. He lived near neighbors to some of the most prominent of the Quakers, and was connected by marriage alliances with some who felt the severity of the laws passed against the sect. He went so far as to censure this law in strong terms in public. For this he was fined by the magistrates. Though indiscreet in speech, the court continued to confer offices of trust and honor upon him,—a most unusual course which shows that his honor and bravery were never doubted In his public and private life he was a man of sound judgment, of good understanding, faithful in performance of duty, liberal in politics tolerant in religion Captain Fuller was also the first regular physician settled in Barnstable His homestead was in the northwest corner of Barnstable, at Scorton Neck He also possessed large tracts in Falmouth and Middleboro, granted for the eminent services he had rendered the Colony His will was dated July 25, 1678 and was proved Oct 30th following His estate was appraised at £1667,04,06, a very large amount for those times Among the items is the following 'Pearls, precious stones and diamonds, at a guess, £200 "

Inventory dated Aug 22, 1676   £1677.04 06

Barnstable Probate Rec

Children

2   Mary², b about 1625 , m April 17, 1650*, Ralph Jones, the Quaker, of Barnstable , many descendants She probably died before 1691, for she is not mentioned in Jones' will of 11th of 3rd month, 1691

    Children Mehitabel³, b 1651 , Matthew³, , Shubael³, Aug 27, 1654, Jedediah³, Jan 4, 1656, John³, Aug 14, 1659, Mercy³, Nov 14, 1666; Ralph³, Oct 1. 1669 , Samuel³, Ephraim³, Mary³

3   Elizabeth², b ——, m April 22, 1652, Moses Rowley, of Falmouth, and East Haddam, Ct She was living in East Haddam in 1714, and earlier All the Rowley families of Falmouth, and East Haddam, Colchester, Chatham, Winchester, Sharon, and Kent, Ct , are descendants

    Children Mary³, b March 20, 1653 , Moses³, Nov 10, 1654, Shubael³, Jan 11, 1660, Mehitabel³ Jan 11, 1660 , Sarah³, Sept 16, 1662, Aaron³, May 1, 1666 , John³, Oct 22, 1667; Matthew³, Nathan³

4   **Samuel²**, b ——, m Mary——

5   **John²**, b ——, m 1, Bethiah —— m 2, Hannah Morton

6   Anne², b——, m Samuel³ Fuller, (*Samuel²*, *Edward¹*)   See Vol 1, page 33

WILL OF CAPTAIN MATTHEW FULLER

This will is recorded in volume three, page 127 of the Plymouth Colony wills and inventories A verbatim copy is found in a volume in the registry of Probate at Barnstable, from which this is copied.

"The five and twentieth day of July In the veere of our Lord one thousand six hundred seaventy and eight, I Matthew Fuller of the Towne of Barnstable in the Collonie of New Plymouth, Being sicke of body, but of Good and perfect memory, thanks be unto almighty God, and Calling to Remembrance the uncertaine state of this transitory life and that all Flesh must yield unto Death. when it shall please God to Call, doe make Constitute and ordaine and declare this my last will and Testament, In manor and forme following, Revoking and Anulling by these presence all and every testament and Testaments will and wills heertofore by mee made and declared either by word or writing, and this to be taken onely

Children Susannah[4] b Jan 12, 1689-90, Joseph[4], Oct
28, 1691, James[4], Dec 18, 1693, Anne[4]. Nov 8, 1695, Matthew[4].
July 10, 1697; Ebenezer[4], March 21, 1698-9, Daniel[4], April 11,
1700, David[4], May 24, 1703, Elizabeth[4], April 19, 1704, Thomas[4],
Feb 6, 1705-6; Mary[4], Dec 22, 1707, Jemima[4], Nov 9, 1709,
Benjamin[4], Dec. 5, 1711, Ebenezer[4], Sept 26, 1714

12 Abigail[3], b

13 **Samuel**[3], b ——1676, m Elizabeth Thacher

5. JOHN[2] FULLER, (*Matthew*[1]), b ——; d in Barnstable 1691-2; m,
1, Bethiah ——, m 2, Mai 24, 1687, Hannah Morton, who survived
him, and m Dec 9, 1695 Capt John Lathrop, of Barnstable

John Fuller resided on the parental estate, at Scorton Neck He was
a physician of some note

His children were

14 Lydia[3], b ——1675, d Nov 6, 1755, in Ct, perhaps at Mansfield, in May 12, 1699, Joseph Dimmock, and had Thomas[4], b
1700, Bethiah[4], 1702, Mehitable[4], 1707, Ensign[4], 1709, Ichabod[4], 1711, Abigail[4], 1714, Pharoah[4], 1717, David[4], 1721

15 Bethiah[3], b Dec 1687; d, Oct 26, 1714, m Feb 20, 1706, Barnabas Lathrop, and had John[4], b Aug 25, 1709, and Hannah[4]
July 16, 1712

16 **John**[3], b Oct 1689, m Thankful Gorham

17 Reliance[3], b Sept 8, 1691, d at Southold, R I, m John Prince
and had John[4], b Aug 10, 1716, Joseph[4]. May 10, 1718,
Rebecca[4], Sept 9, 1719, Benjamin[4], Samuel[4], April 24, 1724,
Hannah[4], Dec 13, 1728

THIRD GENERATION.

7. THOMAS[3] FULLER, (*Samuel*[2], *Matthew*[1]), b about 1661 in Barnstable; d. in his 68th year, according to his gravestone at West Barnstable However, the evidence of the probate records is strong proof
that he d in Nov 1718

He was Captain of the Barnstable militia company, thus worthily
imitating his father and grandfather

He m Dec 29, 1680, Elizabeth Lathrop, who survived him, but the
date of her decease is not found

Children—b in Barnstable

18 Hannah[4], Nov 17, 1681, m Jabez Burseley

19. **Joseph**[4], July 12, 1683, m. Joanna Crocker

20 Mary[4], Aug 6, 1685, d Oct 23, 1756, m Sept 1, 1731, William
Green No Chn

21 **Benjamin**[4], Aug 6, 1690, m, Rebecca Bodfish

22 Elizabeth[4], Sept 3, 1692 m, Oct 31, 1726, Isaac Crocker and settled in East Haddam, Ct, but removed to Colchester, Ct 1729
They had Elizabeth[5], Aug 26, 1727, Mary[5], April 30, 1829, Abigail[5], March 10, 1733.

23   **Samuel⁴**, April 12, 1694, m. Melatiah Bodfish
24   Abigail⁴, Jan 9, 1695-6, d Oct 5, 1724, at Barnstable, m Oct 25, 1721, Jacob Chipman, and left two daughters, Sarah⁵, b Nov 23, 1722, and Abigail⁵, June 16, 1724
25   John⁴, bap April 19, 1696, probably d young   Not named in his father's will

8. JABEZ³ FULLER, (*Samuel²*, *Matthew¹*) b about 1663, in Barnstable, d before June 20 1712, in Middleboro, m about 1686, Mary, dau of Joseph and Elizabeth (Gorham) Hallett, of Sandwich   This marriage is proved by an entry in Plymouth Probate Records, Vol III, pp 131, 348   Children b in Barnstable

26   Samuel⁴, Feb 23, 1687, d before June 24, 1715, leaving no issue
27   **Jonathan⁴**, March 10, 1692, m 1, Eleanor Bennett m 2, Hannah Harlow
28   Mercy⁴, April 1 1693, m April 5, 1716, Jabez, son of Samuel Wood, of Middleboro
29   Lois⁴, Sept 23, 1704, m Nov 25, 1725, Thomas Foster, of Marshfield
30   **Ebenezer⁴** Feb 20, 1707-8, m Martha Jones
31   Mary⁴, about 1710, m James Bearse, Jr
32   Hannah⁴, b ——, mentioned in "Genealogy of Maine families"

9. TIMOTHY³ FULLER, (*Samuel²*, *Matthew¹*), b about 1670, in Barnstable; d Nov 30, 1748, at East Haddam, Ct , m 1, about 1694, Sarah Gates, b March 16, 1670, in Haddam, d about 1712, dau. of Capt George and Sarah (Olmstead) Gates, of Haddam, m 2, about 1714, Mary Champion, b July 31, 1693, in Lyme. Ct , d Dec 12, 1770, at East Haddam, aged 78 years, dau of Thomas and Hannah (Brockway) Champion of Lyme   His will dated Oct 27, 1747, is found in Prob Rec, at Colchester, Ct and mentions four sons; five daughters, wife Mary   His negro man Salem, and negro girl Lois, were left to wife Mary Fuller

Timothy Fuller owned land in East Haddam as early as April 7, 1696 He and wife Sarah were members of the church at East Haddam in 1707, both were buried in the old graveyard near Salmon River Cove He was town blacksmith

Children

33   Timothy⁴, b Aug 29, 1695; d 1714
34   Mary⁴, b Dec 19, 1697; d unmarried
35   **Matthias⁴** b March 24, 1700, m 1, Mary Cone; m 2, Mrs Jemima (Richardson) Hungerford
36   Sarah⁴, b Aug 7, 1702, m April 19, 1722, John Gates, her cousin, at Westchester Parish, Colchester, Ct   She d Aug 25, 1784. Children   Sarah⁵, b Aug 10, 1725, John⁵, Aug 19, 1728; Nehemiah⁵. April 17, 1730; Matthias⁵, Feb. 13, 1733-4, Ezra⁵, July 20, 1736

37 Abigail[4], b July 5, 1704; d 1714

38 Ann[4], b Aug 29, 1707; m Samuel Gates 2d, of East Haddam,
    March 16, 1743, she d Dec 27, 1793 He was b Aug 14, 1715,
    and d Dec, 1788 Her will, dated East Haddam, Aug 17, 1781,
    proves conclusively that Timothy[3] Fuller, m. 2d, Mary Cham-
    pion, for she calls children of both Sarah the first wife, and
    Mary the second, her brothers and sisters I find no record of
    children, and in her will she mentions none

39 **Samuel[4]**, b Sept 1, 1711; m Mercy Price

40 Timothy[4], bap 1715, d young.

41 Mary[4], bap 1717, d. young.

42 Abigail[4], b Oct 19, 1718, m Dec 4, 1746, Deacon and Lieutenant
    Joseph Gates, of East Haddam, b March 28, 1722, d April 17,
    1808 She d Sept 9 1801
      Children Abigail[5], b April 22, 1749, Anne[5], March 21,
    1751; Joseph[5], May 9, 1754, Susannah[5], March 14, 1756, Abi-
    gail[5], Sept 9, 1760

43 Hannah[4], b July 3, 1720; d, before 1768, m Stephen Olmstead of
    Middletown, Ct This Stephen Olmstead was son of John and
    Susannah Olmstead of East Haddam, b Aug 7, 1721 He was
    a Revolutionary Captain, and d of smallpox, April 26, 1778
    He m 2d, Mary ——
      Children Stephen[5], a Baptist Minister, 40 years at Shodack,
    N Y, Johnathan[5], a merchant at Hamilton, N Y, and a bene-
    factor of the college there, Dorathy[5], b 1752, m March 1,
    1776, Elijah Day and d Aug 4, 1846, aged 94 years: Hannah[5],
    Susannah[5], m Jared Parmalee, Anna[5], Mercy[5], Aurelia[5].

44 **Timothy[4]**, b May 30, 1722, m Thankful Gray

45 Noadiah[4], bap July 19, 1724, d young

46 **Thomas[4]** b June 24, 1726, m Hannah Dimmock

47 Mary[4], b March 18, 1731, m Jan 25, 1753, Jedediah Spencer of
    East Haddam
      Children Thaddeus[5], b Sept 16, 1754, Hannah[5], Oct 21,
    1756, Olive[5], Sept 24, 1758, Jonathan[5], Aug 15, 1760, Loley[5],
    Sept 8, 1762, Mary[5], May 21, 1765; Phoebe[5], May 9, 1767; Jede-
    diah[5], July 2, 1769

13. SAMUEL[3] FULLER, (*Samuel[2]*, *Matthew[1]*), b 1676, in Barnstable, d.
Sept 29, 1716, in Mansfield, Ct, m Oct 3, 1700, Elizabeth Thatcher, b
March 1, 1672, in Duxbury

Samuel Fuller resided in Preston and Mansfield, Ct He is called
Sergeant

Children

48 Rebecca[4], July 22, 1701, d 1778, at Scotland, Ct, m. April
    29, 1724, Joseph Allen, of Preston, and had Barnabas[5], b 1730
    (m Elizabeth Fuller dau of Rodolphus Fuller); Jemima[5],
    Betty[5], 1734, Mary[5], 1736; Joseph[5], 1739, Samuel[5], 1740, Ashbel[5],
    1742

49 **Rodolphus[4]**, Aug 22, 1703, m 1, Anne Hall; m 2 Anne Robin-
    son

50 Ruth[4], April 12, 1706; d June 9 1795; in Scotland, Ct, m June
    20, 1725, Peter Robinson, and had Samuel[5], July 6, 1726,
    Experience[5], April 22, 1728, Peter[5], May 19, 1730, Elizabeth[5],

2

23   **Samuel**, April 12, 1694, m, Melatiah Bodfish
24   Abigail', Jan 9, 1695-6, d Oct 5, 1724, at Barnstable, m Oct. 25, 1721, Jacob Chipman, and left two daughters, Sarah⁵, b Nov 23, 1722, and Abigail⁵, June 16, 1724
25   John', bap April 19, 1696, probably d young Not named in his father's will

8. JABEZ³ FULLER, (*Samuel²*, *Matthew¹*), b about 1663, in Barnstable; d before June 20 1712, in Middleboro m about 1686 Mary dau of Joseph and Elizabeth (Gorham) Hallett, of Sandwich This marriage is proved by an entry in Plymouth Probate Records, Vol III, pp 131, 348 Children b in Barnstable

26   Samuel⁴, Feb 23, 1687, d before June 24, 1715, leaving no issue
27   **Jonathan**', March 10, 1692, m 1, Eleano. Bennett m 2, Hannah Harlow
28   Mercy⁴, April 1, 1693, m April 5, 1716. Jabez, son of Samuel Wood, of Middleboro
29   Lois⁴, Sept 23, 1704, m Nov 25, 1725, Thomas Foster, of Marshfield
30   **Ebenezer**⁴ Feb 20, 1707-8; m Martha Jones
31   Mary⁴, about 1710, m James Bearse, Jr
32   Hannah⁴, b ——, mentioned in "Genealogy of Maine families"

9. TIMOTHY³ FULLER, (*Samuel²*, *Matthew¹*), b about 1670, in Barnstable; d Nov 30, 1748, at East Haddam, Ct , m. 1, about 1694, Sarah Gates, b March 16, 1670, in Haddam; d about 1712, dau of Capt George and Sarah (Olmstead) Gates, of Haddam, m 2, about 1714, Mary Champion, b July 31, 1693, in Lyme, Ct , d Dec. 12, 1770, at East Haddam, aged 78 years, dau of Thomas and Hannah (Brockway) Champion of Lyme His will dated Oct 27, 1747, is found in Prob Rec, at Colchester, Ct and mentions four sons, five daughters, wife Mary His negro man Salem, and negro girl Lois, were left to wife Mary Fuller

Timothy Fuller owned land in East Haddam as early as April 7, 1696 He and wife Sarah were members of the church at East Haddam in 1707, both were buried in the old graveyard near Salmon River Cove He was town blacksmith

Children

33   Timothy⁴, b Aug. 29, 1695, d 1714
34   Mary⁴, b Dec 19, 1697; d unmarried
35   **Matthias**⁴ b March 24, 1700, m. 1, Mary Cone, m 2, Mrs Jemima (Richardson) Hungerford
36   Sarah⁴, b. Aug. 7, 1702, m April 19, 1722, John Gates, her cousin, at Westchester Parish, Colchester, Ct She d Aug 25, 1784 Children Sarah⁵, b. Aug 10, 1725; John⁵, Aug 19, 1728, Nehemiah⁵, April 17, 1730, Matthias⁵, Feb 13, 1733-4; Ezra⁵, July 20, 1736

37 Abigail⁴, b. July 5, 1704, d 1714
38 Ann⁴, b Aug 29, 1707, m Samuel Gates 2d, of East Haddam, March 16, 1743; she d Dec 27, 1793 He was b Aug 14, 1715, and d Dec, 1788 Her will, dated East Haddam, Aug 17, 1781, proves conclusively that Timothy³ Fuller, m. 2d, Mary Champion, for she calls children of both Sarah the first wife, and Mary the second, her brothers and sisters. I find no record of children, and in her will she mentions none
39 **Samuel⁴**, b Sept 1, 1711, m Mercy Price
40 Timothy⁴, bap 1715, d young
41 Mary⁴, bap 1717; d young
42 Abigail⁴, b Oct. 19, 1718, m Dec 4, 1746, Deacon and Lieutenant Joseph Gates, of East Haddam, b March 28, 1722, d April 17, 1808 She d Sept 9 1801
    Children   Abigail⁵, b April 22, 1749, Anne⁵, March 21, 1751, Joseph⁵, May 9, 1754, Susannah⁵, March 14, 1756; Abigail⁵, Sept. 9, 1760
43 Hannah⁴, b July 3, 1720; d, before 1768; m Stephen Olmstead of Middletown, Ct This Stephen Olmstead was son of John and Susannah Olmstead of East Haddam, b. Aug 7, 1721 He was a Revolutionary Captain, and d of smallpox, April 26, 1778. He m 2d, Mary ——
    Children   Stephen⁵, a Baptist Minister, 40 years at Shodack, N Y , Johnathan⁵, a merchant at Hamilton, N Y and a benefactor of the college there, Dorathy⁵, b 1752, m March 1, 1776, Elijah Day and d Aug 4, 1846, aged 94 years, Hannah⁵, Susannah⁵, m Jared Parmalee. Anna⁵, Mercy⁵, Aurelia⁵.
44 **Timothy⁴**, b May 30, 1722, m Thankful Gray
45 Noadiah⁴, bap July 19, 1724, d young
46 **Thomas⁴** b. June 24, 1726, m Hannah Dimmock
47 Mary⁴, b March 18, 1731, m Jan 25, 1753, Jedediah Spencer of East Haddam
    Children   Thaddeus⁵, b Sept 16, 1754; Hannah⁵, Oct 21, 1756, Olive⁵, Sept 24, 1758, Jonathan⁵, Aug 15, 1760, Loley⁵, Sept 8, 1762, Mary⁵, May 21, 1765, Phoebe⁵, May 9, 1767, Jedediah⁵, July 2, 1769

13. SAMUEL² FULLER, (*Samuel² Matthew¹*), b 1676, in Barnstable, d Sept 29, 1716, in Mansfield, Ct , m. Oct 3, 1700, Elizabeth Thatcher, b March 1, 1672, in Duxbury
Samuel Fuller resided in Preston and Mansfield. Ct He is called Sergeant
    Children
48 Rebecca⁴, July 22, 1701, d 1778, at Scotland, Ct ; m April 29, 1724, Joseph Allen, of Preston, and had Barnabas⁵, b 1730. (m. Elizabeth Fuller, dau of Rodolphus Fuller), Jemima⁵; Betty⁵, 1734; Mary⁵, 1736, Joseph⁵, 1739, Samuel⁵, 1740; Ashbel⁵, 1742
49 **Rodolphus⁴**, Aug 22, 1703, m 1, Anne Hall, m 2 Anne Robinson.
50 Ruth⁴, April 12, 1706, d June 9, 1795, in Scotland, Ct , m June 20, 1725, Peter Robinson, and had Samuel⁵, July 6, 1726, Experience⁵, April 22, 1728; Peter⁵, May 19, 1730, Elizabeth⁵,

2

Nov 6, 1732, Jacob⁵, Aug 14, 1734, Nathan⁶, July 19, 1736; Abner⁶, Feb 22, 1738 Ruth⁶, Dec 14, 1740, Elias⁵, Aug 22, 1742; Rachel⁶, March 30 1744, Bathsheba⁶, July 31, 1746, Joshua⁵, Sept 24, 1748

51   **Elkanah⁴**, April 24, 1709, m Mary Andrews

52   Waitstill⁴, April 8, 1711, m Feb 21, 1733-4, Thomas Heath

53   Mary⁴, April 5, 1713

54   **Judah⁴**, Aug 25 1715, m Abigail Wentworth

16. JOHN³ FULLER, (*John²*, *Matthew¹*), b Oct, 1689 at Barnstable, d there July 20, 1732, aged 42 years, but his grave stone inscription is, Lieut John Fuller July 24, 1732, in the 43rd year of his age "

He m June 16, 1710, Thankful Gorham, b Feb 15, 1690-1

Children born in Barnstable.

55   Hannah⁴, April 1, 1711, m Sept 3, 1730? Matthias Smith

56   **John⁴**, Aug 3, 1712, m Temperance Gorham

57   Mary⁴, Sept 1, 1715; m Aug 11, 1737, Seth Lathrop She d and he m 2d Aug 8, 1763, Mary⁵ Fuller (No 1, 2d group) of Sandwich, who d Jan 18, 1809, aged 95 years
       Children—all by 1st w Mary   Nathaniel⁵, Dec 27, 1739, Joseph⁵, May 1, 1742, Thankful⁵ Aug 2, 1741, John⁵, April 5 1745, Thankful⁵, Feb 18, 1746-7, Mary⁵, March 24, 1748-9, Benjamin⁵, July 1, 1753, Seth⁵, Dec 1756, Thomas⁵, July 4, 1758

58   Bethiah⁴, Sept 1, 1715 m Dec 20, 1739, Joseph Bursley, Jr, of Barnstable, and had John⁵, Nov 1, 1741, Bethiah⁵, March 2 1743, Lemuel⁵, March 2, 1745, Sarah⁵, Oct 24, 1748, Abigail⁵, Oct 23, 1750, Joseph⁵, March 27, 1757

59   Nathaniel⁴, Dec 10, 1716, m Abigail Hinckley

60   Thankful⁴, Sept 19, 1718, d Jan. 20, 1759 m Oct 25, 1739, Nathan Bassett, Jr, of Middleboro, and had Mary⁵, Sept 22, 1740, Bethiah⁵, Sept 4 1747; Nathan⁵, Dec 30, 1750, Cornelius⁵, Jan 20, 1753, N S John⁵, May 21, 1756, Gersham⁵, Feb 26 1758, Thankful⁵ Nov 30, 1761

Explanation of Group Arrangememt.

Sons of the third generation who married and had children, are made the heads of the groups, and the genealogy of each group is completed by itself with individual numbering relative to the groups

SUCH SONS FORM HEADS OF 14 GROUPS

Group Number	Individual Number	LINEAGE	Place of Birth
1	19	Joseph[4], *Thomas[3] Samuel[2], Matthew[1]*	Barnstable
2	21	Benjamin[4], *Thomas[3], Samuel[2], Matthew[1]*	Barnstable
3	23	Samuel.[4] *Thomas[3], Samuel[2], Matthew[1]*	Barnstable
4	27	Jonathan[4], *Jabez[3], Samuel[2], Matthew[1]*	Barnstable
5	30	Ebenezer[4], *Jabez[3], Samuel[2], Matthew[1]*	Barnstable
6	35	Matthias[4], *Timothy[3], Samuel[2], Matthew[1]*	East Haddam, Ct
7	39	Samuel[4], *Timothy[3], Samuel[2], Matthew[1]*.	East Haddam, Ct
8	44	Timothy[4], *Timothy[3], Samuel[2], Matthew[1]*	East Haddam, Ct
9	46	Thomas[4], *Timothy[3], Samuel[2], Matthew[1]*	East Haddam, Ct
10	49	Rodolphus[4], *Samuel[3], Samuel[2], Matthew[1]*	Preston, Ct
11	51	Elkannah[4], *Samuel[3], Samuel[2], Matthew[1]*	Mansfield Ct
12	54	Judah[4], *Samuel[3], Samuel[2], Matthew[1]*	Preston, Ct
13	56	John[4], *John[3], John[2], Matthew[1]*	Barnstable
14	59	Nathaniel[4] *John[3], John[2], Matthew[1]*	Barnstable

FIRST GROUP

FOURTH GENERATION.

JOSEPH[4] FULLER, AND SOME OF HIS DESCENDANTS.

19. JOSEPH[4] FULLER, (*Thomas[3], Samuel[2], Matthew[1]*), b July 12, 1683, at Barnstable, d there Sept 24, 1745, m Feb 9, 1708-9, Joanna Crocker, b July 18, 1687, d April 13, 1766, dau of Sergt Joseph and Temperance (Bursley) Crocker, of West Barnstable

Children b in Barnstable

1   Rebecca[5], b Dec 29 1709, d July 30, 1732; unmarried
2   Bethiah[5], b March 2, 1712, d July 1, 1737, unmarried
3   Temperance[5], b April 24 1717, m Nov 12, 1736, Abraham Blush and had Abraham[6], b Oct 20, 1737, Elijah[6], March 5, 1738-9; Rebecca[6], Nov 4, 1740, Benjamin[6], May 9, 1743, Elisha[6], April 23 1745, d Nov 17, 1745, Elisha[6], March 1, 1746-7, Martha[6], July 14, 1749, Temperance[6], Nov 21, 1751, Timothy[6], Aug 3. 1756
4   **Timothy[5]**, b April 3, 1719, m 1, Jane Lovell, m 2, Hannah ——.
5   **Matthias[5]**, b Sept 3, 1723, m Lydia Blossom
6   Bathsheba[5], b Aug 10, 1726, d June, 1749
7   **Lemuel[5]**, b Feb 10, 1731-2, m Abigail Jones.

FIFTH GENERATION.

4. TIMOTHY[5] FULLER, (*Joseph[4], Thomas[3], Samuel[2], Matthew[1]*), b. April 3, 1719, at Barnstable, probably the Timothy Fuller of East Hampton, Ct parish, who d Nov 23, 1794, aged 76 years, m 1, Jan 22. 1740, Jane Lovell, dau of Andrew and Lydia Lovell, of Barnstable, he joined the church at Westchester, Ct, July 21, 1751, his wife joined in 1761, he appears on the list of church members in 1776 He settled in Chatham, Ct, in 1755, he m 2, Hannah ——, who survived him

Children recorded at Colchester, Ct

8   Bethiah[6], b May 22, 1742, m May 7, 1760, at Colchester, Thomas Chipman of Barnstable, and had Timothy[7], b Feb 1, 1761; Isaac[7], Sept 12, 1762, Rebecca[7], Jan 26, 1764, Hannah[7] ——
9   Jane[6], b Sept 26, 1744
10   Joanna[6], b. Nov 22, 1747

5. MATTHIAS[5] FULLER, (*Joseph*[4], *Thomas*[3], *Samuel*[2], *Matthew*[1]), b Sept 6 1723, in Barnstable, date of death not found (He was living in Barnstable as late as March 19, 1799), m 1755? (or 1765), Lydia Blossom, b March 19 1729, dau of Joseph and Temperance (Fuller) Blossom, of Barnstable

Children born in Barnstable
11 Temperance[6], b July 4, 1768
12 **Matthias[6]**, b Nov 27, 1769; n Thankful Smith
13 David[6], b July 18, 1771, d Nov. 14, 1772
14 Abraham[6], b. Jan 4, 1773 Nothing more found about him

7. LEMUEL[5] FULLER (*Joseph*[4], *Thomas*[3], *Samuel*[2], *Matthew*[1]), b Feb 10, 1731-32, at Barnstable, d ——, m —— Abigail Jones
Resided at Marstons Mills
Children
15 **Joseph[6]**, b Jan 30, 1761, m Lydia Jones
16 Benjamin[6], b Sept 18, 1763 The Hinckley copy of Barnstable Records says, Benjamin, son of Lemuel Fuller, had his poll tax remitted in 1782, as he was in captivity and remained so until death
17 Samuel[6], b Nov 14, 1769, probably the Samuel Fuller who d May 8, 1859, aged 90 years, unmarried (Sandwich, Mass Rec)
18 **Timothy[6]**, b ——, m Mary (Polly) Rider
19 Hannah[6] b ——
20 Thomas[6], b June 5, 1778, d Sept 30 1779, at Barnstable

SIXTH GENERATION.

12. MATTHIAS[6] FULLER, (*Matthias*[5] *Joseph*[4], *Thomas*[3] *Samuel*[2], *Matthew*[1]), b Nov. 27, 1769, in Barnstable, d May 12 1842, m 1798 Thankful Smith, b Feb 28, 1778 d June 3, 1843, dau of Joseph Smith, of West Barnstable

Children given in Barnstable records
21 David[7], b May 20, 1805, nothing more found about him
22 **Ansel B[7]**, b March 6, 1808, m Sophia Goodspeed
23 Seth[7], b Feb 14, 1810, nothing more found
24 Jonathan Bodfish[7], b July 28, 1813, nothing more found
25 **Joseph Crocker[7]**, b Feb 19, 1815, m 1, Sarah A Wright, m 2, Sarah P Nye
26 Lydia Smith[7], b Feb 9, 1817, d Sept 27, 1833
27 **Abram[7]**, b Aug 11, 1819, m Eunice S Jones
28 Mary Smith[7] b Jan 14, 1821, d April 30, 1884, m Dec 25, 1845, David Jones

It is traditional that there were 12 children born to Matthias[6] Fuller, 8 sons and 4 daughters, and that 3 sons and 2 daus d young or unmarried

15. JOSEPH[6] FULLER, (*Lemuel[5], Joseph[4], Thomas[3], Samuel[2], Matthew[1]*), b Jan 30, 1761, in Barnstable; d July 12, 1830, m Int Pub. Nov 29, 1786, with Lydia Jones, who d Jan 27, 1841 Resided at Marstons Mills

Children

29 Rebecca[7], b April 3, 1790
30 Thomas[7], b March 4, 1794; m about 1819, Zopha Cash (Nantucket Rec) Nothing further found He was a seaman who went on whaling voyages to the Pacific
31 **Joseph**[7], b Sept 27, 1800, m Sophia Wright
32. Susanna[7], b March 23, 1806; perhaps the one published Oct 14, 1831, with Calvin Meiggs

18. TIMOTHY[6] FULLER, (*Lemuel[5], Joseph[4], Thomas[3], Samuel[2], Matthew[1]*), b —— at Marstons Mills, d ——, at ——, m Jan 9, 1792, Mary (Polly) Rider

The History of Wells, Vt, says, "Timothy Fuller came from Barnstable, Mass, in 1794, and settled on the farm now owned by Hiram Francis He married Mary Rider, and raised a large family, all of whom have left town"

Children recorded in Wells, Vt

33. Benjamin[7], b June 16, 1793
34 Abigail[7], b Aug 12, 1795 (An Abigail Fuller m Wm Rider in Wells, Vt May 10, 1819)
35 Hannah[7], b June 5, 1797
36 Lemuel[7], b Aug 18, 1799

SEVENTH GENERATION.

22. ANSEL B[7] FULLER, (*Matthias[6], Matthias[5], Joseph[4], Thomas[3], Samuel[2], Matthew[1]*), b March 6, 1808, in Barnstable, d Feb 8, 1892, at Marstons Mills, m Feb 25, 1836, Sophia B Goodspeed, both of Barnstable She d Feb 21, 1903, aged 90y—4m—6d

Children ·

37 **George Henry**[8], b Dec 5, 1836
38 Lydia G[8], b June 9, 1839, m Feb 16, 1860, William Cobb Resided in S Braintree No children
39 **Ansel E**[8], b April 6, 1841, m Olive B. Hamblin
40 Ada May[8], b Dec 14, 1854, d Feb 24, 1908, at Hyannis, m Sept. 10, 1875, John S Bearse, and had John C[9], b Aug 24, 1877, m June 28, 1899, Laura R Burlingame, of Cotuit, Charles O[9], b Sept 26, 1879, m Dec 24, 1904, Henrietta Crocker, of West Barnstable; William A[9], b May 27, 1883; m June 19, 1903, Anne Harwood, of Centerville, Howard E[9], b Jan. 22, 1890, unmarried (1912)

25. JOSEPH CROCKER[7] FULLER, (*Matthias*[6], *Matthias*[5], *Joseph*[4], *Thomas*[3], *Samuel*[2], *Matthew*[1]), b. Feb 19, 1815, at Barnstable; d June 23, 1888, in Sandwich, m 1, Dec 3, 1855, Sarah Ann Wright, b Jan 17, 1832, d March 1, 1873, dau of Joseph and Rebecca Wright, m 2, Sept 16, 1873, Sarah P Nye, b June 6, 1838, dau. of Warren B and Chloe (Parker) Nye He was a farmer.

Children

41 Charles Crocker[8], b July 16, 1856
42 Clifton Merrill[8], b July 19, 1867; m Dec 13, 1899, Edna Anna[9] Fuller, of Hyannis; b Aug 10, 1876 (No 62 of this group)

27. ABRAM[7] FULLER, (*Matthias*[6], *Matthias*[5], *Joseph*[4], *Thomas*[3], *Samuel*[2], *Matthew*[1]), b Aug 11, 1819, at Barnstable, d. May 1, 1893, m Jan 22, 1850, Eunice S Jones, b Nov 4, 1830, who is living at Hyannis (1912)

Children

43 Mary Eunice[8], b Dec 18, 1851; d Feb 22, 1852
44 **Edward H**[8], b June 15, 1852, m Izetta Anthony
45 **William A**[8], b Nov 20, 1859, m Josephine Coleman.

31. JOSEPH[7] FULLER, (*Joseph*[6], *Lemuel*[5], *Joseph*[4], *Thomas*[3], *Samuel*[2], *Matthew*[1]), b Sept 27, 1800, at Marstons Mills; d Oct 26, 1890; m Oct 28, 1828, Sophia Wright, who d April 28, 1866

Children, recorded in Barnstable

46 **Edwin**[8], b July 1, 1830, m 1, Eloise B Goodspeed, m 2, Sarah A Jagger, m 3, Emily E. Stearns
47 Martha A[8], b July 15, 1832, m Feb 28, 1864, Waterman Wood
48 Chloe H[8], b April 9, 1834, d ——, m. March 1, 1857, James T Lapham, and had Arthur W[9], Nancy[9], and Bessie[9]
49 Susan[8], b Feb 25, 1836, m March 4, 1866, Hiram L Ames
50 **Joseph**[8], b March 19, 1838; m 1, Mary Ellen Hendrick; m 2, Agnes Richards
51 Sophia[8], b July 26 1840; m Feb 4, 1864, Hezekiah H Jones, and had Charles F[9], and Nancy[9]
52 Thomas[8], b Sept 9, 1845, d Feb 27, 1846
53 **Thomas H.**[8], b July 9, 1848; m Lavinia H Fifield

EIGHTH GENERATION.

37. GEORGE HENRY[8] FULLER, (*Ansel B*[7], *Matthias*[6], *Matthias*[5], *Joseph*[4], *Thomas*[3], *Samuel*[2], *Matthew*[1]), b Dec 5, 1836, in Barnstable; m Jan 15, 1857, Esther F Phinney, b 1838, in Barnstable, d June 9, 1906, at Cotuit

He is living (1912) in Cotuit

Children

54 Mary Helen[9], b Nov 18, 1857; d Jan 24, 1908, m 1, Jan 25, 1875 William A Sturgis, m 2, Carlton B Nickerson of Cotuit
55 Henry A[9], b Sept 22, 1859, Resides (1912) at Cotuit, unmarried

56 Naomi P[9], b Nov 4 1864, d May 16, 1868
57 Grafton P[9] } twins, b Nov 1, 1869, { d May 27, 1888
58 George F[9] } { resides (1912) Cotuit, unmarried.
59 Nina L[9], b April 11, 1878, m —— Mitchell, of Quincy

39 ANSEL E.[8] FULLER, (*Ansel B*[7], *Matthias*[6], *Matthias*[5], *Joseph*[4]. *Thomas*[3], *Samuel*[2], *Matthew*[1]), b April 6, 1841, m. June 10, 1868, Olive B. Hamblin, who d June 15, 1909

He resides (1912) at Marstons Mills

Children

60 **Calvin H**[9], b Feb 16, 1869, m Mary A Hallett
61 **Ansel A**[9], b Feb. 14, 1874, m Rose C Cartier
62 Caroline D[9], b July 15, 1875, m July 15, 1892, John A Coleman, and has Alice Ellenwood[10], b March 21, 1894, Frances Austin[10] Jan. 14, 1895 and Marion Rose[10], Dec 5, 1899, resides at Marstons Mills

44. EDWARD H[8] FULLER, (*Abram*[7], *Matthias*[6], *Matthias*[5], *Joseph*[4], *Thomas*[3], *Samuel*[2], *Matthew*[1]), b June 9 1852 in Barnstable, m Aug 1, 1875, Izeta Anthony, b. Oct 5, 1853, at Hyannis They reside at Hyannis

Children

63 Edna A[9], b Aug 10, 1876, m Dec 13, 1899, Clifton Merrill Fuller, No 41 of this group
64. Mina Jones[9], b May 19 1883
65 Frances Porter[9], b Oct 10, 1891

45. WILLIAM A[8] FULLER, (*Abram*[7], *Matthias*[6], *Matthias*[5], *Joseph*[4] *Thomas*[3] *Samuel*[2], *Matthew*[1]), b Nov 20, 1858 at Marstons Mills, m May 16, 1880, Josephine Coleman, b Oct 3, 1861, at Osterville They reside at Hyannis

Children, all born at Marstons Mills

66 Wilhemina[9] b May 9, 1882
67 Leon Clark[9] b Oct 5, 1888 m Oct 5 1910 Edith F Herron They reside in Dorchester (1912)
68 Edwin Coleman[9] b June 10, 1903, d March 11, 1904

46. EDWIN[8] FULLER (*Joseph*[7], *Joseph*[6], *Lemuel*[5], *Joseph*[4] *Thomas*[3] *Samuel*[2], *Matthew*[1]) b July 1, 1830, in Barnstable, m 1, April 6, 1856, Eloise B Goodspeed who d Oct 16 1860, m 2 Oct 23, 1863, Sarah A Jagger, who d Feb 10, 1864; m 3, May 10, 1866, Emily E Stearns, b in Walpole

Children

69 **Edwin F**[9], b Sept 19, 1857; m Jennie W Coleman
70 Charles F[9], b May 17 1860, m Lydia E Savery, Dec 18, 1890
71 Emma E[9], b Nov 4, 1868, d Oct 10, 1890

50. JOSEPH[8] FULLER, (*Joseph[7], Joseph[6], Lemuel[5], Joseph[4], Thomas[3], Samuel[2], Matthew[1]*), b March 19, 1838, in Barnstable, d July 12, 1903, in Chatham, m 1, May 15, 1870, Mary Ellen Kendrick, m. 2, Nov 25, 1891, Agnes Richards, b in Alchester, England

Children: all born in Chatham

72 Lester Quincy[9], b Aug 17, 1873, m June 14, 1906, Idella M E. Bassett

73 Agnes Elizabeth[9], b Feb 25, 1900

53. THOMAS H[8] FULLER, (*Joseph[7], Joseph[6], Lemuel[5], Joseph[4], Thomas[3] Samuel[2], Matthew[1]*), b July 9, 1848, in Barnstable, m. April 14, 1878, Lavinia H Fifield

They reside (1912) at Marstons Mills

Children

74 Ella Burnett[9], b Jan 19, 1884, d Nov 18, 1912, m Nov 12, 1902, Ernest L Goodspeed

75 Thomas Bertram[9], b Feb 12, 1895

NINTH GENERATION

60. CALVIN H[9] FULLER, (*Ansel E[8], Ansel B[7], Matthias[6], Matthias[5] Joseph[4], Thomas[3], Samuel[2] Matthew[1]*), b Feb 16, 1869 at Marstons Mills, m Sept 2, 1892, Mary A Hallett They reside at Marstons Mills

76 Ada Hallett[10], b June 13, 1895

77 Carroll H[10] b Sept 15, 1902

61. ANSEL A[9] FULLER, (*Ansel S[8] Ansel B[7], Matthias[6], Matthias[5] Joseph[4], Thomas[3], Samuel[2], Matthew[1]*), b Feb 14, 1874, m Nov 6, 1898, Rose C Cartier They reside at Marstons Mills

Children

78 Lizzie Dorothy[10], b Oct 20, 1901

79 Orrin Ansel[10], b Jan 6, 1911.

69. EDWIN F[9] FULLER, (*Edwin[8], Joseph[7], Joseph[6], Lemuel[5] Joseph[4], Thomas[3] Samuel[2], Matthew[1],*), b Sept 19, 1875, m Feb 19 1852 Jennie W Coleman, both of Barnstable

Children

80 Miriam Forrest[10], b May 23 1884, at Marstons Mills; m Oct 15, 1902, William R Weeks, b in Canada

SECOND GROUP

FOURTH GENERATION.

BENJAMIN[4] FULLER, AND SOME OF HIS DESCENDANTS

21. BENJAMIN[4] FULLER, (*Thomas*[3], *Samuel*[2], *Matthew*[1]), b Aug 1690, in Barnstable; d there Jan 2, 1748, m 1, March 25, 1714, Rebecca Bodfish, b Feb 22, 1692-3, d March 10, 1727-8, dau of Joseph and Elizabeth (Besse) Bodfish, of West Barnstable, m 2, Feb 20, 1729-30, Mercy Fuller, dau of Joseph[4] Fuller, (Samuel[3], Samuel[2], Edward[1]) and Thankfull (Blossom) Fuller See Vol 1, p 38 "Some descendants of Edward Fuller of the Mayflower" The second marriage is proved by the wills of Joseph[4] and Thankful Fuller, his wife

The latter will—dated Aug 13, 1757—names Grandson Seth Fuller, whc is to pay his mother, Mercy Fuller, a certain legacy

This Benjamin Fuller was a Lieutenant, and is called Junior, to dis tinguish him from Benjamin[4] Fuller, (Samuel[3], Samuel[2], Edward[1])

Children born in Barnstable

1 Mary[5], b July 12, 1714, unmarried in 1741, probably the Mary Fuller of Sandwich, Mass, who m Aug 8, 1763, Seth Lathrop as his 2d wife She d Jan 18, 1809, aged 95 years

2 Lydia[5], b March 23, 1716, d June 29, 1801, m 1742, John Percival of Sandwich, and had Elisha[6], b June 13, 1743, Abigail[6], Oct 22, 1745, Sarah[6], Sept 3, 1747; Elizabeth[6], Nov 3, 1748, Benjamin[6] Jan 13, 1752, John[6], Nov 6, 1754, James[6], March 25, 1757, and Thomas[6], March 11, 1759

3 **Thomas**[5], b June 18, 1718, m Elizabeth Arnold

4 Elizabeth[5] b Sept 30, 1720, m March 22, 1738-9, Isaac, son of Nathan Crocker

5 Benjamin[5], b Oct 28, 1723, m Mary —— He d Nov 11, 1815, aged 93 years, at Millington parish, East Haddam, Ct, wife Mary d there April 28, 1807, aged 86 years, 6 months He came to East Haddam before 1745 and lived in the same house with Joshua Isham, also from Barnstable

   Benjamin Fuller was elected deacon of the church at Milling ton Feb 26, 1778, and resigned March 4, 1796 No record of his family found

6 Abigail[5], b Nov. 29, 1725, d Dec 29, 1726

7 Joseph[5] b Oct 18, 1730, d May 30, 1732

8 Thankful[5], b April 26, 1733, m April 23, 1758, Dr Samuel Gilbert, from Ct He d 1778 in Barnstable Their children were Seth[6], b Feb 4, 1759, Abigail[6], b. Jan, 1762, and Benjamin[6], b June 21, 1764

9   Rebecca⁵, b June 1, 1735
10   Seth⁵, b March 14, 1736-7; m Deliverance Jones

FIFTH GENERATION.

3. THOMAS⁵ FULLER. (*Benjamin⁴, Thomas³, Samuel², Matthew¹*), b
Jan 18, 1718, in Barnstable; d March 6, 1780, aged 63 years⁹ (see note*)
(a record in the church records of Westchester (town of Colchester),
Ct, giving the above date of death probably refers to this Thomas
Fuller, *or to his wife* Since the first name is omitted in the original record, we cannot be sure), m. Nov 10, 1741, at Middle Haddam, Ct,
Elizabeth Arnold, b Jan 26, 1716-17, in Haddam, Ct, d ——, dau of
Dr Joshua and Elizabeth Arnold, of Haddam, Ct Thomas Fuller lived
in Westchester parish from his marriage until about 1745, in Barnstable
1746-1750; then in East Haddam, Hadlyme parish, until about 1755,
finally in Westchester again His wife was a church member in all
these places The above is from H. W Brainard's Mss—In the N. Y
Record Oct 1903, Brainard says he lost trace of them in Westchester,
not finding any further notice of them
  Children
11   Elizabeth⁶, b Jan 21, 1743, (Barnstable Records), m Oct 24, 1765,
       Asa Daniels⁹
12   Thomas⁶, b Aug 14, 1745, in Barnstable, m Lois Giddings?
13   Jacob⁶, b March 6, 1746, in Barnstable, m at Colchester, Ct,
       April 1, 1771, Eunice Williams of Chatham, Ct He was in the
       Lexington Alarm Co, April 19, 1775
14   Hannah⁶, b April 2, 1749, in Barnstble, m April 18, 1779, James
       Young of Middle Haddam, Ct, they removed to Lee in 1778
          Children James⁷ b Jan 31, 1771; Elizabeth⁷, bapt Feb 1,
       1778, at Middle Haddam
15. Ruth⁶, b Nov. 21, 1750, in East Haddam
16   Rebecca⁶, b Sept 2, 1752, in East Haddam, d Oct 15, 1752
17   Benjamin⁶, b June 15, 1754, in East Haddam, d Nov 8, 1775, a
       Revolutionary soldier
18   Joseph⁶, bapt Jan 16, 1757, m ——, Mary ——;

       NOTE—In the published Vital Records of the town of Lee,
     there are records of the death of a Thomas Fuller "Sept 24,
     1808 a 90 (a 90 y—3 mos C R) (husb Lucy, G R)" and
     "Lucy, wid Thomas Fuller, d Sept 26, 1824, a 89."

       There is no further mention of them in these vital records of
     Lee It appears they were members of the Lee Cong Church,
     "Joined on profession," were received July 14, 1793, and died
     members of that church Nothing further shown in Ch
     records The Lee U S census of 1790 mentions this family as
     residing in Lee It has occurred to the compiler that it *may*
     have been Thomas Fuller's wife Elizabeth, who died March 6,
     1780, a 63, that Thomas removed to Lee, when his daughter
     Hannah was probably living, and married for second wife, be-
     fore 1790, Lucy ——, who survived him

10. SETH[5] FULLER, (*Benjamin[4], Thomas[3], Samuel[2], Matthew[1]*), b
March 14, 1736-7, in Barnstable, d ——, m Oct 15, 1759, at Barnstable.
Deliverance Jones

He removed—Otis says, to Kennebec, Maine

He was living in 1787 as a deed (Barnstable recopied deeds) proves—
"Seth Fuller and Deliverance his wife, formerly of Barnstable, to Jonathan Bodfish "

This was a deed of one half of the farm of Joseph Fuller, deceased
who was his grandfather, on his mother's side   She was Mercy[5] Fuller
(Joseph[4], Samuel[3], Samuel[2], Edward[1])   See Vol 1, p 38 "Some Descendants of Edward Fuller of the Mayflower "

Children—the first two recorded in Barnstable
19   Hannah[6], b April 10, 1766
20   Abigail[6], b Nov 25, 1768
21   **Seth[6]**, b ——, m Bathsheba Jones
22   **Benjamin[6]**, b ——, m, Deliverance Jones
23   Thankful[6], b ——, m —— Nathaniel Blackwell, of Madison, Me
24   Mercy[6], b

> Mrs Abbie (Fuller) Chandler, No 45 of this Group, states
> that her "father's grand parents, Seth and Deliverance Fuller
> lived in Barnstable Children   Seth, Benjamin my grand-
> father, Thankful, and Mercy They all settled in Fairfield
> Maine   There were others unknown to us "

SIXTH GENERATION.

18   JOSEPH[6] FULLER (*Thomas[5], Benjamin[4], Thomas[3], Samuel[2] Matthew[1]*), bapt. Jan 16, 1757, at Westchester, Ct , d June 1, 1836, a 79,
m —— Mary —— who d March 17, 1841 a 81

Children born in Westchester (Town of Colchester)
25   **Joseph[7]**, b Aug 12, 1782, m 1, Polly Bonney, m 2, Sally Bonney
26   Ellery[7], b May 25, 1786
27   Lambert[7], b June 7, 1888, m Almda Murdock, and had two
        daughters   All deceased—names and dates not obtained

21. SETH[6] FULLER, (*Seth[5] Benjamin[4], Thomas[3] Samuel[2] Matthew[1]*),
b —— in ——; d —— in ——, m ——, Bathsheba Jones
Children born in ——
28   Aurelia[7] b ——
29   **Charles[7]**, b ——, m ——, ——Tobey
30   Delia[7], b ——, m Samuel S Rogers, of Augusta, Me

22. BENJAMIN[6] FULLER, (*Seth[5], Benjamin[4] Thomas[3], Samuel[2] Matthew[1]*), b ——, in Fairfield, Me , d there, in 1815, m ——, Deliverence
Jones
Children
31   Edward Jones[7] b —— 1804, m ——, Mary Lander

32 **John Jones**[7], b July 22, 1806, m ——, Deborah Rogers
33 Abigail Nye[7], b —— ; m ——, Franklin Blackwell, and had Edwin
      of Winslow, Me , and Russell of Augusta, Me
34 **Warren**[7], b—— , m ——, Hannah Nason

SEVENTH GENERATION.

25. JOSEPH[7] FULLER, (*Joseph*[6], *Thomas*[5], *Benjamin*[4], *Thomas*[3], *Samuel*[2], *Matthew*[1]), b Aug 12, 1782 in Colchester, Ct , d June 18, 1858, m 1, June 15, 1818, Polly Bonney, m 2, Jan 1, 1822, Sally Bonney—sister to first wife. Joseph was in the Ct Militia, war of 1812
   Children
35 Fanny[8], b March 18, 1819
36 Polly Frutilla[8], b June 16, 1821
37 Ellery Briggs[8], b Sept 27, 1823
38. Sarah Matilda[8], b Nov 12, 1824
39 Mary Patterson[8], b April 18, 1826
40 Josiah Bonney[8], b Aug 13, 1827, living 1909, a 81, at Hubbards-
      ville, N. Y.
41 Seth Pierce[8], b Aug 5 1829
42 Lucy Ledoma[8], b June 24, 1831: m and had a daughter who m
      Romaine Risley and resides at Hubbardsville, N. Y
43 Benjamin Florence[8], b July 6, 1833

29. CHARLES[7] FULLER, (*Seth*[6], *Seth*[5] *Benjamin*[4], *Thomas*[3], *Samuel*[2] *Matthew*[1]), b ——, m ——, d —— ; m ——, ——Tobey
   Children
44 Ellen[8], b ——

32. JOHN JONES[7] FULLER, (*Benjamin*[6], *Seth*[5], *Benjamin*[4], *Thomas*[3] *Samuel*[2], *Matthew*[1]) b July 22, 1806, in Fairfield, Me , d Jan 14, 1886, in Augusta, Me , m Dec 25, 1840 Deborah Rogers, of Augusta
   Children
45 Abbie S[8], b Nov 10, 1841, m July 24, 1873, Rev Perry Chandler,
      and had Perry Chandler[9], b June 8, 1874, Ralph H[9], June 5,
      1876, and Webster A[9], Dec 10, 1878 She resides in E Bos-
      ton, Mass.
46 **James Edward**[8], b Dec 17, 1844, m Emily Howard
47 John Martin[8], b Dec 11, 1846, d Jan 27, 1865
48 **Samuel Rogers**[8], b Feb 2, 1852, m Frances Chick

34. WARREN[7] FULLER, (*Benjamin*[6], *Seth*[5], *Benjamin*[4], *Thomas*[3], *Samuel*[2], *Matthew*[1]), b. ——, in ——, d ——, m——, m ——, Hannah Nason
He was a farmer in Fairfield, Me
   Children
49 John Henry[8], b —— ; resides at Somerset Mills Fairfield, Me

EIGHTH GENERATION.

46. JAMES EDWARD[8] FULLER, (*John Jones[7], Benjamin[6], Seth[5], Benja-min[4], Thomas[3], Samuel[2], Matthew[1]*), b Dec 17, 1844, in Augusta, Me, m March 21, 1867 Emily Howard

He resides (1912) in Augusta

Children

50   Florence[9], b July 21, 1868, m April 27, 1895, Thomas C Ingra-ham, and had James[10], Deborah[10], Horace[10], and Howard[10]

51   John H[9], b Dec 10, 1869, m Francis Elliott of Elmira, N Y

52   Edith M[9], b Jan 18, 1879, m Henry T Elmore, of Elmira N Y

53   James Martin[9], b July 26, 1882, d May 15 1905

48. SAMUEL ROGERS[8] FULLER, (*John Jones[7], Benjamin[6], Seth[5], Benja-min[4], Thomas[3], Samuel[2], Matthew[1]*), b Feb 2, 1852 in ——, d July, 1911, in ——, m Feb 22, 1871, Frances Chick

Children born in ——

54   Harry Hull[9] b Aug —, 1872, m ——; resides Atlanta, Ga

55   Emma Alice[9], } twins, b June 8, 1876, { m ——, Ancory Way
56   Grace Mary[9], }   { m ——, Louis Lencke

57   Thaddeus Chick[9] b Sept 30, 1882

58   James Edward[9] b Nov 10, 1890

THIRD GROUP

FOURTH GENERATION.

SAMUEL[4] FULLER, AND SOME OF HIS DESCENDANTS

23. SAMUEL[4] FULLER, (*Thomas*[3], *Samuel*[2], *Matthew*[1]), b April 12, 1694, in Barnstable, d after 1760, in Chatham, Ct ; m Jan 20, 1725-6 Malatiah Bodfish b, April 17, 1696, dau of Joseph and Elizabeth (Besse) Bodfish of Barnstable

April 9, 1750, he bought of John Fuller of East Haddam, Ct , 51 acres of land situated on the east side of the Ct River, in Middletown, now Chatham, two rods from the Haddam line In this deed he is called "of Haddam," and had probably resided in the same locality, now known as "Haddam Neck" for some years before

July 11, 1760, he transferred this land to his son Abijah and perhaps died not long after Malatiah, wife of Samuel Fuller, joined Cong Church at Middle Haddam, Nov 24, 1751

Children born at Barnstable

1 **Abijah**[5]. b Dec 29, 1726, m Esther Arnold
2 Abigail[5], b June 26, 1730

There were also three children that died in infancy

FIFTH GENERATION.

1. ABIJAH[6] FULLER, (*Samuel*[4], *Thomas*[3], *Samuel*[2]. *Matthew*[1]), b. Dec 29, 1726, in Barnstable, d Oct 29, 1804, was buried in the "Young Street graveyard in Chatham, Ct , m 1, Aug 7, 1746, at Middle Haddam, Ct , Esther Arnold, b May 29, 1722, d April 22, 1762

He m 2, Sept 8, 1763, Martha Hale. One record of his first marriage adds the words "in the 20 year of his Age" He returned to Barnstable after his marriage, but came back to Ct in two years, and resided in Chatham until death An old record in possession of Mrs Prudence (Young) Wright, East Hampton, Ct gives his family record and adds "I sot scail from cape cod May ye 2, 1749 Arrived into Connecticut River May ye 11, 1749 " His wife was a member of the West Barnstable Church during their brief residence there, and the eldest child was born and baptized there—the others were born in Chatham

3   Malatiah[6], b Feb 8, 1748, d Sept 1, 1842, m, Dec 17, 1767, Samuel Young, of Chatham, and had Esther[7], b Dec. 27, 1768, Samuel[7], Feb 27, 1771; Elias[7], Feb 26, 1774, Seth[7], Dec. 21, 1776, Zillah[7], April 12, 1780, Eunice[7], Feb 14, 1783, Ezra[7]. Sept 5, 1786

4   **Samuel**[6], b April 4, 1750, m Lydia Brainard.

5   Abijah[6], b July 18, 1753; m Hannah Spencer

6   Joseph[6], b Sept 23, 1757; d Oct 7, 1757

7   Amasa[6], b Sept 10, 1764, d Sept 30, 1765

8   **Amasa**[6], b Sept 12, 1766; m Hannah Brainard

9   Abigail[6], b April 25, 1769, d Nov 16, 1857, at Brooklyn, O ; m about 1796, Ensign Asa Brainard, and had Maria[7], b 1797, in Middle Haddam, Marvin[7], Feb. 9, 1799, Marietta[7], Sept 26, 1801, Simon[7], about 1808, d about Jan, 1815, Martha[7], 1811, d 1838, in Cleveland, O , Louisa[7], April 29, 1814, and Betsy Ann[7], Aug 12, 1817.

SIXTH GENERATION.

4. SAMUEL[6] FULLER, (*Abijah[5], Samuel[4], Thomas[3], Samuel[2], Matthew[1]*), b April 4, 1750 in Middle Haddam parish, Middletown, Ct ; d March 29, 1821, at Butternuts, Otsego Co, N Y , m aged 22, Dec. 19, 1771, Lydia Brainard, b Dec 25, 1746, in Middle Haddam She was living in 1839 at Butternuts

He removed from Middle Haddam to Butternuts about 1803, was a veteran of the Revolutionary war, and a U. S Pensioner.

Children·

10   Sylvester[7], b about 1774, d ——, unmarried

11   Statira[7], b March 6, 1776, m March 1, 1797, Elias Higgins

12   Martha[7], b ——, m ——, Moses Higgins

13   Lydia[7], b ——, d ——, unmarried

14   Deborah[7], b ——, d ——, unmarried

15   Harriet[7], b April 4, 1791, d Aug 20, 1831 in Union Valley, N Y. m Calvin Converse, b Nov 6, 1791, New Canaan, N Y , d Jan 21, 1856

5. ABIJAH[6] FULLER, (*Abijah[5], Samuel[4], Thomas[3], Samuel[2], Matthew[1]*), b July 18, 1753 in Middle Haddam parish, Middletown, Ct , d —— m Aug—, 1774, Hannah Spencer, at East Haddam (Bailey) H W Brainard thinks "that about 1785 he settled in Winchester, Ct and after a few years removed again "

Boyd's "Annals of Winchester" gives Abijah Fuller from Chatham, of Barnhamsted, Ct , 1785

Barnhamsted town clerk writes (1912) "that Abijah Fuller bought land of Samuel Cook, Sept 16, 1783, and sold the same April 16, 1784, and probably remained but a few months in town He was of Winchester when he made the purchase "

The U S Census 1790 does not mention this Abijah Fuller and family in New England or New York

Children born in Middle Haddam

16   Milton[7] bapt 1777
17   Roswell[7], bapt 1777.
18   Joseph[7], bapt 1781
19   Elisha[7], bapt 1783

8. AMASA[6] FULLER, (*Abijah[5] Samuel[4], Thomas[3], Samuel[2], Matthew[1]*), b Sept 12, 1766, in Middle Haddam parish, Middletown, Ct ; d ——; m ——, Hannah Brainard, b Feb 22, 1770, in Middle Haddam

He settled in Ohio

Children

20.   Chauncey[7], b ——, Lived near Cleveland, O.

FOURTH GROUP

FOURTH GENERATION.

JONATHAN⁴ FULLER AND SOME OF HIS DESCENDANTS

27. JONATHAN⁴ FULLER, (*Jabez³, Samuel², Matthew¹*), b March 10, 1692, at Barnstable, d ——, m 1, Feb 14, 1711-12, Eleanor Bennett, born Dec 18, 1689, dau of John Bennett   She died Sept 28, 172(—) in the 38th year of her age   (Mayflower Descendant Magazine, Vols 1 and 5)

The records at Middleboro say she died in 1720? but also give children born in 1721 and 1725 as below, m 2, Dec 17, 1729, Hannah Harlow, both of Middleboro   He resided in Middleboro

Children born in Middleboro

1   Margaret⁵, b Nov 17, 1712
2   Abigail⁵, b March 11, 1714-15
3   **Jabez⁵**, b July 22, 1717, m Hannah Pratt
4   Timothy⁵, b Jan, 1721, joined church 1742, dismissed to Attleboro, 1766
5   Molly⁵, b Sept, 1725, joined church 1742
6   Eleanor⁵, b Feb 28, 1731
7   Ebenezer⁵, b July 22, 1732

FIFTH GENERATION.

3. JABEZ FULLER, (*Jonathan⁴, Jabez³, Samuel², Matthew¹*), b July 22, 1717, in Middleboro (Middleboro records), d ——, 1770, in Medfield, (H W Brainard's Mss), m Dec 27, 1744, Hannah Pratt (Middleboro record)

Children born in Middleboro, dates of birth according to Brainard Mss

8   Sarah⁶, b July 29, 1746
9   Lucy⁶, } twins, b May 13, 1749, } m 1767, Ezra Washburn
10 Peter⁶,
11 **Zenas⁶**, b July 8, 1752, m Rachel Yates
12 Betsy⁶, b Sept 13, 1754
13 **John⁶**, b. June 18, 1756
14 **Amasa⁶**, b March 10, 1759
15 **Andrew⁶**, b May 18, 1761, m Hannah Richards

16   Hannah[6], b March 4, 1764

> NOTE—The records of the town of Middleboro give dates for the births of the above mentioned children of Jabez[5] Fuller differing in every case from those here given, which agree with those given by the descendants—by those in other records, and those given by Prof Brainard

SIXTH GENERATION.

11. ZENAS[6] FULLER, (*Jabez[5], Jonathan[4], Jabez[3], Samuel[2], Matthew[1]*), b July 8, 1752, in Middleboro, d Aug 14, 1819, aged 67, buried in Oak Hill Cemetery, Round Pond, Me. m Dec 27, 1775, Rachel Yates, who d Oct 31, 1847, aged 89-10-17 He removed to Bristol, Me, about 1775 His children, born in Bristol, were

17   **John**[7], b Sept 26, 1776, m Eleanor Chapman
18   Jane[7], b Aug 14, 1778, m. ——Bogart[?] and had several children.
19   Betsy[7], b Sept 21, 1780; m 1, ——Fassett, and had one daughter, m 2, —— Plummer, and had two sons and two daughters, m 3, Wm M McClintock, of Bristol, Me
20   Samuel[7], b Nov 27, 1782, m ——
21   Jabez[7], b Aug 8, 1884, m ——
22   **James Yates**[7] b Nov 27, 1786, m Betsy Ripley
23   Margaret[7], b Sept 2, 1789, never married
24   **Alexander**[7], b July 20, 1792, m Margaret Fountain
25   **Zenas**[7] b April 23, 1794, m Elizabeth Fountain
26   Rachel[7], b Feb 6, 1796, d Oct 10, 1841, m 1821, Wm Cox, had five children

13. JOHN[6] FULLER, (*Jabez[5], Jonathan[4], Jabez[3], Samuel[2], Matthew[1]*), b June 18, 1756, in Middleboro, d Feb, 1839, aged 82, in Pittsfield, Vt. m —— Martha Morton

According to information from the late Mr Newton Fuller, genealogist, of New London, Ct, John, Amasa, Andrew and Hannah Fuller, children of Jabez, removed from Mass to Sherburne, Vt Later Andrew removed to Warren, Me Later, according to the Pierce family genealogy, Nathaniel Morton Fuller of Sherburne, Vt, son of Capt John and Martha (Morton) Fuller, married Anna Pierce

In 1811, John Fuller was on the lists at Sherburne, Vt In 1823, a deed recorded in Sherburne, indicates that he was living in Pittsfield, Vt

According to the U S Pension records, he enlisted in July, 1775, became Captain, later, in the 4th Mass Regt under Col William Shepard, served until June, 1783, applied for pension April 7, 1818, then living at Pittsfield, Vt, 61 years of age

Children born in Sherburne

27   **Nathaniel Morton**[7], b ——, m 1, Hannah; m 2, Anna Pierce
28   **Job Morton**[7], b ——, m Rhoda ——
> Perhaps there were other children

14. AMASA⁶ FULLER, (*Jabez⁵, Jonathan⁴, Jabez³, Samuel², Matthew¹*), b. March 10, 1759, in Middleboro, d. March 10, 1844, in Plymouth, Vt , buried in Sherburne, Vt ; m 1, Oct 18, 1782, in Freetown, Mary Mason, b in Freetown, 1761; d 1802 , m 2, Oct 24, 1803, in Stockbridge, Vt , Lois Barr, who d. Dec 29, 1829, m 3, Widow —— (——) Bates

Amasa Fuller was a soldier of the Revolution, and in his application for a pension April 6, 1818, he was 60 years old, his wife was 11 years younger, his son Silas 30 years younger and a cripple In 1823, his daughter was 15 years old Amasa Fuller enlisted March, 1776, at Roxbury, Mass , and served a year Enlisted again in 1777; went to Ticonderoga, was in the battle of Saratoga , marched to Pennsylvania He held the rank of Sergeant when discharged at West Point, March 5, 1780 He lived later in Sherburne, Vt In 1821 he sold there a piece of land, to Portus Fuller, of Pittsfield, Vt , deed acknowledged before Nathaniel M Fuller, J P.

Children
29   **Silas⁷**, b —— 1783 , m Zilpha Hastings
30   **Portus⁷** b —— 1785, m Submit Ormsby
31   Jabez⁷, b Oct 13, 1787; d Dec 22, 1864, m Hannah Bowen.
32   **Nathan E ⁷** b Dec 29 1791 ; m 1 Almira Fay m 2. Persis Howe Doane
33   Mary M ⁷. b about 1808 , m Jan 14, 1830, Roswell B Adams

15. ANDREW⁶ FULLER, (*Jabez⁵, Jonathan⁴, Jabez³, Samuel², Matthew¹*), b May 18, 1761, in Middleboro, d Jan 21, 1820, at Warren, Me , m April, 1785, Hannah Richards, b at Scituate d March 13, 1845, aged 91

Andrew Fuller was a Corporal in the Revolutionary War , was ordained minister in 1794, in Nobleboro, Me , was pastor at Muscongus Island—Hope, and finally at Warren, Me

Children
34   **William Oliver⁷**, b about 1786, m Mary McIntire
35   Andrew⁷, b —— 1787, d ——1805, at Demaraia, Me
36   Sarah⁷, b —— 1788 , d March 19, 1861, at Warren, Me , m James Chaples
37   **Peter⁷**, b April 30, 1791 , m Phebe Dunbar
38   Priscilla⁷, b ——, d in infancy

SEVENTH GENERATION.

17. JOHN⁷ FULLER, (*Zenas⁶, Jabez⁵, Jonathan⁴, Jabez³, Samuel², Matthew¹*), b Sept 26, 1776, in Bristol, Me , d ——, m ——, Eleanor Chapman

Children
39   Samuel⁸, b ——
40   John⁸, b ——
41   Wm Oliver⁸, b ——

42 **Wilson**, b ——, m ——
43 Martha³, b ——, m Jacob Shepard, and had Clara, who m Albert Barnes and had Mary, who m Amasa Holden
44 Rachel D⁸, b ——, m Abel Merriam, b Feb 16, 1820, and had 7 children.

22. JAMES YATES⁷ FULLER, (*Zenas⁶, Jabez⁵, Jonathan⁴, Jabez³, Samuel², Matthew¹*), b Nov 27, 1786, in Bristol, Me ; d about 1850, in Appleton, Me , m —— Betsy Ripley
Children, born in Appleton, Me
45 **William R**⁸, b Feb 10, 1822, m —— Mahala P Moody
46 **Alexander**⁸, b Feb, 1825, d Dec 23, 1904, in Star Prairie, Wis ; m Matilda Hyde No children, except by adoption
47 **Alden**⁸. b Dec 9, 1827; m Sarah Simmons
48 **Edward A**⁸, b March 19, 1830, m ——, Laura A ——
49 **John Franklin**⁸, b Dec. 12, 1833, m 1, Sarah Philbrick, m 2, Lydia Nicholson

24. ALEXANDER⁷ FULLER, (*Zenas⁶, Jabez⁵, Jonathan⁴, Jabez³, Samuel², Matthew¹*) b July 20, 1792, in Bristol, Me , d May 3, 1853, at Appleton, Me ; m March 22, 1815, Margaret Fountain, b Sept 17, 1792, in Bristol, d Feb 15, 1876, in Appleton
Children
50 **Augustus L**⁸, b June 16, 1816, m Levina H Chapman
51 Martha⁸, b Jan 16, 1822 in Bristol, d April, 1868, in Searsmont, Me , m Sept 17, 1842, Edward Meservey, and had Arista⁹, b July, 1846, Theresa A⁹, b April 18, 1851, and Margaret T⁹, deceased
52 **Lafayette**⁸, b April 15, 1825, m Elizabeth A Chapman
53 Alexander⁸, b Feb 22, 1830, in Appleton, d March 29, 1851
54 Orlando⁸, b May 14, 1837, in Appleton, d Jan 2, 1838

25. ZENAS⁷ FULLER, (*Zenas⁶, Jabez⁵, Jonathan⁴, Jabez³, Samuel², Matthew¹*), b. April 23, 1794, in Bristol, Me , d June 19, 1869, at Appleton, Me , m ——, 1816, Elizabeth Fountain, b April 23, 1790, in Bristol; d July 18, 1880, in Appleton
Children
55 Nancy⁸, b Aug 14, 1818 in Bristol, d Oct, 1877, in Appleton, m Dec, 1837, Jacob Stover, and had Martha A⁹, b Aug 14, 1838 Lysander C⁹, Nov, 1840; Althea⁹, Oct, 1843, Alexander A⁹, May 15 1850, Lizzie,⁹ 1853, Leander⁹, May 13, 1855, Leantha⁹, Sept 14, 1858; Frederick⁹, 1864, and Angie⁹, May, 1867, all b in Appleton
56 **Isaac**⁸, b March 14, 1820, m Jane Glidden
57 Wealthy⁸, b May 13, 1823, d Nov 29, 1895, m Frank Eastman, and had Marietta⁹, b April 24, 1847, Sumner P⁹, May 18, 1851, and Cora⁹
58 Margaret⁸, b Jan 3 1826, m May 7, 1850, Bradbury Boggs, of

Warren, Me, and had Oliver[9], Lizzie[9], Clara A[9], Alexander F[9], Josephine[9], Julia[9], and Bradbury B[9]

59   Elizabeth J[8], b Sept 26, 1829; resides in West Appleton, Me

60   Orissa T[8], b Dec 28, 1832, d at Appleton, Oct 9, 1879; m Horace W Glidden, and had Andrew[9], b March, 1873.

61.   Andrew[8], b March 28, 1837, d. April, 1863, in the army.

27   NATHANIEL MORTON[7] FULLER, (*John[6]*, *Jabez[6]*, *Jonathan[4]*, *Jabez[3]*, *Samuel[2]*, *Matthew[1]*), b ——, in Sherburne, Vt ; d ——, m 1, ——, Hannah ——, who d July 24, 1803—30 days after marriage—aged 19; m 2, Anna Pierce. (Pierce Gene).

A deed recorded in Sherburne, in 1823, indicates that he was a resident of Pittsfield, Vt

Children—recorded at Sherburne.

62.   **John Dnane**[8], b June 18, 1809, m ——, ——.

63   Nancy Ann[8], b March 7, 1811

64   Martha Caroline[8], b Sept 6, 1812

65   Marcia Emeline[8], b Dec 26, 1813

66   Hannah Adaline[8], b Aug 10, 1815
        and perhaps others

28.   JOB MORTON[7] FULLER (*John[6]*, *Jabez[5]*, *Jonathan[4]*, *Jabez[3]*, *Samuel[2]*, *Matthew[1]*), b ——, in Sherburne, Vt., d ——, m ——, Rhoda ——, of Alstead, N H (Dedham, Mass, Record)

Children born in Pittsfield, Vt

67   Anna B[8], b ——, d. Aug 8, 1872, aged 51—7—0

68   Lucius[8], b ——, d about 1812, m ——   He was a surveyor and lived in Pittsfield where his widow was living in 1913
        Perhaps Job Morton Fuller had other children

29.   SILAS[7] FULLER, (*Amasa[6]*, *Jabez[5]*, *Jonathan[4]*, *Jabez[3]*, *Samuel[2]*, *Matthew[1]*), b ——, 1783? (see under Amasa) m ——, d ——, m ——, m. —— Zilpha Hastings

Children.

69   Almira[8], b Feb 27, 1822, in Sherburne, Vt , d Oct 13, 1870, at West Windsor, Vt., m there, March 4, 1846, Frederick Augustus Ely

30.   PORTUS[7] FULLER, (*Amasa[6]*, *Jabez[5]*, *Jonathan[4]*, *Jabez[3]*, *Samuel[2]*, *Matthew[1]*), b ——, 1785, in ——, d. Jan 7, 1839, in ——, m ——, Submit Ormsby, of Stockbridge, Vt, b 1792, d 1837

He resided in Pittsfield, Vt

Children—all born in Pittsfield, Vt.

70   Eliza Ormsby[8], b ——, m ——, Franklin Manley, of Chittenden, Vt , and had Henry[9], Ellen[9], Mary[9], Thomas[9], and Orlin[9]

71.   Hannah Lamantha[8], b ——; m ? William M. Whitcomb, and had Varnam W[9], Erwin[9], Mary Ann[9], Isabelle[9], Nettie[9], and Horace[9]

72 **Francis Portus**[8], b ——, m 1, ——, m. 2, Maria Sawyer
73 Rebecca Lemira[8], b ——; m Charles Lewin of Stockbridge, Vt , and had one child, Mary L[9].
74 Lucinda Abigail[8], b. Nov 18, 1827, in Pittsfield, Vt , d Sept, 1898, in Easthampton; m. May 5, 1845, James M Furman, b June 22 1824, at Fort Covington, N Y.; d Oct, 1899, in Woodstock, Vt Their children were Mary Lucinda[9], b in Chittenden, Vt , June 16, 1846, m. Dec 3, 1888, Joseph Eugen Bishel, of Tries, Germany, reside at Middletown, Ct ; Martha Wiley[9], b April 18, 1849 , Miner LeRoy[9], b Dec 7, 1851 , Marcus M[9], b May 26, 1854, and James Waldo[9], b Feb 22, 1857.
75 Mary F[8], b. ——; m. William Pratt   No children

32. NATHAN E[7] FULLER, (*Amasa*[6], *Jabez*[5], *Jonathan*[4], *Jabez*[3], *Samuel*[2], *Matthew*[1]), b Dec 29, 1791, in Sherburne, Vt ; d Oct 31, 1871, in Bakersfield, Vt , m 1, Feb 16, 1817, Almira Fay, b. May 21, 1792, at Barnard, Vt ; d May 15, 1862, m 2, Nov 1, 1862, Persis (Howe) Doane, b 1808, d Sept 30, 1873

He lived in Bakersfield

Children

76 Lucia Alzina[8], b June 15, 1818, d Oct 10, 1881, in N Y City, m 1836 Noah A Childs, and had Frances[9], Henry[9], Adelia[9], Childe Harold[9], and James[9]
77 Loraine E[8], b April 11, 1820, d April 19, 1896, in Orange, N J , m May 23, 1841, Benjamin F Cairns, b 1821, d 1891, no issue
78 Lawson W[8], b. Oct 28, 1823, d July 14, 1904, in N Y City, m 1, Dec 25, 1851, Mary A Martin, b 1830, d 1865, m 2, Oct 30, 1866, Frances L Wilcox, b 1840; d 1906
79 **Austin A.**[8], b Jan 27, 1825 , m Anna B Moore
80 Hannah A[8], b Jan. 21, 1827, d May 21, 1907, in N Y City, m Jan 20, 1850 Horace Secor, b June 5, 1810, d April 24, 1896 Children—all born in N Y City   Frances L[9], b Dec 9, 1850, d April 14, 1853, Clarence E[9], b June 5, 1854 ; Horace[9] b Nov 18 1856, and Austin A[9], b Feb 3, 1859, d May 18, 1860
81 **Andrew Jackson**[8], b Oct 22, 1828 , m Sarah M Vreeland
82 Julia R[8], b Nov 3, 1831 , d Jan 14, 1875, in N. Y City, m 1852, Jewett B Brigham, b 1826, d 1890 Children   Frank Lawson[9], b Jan 14, 1853, Flora Adelia[9], b June 17, 1857, and Flora Mabel[9], b April 10, 1866
83 **Eliakim F.**[8], b Aug 5, 1833 , d Dec 2, 1898, in N. Y City, m 1, 1862, Mary Wheeler, b 1835, d 1869, m 2, Dec 25, 1872, Martha A Doane, b 1855 , d 1877 , m 3, 1881, Martha ——, who d 1898
84 Adelia D[8], b July 2, 1835; d Dec 31, 1874, at Orange, N J ; m June 20, 1858, J Oscar D Harrison, b 1833 , d 1903 Children born in Orange, N J   A Erminia[9], b May 22, 1859, and Benj L[9], b Dec 19, 1865

34. WILLIAM OLIVER[7] FULLER, (*Andrew*[6], *Jabez*[5], *Jonathan*[4], *Jabez*[3], *Samuel*[2], *Matthew*[1]), b about 1786, d Nov 21. 1813, in Halifax, N S ; m ——, Mary McIntire

In 1813 he was Captain of the sloop Peggy; was taken prisoner by the

British—carried to Halifax, where he died of typhoid fever

Children

85   Andrew[8], b ——, d 1850, in New York, m ——

86   Mary Jane[8], b ——, d Aug 13, 1832, at Hope, Me., m Joshua Pierce, of Hope

37. PETER[7] FULLER, (*Andrew[6], Jabez[5], Jonathan[4], Jabez[3], Samuel[2], Matthew[1]*), b April 30, 1791, d March 20, 1866, m 1811, Phebe Dunbar

He was Sheriff and Deputy Sheriff of Lincoln Co, Me, for 25 years. Resided in Rockland, Me

Children

87   Andrew[8], b. March 26, 1812, d March 31, 1812

88.   Belinda White[8], b. Aug 4, 1813; d Jan. 22, 1896, m Oct. 25, 1846, Samuel Braley, of Oldtown, Me, and had May F[9], b April 6, 1849, Sarah Frances[9], b May 26, 1851, and Eva Rowena[9], b Aug. 28, 1853

89   **William Oliver[8]**, b Feb 11, 1816, m Bethia C Snow

90   **Daniel Dunbar[8]**, b April 5, 1818, m Mary White

91   **Andrew[8]**, b. May 2, 1820, m 1, Sarah Braley, m 2, Elizabeth Gay.

92   Mary W[8], b May 16, 1822, d Feb 19, 1904, m Calvin Bickford, and had Francis Sargent[9], b Oct 1, 1850, and William Oliver[9], b Nov 4, 1854

93   Phebe A[8], b Aug 21, 1826, died young.

94   Eliza A[8], b ——   Adopted

42. WILSON[8] FULLER, (*John[7], Zenas[6], Jabez[5], Jonathan[4], Jabez[3], Samuel[2], Matthew[1]*), b ——, d ——, m ——,

Children

95   Abel[9], b. ——, Resides Rockland, Me *

45. WILLIAM R[8] FULLER, (*James Y[7], Zenas[6], Jabez[5], Jonathan[4], Jabez[3], Samuel[2], Matthew[1]*), b Feb 10, 1822, in Appleton, Me, d about 1858, at Ellsworth, Me, m Oct 17, 1848, Mahala P Moody

Children

96   Aubrey M[9], b Oct 1, 1849, in Kenduskeag, Me   Resides (1909) at Star Prairie, Wis, unmarried   Parents both died when he was very young

46. ALEXANDER[8] FULLER, (*James Y[7], Zenas[6], Jabez[5], Jonathan[4], Jabez[3], Samuel[2], Matthew[1]*), b Feb, 1825, in Appleton, Me, d Dec. 23, 1904, at Star Prairie, Wis, m, 1854, Matilda Hyde

He removed to Star Prairie in 1863

Children

97   They had only an adopted son

      *No reply to request for information

47. ALDEN[8] FULLER, (*James Y.[7], Zenas[6], Jabez[5], Jonathan[4], Jabez[3], Samuel[2], Matthew[1]*), b Dec 9, 1827, in Appleton, Me ; d May 23, 1898, at Star Prairie, Wis ; m. about 1858, Sarah Simmons, of Georgiaville, R I

He removed to Star Prairie about 1865.

Children

98 A son, b ——; killed by falling from a horse, aged about 14 years

99 Ida[9], b May 29, 1869, m Edward Schneider of Amery, Wis

48. EDWARD A[8] FULLER, (*James Y[7], Zenas[6], Jabez[5], Jonathan[4], Jabez[3], Samuel[2], Matthew[1]*), b March 19, 1830, in Appleton, Me , d Oct 24, 1891, probably in Appleton, m ——, Laura A ——, b Jan 5, 1830, in Appleton; d April 20, 1906

Children—probably all born in Appleton

100 Ellen A[9], b Sept 7, 1858, m ——, —— Proctor, and had Frank C[10], b Aug 17, 1883, Edna E[10], b July 29, 1885, Bessie L[10], b Jan 10, 1888, Grace E[10], b Feb 4, 1890; Anne L[10], b Jan 19, 1891, Eva E[10], b Feb 13, 1893, and Leon[10], b Sept 10, 1898

101 Larelos A[9]

102 Marcellus E[9] } twins, b Sept 30, 1860; { d ——.

103 William R[9], b June 20, 1862

104 Carrie E[9], b. Nov 18, 1864, m ——, ——Mehuren, and had Harold E[10], b April 5, 1890, Wm E[10], b Aug. 31, 1896, and Herbert S[10], b Sept 15, 1893

105 Larelos[9], b ——; d ——

106 Edwin[9], b ——, d ——

107 Bessie[9], b ——, d ——

108 Frank[9], b ——, d ——

49. JOHN FRANKLIN[8] FULLER, (*James Y[7], Zenas[6], Jabez[5], Jonathan[4], Jabez[3], Samuel[2], Matthew[1]*), b Dec 12, 1833, in Appleton, Me , m Dec 20, 1854, Sarah Philbrick, at Searsmont, Me , m 2, —— 1866, Lydia F Nicholson, of Providence, R I

He removed to Star Prairie, Wis in 1866, and now resides at Cumberland, Wis

Children

109 **Al DeForest[9]**, b Jan 2, 1856, m Alice McGregor

110 **William Nicholson[9]**, b April 28, 1870, m Anne Grace Pinkerton

111 Elmer B H[9], b Sept 4, 1871, at Star Prairie, Wis ; m Marie May Ross, at Wardner, Idaho, July 2, 1900 No children (1909) Reside at Virginia, Minn

50. AUGUSTUS L[8] FULLER, (*Alexander[7], Zenas[6], Jabez[5], Jonathan[4], Jabez[3], Samuel[2], Matthew[1]*), b June 16, 1816, in Bristol, Me , d Sept 1, 1877 in Appleton, Me , m July 5, 1846, Levina H Chapman, b April 30, 1816, in Appleton, Me , d there Jan 29, 1900

Children born to them were

112   Oren Leroy[8], b May 24, 1847, in Appleton; d there Oct 14, 1851
113   **Albert A.[8]**, b April 10, 1850, m Mary F Mosman
114   Mary E[8], b May 10, 1852, at Appleton, d Jan 23, 1879, at Belfast, Me ; m. Dec 6, 1874. Sylvanus G Cottrell, of Belfast, and had Albert H[10], b Nov 5, 1875
115   Lizzie M[9], b. June 11, 1856, at Appleton

52. LAFAYETTE[8] FULLER, (*Alexander[7], Zenas[6], Jabez[5] Jonathan[4], Jabez[3], Samuel[2], Matthew[1]*), b April 15, 1825, in Appleton, Me , d Nov 4, 1868, at Appleton, m May 3, 1857, Elizabeth A Chapman
Children, born in Appleton
116   **William A.[9]**, b Feb 3, 1858, m Clara A. Barnes
117   Rosanna A[9], b May 18, 1860, m Charles Meader, of Haverhill

56. ISAAC[8] FULLER, (*Zenas[7], Zenas[6], Jabez[5], Jonathan[4], Jabez[3], Samuel[2], Matthew[1]*), b March 14, 1820, in Appleton, Me , d May 8, 1900, in Appleton, m ——, Jane Glidden
Children, born in Appleton
118. **Oren P.[9]**, b Feb 20, 1856; m Mollie J Adams
119   Vesta J[9], b ——, 1859, d Feb, 1861, in Appleton
120   **Charles A.[9]**, b June 14, 1863, m Isabel C Eastman

62. JOHN DUANE[8] FULLER, (*Nathaniel M[7], John[6], Jabez[5], Jonathan[4] Jabez[3], Samuel[2] Matthew[1]*), b June 18, 1809, in Sherburne, Vt , d Jan 3, 1885, m —— ——
He lived for a time in Arcade, N Y
Children
121   Frank[9], b ——   Resides North Fork, Madero Co, Cal
122   Minerva[9], b ——, d ——, m ——, Burt Crawford
123   Mary[9], b ——

72. FRANCIS PORTUS[8] FULLER, (*Portus[7], Amasa[6], Jabez[5], Jonathan[4], Jabez[3], Samuel[2], Matthew[1]*), b ——, in Pittsfield, Vt , d —— in Pittsfield, m 1, —— ——; m 2, Lydia Marie Sawyer, of Sherburne, Vt
Children by first wife
124
125
Children by second wife
126   Emma[9], b ——, m Andrew White of Sherburne, Vt
127   Isabelle[9], b ——, m —— Blaisdell, West Lebanon, N H
128. Minerva[9], b ——, m William Davis, Norwich, N H
129   William[9], b ——, unmarried (1913)

79. AUSTIN A[8] FULLER, (*Nathan E[7], Amasa[6], Jabez[5], Jonathan[4], Jabez[3], Samuel[2], Matthew[1]*), b Jan 27, 1825, in ——, d Nov 21, 1891, in

New York; m. May 29, 1850, Anna B Moore, b April 24, 1831, in New York, d July 21, 1906.

Children, all born in New York:

130 Oscar A⁹, b Jan 16, 1852; d June 13, 1884, unmarried.
131. George B⁹, b Oct 1. 1853, m June 16, 1892, Mary Mosher.
132. Frank W.⁹, b Nov 21, 1855
133 Augustus W⁹, b —— 185?
134 Charles J⁹, b Jan 20, 1861
135 Adelaide A⁹, b Aug 28, 1864
136 Minnie A⁹, b. Nov. 6, 1869
137 **Austin A.⁹**, b July 13. 1871, m Mary McArdle

81. ANDREW JACKSON⁸ FULLER, (*Nathan E⁷, Amasa⁶, Jabez⁵. Jonathan⁴, Jabez³, Samuel², Matthew¹*), b Oct 22, 1828, in ——, d Nov 16, 1891, at Black Creek, Pa , m Feb 11, 1861, Sarah M Vreeland, b Aug 4. 1835, at Ridgefield, N J

Children.

138 **Nathan E.⁹**, b Aug 17, 1862, m Elizabeth B. Cory

83. ELIAKIM F⁸ FULLER, (*Nathan E⁷, Amasa⁶, Jabez⁵ Jonathan⁴, Jabez³, Samuel², Matthew¹*), b Aug 5 1833, in ——; d Dec 2, 1898, in New York. m 1, —— 1862, Mary Wheeler, b ——, 1835, d Nov 21. 1869, m 2, Dec 25, 1872, Martha A Doane, b ——, 1855, d Jan 16, 1877, m 3, ——1881, Martha —— who d 1898

Children

139 Willard Lawson⁹. b Oct 14 1864
140 Arthur Fay⁹. b Oct 21. 1866

89. WILLIAM OLIVER⁸ FULLER, (*Peter⁷, Andrew⁶, Jabez⁵, Jonathan⁴, Jabez³, Samuel², Matthew¹*), b Feb 11, 1816, at Thomaston, Me , m Bethiah Charlotte Snow, of Thomaston

He resided at Rockland, Me

Children

141 Adela Snow⁹, b Aug 11, 1842 m Dec 12. 1867, Cyrus C Hills, of Rockland, and had Harry Chapman¹⁰, b July 9, 1869, Martha Douglas¹⁰, b March 26. 1871, Cyrus Walker¹⁰, b April 30, 1880, Oliver Fuller¹⁰, b Jan 1, 1882.
142 Martha Cobb⁹, b Sept. 19, 1844, m Feb 15. 1881, John Reed, of Damariscotta, Me , and had Edward Veazie¹⁰, b Dec 8, 1882
143 Ambrose Snow⁹, b June 20, 1846, lost at sea Sept 13, 1862
144 Mary⁹, b Nov 21 1852, m Oct. 20, 1860, Edward L Veazie, and had Frank Fuller¹⁰, b Jan 6, 1883 and Edward Reed¹⁰, b Sept 12, 1888
145 **William Oliver⁹**, b Feb 3, 1856, m 1. Elizabeth N. Jones, m 2, Kathleen W Stevens
146 **Frank Washburn⁹**, b Aug 24. 1860, m 1, Hattie O Watts, m 2, Grace Andrews

90. DANIEL DUNBAR[8] FULLER, (*Peter[7], Andrew[6], Jabez[5], Jonathan[4]* *Jabez[3], Samuel[2], Matthew[1]*), b April 5, 1818, in Rockland, Me , d there Nov 6, 1876, m Dec 2, 1841, Nancy T White of Boston, who d Aug 5, 1879

Their children were

147   Mary Frances[9], b Oct 6, 1842 , m Jan 6, 1898, William Harvey, of Boston

148   Belinda B[9], b 1847 , d 1847

91. ANDREW[8] FULLER, (*Peter[7], Andrew[6], Jabez[5], Jonathan[4], Jabez[3],* *Samuel[2], Matthew[1]*), b May 2, 1820, in Rockland, Me , d —— in Albany, N Y , m 1, Sarah Bialey, who d Feb 8, 1855, m 2, Elizabeth Gay

Resided at Camden, Me , and Albany, N. Y , was a manufacturer of woolen goods

Children by first wife

149   Edward Tillson[9], b July 8, 1846, d July 13, 1876, at Camden, Me , m Aug 16, 1867, Cora J Perry

150   **Holly Granger[9]**, b Nov 20, 1847 , m 1, April 2, 1868, Mary J Washburn , m 2, Sept 13, 1876, Hattie King Rogers   Resided in Portland, Me

151   Phebe Luella[9], b ——, d at Camden, Me

152   Duncan McCallum[9] b July 3, 1851 , m Mrs Geo B Bebb, of Searsmont, Me   Res Albany N Y

By second wife

153   Osgood Everett[9], b Sept 21, 1857 , d ——, Albany, N Y , m Ida Marriner

154   Sarah[9], b July 9, 1860 , d Oct 17 1862

NINTH GENERATION.

109. Ai DEFOREST[9] FULLER, (*John F[8], James Y[7], Zenas[6], Jabez[5],* *Jonathan[4], Jabez[3], Samuel[2], Matthew[1]*), b Jan 2, 1856, at Appleton, Me ; m June 7, 1879, Alice McGregor, of New Richmond, Wis

He resides at Tower, Minn (1909)

Children

155   John Alvin[10], b March 23, 1880, at Barronett, Wis

156   Charles Alden[10], b Sept 16, 1882, at Barronett

157   Robert DeForest[10], b Aug. 7, 1887, at Barronett

158   Beatrice W[10], b July 3, 1893, at Tower, Minn

110. WILLIAM NICHOLSON[9] FULLER, (*John F[8], James Y[7], Zenas[6]* *Jabez[5], Jonathan[4], Jabez[3], Samuel[2], Matthew[1]*), b April 28, 1870, at Star Prairie, Wis., m Nov. 30, 1892, at Leon, Wis , Anne Grace Pinkerton

He resides at Cumberland, Wis (1914)

Children, born at Cumberland

159   Donald Pinkerton[11], b Aug 11, 1893

160   William Thomas[10], b May 23, 1895, d Aug 26, 1897
161   Richard C[10], b May 23, 1898

113. ALBERT A[8] FULLER, (*Augustus L.[8], Alexander[7], Zenas[6], Jabez[5], Jonathan[4], Jabez[3], Samuel[2], Matthew[1]*), b April 10, 1850, in Appleton, Me , m Nov. 10, 1878, Mary F Mossman
   Children, born in Appleton:
162   Bertha[10], b March 12, 1880; d March 22, 1880
163   Aubrey L[10], b. Sept. 9, 1885.
164   Maud Sarita[10], b July 27, 1891

116. WILLIAM A[8] FULLER, (*Lafayette[8], Alexander[7], Zenas[6], Jabez[5], Jonathan[4], Jabez[3], Samuel[2], Matthew[1]*), b. Feb 3, 1858, in Appleton, Me , m Aug 22, 1880, Clara A Barnes, of Camden, Me
   Children
165   L Montez[10], b. Sept 14, 1881, d March 29, 1882, in Hope, Me.
166   Vannie Grace[10], b March 22, 1884, in Hope
167   Preston H[10], b Aug 14, 1891, d April 15, 1896, in Camden, Me
168   Maud R[10], b Sept 27, 1898, in Camden

118. OREN P[8] FULLER, (*Isaac[6] Zenas[7], Zenas[6], Jabez[5], Jonathan[4], Jabez[3], Samuel[2], Matthew[1]*), b Feb 20, 1856, in Appleton, Me , m ——, Mollie J Adams, of Searsmont, Me
   Children born in Searsmont, Me
169   Leroy A[10], b July 29, 1881
170   Ruth Edith[10], b Aug 1, 1883

120. CHARLES A[8] FULLER, (*Isaac[8], Zenas[7], Zenas[6], Jabez[5], Jonathan[4], Jabez[3], Samuel[2], Matthew[1]*), b June 14, 1863, in Appleton Me., m ——, Isabel C Eastman
   Children
171   Olney W[10], b March 11, 1892
172   Orrie J[10], b May 3, 1894
173   Gladys M[10], b Nov 29, 1895

137. AUSTIN A[9] FULLER (*Austin A[8], Nathan E[7], Amasa[6], Jabez[5], Jonathan[4], Jabez[3], Samuel[2], Matthew[1]*), b July 13, 1871, in New York , m Nov 7, 1899, Mary McArdle, b Aug 26, 1874 in New York
   Children
174   Austin A[10], b Jan 2, 1901
175   Ethel E[10], b April 9, 1902
176   May G[10], b Jan 6, 1909

138. NATHAN E[9] FULLER, (*Andrew J[8], Nathan E[7], Amasa[6], Jabez[5],*

Jonathan⁴, Jabez³, Samuel², Matthew¹), b Aug 17. 1862, m ——; m
June 28, 1888, Elizabeth B Cory b April 6 1859, m Lima, Ind
 Children, born in Corning, N Y
177   Clarence C¹⁰, b May 30, 1895
178   Alice M¹⁰. b Oct 15, 1898

145. WILLIAM OLIVER⁹ FULLER, (*William O⁸, Peter⁷ Andrew⁶, Jabez⁵,
Jonathan⁴, Jabez³, Samuel², Matthew¹*), b Feb 3, 1856, m 1, Oct 25,
1882, Elizabeth N Jones, who d June 8, 1890, m 2, March 29, 1892,
Kathleen W Stephens, of Baldwin, Kansas
 He resides in Rockland, Me
 Children
179   Douglas Wardwell¹⁰, b Sept 9, 1884   Ensign in U. S Navy
180   Donald Hills¹⁰, b Aug 4, 1886
181   Elizabeth Jones¹⁰, b June 23, 1887
182   Marion Snow¹⁰, b 1889, d 1889
183   Richard Stearns¹⁰, b May 22 1894

146 FRANK WASHBURN⁹ FULLER (*William O⁸ Peter⁷, Andrew⁶,
Jabez⁵, Jonathan⁴, Jabez³, Samuel², Matthew¹*), b Aug 24, 1860, m 1
Dec 27, 1887, Hattie O Watts who d Feb 1, 1896, m 2, March 19, 1900,
Grace Andrews
 Children
184   Helen Whitford¹⁰, b Jan 27, 1882
185   Lucy Andrews¹⁰, b Jan 6, 1902

150. HOLLY GRANGER⁹ FULLER, (*Andrew⁸, Peter⁷, Andrew⁶, Jabez⁵,
Jonathan,⁴ Jabez³, Samuel², Matthew¹*), b Nov 20, 1847, m 1, Mary J
Washburn, m 2, Hattie King Rogers
 Children by first wife
186   A son, b 1869; d 1869
 By second wife
187   Harry Upton¹⁰, b Dec 3 ,1877
188   Florence Luella¹⁰, b July 19, 1879
189   Charles Gilman¹⁰, b Jan 4, 1882

FIFTH GROUP

FOURTH GENERATION.

EBENEZER⁴ FULLER, AND SOME OF HIS DESCENDANTS

30. EBENEZER⁴ FULLER, (*Jabez³, Samuel², Matthew¹*), b Feb 20, 1708, at Barnstable, d ——, m Jan 1, 1729, Martha Jones

Children

1   Martha⁵, b ——; m 1753, Gamaliel Ewer of Barnstable
2   Ebenezer⁵, b about 1735, m Deborah ——
3   Nathan⁵, b ——, m. 1, Mary ——, m 2 ? April 2, 1771, Anna Connett
4   Elizabeth⁵, b ——

The above is from H W Brainard's Mss   I have found nothing more

SIXTH GROUP

FOURTH GENERATION.

MATTHIAS⁴ FULLER, AND SOME OF HIS DESCENDANTS

35. MATTHIAS⁴ FULLER (*Timothy³, Samuel², Matthew¹*), b March 24, 1700 in East Haddam, Ct, d there before Dec 6, 1770, m 1, June 16, 1722, Mary Cone, b Jan 6, 1701, d Nov 16, 1739, dau of Daniel and Mary (Gates) Cone of East Haddam, m 2, April 16, 1741, Mrs Jemima (Richardson) Hungerford, b at Stonington, Ct, dau of Stephen and Lydia Richardson, and widow of Green Hungerford, m 3, ——, Patience ——, who survived him, and is called his widow and relict She was living in Colchester, Ct, Dec 6, 1770 (E Haddam Deeds, vol VIII, p. 380)

Matthias Fuller was a farmer residing at East Haddam, Millington Society He was one of the constituent members of the Millington Church

Children, born in East Haddam

1   **Matthias⁵**, b Jan 15, 1724-5; m. Mary Griswold
2   **Elisha⁵**, b March 4, 1727, m Esther Hungerford
3   **Noadiah⁵**, b Sept 3, 1729; m Lydia Cone
4   **Daniel⁵**, b Feb 5, 1731-2; m 1, Mehitable Cone, m 2, Eunice Andrews
5   Ezra⁵, b Aug 24, 1734, d July, 1736
6   Anne⁵, b Feb. 17, 1736-7, d Sept 9, 1821, at Millington, m June 25, 1761 Nathan Beebe No record of any children found
7   Mary⁵, b Oct 29, 1739, d Feb 2, 1739-40

FIFTH GENERATION.

1. MATTHIAS⁵ FULLER, (*Matthias⁴, Timothy³, Samuel², Matthew¹*), b Jan 15, 1724-5, in East Haddam, Ct, d there March 16, 1788, aged 63 His will dated March 14—proved March 31, 1788, names children given below (Colchester P R Vol V, p 443) He m June 27, 1754, Mary Griswold—parents and date of her death not known

He was a farmer, living in Millington, E Haddam, Ct

Children born in E Haddam

8   Ithamar⁴, b Dec 25, 1754; d Dec 23, 1830 His widow d Jan.
22, 1852⁵

9   Anne⁶, b. Sept 1, 1757, d Feb 7, 1790, at Millington, m. ——
Winslow

10 Mary⁶, b ——, unmarried, 1795

11 John Wilkes⁶, b ——, d Oct 21, 1793, aged 23 years

12 Matthias⁶, b Sept 29, 1773; m Huldah Marvin

2. ELISHA⁶ FULLER, (*Matthias⁵*, *Timothy⁵*, *Samuel²* *Matthew¹*), b
March 4, 1727, in East Haddam, Ct , d Nov 3, 1811, in Richmond, m.
May 5, 1748, at Millington, East Haddam, Esther Hungerford, b May 22,
1728, at E. Haddam, dau of Green and Jemima (Richardson) Hungerford

Elisha Fuller was a lieutenant of militia About 1798 he removed to
Richmond, Mass His wife was admitted member Millington church
Jan. 23, 1757, and at Richmond Cong Church Nov 4, 1804

  Children, born in East Haddam

13 **Elisha⁶**, b. about 1749, m Sarah Sparrow

14 Lydia⁶, b ——, m Feb 1, 1775, Calvin Tilden of Richmond.

15 Uriel⁶, b ——

16 Ezra⁶, b ——

        The last three children were bapt May 8, 1757

        The U S Census of 1790 mentions the family of an Uriel
Fuller in E Haddam of eight persons—2 sons under 16 and 4
daughters

3. NOADIAH⁵ FULLER, (*Matthias⁴*, *Timothy³*, *Samuel²*, *Matthew¹*), b
Feb 5, 1731-2. at East Haddam, Ct , d May 19, 1818⁵, m 1, May, 1756,
1755, Lydia Cone, b Feb. 5, 1732-3, d June 5, 1812, dau of Daniel. Jr.
and Mary (Spencer) Cone.

Noadiah Fuller lived in Millington, E Haddam

  Children, born in E Haddam

17 Mary⁶, bapt. Nov. 15, 1767, m Philemon Tiffany

18 **Noadiah⁶**, b about 1763, bapt Nov 15, 1767.

4. DANIEL⁵ FULLER, (*Matthias⁴*, *Timothy³*, *Samuel²*, *Matthew¹*), b
Feb 5, 1731-2, at East Haddam, Ct ; d May 19, 1818⁵, m 1, May 1756.
Mehitable Cone, b Aug. 11, 1729, d about 1757, dau. of James and
Grace (Spencer) Cone, of E Haddam; m 2, May 25, 1758, Eunice
Andrews, b July 9, 1742, dau of Samuel, Jr. and Jemima (Cone)
Andrews, of E Haddam

Daniel Fuller lived in Millington, E Haddam

Shortly before his death—instead of a will—he made deeds of gifts
to his surviving children, and from these deeds were obtained the
names of his younger children, not recorded elsewhere

  Children, born in E. Haddam

4

19   **Daniel**[6], b. Feb., 1757; m. Louisa Lovell.
20   ?Mehitable[6], b ——
21   Sarah[6], b —— ,1764; d Jan 25, 1833; unmarried
22   **Warren**[6], b. —— 1773; m Deborah Jones
23   Samuel Andrews[6], b 1774; d. 1840 unmarried
24   Huldah[6], b. 1776; d Nov 23, 1856 at Salem, Ct, unmarried
25   **Richardson**[6], b Feb 9, 1780; m Jerusha B Carrier

SIXTH GENERATION.

13.   ELISHA[6] FULLER, (*Elisha*[5], *Matthias*[4], *Timothy*[3], *Samuel*[2], *Matthew*[1]), b about 1749, in East Haddam, Ct., d there Aug. 7, 1778; m Nov. 9, 1770, Sarah Sparrow, b. about 1740; d April 16, 1818, aged 79.
Children, born in E Haddam.

26   **Elisha**[7], b Oct 3, 1771; m. 1, Rachel Brainard, m 2, Mrs Sally (Brainard) Emmons
27   Lydia[7], b about 1773.
28   Eunice[7], bapt Dec 5, 1779, d June 20, 1842, aged 66, in Poolville, N Y, m Dec 28, 1797, Elijah Brainard, of Poolville, and had Sarah S[8], Wm G[8], Elijah[8], Ogden[8], and Ogden A[8].
29   **Ezra Newell**[8], b. about 1778, m Deborah Carrier

18.   NOADIAH[6] FULLER, (*Noadiah*[5], *Matthias*[4], *Timothy*[3], *Samuel*[2], *Matthew*[1]), b about 1763, in East Haddam, Ct, d ——, m ——, Dorothy Church (Kellogg Gen)

Before 1815 he had removed to the town of Chatham, Ct, whence he removed to Genessee Co, N. Y (Brainard Mss)

Noadiah of Ogden (Monroe Co, N Y) (Kellogg Gen)

Children ·
30   **Chauncey**[7], b Sept 5, 1790, m 1, Martha Stewart, m 2, Sarah Ann Beckwith
31.   **Calvin**[7], b June 2, 1793, m. Aspasha Kellogg
32   Eliphalet[7], b ——
33   Harriet[7], b ——, m March 4, 1813, Mumford Ransom
34   Eliza[7], b ——

19.   DANIEL[6] FULLER, (*Daniel*[5], *Matthias*[4], *Timothy*[3], *Samuel*[2], *Matthew*[1]) b Feb, 1757, in Millington, East Haddam, Ct, d there Dec 16, 1789, aged 32 y —10 mos., m. —— Louisa Lovell, who m 2, —— Grover, of North Bolton, now Vernon, Ct

Children
35   **Ambrose**[7], b about 1782
36   Isaac[7], b about 1785.
37   Aaron[7], b 1787, d Sept, 1811, aged 24
38   Pamelia[7], b Sept 19, 1789, m Eli Williams

22. WARREN[6] FULLER, (*Daniel*[5], *Matthias*[4], *Timothy*[3], *Samuel*[2], *Matthew*[1]), b. about 1773, in Millington, East Haddam, Ct · d Feb 24 1840, in Salem, Ct ; m June 5, 1796, Deborah Jones, of Colchester, Ct , b. there 1775, d Feb 8, 1837, at Salem

He was a farmer who lived in Colchester and Salem
Children, all born in Salem, Ct
39   **Amos Jones**[7], b 1798, m. Celinda Miller
40   Mary[7], b —— 1799; d June 19, 1820, unmarried
41. **Daniel**[7], b April 1, 1801, m Mary Sisson
42. Electa J[7], b 1803, d July 8, 1821
43   **Warren**[7], b 1807, m. 1, Electa Williams, m 2, Anne Minard
44   Henry[7], b 1808, d May 28, 1822

25. RICHARDSON[6] FULLER, (*Daniel*[5], *Matthias*[4], *Timothy*[3], *Samuel*[2], *Matthew*[1]), b Feb 9, 1780, in Millington, East Haddam, Ct ; d there Sept. 23, 1858, m Sept 14, 1835, Jerusha B Carrier, of Colchester, Ct , b 1808; d March, 1846

He was a farmer and lived on his father's homestead
Children, born in E Haddam
45   Mary Jane[7], b ——
46   Sarah E[7], b. ——

SEVENTH GENERATION.

26. ELISHA[7] FULLER, (*Elisha*[6], *Elisha*[5], *Matthias*[4], *Timothy*[3], *Samuel*[2], *Matthew*[1]), b Oct 3, 1771, in East Haddam, Ct , d April 3, 1845 in East Hamilton, N Y , m. May 9, 1793, Rachel Brainard, b Dec 23, 1770, in Chatham, Ct ; d Nov 19, 1826, in E Hamilton, m 2, May 1, 1827, Sally (Brainard) Emmons, b. Jan. 28, 1794, in Millington, E Haddam, Ct , d. June 26, 1880, at Dexter, Mich

Children born at East Hamilton
47   Laura[8], b April 9, 1794, d Jan 22, 1829, m 1812, L E Beach
48   Roxy[8], b Jan 30, 1796; d Oct 6, 1821, unmarried
49. Deborah[8], b March 11, 1798, d Aug 25, 1828, in Mich , m 1824, Silas Graham
50. **Sparrow**[8], b Sept 30, 1799; m M Electa Sexton
51   **Lorenzo**[8], b. Feb. 2, 1806, m Martha Haling
52   **Ezra Newell**[8], b Oct 2, 1809, m Louisa Youmans
53. Roxy Jane[8], b May 6, 1828, d Oct. 1878, m July 5, 1846, John Muir, and had Mary A[9], b. May 26, 1847; Frank[9], Feb 7, 1860; Mary[9], Sept 25, 1863
54   Laura Celinda[8], b Aug 12, 1830, d May, 1881, m Nov 2, 1848 William H Lane, and had Herbert D[9], b April 2, 1850, Elisha D[9], Dec 5, 1851, and John H.[9], Dec. 16, 1853
55. Elisha[8], b June 5, 1832, d March 13, 1833
56   Deborah Salome[9], b July 5, 1835; m. Nov 8, 1854, Orsemus C Sawdy, and had Fred S[9], b Dec 31, 1856; Andrew B[9], Aug 19,

1861, Addie⁸, Oct 22, 1865, Fred⁸, July 30, 1868, and Nora⁸, Sept. 27, 1872.

29. EZRA NEWELL⁷ FULLER, (*Elisha⁶, Elisha⁵, Matthew⁴, Timothy³, Samuel², Matthew¹*), b about 1778, in East Haddam, Ct , d. ——— ; m ———, Deborah Carrier.

Children.
57   Jerusha⁸, b Feb 4, 1807, at East Hamilton, N Y., d Nov 20, 1883; m Aug 18, 1829, Ephraim Brainard, and had Mary E⁹, b. July 18, 1830, Lyman⁹, March 2, 1832, and Lydia C.⁹, Sept. 22, 1841.

30. CHAUNCEY⁷ FULLER, (*Noadiah⁶, Noadiah⁵, Matthias⁴, Timothy³, Samuel², Matthew¹*), b. Sept 5, 1790, in East Haddam, Ct ; d ———. m 1, March 25, 1813, at Millington, E Haddam, Martha Stewart, b. 1782; d. Feb 13, 1824, m 2, March 21, 1826, Sarah Ann Beckwith, of E Haddam.

He lived in Millington and Middletown, Ct

Children.
58   Martha Shaw⁸, b Jan 21, 1814, m John L Bacon
59.   **Aaron Chauncey⁸** b June 27, 1815, m Eunice Anne Avery
60   Mary Graves⁸, b. Nov 16, 1816, m. Edmund Daniels
61   William Cone⁸, b March 13, 1819; d. 1847
62   **Joseph Arnold⁸**, b Dec 15, 1820; m. Betsey E. Smith
63   Rhoda L ⁸, b. Sept 15, 1822, d Sept., 1903, in Hartford, Ct , m. Dec 3, 1844, Geo W Woolley of Hartford
64   **John C.⁸**, b March 1, 1824, m Henrietta Ralph

31. CALVIN⁷ FULLER, (*Noadiah⁶, Noadiah⁵, Matthias⁴, Timothy³, Samuel², Matthew¹*), b June 2, 1827; d July, 1837; m. Oct 25, 1823, in Tolland Arpasha Kellogg, b July 16, 1794, d Dec 23, 1891, in Southwick.

He lived in Tolland and West Granville.

Children:
65   Eliza⁸, b May 26, 1824, in Tolland; d Dec. 8, 1838
66   **Henry⁸**, b July 17, 1825, m. 1, Harriet Bridges, m 2, Catherine B Pearl
67   **William⁸**, b. June 4, 1827, m Mrs. Cynthia Clark
68.   Calvin⁸, b Jan 18, 1829, m Mrs Mary Ann Cowles
69.   John⁸, b Sept 12, 1831
70   Harriet⁸, b Aug 4, 1833, d March 12, 1835
71   **Chauncey⁸**, b Oct 16, 1835, m Eliza A Cook.

35. AMBROSE⁷ FULLER, (*Daniel⁶, Daniel⁵, Matthias⁴, Timothy³, Samuel², Matthew¹*), b. Dec 17, 1779, in East Haddam, Ct , d Dec. 17, 1857, aged 78 years, in Springfield, m ——, Chloe Newton, b July 7, 1786, d Nov 23, 1847

Children

72 Laura Pamelia[8], b April 17, 1808, d Sept 3, 1865, m Feb 22, 1827, Joseph W Bly, of Ludlow

73 **Lester K.**[8], b Feb. 21, 1810, m 1, Mary Adams; m 2, Adeline Frost

74 **Aaron**[8], b July 28, 1812, m Jerusha Gale

75 **Francis L.**[8], b Oct 1, 1814, m Dolly Maria Shepard

76 **Samuel**[8], b Sept 7, 1817, m Mary B Frost

77 Daniel[8], b. April 10, 1821; d April 10, 1821

78 William N[8], b June 5, 1823, in Springfield, d May 12, 1902, at Excelsior, Minn; m Susan Russell, March 3, 1851, (both of Wilbraham), daughter of John T Russell No children

79 **Rodney**[8], b Nov 20, 1825, m Elizabeth Campbell

80 Adeline Zerviah[8], b May 20, 1820, m Sept. 29, 1853, Nelson W Morley. Resided in Baraboo, Wis, over 50 years Children Newton F[9], b Oct 12, 1854, m Sept 29, 1883, Sarah Jane Christie Arthur W[9], Nov 1, 1855, m March 5, 1892, Abbie Van Buren Fannie C.[9], June 10, 1859, d May 13, 1888 Lillie A[9], June 27, 1864 Thomas B[9], March 15, 1866 Frank N[9], March 4, 1868, m Dec 24, 1894, Alma B Knapp Lucy M[9], Jan 10, 1870 Charles Lyman[9], May 9, 1872, m Feb 28, 1901, Edna E George

39. AMOS JONES[7] FULLER, (*Warren*[6], *Daniel*[5], *Matthew*[4], *Timothy*[3], *Samuel*[2], *Matthew*[1]), b. about 1798, in Salem, Ct; d there Jan 12, 1846, m Feb 26, 1821, Celinda Miller, b 1796, d Jan 31, 1876, at Waterloo, Ia

Children

81 **Henry Atwood**[8]. b ——; d ——; m Evelyn ——

82. Aurelia[8], b ——, 1822, d ——, 1891; unmarried

41. DANIEL[7] FULLER, (*Warren*[6], *Daniel*[5], *Matthias*[4], *Timothy*[3], *Samuel*[2], *Matthew*[1]), b April 1, 1801, in Salem, Ct, d. there Dec, 1883; m ——, 1837, Mary Sisson, of Swansea, b 1809, d 1861

Children all born in Salem, Ct

83 Ellen Maria[8], b 1839, m Joseph Smith, of Colchester Ct., where she resides (1912) Has seven children George Albert[9], b Feb 1, 1867 William Irving[9], Feb 2, 1868 Anne May[9], Aug 17, 1869 Bertha, March 8, 1871 Nellie Maria[9], Jan 17, 1873 Joseph Henry[9], Sept 20, 1874, and Rose Florence[9], May 24, 1876

84 **George Henry**[8], b Aug 28, 1840; m Emily Halsted.

85 **Sherwood Whitcomb**[8], b July 8, 1842; m Jennie N Morgan

43. WARREN[7] FULLER, (*Warren*[6], *Daniel*[5], *Matthias*[4], *Timothy*[3], *Samuel*[2], *Matthew*[1]), b 1807, in Salem, Ct; d Sept 9, 1858; m 1, Feb 26,

1832, Electa Williams, of East Haddam, Ct ; b 1809, d 1847, m 2, Aug 17, 1849, Anne Minard, b 1816, d 1867.

Children born in Salem, Ct

86   Anna Electa[8], b Sept 5, 1850; d April 6, 1886, m Feb 13, 1877 Frank A. Rugg, of Keene, N H   She left one child, Warren Fuller[9] Rugg

87   Nettie[8], b April 14, 1853, m Sept 17, 1885, John M. Fox, of Salem, and had Anna Elizabeth[9], b Oct 7, 1886   Maria Lathrop[9], Aug 22, 1889, and Henry Warren[9], Sept 25, 1898

88   Alice[8], b June 29, 1855, d Jan. 15, 1870

EIGHTH GENERATION.

50. SPARROW[8] FULLER, (*Elisha[7], Elisha[6], Elisha[5], Matthias[4], Timothy[3], Samuel[2], Matthew[1]*), b Sept 30, 1799, in East Hamilton, N Y , d Feb 5, 1849, in Hamilton, N Y , m 1826, Electa Sexton

They had 4 children

89

90   A son, b ——; resides in Hamilton

91   A daughter, b ——, resides in Hamilton

92

51. LORENZO[8] FULLER, (*Elisha[7], Elisha[6], Elisha[5], Matthias[4], Timothy[3], Samuel[2], Matthew[1]*), b Feb 2, 1806, in East Hamilton, N Y , d there May 17, 1871; m April 14, 1830, Martha Haling

Children

93   Azubah[9], b March 15, 1831, m Jan 8, 1860, Griffith Murphy

94   Lucinda[9], b Oct 31, 1837

95   Sophronia[9], b Dec 20, 1839

      All three were living at the old homestead in E Hamilton, 1908

52. EZRA NEWELL[8] FULLER, (*Elisha[7], Elisha[6], Elisha[5], Matthias[4], Timothy[3], Samuel[2], Matthew[1]*), b Oct 2, 1809, in East Hamilton, N Y , d Dec 31, 1886, in Northeast, Pa , m 1835, Louisa Youmans

Children

96   Julia Delphine[9], b Sept 26, 1835, d Feb 19, 1845

97.   Sophia Youmans[9], b July 8, 1837; m Nov , 1853, John Jacks

98.   Rachel Jennette[9], b March 11, 1840, d 1872; m Feb , 1866, Geo W Butt

99   Melvina[9], b July, 1842, m , 1870, Simeon Royce

100.   Elisha T [9], b May 4, 1845, m 1867, Elizabeth Franklin

101   **Leander Sparrow**[9], b May, 1847, m Betty Bennett

59. AARON CHAUNCEY[8] FULLER, (*Chauncey[7], Noadiah[6], Noadiah[4], Matthias[4], Timothy[3], Samuel[2], Matthew[1]*), b June 27, 1815, at East Haddam, Ct ; d Sept 6, 1896, at Waterford, Ct , m Nov 24, 1851, Eunice Anne Avery, of Groton, Ct , b Nov 21, 1830.

He lived in E Haddam, Middletwn, Groton and Waterford, Ct

Children, all born at Groton, Ct

102 Chauncey A⁹, b Jan 13, 1853, m Dec 20, 1884, Jennie White
103 William⁹, b Sept 2, 1854
104 Ida⁹, b Feb 11, 1857; m J Frank Darrow
105 Jennie⁹, b July 24, 1863
106 George⁹, b Oct 23, 1865

62. JOSEPH ARNOLD⁸ FULLER, (*Chauncey⁷*, *Noadiah⁶*, *Noadiah⁵*, *Matthias⁴*, *Timothy³*, *Samuel², Matthew¹*), b Dec 15, 1820, d ——; m Feb 19, 1844, Betsey E Smith, of Portland, Ct, who d March 21, 1875

He lived in Middletown and Willington, Ct

Children

107 Joseph A⁹, b May, 1847, d 1847
108 Frederick A⁹, b Jan 3, 1852, m E B Lawrence
109. George⁹, b March 2, 1854, d 1859.

64. JOHN C⁸ FULLER, (*Chauncey⁷*, *Noadiah⁶*, *Noadiah⁵*. *Matthias⁴* *Timothy³*, *Samuel², Matthew¹*), b March 1, 1824, d Sept 16, 1896, m Feb 6, 1857, Henrietta Ralph

He lived in Cromwell, Ct , and in Willington, after 1866

He followed the sea for years, and in 1862-5 was a Union soldier

Children

110 Mary C⁹, b Oct 22, 1861
111 John C⁹, b March 15, 1863, d 1875

66. HENRY⁸, FULLER, (*Calvin⁷*, *Noadiah⁶*, *Noadiah⁵*, *Matthias⁴*, *Timothy³*, *Samuel², Matthew¹*), b July 17, 1825, in Tolland, d June 14, 1913, in Westfield; m. 1, Harriet Frances Bridges, b in Warren, m 2, Dec 15, 1856, Katherine Barker Pease, b in Wellbrook, Me, who d May 25, 1888

He was a lawyer, resided in Westfield In 1854 was a member of the Massachusetts Legislature, later he served 6 years as County Commissioner, in 1868, 1874 and 1875 he was a member of the State Senate, in 1875 appointed trial justice, later served 5 years as clerk of the District Court, at time of his death was the attorney and one of the trustees of the Woronoco Savings Bank, was a member of the Congregational Church, and the Western Hampden Historical Society.

Children, b in Westfield

112 Ada⁹, b April 18, 1852, d Oct 7, 1903
113 Katie⁹, b Nov 4, 1857; d Dec 16, 1909, unmarried
114 Infant, b Jan 15, 1860, } d same day
115 Infant, b Jan 15, 1860; } d Jan 21, 1860
116. Henry L⁹, b Dec 3, 1861, d Feb 7, 1864

117   Florence[9], b Feb 27, 1867, m Oct 2, 1901, Milton B Whitney

67. WILLIAM[8] FULLER, (*Calvin[7], Noadiah[6], Noadiah[5], Matthias[4], Timothy[3], Samuel[2], Matthew[1]*), b June 4, 1827, in West Granville; d ——, m Mrs Cynthia Clark
   Children.
118   Calvin C[9], b about 1856 in Hudson, N Y , m Jan 9, 1877, Hattie A Parker, b in Springfield, res Hartland, Ct
119.   Leman C[9], b about 1869 in Southwick, m Louise S Messenger

71. CHAUNCEY[8] FULLER, (*Calvin[7], Noadiah[6], Noadiah[5], Matthias[4], Timothy[3], Samuel[2], Matthew[1]*), b Oct 16, 1835, d ——, m Dec. 15, 1854, in Westfield, Eliza A Cook, who d July 5, 1912, in Southwick
   Children
120   Francis C[9], b May 22, 1856, m Feb. 15, 1880, Mary J Granger
121   John J[9], b ——, 1858, m June 27, 1888, Ellen J Sibley
122   Calvin[9], b May 12, 1860
123   **Lyman C.[9]**, b March 20, 1862, m March 18, 1891, Hattie M Norton
124   Emily E[9], b July 13, 1864, m Oct 22, 1885, Franklin R Palmer, and had Henry F[10], who d April 21, 1905, aged 15 years 2 months 12 days
   Resides in Southwick
125   **Daniel K.[9]**, b —— 1867, m April 2, 1891, Cora A Barnes
126   **Harold H.[9]**, b —— 1870, m April 4, 1891, Carrie H Ellsworth of Becket

73. LESTER KING[8] FULLER, (*Ambrose[7], Daniel[6], Daniel[5], Matthias[4], Timothy[3], Samuel[2], Matthew[1]*), b Feb 21, 1810 in Suffield, Ct , d Oct 31, 1879 in Brimfield, m 1, Oct 23, 1834, Mary Adams who d April 5, 1848, in Wilbraham, m 2, Adeline Frost who d Feb 1 1891, aged 62, in Brimfield
   Children
127   Mary Angeline[9], b ——, 1835, d Sept 8, 1896, in Monson m July 2, 1854, in Palmer, N Wright and had 5 children
128   Rosamond[9], b ——, died young
129.   John K[9], b May 1, 1840, d Jan 25 1914, at Goshen, m Dec 2, 1869, Lucina Plumley
          No children   Resided at Goshen
130   Isabella[9] b Oct. 28, 1846, in Springfield, m 1865, Frank C Webber, had one son, Clarence W.[10]
131   Nancy Melissa[9], b. ——, in Monson, m March 3, 1865, John K Wellman, and had one son and one daughter
132   Alice[9], b March 5, 1848, in Springfield; d Sept 12, 1848, in Wilbraham
133   Lucy A.[9], b Dec. 13, 1852, in Monson, d Dec. 16, 1852

74. AARON[8] FULLER, (*Ambrose[7], Daniel[6], Daniel[5], Matthias[4], Timothy[3], Samuel[2], Matthew[1]*), b July 25, 1812, in Wilbraham, d Oct 17, 1858, in Springfield, m Sept 24, 1834, Jerusha Gale; b at Charlton.
Children:

134   Norman Leslie[9], b July 14, 1839, in Springfield
135   Herbert Newton[9], b May 10, 1841, in Wilbraham.*
136   Sylvester Franklin[9], b Jan 27, 1844, in Wilbraham
         *A Herbert N Fuller of 15th Mass. Regt. d in Andersonville Prison, Feb 20, 1865

75 FRANCIS LORD[8] FULLER, (*Ambrose[7], Daniel[6], Daniel[5], Matthias[4], Timothy[3], Samuel[2], Matthew[1]*), b Oct 1, 1814, in Wilbraham, d June 17, 1881, at Kansas City, Mo , m Sept 11, 1848, Dolly Maria Shepard, of Westfield
Children

137   A dau , b. ——; d ——.
138   A dau , b ——
139   Edward[9], b ——, resides Kansas City.
140   Daniel[9], b ——, resides Kansas City.
         Probably not given in order of birth

76. SAMUEL[8] FULLER, (*Ambrose[7], Daniel[6], Daniel[5], Matthias[4], Timothy[3], Samuel[2], Matthew[1]*), b Sept 7, 1817, in Wilbraham, d March 28, 1875, m April 13, 1843, Mary B Frost, of Wilbraham
Child, b in Wilbraham

141   Charles F[9], b June 16, 1846, d July 27, 1847

79. RODNEY[8] FULLER, (*Ambrose[7], Daniel[6], Daniel[5], Matthias[4], Timothy[3], Samuel[2], Matthew[1]*), b Nov 30, 1825; d Dec 10, 1883, in Trevorton, Pa , m. Oct. 1, 1855, Elizabeth Campbell, b Oct 21, 1836
Children.

142   Laura M[9], b Oct 30, 1856; d May 6, 1904, m. Oct 4, 1881, Kirk
         John Thurston
143   Marion A[9], b Sept 27, 1858, d Aug 19, 1882
144   Chloe M[9], b Sept 30, 1861; d Aug 28, 1881
145   Jesse Ambrose[9], b April 19, 1863; resides at Mound City, Mo
146   Mary E[9], b July 1, 1868, d June 1, 1898
147   Hiram J[9], b July 9, 1870; d June 4, 1904
148. William R[9], b. June 22, 1873
149   Caroline E[9], b. July 8, 1877
150   Maria L[9], b March 18, 1879
151   George R[9], b Aug 8, 1882, d June 13, 1886

81. HENRY ATWOOD[8] FULLER, (*Amos J[7], Warren[6], Daniel[5], Matthias[4], Timothy[3], Samuel[2], Matthew[1]*), b ——, d ——, m ——, Evelyn

Child
152   Rosie[9], b ——, 1854, d ——, 1876, in Waterloo, Ia , m ——, in
          Waterloo, Henry Crumb.

84. George Henry[8] Fuller, (*Daniel[7], Warren[6], Daniel[5], Matthias[4], Timothy[3], Samuel[2], Matthew[1]*), b Aug 28, 1840, in Salem, Ct , m 1870, Emily Halsted, who d. May, 1905.
   He resides in San Francisco, Cal
   Children:
153. George Comins[9], b June 29 1872, in Brooklyn, N Y ; m 1892,
          Anne Gopher

85. Sherwood Whitcomb[8] Fuller, (*Daniel[7], Warren[6], Daniel[5], Matthias[4], Timothy[3], Samuel[2], Matthew[1]*), b. July 8, 1842, in Salem, Ct , m April 26, 1870, in Colchester, Ct , Jennie N. Morgan ; b Aug 28, 1846, in Chesterfield, Ct
   Resides in San Francisco, Cal.
   Children:
154   Henry Hale[9], b May 8, 1872, in Brooklyn, N Y ; m Adah May
          Alen   No children   Resides Los Gatos, Cal

NINTH GENERATION.

101. Leander Sparrow[9] Fuller, (*Ezra N.[8], Elisha[7], Elisha[6], Elisha[5], Matthias[4], Timothy[3], Samuel[2], Matthew[1]*), b May 1847 , m Betty Bennett
   Children, born in Missouri
155   A dau , b ——
156. A dau , b ——

119. Leman C[8] Fuller, (*William[8], Calvin[7], Noadiah[6], Noadiah[5], Matthias[4], Timothy[3], Samuel[2], Matthew[1]*), b about 1869, in Southwick ; m Jan 4, 1890, Louise S Messenger.
   Children
157   Ida Louise[10], b. June 12, 1892

123. Lyman C.[9] Fuller, (*Chauncey[8], Calvin[7], Noadiah[6], Noadiah[5], Matthias[4], Timothy[3], Samuel[2], Matthew[1]*), b March 20, 1862, in Southwick ; m March 18, 1891, Hattie M Norton.
   Children
158   Chauncey N.[10], b Jan 25, 1893
159   Glenwood Lyman[10], b. Oct 18, 1895, in Westfield

125. Daniel K[9] Fuller, (*Chauncey[8], Calvin[7], Noadiah[6], Noadiah[5]*

Matthias[4], Timothy[3], Samuel[2], Matthew[1]), b 1867, in Southwick; m. April 2, 1891, Cora A Barnes

Children, born in Southwick

160 Arthur Barnes[10], b Jan 22, 1894, d Jan 3, 1900
161 Edward King[10], b Sept. 19, 1895.
162 Mary Ellen[10], b ———, 1904

126. HAROLD H.[9] FULLER, (*Chauncey[8], Calvin[7], Noadiah[6], Noadiah[5], Matthias[4], Timothy[3], Samuel[2], Matthew[1]*), b 1870, in Southwick, m April 14, 1891, Carrie H Ellsworth, of Becket; b in Chester

Children·

163 Raymond Ellsworth[10], b May 18, 1893
164 Harold[10], b July 8, 1897, Westfield Records

SEVENTH GROUP

FOURTH GENERATION.

SAMUEL⁴ FULLER, AND SOME OF HIS DESCENDANTS

39. SAMUEL⁴ FULLER, (*Timothy³, Samuel², Matthew¹*), b Sept 1, 1711, at East Haddam, Ct , d Jan 25, 1778, at Rumney, N H , m 1, April 19, 1732, Mercy Price; m 2, June 30, 1749, Sarah Hall ?

Children, born in East Haddam

1 **Samuel⁵**, b Oct 16, 1733 , m Lois Andrews
2 Mercy⁵, b March 9, 1734-5
3 Sarah⁵, b Sept 28, 1736 , m Amasa Ackley ?
4 **Timothy⁵**, b Feb. 10, 1737-8 , m Hannah Fuller
5 Alpheus⁵, b Jan 2, 1739-40
6 Zipporah⁵, b Dec. 2, 1741 , d 1812, at Westmoreland, N Y , m Aug 12, 1762, Daniel Gates, of East Haddam, who d July 13, 1788, aged 48 A soldier in the second French war
7 Thaddeus⁵, b Nov 8, 1743 *
8 Elizabeth⁵, b Nov 13, 1745
9 **Benjamin⁵**, b ——, m 1, ——, m 2, Mrs Lydia Bly
10 Mary⁵, b ——
      *There was a Thaddeus Fuller from Connecticut in the French and Indian war, and a Thaddeus, Jr., in the War of 1812

FIFTH GENERATION.

1. SAMUEL⁵ FULLER, (*Samuel⁴, Timothy³, Samuel², Matthew¹*), b Oct 16, 1733, in East Haddam, Ct , date and place of death not known , m Nov 16, 1758, Lois Andrews , b Aug 31, 1744, at East Haddam, dau of Samuel, Jr , and Jemima (Cone) Andrews

In 1769 he removed with his father to Campton, N H , and afterward to Rumney, N H In 1781 he was living at Thornton, N H

Children, given in New Hampshire Vital Records

11 Mary⁶, b. Feb 29, 1761 , place not given
12 **Samuel⁶**, b Aug 11, 1765 ; place not given, m 1, ——, m 2, ——, m 3, Mary Beach
13. Dorcas⁶, b Nov 27, 1768 , place not given
14 Thomas⁶, b July 7, 1770, at Campton, N H.

15   John⁶, b Sept 17, 1773, at Campton
16   Bethuel⁶, b March 21, 1776, at Campton; said to be the 6th child

4. TIMOTHY⁵ FULLER, (*Samuel⁴, Timothy³, Samuel², Matthew¹*), b Feb 10, 1737-8, in East Haddam, Ct ; d Feb , 1785, in Rumney, N H ; m Jan 31, 1781, Hannah⁵ Fuller, No 6 of the 9th Group who married 2d, Capt Benjamin Hayes of Granby, Ct , Nov. 20, 1792

Timothy Fuller served more than 3 years in the Revolutionary War and was a U. S Pensioner   He lived in East Haddam, Ct , until 1783, and then removed to Rumney, N H

Children, given by New Hampshire Vital Records
17.   "Clerisa" (Clarissa?)⁶, b. July 2, 1782
18   Dilecta⁶, b Aug 12, 1784, in Rumney.

9. BENJAMIN⁵ FULLER, (*Samuel⁴, Timothy³, Samuel², Matthew¹*), b ——, in East Haddam, Ct ; d. ——, 1778, in Rumney, N H ; m 1, ——, m. 2 (?), March 5, 1776, Mrs Lydia Bly, widow of James Bly; both of Rumney, N H. (Haverhill, Mass., Vital Records)   She m. 3d, Abraham Burnham of Rumney

Children:
19   Azubah⁶, b ——, marriage intentions pub March 24, 1779, with Joseph Smith, of Rumney.

SIXTH GENERATION.

12. SAMUEL⁶ FULLER, (*Samuel⁵ Samuel⁴, Timothy³, Samuel², Matthew¹*), b Aug 11, 1765, in East Haddam, Ct , d Jan 13, 1844, in Hume, Alleghany Co , N. Y., m. 1, ——, m. 2, ——, m 3, Mary Beach who survived him and was living in 1853.

He removed with his father to Campton and Rumney, N H , and thence westward   In 1838 he was in Oregon, Ogle Co , Illinois. The above identification is not absolutely sure, but is believed to be correct The party who furnished the information about this family is dead, and the town clerk at Hume; nor the parties he referred to can furnish no information concerning this family.

Children, no place of birth furnished.
20   Judith M ⁷, b Jan 28, 1791
21.   William⁷, b May 28, 1793.
22   John⁷, b Sept 27, 1794
23   Guy⁷, b April 6, 1796
24   Jason⁷, b June 11, 1797.
25   Samuel⁷, b Aug 30, 1800, d young
26   Luman⁷, b June 8, 1802, in Wyoming Co , N Y., d 1865
27   Mary⁷, b Feb 7, 1805
28   Marietta⁷, b March 8 1808.
29   Russell⁷, b. Jan 22, 1812

30. Sarah[7], b. Jan 17, 1814
31. Samuel[7], 2d, b. March 2, 1816.
32. Phillip[7], b June 8, 1818
33 Lucina[7], } twins, b. Nov 15, 1820
34. Lucinda[7], }
35. Lois[7], b Aug 7, 1823
36. Eunice[7], b Nov. 3, 1825
37. Elizabeth[7], b May 17, 1828
38. Levi[7], b Aug 28, 1830.

EIGHTH GROUP

FOURTH GENERATION.

TIMOTHY⁴ FULLER, AND HIS DESCENDANTS

44. TIMOTHY⁴ FULLFR. (*Timothy³, Samuel², Matthew¹*), b May 30, 1722, at East Haddam, Ct , d previous to Aug 4, 1772, when his estate was distributed; m Nov 30, 1749, at Millington, Ct , Thankful Gray, b ——, d Aug 8, 1794, at East Haddam

Children, born at East Haddam

1 Mary⁵, b Sept 12, 1750, d April 22, 1785, m John Howard She left a son, Philemon Fuller Howard, who died Sept 25, 1785.
2 Timothy⁵, b July 25 1752, d Oct 18, 1775
3 Philemon⁵, b April 22, 1755, d Oct. 25, 1775
   Both sons were Revolutionary soldiers and died at Roxbury, Mass

NINTH GROUP

FOURTH GENERATION.

THOMAS⁴ FULLER, AND SOME OF HIS DESCENDANTS

- **46.** THOMAS⁴ FULLER, (*Timothy³, Samuel², Matthew¹*), b June 24, 1726, at East Haddam, Ct ; d June 29, 1797, at Hartland, Ct , m May 15, 1748, Hannah Dimmock, b Nov 25, 1728, at Barnstable, d Feb 28, 1819, at Hartland, Ct , dau of Samuel and Hannah (Davis) Dimmock, of Barnstable, Mass , Saybrook and Tolland, Ct

He is called in 1748, Thomas Fuller 4th, the others being Thomas³, b 1679, (No 18 Edward line) , Thomas⁴, b 1717, (No 52 Edward line), and Thomas⁵, b 1718, (No 3, 2d Group), son of Benjamin⁴, all of whom were living in East Haddam at the time   In 1770, he was elected deacon of the First Congregational church in East Haddam, at which time he is called Sergt Thomas Fuller, 3d, Thomas⁵ having removed, the others being still living

He removed to Hartland after 1772

Children, born in East Haddam

1   **Eliphalet⁵**, b Sept 22, 1749, m 1, Thankful Sparrow ; m 2, Mrs Amy (Morris) Bradley
2   **Samuel⁵**, b Oct 10, 1751 m Mary Dimmock
3   Bethuel⁵, b Jan 9, 1754; d July 14, 1755
4   Bethuel⁵, b Mar 10, 1756, d Sept 19, 1775   He was a Revolutionary soldier in Gen Joseph Spencer's Company
5   Ichabod⁵, b Mar 23, 1758, m Mar 4, 1784, Apphia Sparrow (East Hartland, Ct , Church Records)
6   Hannah⁵, b Aug 15, 1760, m 1, Timothy Fuller No. 4 of Group 7 , m 2, Nov 20, 1792 Benjamin Hayes
7   Anne⁵, b Feb 11, 1763, m , April 17, 1783, Thomas Beman
8   Mary⁵, b Nov 6, 1770, d Dec 15, 1860, at Vernon, O , m Nov 27, 1788, Asa Haines, b April 10, 1765, at Bridgehampton, L I , d Sept 1, 1849, at Vernon, O   Children, b at Hartland, Ct Anna⁶, b May 6, 1789 Asa⁶, Mar 29, 1791, Sylvia⁶, Jan 12, 1794, Harriet⁶, June 19, 1796; Selden⁶, Nov. 27, 1800, David⁶, June 18, 1803, Sarah⁶, Nov 11, 1805 , born in Granby, Ct , Maria⁶, Jan 13, 1808, Clarissa⁶, Nov. 26, 1810, Julia⁶, May 2, 1815

FIFTH GENERATION.

1. ELIPHALET[5] FULLFR, (*Thomas[4], Timothy[3], Samuel[2], Matthew[1]*), b Sept 22, 1749, in East Haddam, Ct , d Mar 20, 1821, in Litchfield, N Y., m 1, Nov 22, 1770, Thankful Sparrow, who d in East Hartland, Ct , Oct 7, 1782, m 2, 1783, Mrs Amy (Morris) Bradley, b in East Haven, Ct , dau of Amos Morris

Children

- 9   **Asa[6]**, b Dec 26, 1784, m Rachel Crosby
10   **Timothy[6]**, b Oct 28, 1787, m Mary Burt.

2. SAMUEL[5] FULLER, (*Thomas[4], Timothy[3], Samuel[2], Matthew[1]*), b Oct 10, 1750, in East Haddam, Ct , d April 4, 1826, at Hartland, Ct , m ——, Mary Dimmock, probably dau of Samuel Dimmock, (H W Brainard's Mss).

He lived in East Hartland, Ct His wife was admitted to communion with the church there, Dec 11, 1791

The U S Pension records say he married, Feb 9, 1778, Mary Gildersleeve, of Chatham, Ct

He enlisted in the Revolutionary War, at East Haddam, Ct , in May, 1776, and served 9 months under Capt Eliphalet Holmes and Col Samuel Selden In 1849 the widow was 95 years of age

Children, born in Hartland

11.   **Samuel Dimmock[6]**. b Nov 30, 1778 , m ——
12   Henry S[6], b Jan 5, 1780 , d Aug 3, 1854
13   **Davis S.[6]**, b Oct 21, 1781, (given also Oct 31, 1782) , m Hannah Bushnell
14   Hannah[6], b Sept 16, 1783 , d Feb 8, 1814, m John Rector or Rudor.
15   Esther[6], b Aug 12, 1785
16   Thomas[6] b Oct 31, 1787
17   Obadiah[6], b July 4, 1790 , d Aug 1, 1791
18   Mary[6], b Sept 14, 1794
      One dau lived in Herkimer Co , N Y.

SIXTH GENERATION.

⌐ **9.** ASA[6] FULLFR, (*Eliphalet[5], Thomas[4], Timothy[3], Samuel[2], Matthew[1]*), b 1784, in Hartland, Ct , d Dec 8, 1828, in Little Falls, N Y , m May 15, 1815, Rachel Crosby, dau Joseph Crosby

Children

- 19   Emmeline[7], b Oct. 4, 1816, d Sept 23, 1850, m June, 1840, at Mohawk, N Y , Charles Benton, and had Burton L B[8], b May 13, 1844
20   Maria Abigail[7], b May 17, 1819 , d Aug 24, 1855, at Little Falls; m Wm Grossbeck, and had Maria[8], Mary[8], and one other child

5

21   **Morris Eliphalet**[7], b June 27, 1821, m 1 Amelia Curtis, m 2, Anna Maxwell
22   **Milton Asa**[7], b Mar 21, 1825, m 1, Gertrude Lansing, m 2, Mary Holcomb

10. TIMOTHY[6] FULLER (*Eliphalet*[5], *Thomas*[4], *Timothy*[3], *Samuel*[2], *Matthew*[1]), b Oct 28, 1787, d ——, m Mary Burt, of Litchfield, N Y. Children
23   Bradley[7], b ——
24   Dwight[7], b ——, m —— Ellsworth Removed to Iowa
25   Elizabeth[7], b ——, m Kilbon Hannah, of Watertown, N Y
26   Mary[7], b ——, m Hiram Holcomb, and had Cornelia[8], and Mary[8] Holcomb, who married Milton Asa[7] Fuller, No 22 this Group.

11. SAMUEL DIMMOCK[6] FULLER, (*Samuel*[5], *Thomas*[4], *Timothy*[3], *Samuel*[2] *Matthew*[1]), b Nov 30, 1778, in Hartland, Ct , d ——, m ——
Children
27   William H[7], b May 15, 1817, in Whately, Mass ; d there June 6, 1883, m Sept 8, 1845, Ruth Brown of Whately He was a farmer in Whately He had no children

NOTE Besides William H. Fuller, the History of Whately by Crafts, mentions Lois Fuller of Hatfield who m Joseph Sanderson, Lydia Fuller, who m, Elihu White, and removed to New York City, thence to Mich , where he died The Whately town records, give the marriage of a Ruth Fuller to Seth Wright Feb 4, 1805, and the death of a Ruth Fuller Aug 5, 1887, aged 66-10-27 Parents of these Fullers not given, and none have been identified The clerk of the Cong Church says, 'no Fuller mentioned in the church records "

13. DAVIS S[6] FULLER, (*Samuel*[5], *Thomas*[4], *Timothy*[3], *Samuel*[2], *Matthew*[1]), b Oct 21, 1781, in East Hartland, Ct , (date also given by correspondent. Oct. 31, 1782), d May 11, 1855, in ——, Indiana, m Oct 17, 1803, Hannah Bushnell, of Granby, Ct , b June 8, 1878 d April 24, 1849
He was one of the pioneer settlers of the "Western Reserve" in Ohio, with his wife, and eldest child in 1805-6; was a saddle and harness maker, served in the War of 1812, and received a land grant of 160 acres
Children, all but the first child, born in Hartford, Ohio
28   Eunice Lavinia[7], b ——, d July 8, 1895, m —— Burr
29   Samuel[7], b Feb 16, 1807, d May 9, 1809
30. **Samuel Davis**[7], b ——, m Eunice Holcomb
31   Henry Haynes[7], b May 30, 1811; d Sept 15, 1828
32   Chloe Corinthia[7], b June 22, 1813, d March, 1878, m Robert McFarlane, and had a son Thomas[8]

33 Harvey Coe[7], b Mar 8, 1816, m Susannah M Grierson
34 Alexander B[7], b Oct 12, 1818, d Dec 30, 1818
35 Alexander[7], b June 4, 1820, m Almira Gates

SEVENTH GENERATION.

21. MORRIS ELIPHALET[7] FULLER, (*Asa[6], Eliphalet[5], Thomas[4], Timothy[3], Samuel[2], Matthew[1]*), b June 27, 1821, in Little Falls, N Y , m 1, Oct 5, 1843, Amelia Curtis, b Dec 4, 1819, in Clinton, N Y , d Jan 23, 1872 m 2, ——, Anna Maxwell

He resides in Schuyler, Neb

Children, by first wife

36 Emma Curtis[8], b Dec 4, 1844, d Sept 18, 1870, m Sept 23, 1869, Breese J Stevens, and had Amelia Emma[9] b Sept 12, 1870
     Resides in Madison, Wis
37 **Edward Morris[8]**, b May 14, 1847; m Jessica Haskell
38 Sarah Amelia[8], b May 2, 1851, m, Feb 7, 1889, Judge Robert Mc-Kee Bashford They reside in Madison, Wis
39 Stephen Asa[8], b Jan 14, 1862, d Jan 16, 1892

22. MILTON ASA[7] FULLER, (*Asa[6], Eliphalet[5], Thomas[4], Timothy[3], Samuel[2], Matthew[1]*), b ——, d ——, 1906, aged 80, m. 1, ——, Gertrude Lansing, m 2, ——, Mary Holcomb

Children, by first wife

40 **Hiram[8]**, b ——
41 **Albert Milton[8]**, b ——
     By second wife
42 Fanny[8], b ——
43 Mary[8], b ——, m. S R Wheeler

30. SAMUEL DAVIS[7] FULLER, (*Davis[6], Samuel[5], Thomas[4], Timothy[3], Samuel[2], Matthew[1]*), b ——, in Hartford, Ohio, d Sept 25, 1891, m May 30, 1831, at Paris, Ohio, Eunice Holcomb, b Feb 7, 1807, in Ct ; d May 10, 1883

Children.

44 Jerusha[8], b June 23, 1835; d Oct 27, 1868, in Chicago, Ill; m ——, —— Rathbone
45 Emeline[8], b ——, died Aug 19, 1837
46 Emeline[8], b June 16, 1838, m Dec 30, 1869, Warren Bates of Hartford, Ohio.
47 Davis C[8], b Nov 14, 1840, d Oct 13, 1870, m Sarah —— No children.

33. HARVEY COE[7] FULLER, (*Davis S[6], Samuel[5], Thomas[4], Timothy[3], Samuel[2], Matthew[1]*), b Mar 18, 1816, in Hartford, O ; d Feb 23, 1889, in Jacksonville, Ill; m Sept, 1839, Susannah Grierson, in Youngstown, O , who d Oct 9, 1874

He removed to Concord, Ill, in 1850, and thence to Jacksonville, Ill.,
in 1860 He was in the saddle and harness making business

Children

48   Mary H⁸, b May 24, 1840, in Youngstown, O , m Dec 25, 1860,
         Thomas J Kirk
49   Louisa M⁸, b. April 14, 1842, in Youngstown
50   **Harvey B⁸**, b May 26, 1845, in Youngstown, m S Ellen Kirk
51   Susannah⁸, b. May 28, 1848, in Youngstown.
52   Helen G⁹, b May 25, 1850, in Youngstown, m ——, Capt William
         Davis, Jr , and has Marietta⁹, b July 31, 1880; Helen⁹, Nov. 23,
         1883, and Anna⁹, b Nov 16, 1885.
53   Albert C⁸, b Nov , 1854, in Concord, Ill., d Aug , 1863
54   Grace L⁸, b July 27, 1857, in Concord, m Sept 14, 1882, Lieut.
         M M Moxon, and had Edith E⁹, b. June 28, 1883, Glennway⁹,
         Sept , 1884, Kimball W.⁹, Aug 24, 1886, Margaret⁹, Aug , 1881;
         Marion⁹, ——, Ethan D⁹, ——, d 1893, and Bruce Ethan⁹, Feb.
         19, 1887
              They reside in Waukesha, Wis
55   Edith Clare⁸, b. ——, in Jacksonville, Ill ; died young

SEVENTH GENERATION.

35. ALEXANDER⁷ FULLER, (*Davis S⁶, Samuel⁵, Thomas⁴, Timothy³,
Samuel², Matthew¹*), b June 4, 1820, in Hartford, Ohio, d Sept 16,
1907, at his home in Streator, Ill ; m Jan , 1842, in Youngstown, O ,
Almira Gates.

He was one of the oldest residents of Streator.

Children, born in Youngstown, Ohio

56   **Dwight W.⁸**, b ——, m Ellen Fell
57   Candace⁸, b ——, m J A Gray, had two sons and one daughter
         Lived in Chicago, Ill
58   Elizabeth⁸, } twins, b. ——. { m —— —— Bennison and has one son
59   Caroline⁸, }   { m Dr Charles E Steward No children

EIGHTH GENERATION.

37. EDWARD MORRIS⁸ FULLER, (*Morris E⁷, Asa⁶, Eliphalet⁵, Thomas⁴,
Timothy³, Samuel², Matthew¹*), b May 14, 1847, m June 13, 1876, Jessica Haskell, b June 24, 1852

They reside in Madison, Wis

Children

60   Shirley⁹, b May 29, 1877; m Louis M Hobbins, and had Mary
         S F¹⁰

40. HIRAM⁸ FULLER, (*Milton Asa⁷, Asa⁶, Eliphalet⁵, Thomas⁴, Timothy³, Samuel², Matthew¹*) b ——, m ——, Julia Reynolds

Children

61   Gertrude⁹, b

41. ALBERT MILTON[8] FULLER, (*Milton A[7], Asa[6], Eliphalet[5], Thomas[4], Timothy[3], Samuel[2], Matthew[1]*), b ——; m ——, Elizabeth Magaw
He resides in Meadville, Pa
Children

62 Marian[9], b ——

63 Frederick[9], b ——.

64 Marguerite[9], b ——

50. HARVEY B[8] FULLER, (*Harvey C[7], Davis S[6], Samuel[5], Thomas[4], Timothy[3], Samuel[2], Matthew[1]*), b May 26, 1845, in Youngstown, Ohio; m Feb 23, 1871, at Chicago, Ill, S Ellen Kirk, b in Youngstown, O.
He is a manufacturer in St Paul, Minn
Children

65 Albert M[9], b Nov. 15, 1871.

66 Gertrude[9], b Oct 27, 1873; m June 1, 1904, Dr C W Russell.

67. Roger K[9] b Dec 20, 1877.

68 Paul G[9], b July 5, 1881, died young

69 Alice[9], } twins, b Nov 23, 1883 { d Dec 31, 1883
70 Mary[9], { d Oct 8, 1884

71 Harvey B[9], } twins, b Sept 21, 1885
72 Helen[9],

56. DWIGHT W[8] FULLER, (*Alexander[7], Davis S[6], Samuel[5], Thomas[4], Timothty[3], Samuel[2], Matthew[1]*), b ——, d July 25, 1892; m Dec 28, 18—? Ellen Fell
Children

73 Leona[9], b ——; m ——

74 Lewis[9], b ——, d ——, m ——; no children

TENTH GROUP

FOURTH GENERATION.

RODOLPHUS⁴ FULLER, AND SOME OF HIS DESCENDANTS

49. RODOLPHUS⁴ FULLER, (*Samuel³, Samuel², Matthew¹*), b Aug 22, 1705, in Preston, Ct , d ——, m 1, Nov 1, 1727, Anne Hall, dau of Capt William and Esther Hall, b June 1, 1706, at Mansfield, Ct ; d April 24, 1755 , m 2, Oct 10, 1755, Anne Robinson, b Aug 20, 1708, probably in Chilmark, Mass , dau of Lieutenant Peter and Experience (Manton) Robinson

Rodolphus Fuller joined the church in Preston, Sept 23, 1726.

Children, born in Mansfield, Ct

1. Elizabeth⁵, b Nov 7, 1728, d 1815, in Canterbury, Ct , m April 21, 1750, or 1752, Barnabas Allen
2. Samuel⁵, b July 18, 1731 , d Aug 18, 1731
3. Lydia⁵, b Nov 19, 1733
4. Silas⁵, b Sept 22, 1735, d April 2, 1752
5. Bela⁵, b March 13, 1736-7 , bapt June 8, 1737 (Dimmock)
6. Anne⁵, b Oct 24, 1738; d 1739
7. Samuel⁵, b Feb 3, 1758.
8. Anne⁵, b Nov 1, 1759; d Nov 22, 1759

ELEVENTH GROUP

FOURTH GENERATION.

ELKANAH[4] FULLER, AND SOME OF HIS DESCENDANTS.

51. ELKANAH[4] FULLER, (*Samuel[3], Samuel[2], Matthew[1]*), b April 24, 1709, at Mansfield, Ct ; d ——; m. May 9, 1731, Mary Andrews, b Dec. 2, 1710, at East Haddam, Ct ; d Sept 13, 1740, at Mansfield, dau of Samuel and Eleanor (Lee) Andrews, m 2, Naomi ——; m 3, April 6, 1767, widow Lydia Hooker, at which time he was "of Newtown, Sussex Co, N J"

Sept 21, 1773, he bought land in Chatham, Ct, and took the oath of fidelity there Sept. 15, 1778

Dec 21, 1793, he had removed with Timothy Percival to Freehold, Albany Co, N Y, where he probably died

Children recorded in Mansfield, Ct

1   Sarah[5], b Oct 9, 1732
2.   Samuel[5], b Sept. 25, 1733, d Dec 30, 1737
3   Eleanor[5], b Aug 23, 1735, d April 15, 1737
4   Mary[5], b Jan 1, 1737, d March 12, 1819, in Boone Co, Ky, m about 1758, Timothy Percival who d June 16, 1815, in Boone Co, Ky Children Jabez[6], b July 10, 1760; Elkanah[6], ——, Timothy[6], ——, Mary[6], Elizabeth[6], Anna[6], and Lydia[6]
5   Bethiah[5], b Feb 9, 1837-9, bapt April 8, 1739
6   Samuel[5], b Feb. 9, 1743-4
7   Bethany[5], b March 12, 1746

TWELFTH GROUP

FOURTH GENERATION.

64. Judah[4] Fuller, (*Samuel[3], Samuel[2], Matthew[1]*), b Aug. 25, 1715, in Preston, Ct ; d ——; m Feb 11, 1745-6, Abigail Wentworth; b March 14, 1723, dau of Aaron and Elizabeth Wentworth

Judah Fuller lived in Norwich, Ct , but his name does not appear in land, probate or church records, and no further account of him or his family is found after birth of Lemuel[5], at Norwich

Children

1   Samuel[5], b. Dec. 15, 1746
2   Elizabeth[5], b Sept 18, 1749.
3   Asa[5], b Nov 10, 1752
4   Lucy[5], b July 9, 1754
5   Lemuel[5], b July 14, 1757 , m 1, Eleanor ——? , m 2, Polly (——) Davis

Note —In 1778 and 1779 there were Asa and Lemuel Fuller in Lyman, N H , who signed pettition about taxes   In 1778 Asa Fuller of Lyman m Elizabeth Fuller? of Rumney, and Asa and Elizabeth had, b in Rumney, Sarah, Jan 2, 1780, Lucinda, Feb 26, 1782, Molly, also given Polly, (perhaps both), July 5, 1784; Hannah, Oct 23, 1786, Betsey, May 8, 1789, John, b Aug 28, 1793 (perhaps the one who m Mary Gould of Plymouth, N H , who d at Rumney, July 30, 1887), and Timothy, b Nov 11, 1795   Was this Asa[5] of Judah[4] Fuller?

FIFTH GENERATION.

Lemuel[5] Fuller, (*Judah[4], Samuel[3], Samuel[2], Matthew[1]*), b. July 14, 1757, in Norwich, Ct ; d Sept 26, 1840, in Bristol, N H , m 1, Elana (Eleanor?) ——, who d Dec. 5, 1803, m 2, June 14, 1817, in Corinth, Vt , Polly (——) Davis, widow of Erskine Davis

In 1855, Polly Fuller was living in Danbury, N H , 75 years of age. In 1828, Lemuel Fuller was 70 years old, his wife, Polly, 49, dau Polly, 8, and dau Hannah, 6 years of age   His dau ? Mary D lived in Alexandria, N H , in 1852

Lemuel Fuller enlisted in the Revolutionary army Nov 28, 1775, for

1 year in Ct, in Capt Joseph Jewett's Co, Col Jedediah Huntington Regt ; served until Jan 1, 1777

The U S Pension records—from which most of the above was taken—call him "of Hanover, N H."

The town clerk of Bradford, Vt, who furnishes the above items in regard to Lemuel's first wife, makes the following statements in regard to Lemuel Fuller and his family "land was deeded to Lemuel Fuller, Sept 16, 1786, and his residence was given as Piermont, N H , and the consideration was 450 bushels of wheat In 1792, he was deeded land by the committee appointed by the Legislature, and his residence was given as Bradford, Vt " He gives date of death of Lemuel's wife, "Dec 6, 1816," and again "Dec 11, 1816, aged 54 years," but does not find Lemuel's death record.

He gives record of Lemuel's children as follows

6   Gibbs⁶, b. Feb 21, 1786.
7   Pheba⁶, b. Aug 24, 1791
8   Dan Malta⁶, b June 15, 1792
9   Lemuel⁶, b Aug 9, 1794
10 Levi Roger⁶, b Sept 21, 1797 , d March 18, 1798
11 Lucy Fuller⁶, b March 24, 1799
12 Christopher⁶, b Aug 16, 1802, d Sept 7, 1802
13 Elana⁶, b Dec 5, 1803
14 Polly⁶, b July 31, 1819
15 Hannah⁶, b Oct 21, 1821

"Lemuel and Polly Fuller deeded lands, May 21, 1822, for one thousand dollars This is the last record of that name on the books."

THIRTEENTH GROUP

FOURTH GENERATION.

JOHN⁴ FULLER, AND SOME OF HIS DESCENDANTS

56. JOHN⁴ FULLER, (*John³, John², Matthew¹*), b Aug 3, 1712, in Barnstable, d there before March 7, 1759 (Inventory of his estate was taken April 17, 1759), m Oct 29, 1741, Temperance Gorham, b July 23, 1721, in Barnstable; d Nov 9 1815 and was buried in Evergreen Cemetery, Wayne, Me, dau of Job and Desire (Dimmock) Gorham of Barnstable

Children, born in Barnstable, Mass

1 Desire⁵, b Aug 1, 1742, m Sept 29, 1767, John Smith of Barnstable
2 **John⁶**, b June 23, 1744, m Anna Tobey
3 **Edward⁵**, b Dec 26, 1746, m Mary Jones
4 **Francis⁵**, b Mar 10, 1749, m Hannah Cobb
5 **Job⁵**, b Nov 25, 1751, m Elizabeth Wing
6 **Thomas⁵**, b May 9, 1754, m Lydia Paige
7 Isaac⁵, bapt 1757 I find no further account of him

NOTE—According to H W Brainard all descendants of John⁴ Fuller and Temperance (Gorham) Fuller are Mayflower descendants, his wife Temperance Gorham being descended from Capt John Gorham, whose wife was Desire Howland, dau of Pilgrim John Howland

FIFTH GENERATION.

2. JOHN[6] FULLER, (*John[4], John[3], John[2], Matthew[1]*), b Jan 23, 1744, in Barnstable, d Nov 2, 1829, in Livermore, Me, m Dec 17, 1767, in Sandwich, Anna Tobey, b Jan 27, 1747, in Boston; d June 27, 1837, in Livermore

John[4] Fuller removed his family to Winthrop, Me, in April, 1773

Children, the first two b in Barnstable, the others in Winthrop.

8   **Isaac[6]**, b Aug 5, 1769, m Nancy Whittaker
9   **Abram[6]**, b Dec 16, 1771, m. Desire Foster.
10   Nathan[6], b Oct 21, 1774, d ——, m —— Mary ——, who m 2d
     Samuel Neat(?) of Boston I have found no record of children
11   Anna[6], b. Sept. 16, 1777, d Nov 6, 1797
12   **John[6]**, b Feb 13, 1779, m 1, Betsey Eldred; m 2, Mrs Laura
     (Chase) Livermore
13   Lydia[6], b July 20, 1782, m 1804, Samuel Chandler, of Wilton, Me
14   Desire[6], b Apr 2, 1785; m, 1801, Henry Caswell
15   **Thomas[6]**, b Sept 26, 1787, m Nancy Wood
16   Addison[6], b Dec 27, 1790, d 1805
17   Abigail[6] (Nabby) b Dec 13, 1793, d June, 1828, m, 1811, Rev.
     Henry Hawkins, and left one child, Fidelia[7] Hawkins

3. EDWARD[6] FULLER, (*John[4], John[3], John[2], Matthew[1]*), b Dec 28, 1746, in Barnstable, d 1831 in Pittston, Me, m Dec 26, 1771, Mary Jones of Barnstable.

He was in 1771 a resident of Sandwich

The "History of Pittston, Me" gives names of children as follows

18   Abigail[6], b Aug 26, 1773, m Levi French, and had a son—the late
     David French of Mt Vernon, Me, whose dau, Mrs Josephine
     L F Richards, resides in Newcastle, Ind (1912)
19   Olive[6], b Jan 6, 1778, d young
20   Catherine[6], b July 16, 1780, d ——; unmarried
21   Edward[6], b June 17, 1783, m Liberty Williams.
22   **Allen[6]**, b Apr 23, 1786, m Nancy Kinney.
23   **Thomas[6]**, b Feb 29, 1788, m Abigail Day
24   Samuel[6], b June 15, 1792
25   Francis[6], b Feb 1, 1793
26   Betsey[6], b ——, m —— Stilphen

4. FRANCIS[6] FULLER, (*John[4], John[3], John[2], Matthew[1]*), b March 10, 1749, in Barnstable, d May 28, 1844, at Vassalboro, Me ; m Oct 15 1772, Hannah Cobb, b Mar 11, 1753, in Barnstable, d Oct. 19, 1816, at Readfield (once a part of Winthrop, now Manchester) Me, dau of Ebenezer and Mary (Smith) Cobb of Barnstable, and granddau of Matthias and Hannah (Fuller) Smith (Hannah[4] Fuller, Nathaniel[3], John[2], John[2], Matthew[1]) of 14th Group

Francis Fuller settled in Winthrop about 1772

Children born in Winthrop, Me (portion now called Manchester)

(These dates of birth of children are said to be from Temperance[6] (Fuller) Russell copy of the family Bible Records) ·

27   Hannah[6], b Aug 19, 1773, d. June, 1840, m Peter Haines, had one son, Francis[7] Haines

28   Mary[6], b May 1, 1775, m John Weymouth

29   Sarah[6], b Jan 22, 1779, d Jan 19, 1873, in Manchester, Me, m, 1809, Richard Hilton, and had Catherine[7], b 1809, Caroline[7], Sarah[7], James[7], Abigail H[7], George W[7], b June 24, 1816, William[7], Greenleaf[7], b July 9, 1820, and Mary Ann[7]

30   **Francis**[6], b Aug 16, 1780, m Sarah Dinsmore

31   **Edward**[6], b Jan 22, 1782, m 1, Temperance Fuller, m 2, Elvira Frost.

32   **David Crocker**[6], b Dec 7, 1785; m 1, Lavinia Estey, m 2, Maria Lovejoy

33   James Blossom[6], b Dec 29, 1786, d about 1816, m twice, had two children

34   Gorham[6], b Sept 23, 1788, d Sept 1, 1811, unmarried

35   **William C**[6], b Nov 25, 1791, m Nancy Melvin

36   Temperance[6], b Aug 12, 1793; d Dec 23, 1878, m Jan 24, 1822, Isaac Russell, and had Joseph F[7], b Jan 22, 1823, Leonard W[7] and Eben F[7], twins Aug 3, 1824, Mary Ann F[7], July 30, 1826, Rebecca Marilla[7], Jan 22, 1828, Francis F[7] and Abel H[7], twins, Aug 5, 1824, Isaac N[7], Feb 8, 1831, Eliza F[7], Dec 7, 1833, Hiram F[7], Oct 22, 1836

37   **Eben**[6], b Feb 25, 1795, m Martha Williams

5. JOB[5] FULLER, (*John[4], John[3], John[2], Matthew[1]*), b Nov 25, 1751, in Barnstable, d ——, m. ——, Elizabeth Wing, who d Aug 1826

The John Wing Genealogy states that Job Fuller removed to Wayne, Kennebec Co, Me, in 1773, and the U S Census of 1790 mentions Job Fuller's family of 5, in New Sandwich, Lincoln Co, Me

The Wing record gives three children

38   Temperance[6], b June 29, 1773, in Sandwich, d —— unmarried

39   Mary[6], b July 19, 1775, in Wayne; m —— Sweet

40   Job[6], b Nov. 6, 1784, in Wayne, d Nov. 25, 1803

6. THOMAS[5] FULLER, (*John[4], John[3], John[2], Matthew[1]*), b May 9, 1754, in Barnstable, d Dec 1, 1823, in Hardwick, Vt ; m Nov 26, 1778, Lydia Paige, dau of Col Timothy Paige She d July 8, 1810, aged 55 Thomas Fuller came to Hardwick, Mass, when about 16 years old, lived later in Barre, Mass, removed to Westminster, Vt., in 1786, and to Hardwick, Vt, in 1798, where he was deacon of the church at the time of his death He served nearly two years in the Revolutionary War—enlisting twice, became 1st sergeant and received a pension

Children

41   **Martin**[6], b June 6, 1780, m Letitia Duncan

42   **Thomas**[6], b Mar 24, 1782; m Sarah House

43 Lydia[6], b June 6, 1784, d Nov 6, 1846; m Daniel Weld, and had
John Fuller[7], b Dec 11, 1808, Daniel[7], b Nov 20, 1810, Moses[7],
b Jan 18, 1813, Eben[7], b Jan 4, 1815, Martin[7], b Oct 15, 1817,
and Charles Stevens[7], b May 5, 1819 The second son, Daniel[7],
married and had a son, Austin[8] Weld, who was adopted by
Austin Fuller (No 47 of this Group) and named Austin Weld
Fuller

44 Melinda[6], b Feb 3, 1787, d Feb, 1857, m Capt Charles Stevens
Children Harriet[7], b Sept 27, 1808, d Feb 27, 1815 Horatio
N[7], b Oct 9, 1811, d Oct 7, 1827 Roxana[7], b Jan 28, 1814,
d Nov 11, 1827 Harriet 2d[7], b Mar 28, 1817, d Mar 12, 1895
Charles E[7], b Mar 27, 1821, d Sept 6, 1909, Hiram[7], b May 21,
1825, d June 9, 1862 Albert N[7], b Mar 4, 1829, d Nov 8, 1902

45 A son, b Mar 7, 1789, d Mar 12, 1789
46 **Timothy Paige[6]**, b Mar 30, 1790, m Rebecca Duncan
47 **Austin[6]**, b Apr 23, 1792, m Betsey Maynard
48 **Francis Enos[6]** b Mar 30 1794, m 1, Martha Worcester; m 2,
Hannah Worcester

49. Rebecca Paige[6], b Feb 29, 1796, d Sept 1872, m Alvin House of
Enosburg, Vt, and had Thomas Fuller[7], b about 1824, d June
23, 1884, Henry M[7], b about 1830, d Apr 13, 1878, Fidelia L[7],
b ——, d Feb 5, 1823, Timothy P[7], b ——, d June 18, 1833,
Mary F[7], b about 1832 d July 4, 1849, Lydia R[7], d about 1836,
d Dec 28, 1897, and Charles E[7], b about 1839, d Mar 29, 1870

50 John Washington[6], b Jan 4, 1799, d Aug 15, 1803

SIXTH GENERATION.

8. ISAAC[6] FULLER, (*John[5], John[4], John[3], John[2], Matthew[1]*), b Aug 5,
1769, in Barnstable, d Mar 28, 1851, in Livermore, Me , m Sept 19,
1788, Nancy Whittaker, of Winthrop, Me, b Jan 7, 1774, d July 25,
1845, dau of Oliver and Philena (Gay) Whittaker

Isaac Fuller removed from Winthrop, Me , to Livermore about 1794
Children
51 Philena[7], b Feb 22, 1793, d Aug 4, 1843, at New Bedford, m
Mar 7, 1812, Leonard Shaw, of Middleboro
52 Hannah[7], b Nov 29, 1794, at Livermore, d Aug 5, 1829, m Mar
1820, Alexander Nelson
53 Anne[7], b June 28, 1796, d Aug 14, 1880, at Jay, Me , m 1, Mar 20,
1832, Moses Walton, m 2, Isaac Rich
54 Betsey[7], b Jan 25, 1798, d Dec 3, 1857, m 1, Nov 29, 1821, William Cooper m 2, Isaac Rich
55 Jesse Lee[7], b June 2, 1800, d Oct 4, 1818
56 Selah Gay[7], b Apr 8, 1804; d Nov 5, 1825, m Bradford Plummer
57 Isaac[7], b Jan 27, 1812, d July 31, 1887, at New Gloucester, Me ,
m Nov 26, 1833, Mary Leach No children
58 Nancy[7], b Dec 20, 1814 d Sept 24 1818

9. ABRAM[6] FULLER, (*John[5], John[4], John[3], John[2], Matthew[1]*), b Dec
16, 1771, in Barnstable d Dec. 8, 1856, at Lagrange, Me , m Feb 2,

1800, Desire Foster, b Nov 5, 1772, in Rhinebeck, N Y, d Jan 7, 1865, in Lagrange, Me ; dau of Lieut Samuel Foster

Children

59 **Orrin**[7], b Feb 4, 1803, m Mary Hobbs
60 **Samuel Foster**[7], b Mar 31, 1804, m Betsey Morrison
61 **John H**[7], b Aug 7, 1806, m Hannah C Hinds
62 **Michael**[7], b May 6, 1809, m Sarah Kelliher
63 Catherine Barton[7], b Jan 19, 1811, at Livermore, Me ; d Oct 22, 1839, at East Livermore, Me, m Cyrus Morrison of Lagrange
64 Frances Marie[7], b Dec 6 1815, at Bangor, Me, d Aug 1, 1896, at Minneapolis, Minn

12. JOHN[6] FULLER, (*John[5], John[4], John[3], John[2], Matthew[1]*), b Feb 13, 1779, at Winthrop, Me, d ——, m 1, 1804, Betsey Eldred, of Pittston, Me, who d 1826, m 2, Mrs Laura (Chase) Livermore, b Mar 11, 1784, in Tisbury, Martha's Vineyard, Mass ; dau of Thomas Chase

In 1810 John Fuller moved to Livermore and on Mill Brook built and operated saw and grist mills, fulling and carding machines

Children

65 Anne[7], b ——, m —— Kimball
66 Reuben[7] b ——, lived at Monmouth, Me
67 Sarah[7], b ——
68 Betsey[7], b ——, d Dec, 1888, at Livermore, m 1, ——, m 2, Oct 31, 1850, Josiah Ladd, of North Livermore, and had dau Sarah Elizabeth[8], b Dec 30, 1852, d July 18, 1855
69 John[7], b ——, m —— Haskell

51. THOMAS[6] FULLER, (*John[5], John[4], John[3], John[2], Matthew[1]*), b Sept 26, 1787, in Winthrop, Me, d Mar 9, 1820, in Portland, Me, m ——, Nancy Wood

Children (3 daughters)

70 —— b
71 —— b
72 —— b

22. ALLEN[6] FULLER, (*Edward[5], John[4], John[3], John[2] Matthew[1]*), b Apr 23, 1786, in Pittston, Me, Me, d ——, m ——, Nancy Kinney

Children

73 Cordelia[7] b ——, d at Farmington, Me ; m Wilson Greaton
74 **Samuel Franklin**[7], b 1816, m 1, Judith Parker Talcott, m 2, Lucinda Bailey
75 Caroline[7], b ——, m 1, John Caswell, m 2, Bowdin Caswell Had Ellen L.[8], William A[8], Hannah D[8], Charles K[8], and George M[8]
76 Hannah[7], b ——, d —— in Industry, Me, m Richard Caswell

77   Elizabeth[7], b ——, m Henry Caswell, and had Frank[8], Carroll[8], and three daughters.

23. THOMAS[5] FULLER, (*Edward[6], John[4], John[3], John[2], Matthew[1]*), b Feb 29, 1788, in Pittston, Me , d Oct 7, 1869, in ——, m 1817 or 18, Abigail Day, of Damariscotta, Me , who d Oct 22, 1869
   Children

78   **Benjamin Franklin[7]**, b Dec 5, 1819, m Hannah Edwards Folsom
79   Joseph E [7], b —— 1821, d 1836
80   Mary Ann[7], b Dec 15, 1823, d June 6 1907, m Capt Theodore Brown, of Pittston, and had Eudora[8], and Anne[8]
81   Martha Jane[7], b ——, m May, 1846, Moses B Bliss, of Wilbraham, Mass , resided (1909) in Santa Cruz, California Children, Charles L [8], Wilbur F [8], Frederic[8], and Jennie F [8]
82   Sarah Abigail[7], b ——, d 1854, m Capt Ira Maxey, of Gardiner, Me , and had Frederic H [8]

30. FRANCIS[6] FULLER, (*Francis[5], John[4] John[3], John[2], Matthew[1]*), b Aug 16, 1780, in Winthrop Me d Sept 1855, m Dec 5, 1803, Sally Dinsmore, b Dec 16, 1787, in Pownalboro, now Dresden, Me., d Oct 15, 1864, at Etna, Me
   Children

83   Stephen[7], b April 24, 1804; d 1806
84   Francis[7], b June 24, 1805, d the same day
85   Polly[7], b Sept 1, 1806, d Feb 1, 1807
86   Sally De Wolf[7], b Mar 3, 1808; d Nov 24, 1895, m July 4, 1825 Amos Friend, and had Edward[8], Eliza[8], Diantha[8], Albin[8], and Varila[8]
87   Edward[7], b Feb 6, 1810, d June 1, 1812
88   Betsey Brown[7], b Nov 11, 1811, d July 19, 1890, m 1, Leonard Maxey, and had John C [8], and Almira[8], m 2, Alvin Barden, and had Horatio[8], Bunyan A [8], Martin L [8], Judson W [8], and Frank[8]
89   **Edward Gorham[7]**, b April 28, 1814, m 1, Abigail Reed, m 2, Phebe Ann Cahler, m 3, ——, m 4 ——
90   Pamelia[7], b Mar 28, 1816, d July 25, 1826
91   Horatio[7], } twins, b June 3, 1818, { d Feb 3, 1834
92   Varila[7],   { d Nov 7, 1895, in Hyde Park, Mass , m May 29, 1843, William Dyer, and had Mary Jane[8], b July 13, 1845, Sarah E [8], b May 13, 1847, William Fuller[8], b Sept 9, 1850 (Res St Jo Mo 1912), Frank[8], May 24, 1852, Caroline E [8], April 27, 1854 All b in Waterville, Me
93   Abigail Dinsmore[7], b June 17, 1820, d Feb , 1883, m 1837, Asa Sylvester, and had Pamelia[8], Pauline[8], Frances[8], Edwin[8], Henry[8], and Ernest E [8]
94   **John Dinsmore[7]**, b Dec 26, 1826; m Charlotte Reed
95   Clara Emerson[7], b July 22, 1829, m 1, Sept , 1853, George Day, and had Frank[8] and Albert Rufus[8], m 2, Oct. 16, 1878, Samuel Burrill

31. EDWARD⁶ FULLER, (*Francis⁵, John⁴, John³, John², Matthew¹*), b. June 22, 1782, in Winthrop, Me , d Aug 26, 1856, at Readfield, Me , m 1, Temperance⁷ Fuller (James⁶, James⁵, Benjamin⁴, Samuel³, Samuel², Edward¹) , b about 1782, in Barnstable , m 2, Elvira Frost.

Edward Fuller was a lawyer

Children by first wife

96   Mary Ann⁷, b ——

97   **Hiram⁷**, b ——, m Sarah Whittier

98   George Gage⁷ b ——

99   James⁷, b ——

Children by second wife

100   William Henry⁷, b ——   Was living in Skowhegan, Me, in 1907

101   Gorham⁷, b ——, d young

102   Helen Louise⁷, b ——, in Daniel Church, of Portsmouth, N H

103   Mary Frances⁷, b ——, living (1898) in Portsmouth, N H

32. DAVID CROCKER⁶ FULLER, (*Francis⁵, John⁴, John³, John², Matthew¹*) b Dec 8, 1785, in Winthrop, Me , d Aug 16 1857, at Winthrop, m 1, Dec 29, 1811, Lavinia Eastey, b Oct 27, 1782, d Dec 6 1812, m 2 Sept 12, 1813, Maria Lovejoy, at Fayette, Me

Children, born in Readfield, Me

104   Charles H⁷, b Sept 21 1812, d May 2 1816

105   Lavinia Eastey⁷, b Jan 31, 1815 , d July 28, 1885, at Hallowell, Me

106   **Lorin Lovejoy⁷**, b Jan 25, 1820, m Lucy P Lovejoy

107   **Ruel Boutelle⁷**, b Aug 8, 1824, m Harriet Atwood Houghton

35. WILLIAM C⁶ FULLER, (*Francis⁵, John⁴, John³, John², Matthew¹*), b Nov 23, 1791, in Winthrop, Me , d Sept 16, 1861, in Readfield, Me , m Nov 25, 1816, Nancy Melvin, b June 3. 1791 , d Sept 13, 1861

Children, born in Winthrop

108   Edward⁷, b June 8, 1820 , d Oct 8, 1840

109   Emily Ann⁷, b Jan 4, 1825 , d Jan 29, 1903, m Mar 24, 1844, George Washington Hinton, and had Nancy Elizabeth⁸, b July 27, 1845 , m June 12, 1888, William K Atkinson, and resides in Readfield, Me , Edna Ann⁸, May 19, 1849, d Sept 24, 1855; George William⁸, Nov 13, 1852, m Sept 12, 1882, Elizabeth Mills No issue

37. EBEN⁶ FULLER, (*Francis⁵, John⁴, John³, John², Matthew¹*), b Jan 25, 1795, in Winthrop, Me , d Oct 6, 1873, in Augusta, Me , m Dec 21, 1821, Eliza Williams, b Oct 30, 1799, in Augusta , d there Aug 28, 1883, dau of Capt Seth Williams   Eben⁶ Fuller was for many years a druggist in Augusta

Children, born in Augusta

110.   Francis Williams⁷, b Jan 15, 1823, d Feb 17, 1863, Sacramento, Cal , unmarried

111   Louisa Lithgow⁷, b Jan 1, 1825, d Jan 7, 1829

112 **Henry Lucins**[r], b Mar 20, 1827; m. Maria E Fowler
113 Louisa Lithgow[r], b Dec 4, 1829, d Aug 1, 1887, at Orange, N J,
    m. Oct. 17, 1853, Oliver H Merrill. No issue
114 Eliza Williams[r], b Mar. 4, 1832; d Sept 25, 1849
115 Ruel Williams[r], b Mar 31, 1834, d. ——, 1838
116 Hannah Bridge[r], b Mar 7, 1835; d. Sept 20, 1909, unmarried
117 Pauline Jones[r], b Mar 2, 1838, m April 24, 1866, Capt John D.
    Myrick, who d Dec 27, 1882   They had a dau, Eliza Williams
    Myrick, b Sept 29, 1868, d Nov 3, 1906, unmarried
118 Helen Williams[r], b Jan 15, 1842
    The last two are living in Augusta (1912)

41. MARTIN[6] FULLER, (*Thomas[5], John[4], John[3], John[2], Matthew[1]*), b
June 8, 1780, probably in Hardwick, Mass, d Oct 18, 1816, in Hardwick,
Vt ; m Mar 3, 1807, Letitia Duncan, of Hancock, N H.
    Children, born at Hardwick, Vt
119 **Thomas James Duncan**[r], b Mar 17, 1808, m 1, Elizabeth Tit-
    comb; m 2, Jennie Elizabeth Dolittle
120 Lydia[r], b July 2, 1810, d Dec 7, 1844, m Feb 29, 1844, Rev. Levi
    Stone; had a son that d young
121 Mary[r], b Jan 13, 1812, d Nov. 1, 1908; m Stearns Foster, and
    had Mary[8] and William[8]
122 **Hiram,**[r] b. Oct 22, 1815; m Laurilla H Cram

42. THOMAS[6] FULLER, (*Thomas[5], John[4], John[3], John[2], Matthew[1]*), b
Mar 24, 1782, probably in Hardwick, Mass ; d Feb 23, 1860, m. ——,
Sally House of Bennington, Vt
    He was a merchant in Enosburg, Vt., Deacon and Representative
    Removed later to Boston, Mass
    Children—probably b. in Enosburg
123 Cordelia H L[r], b. Dec. 27, 1810, d Nov 7, 1841, m Hon Horace
    Eaton, late Governor of Vt   Left no children
124 Thomas H[r], b Mar. 13, 1815
125 Charles E[r], b. June 8, 1817; d Sept 12, 1835
126 Martin Kimball[r], b Apr 21, 1823, d Aug 24, 1838
127 Mary C[r], b. Oct 28, 1824; d Nov 16, 1847
128 Sarah E.[r], b. July 15, 1826; d July 26, 1845
129. Martha R.[r], b. Mar 24, 1828; m A C. Chandler, of Boston, Mass
130 Frances Maria[r], b Feb 19, 1831; d Feb 26, 1852

46. TIMOTHY PAIGE[6] FULLER (*Thomas[5], John[4] John[3], John[2], Matthew[1]*), b Mar 30, 1790, in Westminster, Vt ; d July 21, 1854, in Hancock, N H , m Nov 14, 1816, Rebecca Duncan, of Hancock, N H,
who d. there Jan 29, 1854
    Resided in Bakersfield, Vt , was Judge of County Court.
    Children:
131. A son, b Sept 30, 1817; d Sept. 30, 1817

6

47. AUSTIN[6] FULLER, (*Thomas[5], John[4], John[3], John[2], Matthew[1]*), b Apr 13, 1792, at Westminster, Vt., d Sept. 29, 1870, at Saratoga, N Y, m Jan. 1, 1817, Betsey Maynard

He was a merchant, manufacturer, Representative, Justice of the Peace, Judge of the County Court, and one of the prominent men of his day and generation   He built at Enosburg, Vt., the first starch factory in the state and the second in New England

He removed from Hardwick, Vt, to Bakersfield, Vt, about 1815; to Enosburg, Vt, 1822, and to Saratoga, N Y, in 1866

Children.

132   Austin Weld Fuller, an adopted son
　　Austin Fuller's sister Lydia (No 43, this Group) m Daniel Weld and among other children had Daniel Weld, Jr, b Nov 20, 1810, d Dec. 2, 1848, m Jan 14, 1837, Mary Harlow of Cornish, N H, b Jan 14, 1814; d Sept 25, 1858   Their third child, b Sept 8, 1841, was a son, and was named Austin after No 47 of this Group, who adopted Austin Weld, and changed his name to Austin Weld Fuller.   Austin Weld Fuller grew up to manhood, and on Aug 9, 1862 enlisted in C I, 10th Vermont Regt, rose from the ranks and was brevetted 1st Lieut. and Capt of Vols. after the battle of Cedar Creek, where he was severely wounded. He afterwards, as 2d Lieut 9th Veteran Reserve Corps, served at the "White House" in the Fall of 1865, and in Freedman's Bureau in N C in 1868   Later he was postmaster under President Harrison for 4 years at St Albans, Vt, and was also in mercantile business there. He m Apr 25, 1867, Mary Robbins of Washington, D C, who d May 9, 1903   No children He removed in 1906 to Cambridge, Mass, where he now (1914) resides

48. FRANCIS ENOS[6] FULLER (*Thomas[5], John[4], John[3], John[2], Matthew[1]*), b Mar 20, 1794, in Hardwick, Vt; d Feb 24, 1869, m 1, Sept 30, 1819, Martha Worcester of Hollis, N. H, who d Feb. 24, 1824; m 2, Oct 17, 1825, Hannah Worcester   Martha and Hannah were sisters of the compiler of Worcester's Dictionary

Children
133   Samuel W[7], b Apr 25, 1822, d Oct 25, 1873, in Chicago, Ill

SEVENTH GENERATION.

59. ORRIN[7] FULLER, (*Abram[6], John[5], John[4], John[3], John[2], Matthew[1]*), b Feb 4, 1803 in Livermore, Me, d Nov 17, 1869, in Lagrange, Me.; m June 26, 1827, Mary Hobbs, who d July 29, 1906, in Lagrange

Children, born in Lagrange
134   **Origen[8]**, b. Mar 15, 1829, m Priscilla Henderson
135   **Lewis H[8]**, b June 28, 1831 m Mary E Joy.
136   Catherine M[8], b Dec. 27, 1833, m Nahum Coburn, now dead, left children   She was living (1909) in Arlington, Wash
137   Emily J[8], b ——; d ——
138   Viola M[8], b ——, d May 24, 1868

AUSTIN FULLER——168.

139. Flora[8], b ——, d Oct 25, 1868
140 Leroy[8], b ——, d Sept 24, 1851

60. SAMUEL FOSTER[7] FULLER, (*Abram[6]*, *John[5]*, *John[4]*, *John[3]*, *John[2]*, *Matthew[1]*), b Mar 31, 1804, in Livermore, Me , d —— in Minneapolis, Minn , m Mar 4, 1833, in Livermore, Betsey Morrison, who d Dec 7 1882

Children

141 Dorilus Morrison[8], b ——; d ——
142 Mandel M[8], b Nov. 17, 1838, d —— at Lookout, Dakota(?)
143 **Charles Augustus** , b Apr 16, 1841; m Helen Bartlett
144. Columbia Morrison[8], b Nov 30, 1842, d July 21, 1905, in Minneapolis, Minn., m Sept 10, 1862, in West Cambridge, Mass , Ami L Danforth, and had Ray S[9], b Aug 2, 1876 in Somerville, Mass.
145 Frances Abbie[8], b. July 10, 1844; d July 12, 1850, at Bangor, Me
146 Florence Lizzie[8], b Mar 2, 1846, d Aug 5, 1851
147 **Frank Russell[8]**, b Dec. 29, 1847, m Martha W Skilling
148 Fanny Maria[8], b Dec 6, 1850, at Bangor, Me , d Aug 1, 1896, in Minneapolis, Minn

61. JOHN H[7] FULLER, (*Abram[6]*, *John[5]*, *John[4]*, *John[3]*, *John[2]*, *Matthew[1]*), b Aug 7, 1806, in Livermore, Me ; d ——, m —— 1829, Hannah C Hinds, b Apr 18, 1809, at Livermore; d Oct 18, 1889, at San Francisco, Cal

Children.

149. Florette[8], b ——, m Oct 23, 1852, Henry Ames
150 Hinds[8], b ——; d ——; m ——
151. Frederick[8], b ——
152. Helen M[8], b ——, m Samuel Springer, who is dead She resides in Oakland, Cal
153. Eliza[8], b ——, m Abner McKinley and had a dau, Helen[9], b ——

62. MICHAEL[7] FULLER, (*Abram[6]*, *John[5]*, *John[4]*, *John[3]*, *John[2]*, *Matthew[1]*), b May 6, 1809, in ——; d Apr 11, 1903, in Lagrange, Me ; m ——, Sarah Kelliher.

He lived in Lagrange

Children:

154 Ellen F.[8], b July 15, 1837; d Dec 5, 1860
155 A Bartlett[8], b Aug 24, 1839, d ——, 1840
156 Thomas F[8], b Oct 29, 1841; d Feb. 15, 1842
157. Desire F[8], b Apr 10, 1843, d Apr 20, 1859
158 Marshall T.[8], b July 10, 1845.

74. SAMUEL FRANKLIN[7] FULLER, (*Allen[6]*, *Edward[6]*, *John[4]*, *John[3]*,

John², Matthew¹), b ——, 1816, in Pittston, Me , d July 3, 1883, in
Industry, Me , m 1, July 4, 1840(?) Judith Parker Talcott; m 2, ——,
Lucinda Bailey
Children
159   Augusta Allen⁸ b Aug 28, 1847, in New Portland, Me , m Jan 1,
      1865, Charles M Partridge Reside in Farmington, Me , children
      all born there, except Nellie, b at Strong, Me   Frank C⁹, b
      Nov 5, 1865; Mamie A⁹, Mar 3, 1868; Bertha L⁹, Apr 3, 1871;
      Anne G⁹, Jan 28, 1873; Nellie⁹, June 13, 1874, Lewis⁹, Sept 12,
      1875; Fred E⁹, May 1, 1878, Wilfred D⁹, July 6, 1879, Merton
      R⁹, June 29, 1882, and Artemas A⁹, Aug 8, 1889
160   **Charles⁸**, b. ——, 1873 , m Lizzie D. Weymouth.
161   **Frank⁸**, b ——
162   **Joseph D.⁸**, b. Mar. 22, 1887; m. Rose E Blaisdell

78. BENJAMIN FRANKLIN⁷ FULLER, (*Thomas⁶, Edward⁵, John⁴, John³,
John², Matthew¹*), b Dec 5, 1819, in ——, d Feb 18, 1904; m Sept 25,
1844, Hannah Edwards Folsom, who d. June 26, 1900
He was a farmer, and being a man of excellent judgment represented
his town in the Legislature in his earlier years, and did much business
in the line of settling estates
Children:
163   Lizzie L⁸, b Nov 24, 1845, m Jan 9, 1877, Capt George F Jewett,
      who was b Mar 9, 1837, in Pittston, Me , and d Feb 18, 1908.
      They had a son, Frank Fuller⁹ Jewett, b Mar 20, 1884.

89. EDWARD GORHAM⁷ FULLER, (*Francis⁶, Francis⁵, John⁴, John³,
John², Matthew¹*), b Apr. 28, 1814, in ——, d ——, m 1, Abigail Reed,
m 2, Phebe Ann Cahler; m 3, ——; m 4, ——
Children by first wife:
164   Parmenas Dyer⁸, b ——, m 1, ——, m 2, ——, m 3, ——
165   Frederick⁸, b ——, never married
166   Gerome⁸, b ——; d young
167   Edward⁸, b ——, m ——, resides in Boston, Mass
168   Selden⁸, b. ——, d July 7, 1904, unmarried
169   Clara⁸, b Nov 27, 1850, at Herman Me , m Oct 14 1886, Herbert
      L Pendleton; no children, resides Boston, Mass
   Children by second wife:
170   **Charles F.⁸**, b Nov 5, 1864, m ——
171   **Simeon⁸**, b Mar 23, 1867, m. ——
172   Anne⁸, b Jan 1, 1872.
   No children by 3d and 4th wives

94 JOHN DINSMORE⁷ FULLER, (*Francis⁶, Francis⁵, John⁴, John³, John²,
Matthew¹*), b Dec 26, 1826, in ——; d ——; m ——, Charlotte Reed.
   Children:
173   Henry⁸, b ——, m 1, Rachel Mayhew; m 2, Mrs Alice Patton

174 Georgia⁸, b ——, m ——, Alexander Huges(?) and had Gertrude⁹, Harry⁹, and Carl⁹

97. HIRAM⁷ FULLER, (*Edward⁶, Francis⁵, John⁴, John³, John², Matthew¹*), b ——, probably in Readfield, Me ; d during the winter of 1895-6; m ——, Sarah Whittier, who d about 1893
Children as given in Nason's "History of Old Hallowell, Me":
175 Martha⁸, b ——; d ——
176 George⁸, b ——; d ——
177 Charles⁸, b. ——, d ——
178 Brenda⁸, b. ——, m ——, —— Freese and had one child, husband and child dead; she resides in Hallowell, Me

106. LORIN LOVEJOY⁷ FULLER (*David C⁶, Francis⁵, John⁴, John³, John², Matthew¹*), b. Jan. 25, 1820, in Readfield, Me ; d. July 15, 1895, in Malden, Mass , m 1, Nov. 8, 1852, at Sebec, Me , Lucy Pierce Lovejoy, m 2, June 20, 1889, at Malden, Mrs Anne W Hornsby
Children
179 **Henry Lorin⁸**, b Jan 27, 1857; m. Desiah Freeman Berry
180 Maria Louise⁸, b Mar 12, 1858, in Melrose, Mass.
181 Everett Lovejoy⁸, b July 1, 1860. in Melrose
182 Lucy Alma⁸, b. Sept 11, 1863, in Malden, Mass

107. RUEL BOUTELLE⁷ FULLER, (*David C⁶, Francis⁵, John⁴, John³, John², Matthew¹*), b Aug 1, 1824, in Readfield, Me ; d Feb 25, 1894, in Wilton, Me ; m ——, Harriet Atwood Houghton
Resided in Wilton, Me. Was P. M. at Wilton 20 years; J. P 32 years, and Senator from Franklin Co, Me., in 1868
Children
183 Frederick Lorin⁸, b Apr 24, 1852, d Mar 31, 1855
184 **Frank Boutelle⁸**, b Aug 28, 1853; m Cordelia Libby Newman.
185 George Gage⁸, b Apr. 19, 1855.
186 Alice Eliza⁸, b Apr 4, 1865

112. HENRY LUCIUS⁷ FULLER (*Eben⁶, Francis⁵, John⁴, John³, John², Matthew¹*) b. Mar. 20, 1827, in Augusta, Me ; d. Sept 17, 1875, in Augusta; m Nov 20, 1871, Maria E Fowler
Children·
187 Alice⁸, } twins, b ——,1872, { d ——
188. Florence⁸, } { d ——.
189. Henry M ⁸, b Oct. 23, 1875; d Sept 16, 1880

119. THOMAS JAMES DUNCAN⁷ FULLER (*Martin⁶, Thomas⁵, John⁴, John³, John², Matthew¹*), b Mar 17, 1808, in Hardwick, Vt , d Feb 13,

1876, near Upperville, Va , m 1, June 6, 1836 Elizabeth Titcomb, who
d Sept 13, 1864, m 2, July 26, 1869, Jennie Elizabeth Doolittle

He settled in Calais Me , began the practice of law, was elected
member of Congress from Maine from 1849 to 1857, was appointed
Second Auditor of the Treasury by President Buchanan, and served
until 1861, and later practiced law in Washington, D C

Children by first wife

190   William D [8], b May 22, 1837 ; d Mar 11, 1886   He graduated
      from the West Point Military Academy, served in the war of
      the rebellion, was brevetted major for gallant and meritorious
      services at the battle of Gettysburg, resigned from the army
      July 22, 1872, purchased a fine farm at Upperville, Va , where
      he remained until after his father's death there, when he re-
      moved to Florida   There were other children by first wife that
      died in infancy

Children by second wife

191   **Thomas J. D.**[8], b Aug 18, 1870, m Elizabeth Ashmead Shaeffer

122. HIRAM[2] FULLER (*Martin[6], Thomas[5], John[4], John[3], John[2], Matthew[1]*), b Oct 22, 1815 ; d Dec 2, 1900, m Jan 25, 1847, Laurilla H
Cram of Antrim, N H , b Aug 28, 1826   He lived in Hancock, N H.

Children.

192   Elizabeth E [8], b Feb 13, 1849, m Isaac Patten Allen, and had Ar-
      thur[9], Sidney De Witt[9] and Christie I[9]

193   Martin[8], b Sept 11, 1853; unmarried; resides San Francisco

194   Helen[8] b Dec 15, 1855, m Feb 2, 1875, Edward Osborn Fowle,
      of Boston, who d in 1909, had one son, Frank Fuller[9] Fowle

195   Susan L [8], b Dec 1, 1857, m July, 1878, George Hamilton Mur-
      dock, and had Laurilla[9] and Hamilton[9], twins, b July 1879, and
      Percy[9], b Aug , 1880, at San Francisco.

EIGHTH GENERATION.

134. ORIGEN[8] FULLER (*Orrin[7], Abram[6], John[5], John[4], John[3], John[2],
Matthew[1]*), b Mar 15, 1829, in Lagrange, Me , m Nov 1, 1854, Priscilla
Henderson, who was b in Lagrange June 27, 1833, and d there July
23, 1899

They had two children

196   Mary[9], b June 4, 1857, d. May 9, 1907, m. Edgar Marsh, and had
      Maynard M [10], Hugh A [10], and Clifton F [10]

197   Alice[9], b Oct 29, 1864

135. LEWIS HOBBS[8] FULLER (*Orrin[7], Abram[6], John[5], John[4], John[3],
John[2], Matthew[1]*), b. June 28, 1831, in Lagrange, Me.; d Dec 19, 1902,
in San Mateo, Cal ; m Mar 20, 1869, in Sacramento, Cal , Mary E Joy,
who resides at San Mateo (1909).

Their children were:

198   Viola[9], b July 8, 1871, in Sacramento; d Apr. 16, 1873

199   Marion[9], b Dec 11, 1876, in San Francisco.
200   Lewis Everett[9], b Nov 10, 1882, in San Francisco

143. CHARLES AUGUSTUS[8] FULLER (*Samuel F*[7], *Abram*[6], *John*[5], *John*[4], *John*[3], *John*[2], *Matthew*[1]), b Apr. 16, 1841, d. —— at Mound, Minn ; m ——, Helen Bartlett
   Children
201   A daughter[9], b, ——, d ——
202   Frances Daisy[9], b ——

147. FRANK RUSSELL[8] FULLER (*Samuel F*[7], *Abram*[6], *John*[5], *John*[4] *John*[3], *John*[2], *Matthew*[1]), b Dec 29, 1847, m ——, Martha W Skilling
   He resides in Bangor, Me
   Children.
203   Winifred Clara[9], b Oct 26, 1872; m 1, George Hemstead Sharp, m 2, Calvin Seavey Batchelder By first husband had George H[10], b Dec 22, 1891; by second husband, Donald Fuller[10], b July 15, 1896, Maude M[10], Jan 11, 1898; Russell M[10], ——; d. ——; Winifred[10], Mar. 6, 1903, and Cecile Miriam[10], May 7, 1907

160. CHARLES[8] FULLER (*Samuel F*[7], *Allen*[6], *Edward*[5], *John*[4], *John*[3], *John*[2], *Matthew*[1]), b ——, 1873; m. Oct 21, 1893, Lizzie D Weymouth
   Resides in North Chesterville, Me
   Children.
204   Doris[9], b ——, 1895
205   Methel[9], b ——, 1900
206.   Clarence[9], b ——, 1903

162. JOSEPH D[8] FULLER (*Samuel F.*[7], *Allen*[6], *Edward*[5], *John*[4], *John*[3], *John*[2], *Matthew*[1]), b. Mar. 22, 1887, d May 17, 1906, at Sprague's Mill, Me ; m Nov 10, 1903, Rose E Blaisdell
   Children
207   Velma Mae[9], b. Oct 25, 1904

170. CHARLES F[8] FULLER (*Edward G*[7], *Francis*[6], *Francis*[5], *John*[4], *John*[3], *John*[2], *Matthew*[1]), b Nov 5, 1864; m ——.
   Resides in Ellsworth, Me
   Children
208   Marian De Wolf[9], b ——
209   Eva Gertrude[9], b ——

171. SIMEON[8] FULLER (*Edward G*[7], *Francis*[6], *Francis*[5], *John*[4], *John*[3], *John*, *Matthew*), b Mar. 23, 1867; m ——.

Resides in Ellsworth, Me
Children, 3
210
211
212

179. HENRY LORIN⁸ FULLER (*Lorin L⁷, David C⁶, Francis⁵, John⁴, John³, John², Matthew¹*), b Jan 27, 1857, in Melrose, Mass ; m July 26, 1887, Desiah Freeman Berry, of West Yarmouth, Mass
Resides in Malden, Mass , is in the insurance business
Children
213   Ernest Lorin⁹, b May 31, 1888, in Malden, Mass

184. FRANK BOUTELLE⁸ FULLER (*Ruel B⁷, David C⁶, Francis⁵, John⁴, John³, John², Matthew¹*), b Aug 28, 1853, in Wilton, Me ; m Sept 13, 1881, in Wilton, Cordelia Libby Newman, b Apr 8, 1857, in Cambridge, Mass
He is a physician in Pawtucket, R. I.
Children
214   Margaret Mary⁹, b Apr 25, 1886, in Pawtucket

191. THOMAS JAMES DUNCAN⁸ FULLER (*Thomas J D⁷, Martin⁶, Thomas⁵, John⁴, John³, John², Matthew¹*), b Aug 18, 1870; m Nov 2, 1892, Elizabeth Ashmead Schaeffer, b Feb. 1, 1872, in Ithaca, N Y.
Mr. Fuller is an architect in Washington, D C
Children
215   Thomas J D⁹, b Aug 6, 1893, now (1913) in the Junior Class in Harvard University
216   Charles Ashmead⁹, b Oct 10, 1894
217. Evelyn Schuyler⁹, b June 10, 1897
218   Elizabeth⁹, b July 26, 1899, d. Nov 3, 1905.

FOURTEENTH GROUP

FOURTH GENERATION.

NATHANIEL FULLER⁴, AND SOME OF HIS DESCENDANTS

59. NATHANIEL FULLER (*John³, John², Matthew¹*), b Dec 10, 1716, Barnstable, d ——; m 1, Feb 22, 1738-9, Abigail Hinckley, b July 30 1718, d about 1760, m 2, Nov 8, 1781 Hannah West, of Barnstable

In deeds at Barnstable (re-copied after 1827) is· Sandwich, Vol 2 "Nathaniel Fuller of Sandwich to Samuel Fuller of Sandwich, all my real estate in Sandwich" Sept 5, 1796

"Capt Nathaniel Fuller, first of Sandwich, afterwards of Barnstable, was in the French War He brought home the smallpox and his wife, and daughters, Thankful and Abigail, died of that disease Capt Nat,' as he was familiarly called, was stern in his manner, and very decided in the expression of his opinions He was not an industrious man, and therefore not prosperous in business "

1 Thankful⁵, b ——, d about 1760
2 Abigail⁵, b ——, d about 1760.
3 Hannah⁵, b Aug 12, 1741, m May 23, 1762, Matthias Smith
4 **Joseph⁵**, b May 9 1758, m Tabitha Jones
5. **Nathaniel⁵**, b Jan 3, 1762, m Rachel Jones
6 Mary⁵, b ——, m Lazarus Ewer

FIFTH GENERATION.

4. JOSEPH⁵ FULLER (*Nathaniel⁴, John³, John², Matthew¹*), b May 9, 1758, at Sandwich; d there "Aug. 16, 1845, aged 88 years" (H W Brainard's "Additions and Corrections"), d there "Aug 16, 1846" (Sandwich Rec); m 1, Tabitha Jones, b July, 1760, dau of Josiah Jones of Sandwich, m 2, Phebe Hoxie, of Sandwich, who d there Nov 25, 1880, aged 88 years, dau of Jesse and Rebecca

Joseph Fuller was a Lieutenant in the Revolutionary War and a Revolutionary pensioner

Children.

7. **Benjamin⁶**, b ——, d ——, m Lucy ——

8   Joseph⁶, b Mar 1, 1786, m Mercy Holway
9   Mary Smith⁶, b Jan 5, 1791, d Oct 11, 1884, m Apr 13, 1820,
     Rufus Conant, at Provincetown, Mass Children   Benjamin
     F⁷, b Mar 7, 1821, Abigail Freeman⁷, Nov 4, 1822, Cassandra⁷,
     June 10, 1825, George⁷, May 8, 1827, Rufus⁷, Apr 27, 1829,
     Joseph F⁷, May 16, 1831, at Sandwich, Mass , Mary M⁷, Sept 8,
     1834—all except Joseph F⁷ b at Provincetown, Mass
10   A child, b ——, d Dec, 1795.
11   Abigail⁶, b ——, m Joshua Freeman
12   Thankful⁶, b ——; m Reuben Baldwin, and had Charles⁷, Joseph
     F⁷, and Amos⁷
13   **Nathaniel⁶**, b June 25, 1799, m Dorcas Myrick

5. NATHANIEL⁵ FULLER (*Nathaniel⁴, John³, John², Matthew¹*), b Jan
3, 1762, in Barnstable, d Apr 9, 1840, in East Sandwich, where he had
lived, and is buried, m Mar 18, 1791, Rachel Jones, b May 23, 1770; d
May 10, 1841 (town records), (Apr 10, 1841, Brainard Mss.), dau of
Samuel Jones, of Sandwich
   Children, born in Sandwich
14   Ruhama⁶, b. Oct 4, 1791, d Sept 5, 1840
15   **Samuel⁶**, b Nov. 14, 1793, m Hannah Chipman
16   James Henry⁶, b Nov 4, 1798; m Dec 2, 1824, Abigail Chipman,
     "both of Barnstable"; nothing further found
17. David⁶, b Oct 27, 1806, d Apr. 26, 1882, at Sandwich
18   Anna⁶, b Apr 4, 1809
19   A child, b ——, d Dec 28, 1795

SIXTH GENERATION.

7. BENJAMIN⁶ FULLER (*Joseph⁵, Nathaniel⁴, John³, John², Matthew¹*),
b ——, d ——; m ——, Lucy ——
   He settled in New York city; was in the ship-rigging business; was
living in 1861 in New York city
   Children
20   Benjamin⁷, b. ——; d ——.
21   Julia⁷, b ——, m (?)
22   A dau, b ——; m ——, Ricker, and had son, Benjamin⁸ Ricker,
     and other children.
   Benjamin⁶ Fuller probably had other children

8. JOSEPH⁶ FULLER (*Joseph⁵, Nathaniel⁴, John³, John², Matthew¹*), b
Mar 1, 1786, at Sandwich, d there Feb 8, 1871; m Mercy Holway, who
d Apr 20, 1876, aged 83 y. 6 d
   Children
23   Mary S⁷, b. Feb 3, 1811; d Sept 20, 1894, m Joseph B Hutchins
24   Franklin⁷, b Dec 6, 1813, d June 1, 1817
25   Golima⁷, b Jan 7, 1816, d Nov. 25, 1817.

26　Golina[7], b July 3, 1818, d ——, m Edmund Freeman
27　Franklin[7], b Oct 28, 1820
28　Tabitha[7], b Jan 10, 1823, in Provincetown, Mass , d Jan 9, 1908, in Wareham, Mass , m Dec 26, 1844, Heman Nye, and had Southworth Howland[8], b Aug 29, 1848, Everett Irving[8], Aug 2, 1851, Andrew William[8], Oct 20, 1856, and Anne Matilda[8], May 12, 1860
29　**Thomas Holway[7]**, b July 30, 1824, m Mary F Freeman
30　Mercy Holway[7], b Dec 10, 1827, living (1905) in Brockton, Mass
31　Isaiah Gifford[7], b July 27, 1830, m Frances Delia Talbot
32　Sarah H [7], b Dec 14, 1834, d Feb 26, 1901, m Nov. 23, 1854, George W H Chipman

13. NATHANIEL[6] FULLER (*Joseph[5], Nathaniel[4], John[3], John[2], Matthew[1]*), b June 25, 1799, in Sandwich, d there Mar 11, 1852; m Dorcas Myrick, of Orleans, who d Oct 9, 1890, aged 89 y. 10 mos
　Children·
33　Nancy[7], b Nov 25, 1827, d July 10, 1845
34.　**Obed L [7]**, b Nov 29, 1829; m Cordelia F Fisher
35　Eliza Allen[7], b. Mar 6, 1832, m July 1, 1853, Samuel Jenkins
36　Hannah Ann[7], b Sept 14, 1835; m 1, Peter Blossom, m 2, ——, —— Childs
37　Benjamin[7], b Mar 11, 1841; d. Aug 22, 1864.

15. SAMUEL[6] FULLER (*Nathaniel[5], Nathaniel[4], John[3], John[2], Matthew[1]*), b Nov 14, 1793, in Sandwich, Mass , d ——, m May 23, 1822, Hannah Chipman.
　Children, born in Sandwich
38　Elizabeth Ann[7], b Oct 10, 1823; m. Oct. 10, 1843, Loramus Crowell
39　Abigail F [7], b June 19, 1825
40　**Sylvester Brown[7]**, b Apr 17, 1829, m Mary Chester Pomeroy

SEVENTH GENERATION.

29. THOMAS HOLWAY[7] FULLER (*Joseph[6], Joseph[5], Nathaniel[4], John[3], John[2], Matthew[1]*), b July 30, 1824, in Sandwich, d ——; m Dec 3, 1848, Mary F Freeman, of Sandwich
　Children, recorded in Sandwich
41　Mary Isadore[8], b Mar 2, 1851
42　Thomas H [8], b Nov 23, 1852
43　Lunnetta F [8], b Feb 8, 1855, d Aug 8 1855.
44　Charles C [8], b Aug 7, 1860

31. ISAIAH GIFFORD[7] FULLER (*Joseph[6], Joseph[5], Nathaniel[4], John[3], John[2], Matthew[1]*), b July 7, 1830, in Provincetown, d May 4, 1908, in Newton; m May 11, 1854, Frances Delia Talbot who d Sept 26, 1900

Children

46   Orrin Mayo[8],)   d May 27, 1866, Portsmouth, R I
                     } twins, b Dec 30, 1854, in Sandwich,
45   Oscar Talbot[6],)   d June 15, 1872, Haverstraw, N Y

47   **Joseph Allen**[8], b Oct 14, 1857, m Emma Gardner Field

48   Eva May[8], b May 1, 1860, in Portsmouth, R I, m Sept 10, 1889,
         Philip Tripp Davis, and had Gladys Frances Davis, b Jan. 16,
         1891, and Lester Tripp Davis, b Apr. 22, 1892, both born at Fall
         River

      They reside at Newton Highlands

49   **Henry Russell**[8], b July 21, 1862, m Anne Harrison

50   Hannah Frances[8], b July 21, 1865, in Portsmouth, R I, d there
         Mar 15, 1870

34. OBED L[7] FULLER (*Nathaniel[6], Joseph[5] Nathaniel[4], John[3], John[2], Matthew[1]*), b Nov 29, 1829, in Sandwich; d there Jan 12, 1860; m Jan 3, 1853, Cordelia F Fisher, b 1833

He was a glass cutter, and lived in Sandwich

Children

51   Nancy Maria[8], b Sept 18, 1854

52   Eudora Frances[8], b Sept 20, 1856

40. SYLVESTER BROWN[7] FULLER (*Samuel[6], Nathaniel[5], Nathaniel[4], John[3], John[2], Matthew[1]*), b Apr 17, 1829, in Sandwich, d ——; m Sept 25, 1851, Mary Chester Pomeroy, b July 9, 1831, in Hadley

Children, born in Amherst

53   **Charles Sylvester**[8], b Sept 6, 1852, m Addie Gertrude Usher

54   **George Arthur**[8], b Nov 19, 1855; m Lucy Abbie Burnham

55   Henry Howland[8], b Aug 2, 1858, d Dec 22, 1881, unmarried

56   Sarah Elizabeth[8], b Jan 5, 1861, m Sept 1, 1885, Charles S
         Crossman, and had Maria F[9], b Aug 29, 1887, Charles H[9],
         Nov 18, 1890, Elizabeth B[9], June 10, 1894, and Lincoln H[9],
         Mar 4, 1901

57   **Frederick Pomeroy**[8], b Mar 20, 1863, m Hattie Florence Ricker

EIGHTH GENERATION.

47. JOSEPH ALLEN[8] FULLER (*Isaiah G[7], Joseph[6], Joseph[5], Nathaniel[4], John[3], John[2], Matthew[1]*) b Oct 14, 1857, in Dighton, d Feb 20, 1907, in Dorchester, m Dec 5, 1883, Emma Gardner Field

Children

58   Cora Field[9], b Sept 25, 1884, in Fall River

59   Howard Allen[9], b Nov 28, 1887, in Dorchester

49. HENRY RUSSELL[8] FULLER (*Isaiah G*[7], *Joseph*[6], *Joseph*[5], *Nathaniel*[4], *John*[3], *John*[2], *Matthew*[1]), b July 21, 1862, in Portsmouth, R I ; m Nov 22, 1887, Anne Harrison
  Children, born in Fall River
60 Ernest Harrison[9], b Oct 11, 1890
61 Marion Russell[9], b Aug 25, 1893.

53. CHARLES SYLVESTER[8] FULLER (*Sylvester B*[7], *Samuel*[6], *Nathaniel*[5], *Nathaniel*[4], *John*[3], *John*[2], *Matthew*[1]), b Sept 6, 1852, in Amherst; m May 26, 1880, Addie Gertrude Usher, b Jan 10, 1856, in Lynn.
  Children
62 Lawrence U[9], b Mar 31, 1881
63 Harold Sylvester[9], b Sept 23, 1889.
64 Charles Kenneth[9], b July 14, 1891.
65 Donald Wellington[9], b Oct 27, 1893
66 Madeline[9], b Dec 12, 1897.

54. GEORGE ARTHUR[8] FULLER (*Sylvester B.*[7], *Samuel*[6], *Nathaniel*[5], *Nathaniel*[4], *John*[3], *John*[2], *Matthew*[1]), b Nov 19, 1855, in Amherst; m June 12, 1879, Lucy Abbie Burnham, b Nov 14, 1856, at Essex
  Children .
67 Sarah Elizabeth[9], b Mar 16, 1880, d Apr 16, 1889, at Essex
68 Henry Howland[9], b and d in June, 1884

57. FREDERICK POMEROY[8] FULLER (*Sylvester B.*[7], *Samuel*[6], *Nathaniel*[5], *Nathaniel*[4], *John*[3], *John*[2], *Matthew*[1]), b Mar 20, 1863, in Amherst; m Dec 22, 1885, Hattie Florence Ricker, b Oct 30, 1863, in Dover, N H.
  Children
69 Henry Howland[9], b Jan 8, 1887, in Lynn
70 Raymond Ricker[9], b Mar 6, 1888, in Lynn
71 Morris Wiggin[9], b July 22, 1891, in Lynn.
72 Louise[9] b Aug 6, 1895, in Salem

JOHN[1] FULLER, of NEWTON,

AND SOME OF HIS DESCENDANTS.

AMERICAN FULLER GENEALOGY.

JOHN[1] FULLER OF NEWTON AND SOME OF HIS DESCENDANTS.

JOHN[1] FULLER, one of the first settlers of Cambridge Village, was born in England in 1611, came to America about 1635, and settled in Cambridge Village—now called Newton—about 1644.

Newton was established as a town in 1691, and in 1873 was incorporated as a city.

In December, 1658, John[1] Fuller bought 750 acres of land for about $1.00 per acre, the tract being bounded on the north and west by Charles River. Later he increased his holdings to upwards of 1,000 acres, and became one of the two largest land owners in the village. His tract was long known as the "Fuller Farm."

He divided his land among his children in his lifetime, confirming the division by his will, with the proviso that they should not sell to any stranger, until they, or their next relation, should have the offer of it. Twenty-two of his descendants, it is said, went into the army of the Revolution. Pope in his "Pioneers of Massachusetts" says he was a farmer and a maltster.

He made his will in 1696, and died "Feb. 7, 1697-8, aged 87," according to his gravestone record.

His wife's name was Elizabeth ——. She d. Apr. 13, 1700.

Their children were all born in Newton, as follows:

1. **John[2]**, b. ——, 1645; m. 1, Abigail Boylston; m. 2, Margaret Hicks.
2. Jonathan[2], b. ——, 1648; d. Aug. 12, 1722, a. 74; m. May 2, 1684, Mindwell Trowbridge, who d. Feb. 22, 1758, a. 96. No issue.
3. Elizabeth[2], b. ——; d. Nov. 28, 1685; m. 1663, Job Hyde.

7

4   **Joseph**[2], b Feb 10, 1652, m Lydia Jackson.
5   **Joshua**[2], b Apr 2, 1654, m. Elizabeth Ward
6   **Jeremiah**[2], b Feb 4, 1658, m 1, Mary —, m 2, Elizabeth —
7   Bethia[2], b Nov 23, 1661, m Feb 27, 1684-5, Nathaniel Bond
8   Isaac[2], b. Dec 2, 1665, d Oct 6, 1691, unmarried

SECOND GENERATION.

JOHN[2] FULLER (*John*[1]), b —, 1645, in Newton, d Jan 21, 1720, m 1, —, 1682, Abigail Boylston; m 2, Oct 14, 1714, Margaret Hicks.
Children
9   Sarah[3], b Oct 5, 1683
10. **John**[3], b Sept 2, 1685, m. —, Sarah —   Bond says m Susan Chinery (History of Watertown, Mass)
11 Abigail[3], b Mar 8, 1688
12 **James**[3], b Feb 4, 1690, m. Abigail Leomans
13 Hannah[3], b Aug 31, 1693; d Mar 3, 1781
14 **Isaac**[3], b Nov. 22, 1695, m Abigail Park
15 Jonathan[3], b Feb 13, 1698, d Mar 26, 1698
16 **Jonathan**[3], b Mar 28, 1700, m Elizabeth Woodward
17 **Caleb**[3], b Feb 24, 1702, m Temperance Hyde

JOSEPH[2] FULLER (*John*[1]), b Feb 10, 1652, in Newton, d Jan 5, 1740, m Dec 13, 1680, Lydia Jackson, who d Jan 12, 1726, dau of Edward and Elizabeth (Newgate) Jackson
Children:
18 **John**[3], b Dec 15, 1681, m Hannah (Jackson) Trowbridge.
19 **Joseph**[3], b July 4, 1685; m Sarah Jackson
20 **Jonathan**[3], b Jan 7, 1686; m Sarah Mirick
21 Lydia[2], b. Feb 15, 1692, m Ebenezer Stratton
22 **Edward**[3], b Mar 7, 1694, m Esther Cowdin
23 **Isaac**[3], b Mar 16, 1698, m Hannah Greenwood
24 Elizabeth[3], b July 1, 1701, m —, 1720, Josiah Bond, and had Elizabeth[4], Jonas[4], Josiah[4], Jonas[4] 2d, Sarah[4], Henry[4], Lydia,[4] and Anna[4]

JOSHUA[2] FULLER (*John*[1]), b Apr 2, 1654, in Newton, d June 27, 1752, m 1, June 7, 1679, Elizabeth Ward, who d Aug 17, 1691, m 2, —, Hannah —, who d Nov 28, 1739, m 3, July 19, 1742, Mary Dana.
Children
25 Elizabeth[3], b Feb 22, 1679-80, m Dec 31, 1702, Isaac Shepard, and settled in Norton, Mass; m 2, — Allen
26 Hannah[3], b July 8, 1682, m Stephen Cook, settled in Watertown, Mass, and had Mary[4], Hannah[4], James[4], Peter[4], Susanna[4], Abigail[4], and John[4]

27 Experience[3], b Nov 5, 1685; m 1, —— Mason; m 2, Jan 27, 1714-15, John Child

28 Mercy[3], b Mar 11, 1688-9; m Mar 22, 1710, Aaron Cady

29 Sarah[3], b. ——, 1695; m Richard Park, Jr , settled in Framingham, Mass , and had William[4], Thomas[4], and 4 daughters He m 2, Esther Fuller

30 Abigail[3], b about 1797, m Dec 3, 1718, Joseph Garfield

31 Ruth[3], b ——; m about 1723, Ebenezer Chinery, as his 2d wife

JEREMIAH[2] FULLER (*John*[1]), b Feb 4, 1658, in Newton, d Dec 23, 1743; m 1, Mary ——, who d Aug 17, 1689, m 2, Elizabeth ——, who d. ——, 1700, m 3, Thankful ——, who d 1729, m. 4, Rachel ——, who d 1742

He is called Lieut. Jeremiah Fuller

Children by second wife

32 Elizabeth[3], b Apr. 14, 1694; d June 22, 1694.

33 Jeremiah[3], b July 3, 1697; d May 4, 1703

By third wife

34 **Thomas**[3], b. Sept. 12, 1701; m. Elizabeth Ball

35 **Joshua**[3], b Apr 12, 1703; m 1, ——, m 2, Anna Stearns

36 Thankful[3], b Dec. 23, 1704, m Mar 15, 1729, Noah Wiswell, and had Jeremiah[4], Thankful[4] 1st, Thankful[4] 2d, Mary[4], Sarah[4], Esther[4], Noah[4], Ebenezer[4], Margaret[4], Hannah[4], Thomas[4], and Elizabeth[4].

37 Jeremiah[3], b Nov 1, 1707, d Aug 28, 1711

38 Elizabeth[3], b Aug 24, 1709, d Aug. 28, 1711(?)

39. **Josiah**[3], b Dec 2, 1710, m Abigail Williams

GROUP ARRANGEMENT.

There are 13 sons in the third generation who married and had children These are made heads of 13 groups in the order of their individual numbering   Each child has its individual number relative to the group, proceeding by generations as before.

Group No.	Individual No	HEADS OF GROUPS, AND LINEAGE	Date of Birth
1	11	John³, *John²*, *John¹*	Sept 2, 1685
2	13	James³, *John , John .*	Feb. 4, 1690
3	15	Isaac³, *John², John¹.*	Nov 22, 1695
4	17	Jonathan³, *John², John¹*	Mar. 28, 1700
5	18	Caleb³, *John², John¹*	Feb 24, 1702
6	19	John³, *Joseph², John¹*	Dec. 15, 1681
7	20	Joseph³, *Joseph², John¹.*	July 4, 1685
8	21	Jonathan³, *Joseph², John¹*	Jan 7, 1686
9	23	Edward³, *Joseph², John¹.*	Mar. 7, 1694
10	24	Isaac³, *Joseph², John¹*	Mar 16, 1698
11	35	Thomas³, *Jeremiah², John¹*	Sept 12, 1701
12	36	Joshua³, *Jeremiah², John¹*	Apr 12, 1703
13	40	Josiah³, *Jeremiah², John¹*	Dec. 2, 1710

FIRST GROUP

THIRD GENERATION.

JOHN³ FULLER AND SOME OF HIS DESCENDANTS

11. JOHN³ FULLER (*John²*, *John¹*), b Sept 2, 1685, in Newton, Mass , d Apr. 7, 1737 (Newton V R), m "Aug , 1709 ——" (Newton V R); m "Aug , 1709, Sarah ——" (Jackson's Hist Newton) , m "Aug , 1709, Susan Chinery" (Bond's Hist Watertown, Mass)

Children, born in Newton

1 Mindwell⁴, b Sept 9, 1710
2 Elizabeth⁴, b June 27, 1712
3 James⁴, b Feb 9, 1714-15
4 Abigail⁴, b Apr 9, 1717.
5 Mary⁴, b June 2, 1720
6 Jerusha⁴, b Oct 16, 1722
7. Eunice⁴, b Aug 6, 1725
8 Rebecca⁴, b Sept 21, 1730
9 Sarah⁴, b July 8, 1733
10. Elisha⁴, b Oct 11, 1735—not given in Newton V R , but mentioned by Jackson and by Bond I notice that all give *Jonathan and Sarah* an Elisha, born Oct 11, *1725*

I find nothing in the published Newton Vital Records that seems to relate to marriages or deaths of any of the above children, but in Boston Vital Records I find an Elizabeth Fuller and Walter Hallowell, and an Abigail Fuller and William Wetherell, whose marriage intentions are of same date—Mar 30, 1739, and a James Fuller who m. Elizabeth Stevens, Jan 8, 1740; names of parents not given.

SECOND GROUP.

JAMES[3] FULLER AND SOME OF HIS DESCENDANTS

13. JAMES[3] FULLER (*John*[2], *John*[1]), b Feb 4, 1690, in Newton, Mass ; d. ——; m Dec 12, 1717, Abigail Youmans.

He removed to Ashford, Ct , and thence to Union, Ct , where he bought land of William Ward, Mar 9, 1732, and where he was Town Clerk in 1737 (Lawson's Hist of Union, Ct)

Children

1   Dinah[4], b Dec 29, 1718; m May 31, 1736, Nathaniel Walker, and had Phebe[5], b Dec 13, 1736, Judith[5], May 6, 1741; Zerviah[5], Dec 20, 1742, Rebecca[5], Sept 10, 1744, Hezekiah[5], Apr 18, 1746; Stephen[5], Jan 1, 1748, James[5], Feb 9, 1755, Keturah[5], Oct 6, 1756, and Simonds(?) , lived in Hampton, Ct

2   Abigail[4], b ——, 1719, m. Nov 9, 1749, Benjamin Walker

3   Elizabeth[4]. b June 15, 1721, d Mar 12, 1747; m Nov 23, 1739, Daniel Badger, Jr , and had 5 children

4   **William**[4], b Mar 13, 1722-3, m Mehitable Tyler.

5   **Hezekiah**[4], b Mar. 2, 1724-5; m 1, Margaret Tyler, m 2, Margaret Graham

FOURTH GENERATION.

4. WLIIAM[4] FULLER (*James*[3], *John*[2], *John*[1]), b Mar 13, 1722-3 (Hist of Union, Ct) , d. ——, m Dec 10, 1746, Mehitable Tyler (Union, Ct , Records)

Children :

6   **Hezekiah**[5], b Nov 25, 1747; m Tryphena Lamkin.

7   Dorothy[5], b Oct. 21, 1751

8   Isaac[5], b Feb , 1756, m. Aug 7, 1777, Judith Buel (Wales, Mass , Rec)

9   Calvin[5], b May 6, 1758

10   Abigail[5], b Aug 30, 1763

11   **Luther**[5], b. May 10, 1766

12   Abner[5], b Feb 29, 1768

13   John[5], b Nov 22, 1771.

NOTE—Isaac, probably the Revolutionary Pensioner of Le Ray Jefferson Co , N Y , whose pension papers state "he was 76 years old in

1832, that he m Elizabeth Chamberlain, Oct 10, 1814," probably as second wife Calvin, probably the one on the lists for short time levy in 1779 from Somers, Ct See under Luther, No. 11, about Somers

5. HEZEKIAH[4] FULLER (*James[3], John[2], John[1]*), b Mar 2, 1724-5, d Mar 19, 1799, in Stafford, Ct ; m 1, Feb 14, 1748, Margaret Tyler, who d Feb 21, 1772, m 2, Margaret Graham, who was of Scotch-Irish descent, her parents coming from the north of Scotland and making their home in Union, Ct Hezekiah Fuller was a wheelwright by trade, having served seven years' apprenticeship with a master in Holland, Mass., later he removed to Stafford, settling near what was known as the Fisk place, and later as the Plymptom place He bought property in Stafford Apr. 10, 1770.

Children

14 Amos[5], b July 10, 1752, m 1778, Thankful Fay(?) (Brimfield Rec)
15 Asa[5], b Mar 28, 1758; probably died young
16 Elizabeth[5], b Sept 6, 1760.
17 **James[5]**, b Mar. 21, 1763; m Lucretia White
18 **Phineas[5]**, b. Aug 28, 1765, m. Elizabeth Durkee
19 Adna[5], b Mar 8, 1768
20 Chloe[5], b Feb. 3, 1772.
21 Margaret[5], b Jan 12, 1776, died young
22 **Asa[5]**, b Jan 12, 1778, m Rachel Trask
23 **Amasa[5]**, b Aug 19, 1780, m Orinda Washburn

FIFTH GENERATION.

6. HEZEKIAH[5] FULLER (*William[4], James[3], John[2], John[1]*), b Nov 25, 1747, d ——; m ——, Tryphena Lamkin

The History of Union, Ct., states that Hezekiah Fuller lived in Lancaster, N. H.

The History of Lancaster, N H , states that Hezekiah Fuller leased a mill there in 1773, and that he was carried away by Indians in 1779

Volume 12 of Town Papers of N. H mentions Hezekiah Fuller as a signer of a road petition in 1778 and Volume 13 as a signer of a petition in Stratford, N H , in 1791

The U S Census of 1790 mentions no Fuller families in Lancaster, but gives 12 persons in the family of Hezekiah Fuller of Stratford Records of deeds in Lancaster show dealings in lands in Stratford by Hezekiah, and by Luther Fuller of Brunswick, Orange Co, Vt.

Hammond's "Town Papers of New Hampshire," referring to a petition by 12 signers in Lancaster, asking the authorities for assistance on account of an Indian raid and their capture of two men, says "the two men referred to were Joseph Barlow and Hezekiah Fuller." What disposition their captors made of them we do not know Their names figure in business transactions at a subsequent date, from which we may infer that they either escaped or were ransomed It was a matter of frequent occurrence for towns to pay the ransom of such captures

The Berlin (N H) "Independent" of Feb 16, 1898, printed portions of an address including mention of the family of Hezekiah Fuller and Tryphena Lamkin as follows

"Hezekiah and Luther, sons of William, settled in Stratford, N H, Hezekiah where his grandson, William G Fuller, now lives We place Mr. Fuller here since the members of his family are descendants of Joshua Lamkin

Children:

24 **Jason**[6], b ——, m Ruth Aldrich, lived in Belchertown, Mass.; had 6 sons and 4 daus

25. Amerillis[6], b ——, m Isaac Schoff, had one son, Henry D[7]

26 **Jeremiah**[6], b ——; m ——

27. Rhoda[6], b ——, m 1, —— Hilton; m 2, —— Smith

28 Samantha[6], b ——, m John Stevens, and had Warren[7], Abner[7], Mahala[7], Harriet[7], Isaac[7], Walter[7], Eddie[7], Samantha[7], and Melissa[7]

29 Ann[6], b ——, m William Styles, and had William[7], Mehitable[7], George[7], Hannah[7], and Roxy[7]

30 **Samuel**[6], b ——, m Almira Fuller.

31 Mehitable[6], b ——; m Simeon Lindley, and had Jessie[7], George[7], Ralph[7], Frank[7], and Louisa[7]

32 **Grant**[6], b ——, m 1, Abigail Clough, m 2, Mary Thompson "

11. LUTHER[5] FULLER (*William*[4], *James*[3], *John*[2], *John*[1]), b May 10, 1766, in Union, Ct, d Oct 1841, in ——. m ——, 1803, Lydia ——, who d. 1837.

In the U S Pension Records it is found that Luther enlisted in Somers, Ct, about May, 1780, in Capt Wales' Co and served 6 months; enlisted again Jan, 1781, at Brimfield, Mass, under Capt Aaron Charles, served in all 28 months

After the war he lived in Stratford and Colebrook, N H His father removed to Brimfield, Mass, and then in 8 to 10 years in Somers, Ct

Children.

33 Peter C[6], b ——, 1806, and probably others

17. JAMES[5] FULLER (*Hezekiah*[4], *James*[3], *John*[2], *John*[1]), b Mar 2, 1763, d ——; m Oct 5, 1786, Lucretia White, ' both of Stafford, Ct "

The U S Census, 1790, gives the family of James Fuller, consisting of 5 persons, in Western, now Warren, Mass

He removed with wife, Frederick W and Eudotia to Vershire, Vt, in 1791

Children

34 Frederick White[6], b July 30, 1787

35 Eudotia[6], b Apr 21, 1790, in Warren, Mass ; m Samuel H Moore, and lived in Norwich, Vt

36 James[6], b Sept 5, 1792, in Warren, Mass

37   Orinda⁶, b Feb 12, 1795
38   Delilah⁸, b Aug 14, 1797
39   Elmira⁶, b Sept 27, 1799
40   Hezekiah⁶, b Sept 25, 1802, m, Persis Austin
41   Lucretia⁶, b Apr 16, 1808

18. Phineas⁵ Fuller (*Hezekiah⁴, James³, John², John¹*), b Aug. 25, 1765 (Hist Union Ct), d Oct 12, 1852 aged 87 (Brimfield, Mass , Rec), m Sept 13, 1792, Elizabeth Durkee, who d Aug 15, 1848, aged 77 years

He lived in South Brimfield, now known as Wales, Mass , for about 5 years, and then removed to Brimfield

Children—buried in Brimfield Cemetery—places of birth not given
42   Eliza⁶, b about 1794, d Mar. 5, 1864, aged 70, unmarried
43   Asenath⁶, b about 1795, d Mar 26, 1796
44   Minerva⁶, b about 1800, d Jan 5, 1812 aged 12 years.
45   Lucy⁶, b about 1802, d Nov 21, 1836, aged 34 years
46   Mary C⁶, b about 1808; d Oct 31, 1848, aged 40 years ; unmarried

22. Asa⁵ Fuller (*Hezekiah⁴, James³, John², John¹*), b Jan 12, 1778 (Stafford, Ct , Rec); d Sept 7, 1862, aged 83-5-12 (Chicopee, Mass Rec), m ——, Rachel Trask, who d 1847, aged 67, in Springfield, Mass

Children (perhaps not mentioned below in order of births)
47   Rhoda⁶, b ——, m. Nov 4, 1823, Seth Clough
48   **Orrin**⁸, b about 1803 , m Mary Cooley
49   **Anson**⁶ b about 1807, m Diana Clough
50   Maria⁶, b ——, m Anthony Slater
51   Lucinda⁸, b ——, m —— Slater
52   **Alvin**⁶, b about 1816, m Mary Ann Huntley
53   **Dexter**⁶, b about 1819, m Delia A Clough
54   **Heman**⁶, b Feb 20, 1822, m Harriet A Hamilton
55   Emily⁸, b ——, m Dec 4, 1848, Harrison Burnett

23. Amasa⁵ Fuller (*Hezekiah⁴, James³, John², John¹*), b. Aug 19, 1780, in Sttafford, Ct d there Apr 21, 1846 , m ——, Orinda Washburn

Children, probably not given in order of birth
56   Albert⁸, b ——, d ——, m ——, "left no living sons "
57   Henry⁶, b ——, d ——, 1892, m ——, "wife and dau died before him."
58   **Robert Stanbross**⁶, b ——, m Hannah E Bugbee
59   Anne J⁶, b ——, at Stafford , d Apr 5, 1906, in Chicopee, Mass , unmarried
60   Emily S⁸, b ——, at Stafford , d Aug 22, 1906, in Chicopee, unmarried

There were 6 children who died unmarried Emily S was the youngest, and furnished most of the bove information shortly before her death

SIXTH GENERATION.

24. JASON[6] FULLER (*Hezekiah[5], William[4], James[3], John[2], John[1]*), b about 1788, d Sept 30, 1848, aged 60 (G S Record, South Belchertown), m —— Ruth Aldrich, who d Nov 17, 1848, aged 57 (G S Rec)

He was a farmer; lived in Belchertown

Children, all born in Belchertown

61   Eliza[7], b about 1812; d Feb 24, 1883 (G S Rec , Palmer, Mass , 4 corners) , m Int Pub Aug 9 1834, with Joseph Smith Hastings   Their children were Eliza Jane[8], Maria[8], and Laura[8]

62   Hannah W [7], b Sept. 29, 1814; d Feb 24, 1892, aged 78 , m 1, Apr 18, 1839, Ebenezer Walker, who d Jan 27, 1846 , m. 2, Sept 30, 1847, James M Stevens   By first husband Jane[8], b Sept. 29, 1843; by second husband, Ruth[8] b July 8 1847, Minerva[8], b Mar 23, 1850, Ora[8], June 5, 1852, Juliette[8], Apr 25, 1854, and Marshall[8], Oct 14, 1857

63. Jeremiah[7], b about 1816, d. Dec 20, 1877, aged 61 (G S Rec) , m Mary Nancy Cleveland, b Mar. 18, 1813, d Sept 7, 1875 , no children

64   **Willis[7]**, b about 1818 , m 1, Emeline Chapin , m 2, Clymenia P Arnold

65   **Alvin[7]**, b about 1821 ; m Mary K Works

66   **Olney[7]**, b Oct 27, 1823, m Maria P Anderson

67   **Grant[7]**, b —— , m 1, Cynthia A Braman , m 2, Harriet ——

68   **William[7]**, b Sept 26, 1828, m Jane L French

69   Sarah[7], b ——; m Adoniram Judson Barrett, who is dead   They had a son George[8], residing (1912) in Cleveland, Ohio, and dau Sarah[8], who d Apr 14, 1860

70   Mary L [7], b ——, m 1, May 6, 1852, Washington L Walker, m 2, —— Wilbur   One son by first husband, 2 sons by second husband

71   James[7], b ——; m 1, Jan 25, 1868, Bridget Hartigan (Holyoke Rec) , m 2, May 25, 1868, Olive A Moulton (Chicopee Rec.) , m 3, —— No children

26. JEREMIAH[6] FULLER (*Hezekiah[5], William[4], James[3], John[2], John[1]*), b probably in Stratford, N H , d in the war of 1812, m. ——

Children.

72   George[7], b ——

73   Jeremiah[7], b ——

30. SAMUEL[6] FULLER (*Hezekiah[5], William[4], James[3], John[2], John[1]*), b probably in Stratford, N H ; m ——. Almira Fuller

Children.

74   Deborah[7], b ——.

75   Clark[7], b ——

76. Monroe[7], b. ——

77   Angelina[7], b ——

32. GRANT[6] FULLER (*Hezekiah[5]*, *William[4]*, *James[3]*, *John[2]*, *John[1]*), b
July 16, 1788, in Stratford, N H.; d Mar 24, 1849, m 1, Abigail Clough,
m 2, Mary Thompson
Children, born in Stratford(?)
78. Dulcinea[7], b ——, m Seth Chase
79 Persis Elvira[7], b ——, m David Emerson, and had William[8] and
Mary[8].
80 Martha[7], } b ——, twins, { died young
81 Mary[7], } { died young.
82 Samuel Allen[7], b ——; d young
83 **William Grandison**[7], b Nov 3, 1822, m Ann E Merriam

48. ORRIN[6] FULLER (*Asa[5]*, *Hezekiah[4]* *James[3]*, *John[2]*, *John[1]*), b about
1803, in Stafford, Ct , d Dec 27, 1877, aged 74 y 11 m 11 d (Chic-
opee, Mass, Records); m Apr 30, 1830, in Enfield, Ct Mary Cooley,
"both of Springfield"
Children
84 Henry O [7], b ——, d young, in Chicopee
85 **Andrew**[7] b about 1836, m Frances J Hamilton
86 Mary J [7], b May 10, 1838, in Chicopee, m Sept 16, 1860, Henry
Clay Hamilton, b Apr 9, 1834, in Pelham, Mass Children ·
Gertrude[8], b June, 1865, in Springfield, Mabel Frances[8], b June
23, 1867, m Dec 25, 1888, Louis J Chandler

49. ANSON[6] FULLER (*Asa[5]*, *Hezekiah[4]*, *James[3]*, *John[2]*, *John[1]*), b about
1807 in Stafford, Ct , d May 11 1853, in Chicopee, Mass , aged 46 y
5 m 3 d , m Apr 9, 1838, Diana Clough, b in Ludlow, Mass , d. Aug
12, 1896
87 Laurinda[7], b about 1839 in S Hadley, Mass , d Dec 31, 1857
88 Mary C [7], b about 1842; m June 23, 1862, Oliver Welden
89 **Henry A.**[7], b Nov 28, 1844, m 1, Emily Wardwell, m 2, Emma
Crowe
90 Ellen S [7], b Jan 16, 1847, d Sept 12, 1848
91 Albert H [7], b ——, d. July 29, 1853
92 Anson Herbert[7], b July 2, 1853, d Mar 26, 1858

52. ALVIN[6] FULLER (*Asa[5]*, *Hezekiah[4]*, *James[3]*, *John[2]*, *John[1]*), b about
1816 in Stafford, Ct , d Dec 18, 1859, aged 43 y 9 d , m ——, Mary
Ann Huntley
Children recorded in Springfield and Chicopee, Mass
93 Harriet L [7], b Dec 17, 1843, m Nov. 17, 1860, George H Hubbard
94 Mary E [7], b June 26, 1846
95 Alvin Elbridge[7], b Feb 4, 1848, m ——, had 4 children; resides
in Maine (1906)
96 Arthur E [7], b Aug 11, 1850; m ——, had 1 son, resides Bridge-
port, Ct (1906)

53. DEXTER[6] FULLER (*Asa*[5], *Hezekiah*[4], *James*[3], *John*[2], *John*[1]) b about 1819, in Springfield, Mass , d there Sept 14, 1847, aged 28 , m 1, May 10, 1841, Adelia A Clough , m 2, —— Welden

Children, recorded in Springfield and Chicopee, Mass

97   Merrick D[7], b Sept 16, 1846

98   **Dexter N.**[7], b ——, m Aug. 3, 1867, Mary A Crawford

54. HEMAN[6] FULLER (*Asa*[5], *Hezekiah*[4], *James*[3], *John*[2], *John*[1]), b Feb 20, 1822, d Feb 3, 1892, in Chicopee, Mass , aged 69 y 11 m 13 d , m July 2, 1845, Harriet Augusta Hamilton, b in Pelham, Mass . dau of Joseph and Sylvia Hamilton   She d Jan 27, 1913, aged 90 years at Chicopee Falls, Mass

Children, born in Chicopee

99   Mary C[7], b Aug 26, 1848, m Sept 11, 1873, Wilson Payne.

100   Alice F[7], b Apr 30, 1859, d Nov 22, 1859

58. ROBERT STANBROSS[6] FULLER, (*Amasa*[5], *Hezekiah*[4], *James*[3], *John*[2], *John*[1]), b ——, d July 3, 1895, in Hartford, Ct , m June 23, 1842, in Stafford, Ct , Hannah E Bugbee, who d. 1888

Children

101   **Albert K.**[7], b May 6, 1844, m S Emma Parker

SEVENTH GENERATION.

64. WILLIS[7] FULLER, (*Jason*[6], *Hezekiah*[5], *William*[4], *James*[3], *John*[2], *John*[1]), b about 1818 in Belchertown; d there Nov 8, 1884; m 1, Int Pub May 3, 1840, with Emeline Chapin, who d May 31, 1869, aged 53 , m 2, Jan 29, 1870, Clymenia P Arnold, who d 1913

He was a farmer in South Belchertown

Children

102   Henrietta[8], b about 1843 , d May 26, 1860

103   Ellen H[8], b Mar 19, 1845 , resides in Monson, Mass , m Nov 26, 1866, Linus H Hatch, and had Forrest G[9], b Mar 11, 1868 , Willis C[9], Jan 28, 1870, Linus M[9], Jan 28, 1874, and Harold F[9], Feb 6, 1875

104   Louisa A[8], b Nov 6, 1848; d Sept 14, 1889, m May 3, 1865, George W Aldrich

65. ALVIN[7] FULLER, (*Jason*[6], *Hezekiah*[5], *William*[4], *James*[3], *John*[2], *John*[1]), b about 1821 in Belchertown , d Oct 14, 1855 , m Dec 18, 1845, Mary K Works (Belchertown Records)

Children .

105   Marthaett[8], b Dec 26, 1846; living 1908 in South Bend, Indiana , unmarried

66. OLNEY[7] FULLER, (*Jason[6], Hezekiah[5], William[4], James[3], John[2], John[1]*), b Oct 27, 1823, in Belchertown; d Feb 28, 1908, in Mendota, Ills ; m 1849, Maria P Anderson, b Feb 8, 1822, in Monson, Mass , d May 13, 1904, in Oshkosh, Wis.

Children

106 Esther M[8], b Aug 18, 1850, m Dec 22, 1875, in Milton, Wis , Charles H Teeter, and had Heber F[9], b Apr 16, 1878, in Milton, d May 17, 1879, Jennie M[9], Jan 5, 1880, in Clinton, Wis, and Ray O[9], Mar 13, 1887 They resided a few years near Milton, Wis, and then removed to Los Angeles, Cal, where they now (1912) reside

107 Charles O[8], b June 6, 1858, d Apr 14, 1859

67. GRANT[7] FULLER, (*Jason[6], Hezekiah[5], William[4], James[3], John[2], John[1]*), b ——, in Belchertown, d about 1895 in Earlville, Ill, m 1, June 15, 1848, Cynthia A Braman, who d in Earlville; m 2, Harriet —— Children, all by first wife.

108 Frank[8], b ——, d in Iowa; m ——, and had one dau.

109 Frances[8], b ——

110 Emma[8], b ——

68. WILLIAM[7] FULLER, (*Jason[6], Hezekiah[5], William[4], James[3], John[2], John[1]*), b Sept 26, 1828, in Belchertown, Mass ; d Oct 3, 1895, aged 67 (Springfield, Mass, Record), m Jan 8, 1851, Jane L French, b Mar 6, 1828, in Williamsburg, Mass (Wilbraham, Mass, Rec), d May 9, 1900

Children

111 **William J.[8]**, b. Apr 27, 1852; m 1, Emma E. Clough , m 2, Martha V Crowe

112 Nellie[8], b Jan 23, 1863, d July 24 1864

113 Jennie L[8], b Dec 17 1857; d July 30, 1858

83. WILLIAM GRANDISON[7] FULLER, (*Grant[6], Hezekiah[5], William[4], James[3], John[2], John[1]*), b Nov 3, 1822, in Stratford, N H , d there June 24, 1900; m ——, Ann E Merriam

Children, all born in Stratford

114 Sarah Helen[8], b Sept 8, 1856

115 Abbie Mary[8], b May 2, 1859

116 Frederick H.[8], b Oct 31, 1866; d Mar. 11, 1868

117 **Edward Byron[8]**, b Feb 3, 1869 , m. Anne Phillips

85. ANDREW[7] FULLER, (*Orrin[6], Asa[5], Hezekiah[4], James[3], John[2], John[1]*), b about 1836 in Springfield, Mass , d June 7, 1905, in Chicopee, Mass , m Oct 25, 1860, Frances Jeanette Hamilton

Children, recorded at Chicopee

118   Edna J[8], b Nov 3, 1870, m. Aug. 8, 1893, Cecil Adams.
119   Charles O[8], b July 9, 1873; d May 3, 1876
120   Frances M[8], b Sept 4, 1875, d Mar 20, 1876
121   Frederick H.[8], b Dec 12, 1877; m June, 1906, Elizabeth Opper-
           thwaite; resides (1906) in Chicopee

89. HENRY A[7] FULLER, (*Anson[6], Asa[5], Hezekiah[4], James[8], John[2], John[1]*), b Nov 28, 1844, in Springfield, Mass (part now Chicopee, Mass), m 1, Sept 17, 1867, Emily Wardwell, m 2, Jan 1, 1895, Emma Crowe

   He resides in Vermont

   Children
122   A dau, b ——

98. DEXTER N[7] FULLER, (*Dexter[3], Asa[5], Hezekiah[4], James[3], John[2], John[1]*), b ——, in Chicopee, Mass; m ——, Mary A Crawford

   Children:
123   Jennie A[8], b Nov 11, 1870

101. ALBERT K[7] FULLER, (*Robert S[6] Amasa[5], Hezekiah[4], James[3], John[2], John[1]*), b May 6, 1844, d ——, m July 16, 1869, Emma Sarah Parker, b Jan 4, 1843

   Children·
124   Bertie E[8], b May 5, 1870, in Windsor, Ct, d Feb 29, 1884. at
           Feeding Hills, Mass
125   Jennie Emma[8], b May 8, 1874, at Windsor
126   Albert Edward[8], b Oct 16, 1877, at W Hartford, Ct

EIGHTH GENERATION.

111. WILLIAM J[8] FULLER, (*William[7], Jason[6], Hezekiah[5], William[4], James[3], John[2], John[1]*), b Apr 27, 1852, in Palmer, Mass, d Nov 9, 1912, in Springfield, Mass. m 1, Nov 29, 1877, Emma E Clough, who d Apr 20, 1878, m 2, Sept 25, 1879, Martha V Crowl, b at Harpers Ferry, Va

   He resided in Springfield, Mass.

   Children
127   **Alvin W.[9]**, b Aug 23, 1883, m Edythe D Janes.

117. EDWARD BYRON[8] FULLER, (*William G[7], Grant[6], Hezekiah[5], William[4], James[3], John[2], John[1]*), b Feb 3, 1869, in Stratford, N H., m Anne Phillips

   Resides in Coos, N H

   Children.

128   Pauline Alice⁹, b Dec. 4, 1903, in Stratford, N H
129   William Morrison⁹, b Oct 4, 1910

NINTH GENERATION.

127. ALVIN W⁹ FULLER, (*William J*⁸, *William*⁷, *Jason*⁶, *Hezekiah*⁵, *William*⁴, *James*³, *John*², *John*¹), b Aug 23, 1883, in Springfield, Mass ; m June 4, 1907, Edythe D Janes of Springfield, where they now (1912) reside
  Children
130   Vera¹⁰, b Feb. 24, 1911

THIRD GROUP

THIRD GENERATION.

ISAAC³ FULLER AND SOME OF HIS DESCENDANTS

15. Isaac³ Fuller, (*John² John¹*), b Nov 22, 1695, in Newton, d there 1755, aged 61; m July 19, 1721, Abigail Park

Children, recorded in Newton Vital Records.

1   John⁴, b July 13, 1722; d July 31, 1722
2   **Abijah⁴**, b June 1, 1723, m Lydia Richardson
3   **Samuel⁴**, b Nov 26, 1724, m Lydia Stearns
4   **Richard⁴**, b Oct 23, 1728 } twins; { m Eunice Childs.
5   Priscilla⁴, b Oct 23, 1728 } twins; { d 1763, unmarried
6   Abigail⁴, b —— , d Apr. 15, 1753

FOURTH GENERATION.

2. Abijah⁴ Fuller (*Isaac³, John², John¹*), b June 1, 1723, in Newton, d there Mar 2, 1798; m Jan 16, 1755, Lydia Richardson of Holden.

Children.

7   Sybil⁵, b. May 27, 1756
8   Rhoda⁵, b Oct 31, 1758
9   Lemuel⁵, b. Jan 26, 1761
10 Esther⁵, b June 9, 1763
11 **Elijah⁵**, b Feb 11, 1766, m Lucretia Smith
12 Ezekiel⁵, b Feb 2, 1768
13 **Amasa⁵**, b Oct 23, 1770
14 **Isaac⁵**, b May, 1775; m Aug 7, 1797, Patty Howe of Holden

3. Samuel⁴ Fuller, (*Isaac³, John², John¹*), b Nov. 26, 1724, in Newton; d ——; m Oct 9, 1746, in Waltham, Lydia Stearns, who d Sept 30, 1753

Children

15 Samuel⁵, b Jan 7, 1746-7; probably died young
16 Samuel⁵, b May 2, 1748, d Nov 29, 1752
17 Sarah⁵, b Oct 26, 1749

18   Lois[5], } twins, b Oct 23,1725
19   Lydia[5],}   m June 10,1772, Silas Stearns of Weston

4.   RICHARD[4] FULLER, (*Isaac[3], John[2], John[1]*), b Oct 23, 1728, in Newton; d ——, m Nov. 16, 1757, Eunice Childs.
  Children
20   Eunice[5], b Dec 24, 1766

FIFTH GENERATION.

11. ELIJAH[5] FULLER, (*Abijah[4]. Isaac[3] John[2], John[1]*), b Feb 11, 1766
in Newton, d 1822, in Marlboro, N H ; m July 11, 1790, Lucretia
Smith of Holden, who d. 1863, aged 97
  They removed to Marlboro in 1797
  Children, the first 3 b in Hubbardston, the others in Marlboro, N H
21   A dau, b May 29, 1791
22   A dau, b Sept 12, 1792
23   **Isaac[6]**, b Nov. 14, 1794, m Temperance Hinckley
24   Martha[6], b Dec 14, 1797; m Abel Garfield, of Troy, N H
25   Lydia[6], b June 9, 1800, d Mar 11, 1811
26   Lucretia[6], b Aug 1, 1805; m John E Jackson.
27   Elijah[6], b Apr 6, 1808, d Jan 19, 1812.
28   Harriet[6], b Apr. 21, 1810

13. AMASA[5] FULLER, (*Abijah[4], Isaac[3], John[2], John[1]*), b Oct 23, 1770,
d ——; is probably the Amasa Fuller who m Dec 11, 1793, Mehitable
Hearsey, "both of Dorchester "
  Children, recorded in Dorchester
29. Nathaniel[6], b Apr 2, 1794
30. Elijah[6], b Mar 10, 1796
31   Clarissa[6], b Jan 15, 1798
32   Isaac Richardson[6], b Sept 6 1800

14. ISAAC[5] FULLER, (*Abijah[4], Isaac[3], John[2], John[1]*), b. May, 1775,
d 1819; m Aug 7, 1797, Patty Howe of Holden, who d Aug 16, 1836
  Removed to Marlboro, N H, about 1797; he is called Capt. Isaac
Fuller
  Children, all but the first child born in Marlboro, N H
33   **Amasa[6]**, b. Dec 7, 1797, m 1, Anna Bemis, m 2, Hannah Jackson;
       m 3, Mrs Mary (Knight) Hager; m 4, Mrs Lovey P Kidder
34   Lucretia[6], b Jan 11, 1800; d. June 11, 1873; m Ezra Alexander,
       resided in Fitzwilliam, N H
· 35   Patty[6], b Sept 6, 1802, d Sept 3, 1840; m David Jackson of Wal-
       lingford, Vt
36   Nancy[6], b Jan 1, 1805; m Aug 17, 1823, Andrew Sherman, who
       d May 26, 1871

8

37   Dorothy[6], b Apr 5, 1807, d June 22, 1807
38   Stillman[6], b July 22, 1808, d Mar 16, 1809
39   Lydia[6], b Feb 9, 1810; m Rufus Jackson; lived in Wallingford, Vt.
40   Isaac[6], b Aug 1, 1812, d July 3, 1814
41   Harriet[6], b Feb 28, 1815, d Sept 14, 1818.
42   Eliza[6], b June 28, 1817, m Loring G Sherman, and lived in
      Brookfield Children Maria L[7], b Nov 4, 1838, d young;
      Helen M[7], May 16, 1840, George L[7], Oct 10, 1842, killed at
      Spottsylvania, Va, May 13, 1864, John F[7], Jan 26, 1846; Emma
      E[7], Dec 1, 1848, and Maria L[7], Nov 17, 1851

SIXTH GENERATION.

23. Isaac[6] Fuller, (*Elijah*[5], *Abijah*[4], *Isaac*[3], *John*[2], *John*[1]), b. Nov.
14, 1794, in Hubbardston, d Dec 14, 1833, in Troy, N H, m Feb 7,
1818, Temperance Hinckley, of Barnstable; b Nov. 11, 1792
   Children
43   Martha H[7], b Mar 15, 1819, m Peleg S Sherman, of Mt
      Holly, Vt.
44   **Isaac Richardson**[7], b Aug 13, 1820, m Laura Jackson, of Mt
      Holly, Vt
45   Lydia[7], b June 12, 1822, m Apr 6, 1843, Winthrop Knights
46   William[7], b Mar 15, 1824; d Apr 12, 1825
47   Charles[7], b Apr 13, 1827, d Feb. 1, 1832
48   Harriet E[7] b Nov 1, 1829, m Nov 12, 1851, Joseph E Lawrence

33. Amasa[6] Fuller, (*Isaac*[5], *Abijah*[4], *Isaac*[3] *John*[2], *John*[1]), b Dec 7,
1797, in Holden, d July 18, 1879, in Swanzey, N H, m 1, Anna Bemis,
who d June 19, 1826, m 2, Jan. 11, 1827, Hannah Jackson, of Wallingford, Vt, b Nov 5. 1803, m 3, Oct 2, 1845, Mrs Mary (Knight)
Hagar. of Troy, N H, b Feb 14, 1802, m 4, Mrs Lovey P Kidder, b
Oct 6, 1813, d Sept 30, 1900, in Swanzey
   Children
49   **Isaac**[7], b Aug 10, 1819, in Troy, N H, m Hepzibah Garfield
50   Elmira[7], b Apr 9, 1822, d May 4, 1847, in Swanzey, N H, m
      July 16, 1846, Stephen Harris, of Troy, N H
51   Anna[7], b Feb 14, 1826, d Nov 23, 1826
52   A dau, b June 11, 1828, d July 18, 1828
53   A son, b Apr 27, 1829, d Apr 30, 1829
54   Flvira[7], b Sept 21, 1830, d Mar 14, 1832
55   A dau, b Mar 1, 1832, d Mar 6, 1833
56   Amasa[7], b Sept 28, 1833; m Georgiana D Taylor
57   **Levi A.**[7], b May 4, 1836, m 1, Elvira L Bemis, m 2, Emily L
      Adams
58   A son, b July 1, 1838, d young
59   **Erwin J.**[7], b Sept 19, 1839, m Czarina W Jacobs

SEVENTH GENERATION.

44. Isaac Richardson[7] Fuller, (*Isaac[6], Elijah[5], Abijah[4], Isaac[3], John[2], John[1]*), b Aug 13, 1820, in Troy, N H , d ——, m ——, Laura Jackson, who d Apr 16, 1913, aged 92 y 3 m , at East Wallingford, Vt , "widow of Richardson Fuller"
Children

60   Elwin[8], b ——, d before his mother   Probably other children. since the obituary notice of Mrs Fuller's death mentions grandchildren, George H Fuller of Winchendon and F R Fuller of Rensselaer, N Y , and also 3 great grandchildren   No reply received to requests for further information

49. Isaac[7] Fuller, (*Amasa[6], Isaac[5], Abijah[4], Isaac[3], John[2], John[1]*) b Aug 10, 1819, in Troy, N H , d Nov 7, 1866, m Dec 12, 1843, Hepzibah Garfield, b Mar 2, 1825, in Troy, N H
Children .

61.   Julia M[8], b Feb 4, 1847, d July 28, 1868 , m July 16, 1868, Edwin F. Stockwell, of Keene, N H , who d Apr 26, 1871

62   George E[8], b Dec 13, 1850; m Jan 24, 1872, Mattie A Alexander, b Swanzey, N H , Dec 24, 1853

63   **Frederic A.[8]**, b Sept 2, 1853; m Fanny M Blanding

64   **Andrew I.[8]**, b Sept 22, 1858, m Bessie A Gates

56   Amasa[7] Fuller, (*Amasa[6], Isaac[5], Abijah[4], Isaac[3], John[2], John[1]*), b Sept 28, 1833, probably in Troy, N H ; d June 21, 1911, in Concord N. H , m 1, Sept 13, 1855, Georgiana D Taylor, of Winchendon, b Sept 13, 1834, d July 4, 1896; m 2, Lizzie McCarley, of Troy, N H
Children

65   Edward S[8], b June 25, 1866—an adopted son

66   Ernest Jackson[8], b June 9, 1904 , d Aug 26, 1910

57. Levi A[7] Fuller, (*Amasa[6], Isaac[5], Abijah[4], Isaac[3], John[2] John[1]*), b May 4, 1836, probably in Troy, N H , m 1, Feb 22, 1860, Elvira L Bemis, b June 4, 1839; d Nov 15, 1865, m 2, Oct 30, 1866, Emily L Adams, of Swanzey, N H., b July 28, 1848

Resides at Marlboro Depot, N H , manufacturer chair stock, shingles and lumber (1914)

67   Cora A.[8], b June 24, 1862 , d July 27, 1862.

68   **Elmer A.[8]**, b Dec 27, 1863 , m Hattie C L Wilson

69   Ida Emily[8], b Nov. 16, 1871; m Nov 12, 1896, Frederick J Farrar, of Troy, N H , b July 28, 1871, and had Dorothy Emeline[9], b June 15, 1898, Charlotte Emily[9], Aug 6, 1902; d Sept 14, 1907 , Wilhelmina Fuller[9], Aug. 24, 1905, and Frederick Adams[9], July 24, 1907.   They reside in Troy

70   **Walter Thomas[8]**, b July 6, 1876; m Charlotte B Farrar

71   **Arthur Levi[8]**, b July 2, 1882; m Laura Sophia Holden. Dec 17, 1910   They reside in Ellwood City, Pa

72   Cora Anstris[8], b July 2, 1887, m Dec. 5, 1909, Franklin Ripley, Jr ,
      of Troy, N H. Their son, Franklin Fuller[9], was b Jan 26,
      1911   They reside in Troy

59.   ERWIN J [7] FULLER, (*Amasa*[6], *Isaac*[5], *Abijah*[4], *Isaac*[3], *John*[2], *John*[1]),
b Sept 19, 1839, in Troy, N H ; m 1, Sept 16, 1865, Czarina W.
Jacobs, b June 8, 1841, in Royalston, Mass , d May 8, 1890, m 2.
June 14, 1894, Georgia A Cook, of Perry, Ga , b Feb 5, 1861.   ³
   Resides in Dublin, Ga
   Children
73   Nettie C [8], b June 16, 1866, in Royalston, Mass , m. in Perry, Ga ,
      Mar 16, 1892, W H Vallette, b June 14, 1861, in Conn , and had
      Carle James[9], b Mar 14, 1893, d Mar 16, 1893, and Czarina
      Mary[9], b Dec 17, 1895
74   Winfied E [8], b. Aug 5, 1868, in Leominster, Mass
75   **Herbert W.**[8], b Dec 22, 1870, in Leominster , m. Sally Pierce
      Wright

EIGHTH GENERATION.

63.   FREDERICK A [8] FULLER, (*Isaac*[7], *Amasa*[6], *Isaac*[5], *Abijah*[4], *Isaac*[3]
John[2], *John*[1]), b Sept 2, 1853, m Apr 8, 1874, Fanny M Blanding, b
Apr 24, 1853
   Children
76   Winfred I [9], b Oct 29, 1875.

64.   ANDREW J [8] FULLER, (*Isaac*[7], *Amasa*[6], *Isaac*[5], *Abijah*[4], *Isaac*[3],
John[2], *John*[1]), b Sept 22, 1858; m Oct 18, 1876, Bessie A Gates
   He resides in Keene, N. H
   Children
77   Julia M [9], b Mar 14, 1879

68.   ELMER AMASA[8] FULLER, (*Levi A* [7], *Amasa*[6], *Isaac*[5], *Abijah*[4], *Isaac*[3],
John[2], *John*[1]), b Dec 27, 1863, m Oct 28, 1885. Hattie C L Wilson,
of Sullivan, N H
   Resides in Danvers
   Children
78   Julian Elmer[9], b Oct 24, 1886; d June 26, 1910

70.   WALTER THOMAS[8] FULLER, (*Levi A* [7], *Amasa*[6], *Isaac*[5], *Abijah*[4],
Isaac[3], *John*[2], *John*[1]) b July 6, 1876, d July 13, 1911. in Woodville,
N H ; m Dec 2, 1901, Charlotte B Farrar, of Troy, N H , b June
10, 1877   They resided in Woodville
   Children
79   Emily Farrar[9], b Sept 20, 1902
80   Elizabeth Charlotte[9], b Sept 10, 1903

81   Sumner Levi[9], b July 23, 1908
82   Anstris[9], b Dec 12, 1910, d Dec 13, 1910

71. ARTHUR LEVI[8] FULLER (*Levi A[7]. Amasa[6], Isaac[5] Abijah[4], Isaac[3], John[2], John[1]*), b July 2, 1882, m Dec 17, 1910, Laura Sophia Holden, of Proctor, Vt , b July 6, 1886
  They reside in Ellwood City, Pa
  Children
82a Roger Holden[9], b Nov 11, 1913

75. HERBERT W[8] FULLER, (*Erwin J[7], Amasa[6], Isaac[5], Abijah[4], Isaac[3], John[2], John[1]*), b. Dec 22, 1870, in Leominster, m in Dublin, Ga, Feb 17 1904, Sally Pierce Wright, b July 29, 1877, in Milledgeville, Ga
  Children
83   Erwin Pierce[9], b May 30, 1905
84   Herbert Stanley[9], b Oct 1, 1906, d July 24, 1908

FOURTH GROUP

THIRD GENERATION.

JONATHAN³ FULLER, AND SOME OF HIS DESCENDANTS.

17. JONATHAN³ FULLER, (*John²*, *John¹*), b Mar. 28, 1700, in Newton, d there Mar 31, 1783; m Jan 2, 1725, Elizabeth Woodward, b.
Nov 1, 1706, dau of Daniel Woodward

Children recorded in Newton

1   Keziah⁴, b Oct 7, 1725, d. Feb. 4, 1741
2   **Jonas⁴**, b Apr 23, 1727, m Jerusha Coller.
3   Huldah⁴, b Feb 10, 1729, m Mar, 1749, Joshua Jackson, and had
        Joshua⁵, b Oct 8, 1751; Daniel⁵, July 23, 1753, Nathaniel⁵, July
        8, 1755, Josiah⁵, Mar 3, 1757, Keziah⁵, Nov 22, 1758, Jona-
        than⁵, Nov 8, 1760, Moses⁵, Aug 23, 1763; Keziah⁵ 2d, Grace⁵,
        Hezekiah⁵, Lucretia⁵, Ruth⁵ and Elizabeth⁵
4.   Elizabeth⁴, b Nov 10, 1730, m Sept 14, 1756, Samuel Gooding, of
        Watertown, Mass.
5.   **Daniel⁴**, b Aug 13, 1732, m Lydia Fuller
6   Grace⁴, b June 14, 1734
7   Eleanor⁴, b Mar 14, 1736
8   **Amos⁴**, b Feb 7, 1738
9   Thaddeus⁴, b Feb 17, 1740
10   Mary⁴, b Sept 18, 1744

FOURTH GENERATION.

2. JONAS⁴ FULLER, (*Jonathan³*, *John²*, *John¹*), b. Apr 23, 1727, in
Newton, d June 20, 1799, in Needham, m Sept 6, 1753, Jerusha Coller,
b Nov 19, 1735, dau of Uriah and Abigail (Ockelton) Coller

Children, all born in Needham

11   Elijah⁵, b June 2, 1754, d 'in the army" Sept 20, 1776
12   Keziah⁵, b Oct 14, 1756
13   Elisha⁵, b Aug 24, 1759
14   Levi⁵, b Nov 12, 1761
15   Dorcas⁵, b Feb 12, 1765
16   Eleanor⁵, b May 27, 1767

17 Hepzibah[6], b July 5, 1773
18. **Ezra**[6], b Apr 17, 1776; m Mary Woodcock
19 Achsah[5], b. Mar. 23, 1779

5. DANIEL[4] FULLER, (*Jonathan*[8], *John*[2], *John*[1]), b Aug 13, 1732, in Newton, d there Sept 26, 1786, aged 54, m. June 30, 1756, Lydia[4] Fuller, (No 7 10th Group), b Oct 23, 1737; d. Oct 4, 1806
   Children recorded in Newton.
20 Isaac[5], b Nov 4, 1756, d Apr 30, 1771
21 Miriam[5], b Mar 6, 1759
22 Lydia[5], b ——, d Oct 23, 1802, aged 42
23 Jemima[5], b ——
24 Grace[5], b ——
25 Nancy[5], b ——
26. Lucy[5], b ——
27 Hannah[5], b ——
28 Daniel[5], bapt Jan 18, 1784

8. AMOS[4] FULLER, (*Jonathan*[8], *John*[2], *John*[1]), b Feb 7, 1738, in Newton, d. ——
   He is probably the Amos Fuller of Marlboro, Mass who m Mar. 25, 1762, Mary Cooledge, as given in Bailey's "Early Mass Marriages" and also in the Bolton vital records, which last gives also the dates of birth of the 5 children of Amos and Mary mentioned below.
   Mass "Soldiers and Sailors of the Revolution," mentions Amos of Bolton in the service
   The U. S Census, 1790, mentions Amos Fuller family of 7 with a son over 16 years of age, and 4 daughters, in Boylston, Mass
   The Boylston vital records, by Rice, gives date of death of Rachel, dau of Amos and Mary Fuller—the date of death of a Mrs ? Hannah Fuller, and the date of marriage of a Molly Fuller Hence it is probable that Amos removed after 1774 to Boylston, with all of his family.
   Children, all born in Bolton, Mass
29. Hannah[5], b Oct 7, 1762, d in Boylston, Aug 27, 1839, aged 77
30 Lucy[5], b Nov 9, 1766
31 Molly[5], b. Sept. 30, 1764, m at Boylston, Jan 18, 1791, Henry Smith
32 Rachel[5], b Sept 9, 1769; d Sept. 14, 1850, aged 82, at Boylston
33 Silas[5], b Sept 5, 1774 No further record of Silas found

FIFTH GENERATION.

18. EZRA[5] FULLER, (*Jonas*[4], *Jonathan*[8], *John*[2], *John*[1]), b Apr 17, 1776, in Needham; d there Feb 17, 1879; m. Nov 27, 1803, Mary Woodcock, b Dec 28, 1777, d. June 23, 1846, in Needham.

Children, born in Needham

34   Mary⁶, b Nov 8, 1804, d Feb 12, 1861, m Ben Richardson   No children

35   Otis⁶, b Dec 29, 1806, left home before he was 20, and never heard from

36   Hannah Washburn⁶, b Mar 1, 1808, d Dec, 1908, m Int Pub Oct 20, 1833, with Oliver Felch, of Natick   Children Lucy Ann⁷, b June 13, 1835, Oliver Amandus⁷, Nov 17, 1836, John Francis⁷, Oct 7, 1839, Hannah Maria⁷, Oct 15, 1843, Charles Benjamin⁷, May 1, 1845, Mary⁷. Sept 17, 1847, George⁷, Feb 16, 1850, and Harrington⁷, b Sept 17, 1851

37   Ezra⁶, b Mar 27, 1810, d in childhood

38   Sarah Ann⁶, b Aug 8, 1812, m Feb 18 1838, Charles Winslow, of Worcester, and had Belle, who m ——Disney

39   **Ezra⁵**, b Apr 9, 1815, m Catherine Elizabeth Smith

40   Lucy Mills⁶, b Mar 25, 1818, d. May 22, 1820

41   **Samuel Francis⁶**, b May 8, 1821, m Helen Maria Rittenhouse

SIXTH GENERATION.

39. Ezra⁶ Fuller, (*Ezra⁵, Jonas⁴, Jonathan³, John², John¹*), b Apr 9, 1815, in Needham, m Feb 3, 1842 Catherine Elizabeth Smith, of Needham, b Sept 30, 1820; d Mar 19, 1907

Children, all born in Needham

42   Ezra Newell⁷, b May 18, 1843, d in the Union Army at Newbern, N C, Feb 21, 1863—unmarried

43   Timothy Otis⁷, b Feb 2, 1845, m Abby Ella Mills, resides at Needham

44   Catherine Rosine⁷, b Oct 21, 1847, resides at Needham

45   Smith Eugene⁷ b Nov 15, 1849, went west about 1880 and nothing has been heard of him for many years (1908).

46   Frank Henry⁷, b Nov 4, 1852, resides in Needham

41. Samuel Francis⁶ Fuller (*Ezra⁵, Jonas⁴, Jonathan³, John², John¹*), b May 8, 1821, in Needham, d there Aug 14, 1895; m July 3, 1843, Helen Maria Rittenhouse, b at Newton Lower Falls, living (1911) in Chelsea, aged 85

Children—Owing to lack of replies to requests for information these may not be listed in order of birth

47   **Francis Llewellyn⁷**, b ——; m ——.

48   George Albion⁷, b Aug 5, 1851, in Natick, m 1, Jan 1, 1889, Georgia Davenport-Boynton, who d Jan 13, 1908, m 2, Nov 26, 1908, Lottie Jane Draper, of Onset (Wareham), resides (1911) Greenwich

49   **Frederick Winslow⁷**, b ——, m ——

50   **Herbert LeRoy⁷**, b ——, m Margaret E Bartlett

51   Wallace Clifton⁷, b ——, m ——, resides in Chelsea

52   Clarence Eugene⁷, b ——, m Alice Sumner, resides in Brookline

SEVENTH GENERATION.

47. FRANCIS LLEWELLYN[7] FULLER, (*Samuel F*[6], *Ezra*[5], *Jonas*[4], *Jonathan*[3], *John*[2], *John*[1]), b ——, m 1, Sarah Louise ——, m 2, ——
Resides in Needham (1911)
Children:
53   A son, b ——, d ——
54   Irving[8], b ——, resides at Waverly

49. FREDERICK WINSLOW[7] FULLER, (*Samuel F*[6], *Ezra*[5], *Jonas*[4], *Jonathan*[3], *John*[2], *John*[1]), b ——, m Natick, d Mar 9, 1910, in Sherborn; m Carrie E Clement, who d Mar 27, 1910
Children:
55   Ethel[8], b ——
56   Edward[8] b ——
57   Walter Frederick[8], b Feb 6, 1882, in Sherborn

50. HERBERT LeROY[7] FULLER, (*Samuel F.*[6], *Ezra*[5], *Jonas*[4], *Jonathan*[3], *John*[2], *John*[1]), b ——, probably in Needham, m Apr 30, 1882, Margaret E Bartlett
Resides in Walpole
Children
58   LeRoy Otis[8], b June 23, 1883, m July 2, 1904, Elizabeth V. McAdams
59   Chester Andrew[8], b Jan 23, 1884
60   Violet Miriam[8], b June 14, 1885, m Feb 4, 1905, Oscar Springfield Reed, and has Wendell Jewell[9], b Aug 29, 1906, and Lester Fuller[9], b Feb 28, 1908
61   Waldo Oscar[8], b Nov 25, 1886
62   Ethel Margaret[8], b Sept 28, 1888, m Feb 5, 1907, Charles Alfred Cook, and has Mildred Ethel[9], b Oct 4, 1908
63   Gladys Warren[8], b Dec 19, 1896

FIFTH GROUP

THIRD GENERATION.

CALEB² FULLER, AND SOME OF HIS DESCENDANTS

18. CALEB³ FULLER, (*John²*, *John¹*), b Feb 24, 1702, in Newton, d there Feb. 21, 1770, m 1, Jan 20, 1724-5, Temperance Hyde, who d Aug 25, 1749, m 2, Dec 27, 1750, Mary Hovey

Children, recorded in Newton.
1   **Ephraim⁴**, b Dec 31, 1725. m Esther Warren
2   Nehemiah⁴, b Sept 16, 1727, d Aug 6, 1735
3.   **William⁴**, b. June 2, 1732, m. Elizabeth——
4   Bethia⁴, b Nov 13, 1734; d before 1788; m Jan 24, 1750, John Murdock of Uxbridge
5   Ann⁴, b Mar 27, 1739, d Feb. 12, 1745

FOURTH GENERATION.

1. EPHRAIM⁴ FULLER, (*Caleb³*, *John²*, *John¹*), b Dec. 31, 1725, in Newton; d there Nov 19, 1772, m Nov 6, 1746, Esther Warren, who d 1784

Children recorded in Newton Vital Records
6   Lucy⁵, b Mar 30, 1747
7   Esther⁵, b Sept 24, 1749
8   Anna⁵, b —— 1751; d Mar 2, 1813
9   Elizabeth⁵, b ——, m Sept 15, 1778, Thomas Bogle
10   **Ebenezer Warren⁵**, b Feb 11, 1769, m Betsey Wheeler.

3. WILLIAM⁴ FULLER, (*Caleb³*, *John²*, *John¹*), b June 2, 1732, in Newton, d. there Dec 12, 1802, m ——, Elizabeth ——

Children
11   **Nathaniel⁵**, b Dec 25, 1760
12   Caty⁵, b. Feb 23, 1763, in Cambridge, m Nov 20, 1794, Nahum Smith, of Needham

FIFTH GENERATION.

10. Ebenezer Warren[6] Fuller, (*Ephraim[4], Caleb[3], John[2], John[1]*), b Feb. 11, 1769, in Newton, d Oct 11, 1841, in Lancaster, m Sept 6, 1791, Betsey Wheeler (The late Newton Fuller, genealogist, gave this date for this marriage in a letter of Dec 2, 1902)

    Children

13   **Ephraim[6]**, b Jan 9, 1793, m 1, Susan Hayward; m 2, Judith Goss
14   Alden[6], b Sept 26, 1796
15   Ebenezer[6], b March 10, 1803
16.   William[6], b July 29, 1808, in Concord; d June 3, 1900, aged
        91 y, 10 m, 4 d, buried in Nashua, N H ; son of Ebenezer and
        Betsey (Wheeler) Fuller, she b in Halifax
17   Jeremiah[6], b July 16, 1810.

Note—The Littleton, Mass, V. R give the marriage of an Ebenezer Fuller of Acton, to Miss Betsey Wheeler, of Littleton, Aug 11, 1792

The Lancaster records give Ephraim as son of Ebenezer, b in Boxboro and Betsey, b in Halifax, N. S.

11. Nathaniel[5] Fuller, (*William[4], Caleb[3], John[2], John[1]*), b Dec 25, 1760, in Newton, d Dec 22, 1817, m June 21, 1786, Elizabeth Jackson

    Children:

18   **Nathaniel[6]**, b Aug 1, 1788; m Sarah Pool
19   Anna[6], bapt July 6, 1800, aged 10 years
20   Josiah[6], bapt July 6, 1800, aged 8
21.   **Abijah Jackson[6]**, bapt July 6, 1800 aged 6; m Eunice Morse (?)
22   Eliza[6], bapt July 6, 1800, aged 3, d Sept 27, 1865, unmarried
23   Eunice[6], bapt July 6, 1800 aged 8 months.
24   **Joseph[6]**, bapt Aug 15, 1802, m Mary Snell
25   William[6], bapt Feb 3, 1805, d April 13, 1863, at Framingham; m
        Sarah A Cutter, who d. March 6, 1881

SIXTH GENERATION.

13. Ephraim[6] Fuller, (*Ebenezer W[5], Ephraim[4], Caleb[3], John[2], John[1]*), b Jan 9, 1793, d Jan 5, 1876, in Lancaster; m 1, March 7, 1818, Susan Hayward, who d May 1, 1833; m 2, Dec 31, 1833, Judith Goss

    Children, born in Lancaster

26   Susan Hayward[7], b Sept 7, 1819
27   Francis Faulkner[7] b Jan 8, 1822, d July 20, 1829
28   **Andrew Lovell[7]**, b June 6, 1824; m Olive Howard
29   Abigail L[7], b 1829, d Feb 5, 1829
30   Francis Faulkner[7], b Feb 5, 1830, d May 24, 1832.
31   Ephraim Hayward[7], b April 25, 1833, d Sept 16, 1833
32   George Walton[7], b Dec 4, 1834, d March 21, 1836
33   William Alden[7], bapt July 2, 1837.

34   Infant, b ——— 1837, d Dec 22, 1837, aged 6 hours
35   Nancy Goss[7], bapt June 7, 1840
36   Franklin Warren[7], b ———, 1842, d Feb 4, 1845

16. WILLIAM[6] FULLER, (*Ebenezer W[6]*, *Ephraim[4]*, *Caleb[8]*, *John[2]*, *John[1]*), b July 29, 1808, in Concord, d June 3, 1900, in Easton, buried in Nashua, N H , m 1 Sept 27, 1832, Lydia Wyman, "both of Concord" She d Oct , 1834 aged 19, m 2, Sarah ——— *

Children
37   Lydia Ann[7], b Sept 23, 1834, (Concord Records), d Jan 3, 1843, aged 8 years, daughter of William and Lydia Fuller Gravestone Record, Woodlawn Cemetery, Nashua, N H
38   A child that d Feb 7, 1858, aged 4 months, born to William and Sarah Fuller, in Hancock, N H , buried in same lot with Lydia Ann, according to the undertaker's record No other stone in the lot April, 1914, but that for Lydia Ann

Perhaps there were other children Lydia Ann's remains had been removed from the old Spring St Cemetery to Woodlawn.

* A William Fuller, m Dec 27, 1835, Sarah Ann Connor of Hopkinton, according to Dunstable Vital Records

18 NATHANIEL[6] FULLER, (*Nathaniel[5]*, *William[4]*, *Caleb[3]*, *John[2]*, *John[1]*), b Aug 1, 1788, in Newton d ———, m Oct 14, 1810 Sarah Pool
Children, all recorded in Newton
39   **George[7]**, b Oct 22, 1812, m Mary Jackson Call
40   Mary Ann[7], b Jan 10, 1815, m Sept 5, 1842, George Trowbridge, and had Harriet L[8], b June 5 1843, and George[8], Nov. 24, 1846
41   **Gilman[7]**, b Oct 7, 1818, m 1, Mary E Bowers, m 2, Susan A Bowers, m 3, Harriet M Harriman
42   Gustavus[7], b Dec 2, 1821, d April 7, 1856, in Newton, unmarried
43   Harriet Newell[7], b Sept 25, 1825; d Oct 19, 1829
44   Joseph Jackson[7], bapt Oct 12, 1828
45   Abigail Jackson[7], bapt May 6, 1832
46   Caroline Elizabeth[7], bapt May 6, 1832; m May 1, 1854, Wm R Small

21. ABIJAH JACKSON[6] FULLER, (*Nathaniel[5]*, *William[4]*, *Caleb[3]*, *John[2]*, *John[1]*), bapt July 6, 1800, aged 6 years; d ———; m May 3, 1820, Eunice Morse (?) who d June 5, 1821.
Children
47   Eunice[7], b May 29, 1821; d March 11, 1846, at Waltham; m Dec 14, 1840, William P. Child, and had 3 children

24. JOSEPH[6] FULLER, (*Nathaniel[5]*, *William[4]*, *Caleb[3]*, *John[2]*, *John[1]*), b Aug 5, 1802, in Newton; d ———; m May 17, 1836, Mary Snell, who d Oct , 1809

He came to Framingham in 1836, removed to Holland, and later returned to Framingham.

Children

48   Edward Porter[7], b Aug 28 1837, d July 7, 1855
49   Harriet Eliza[7], b Apr 9, 1839, d Aug 26, 1839
50   Joseph Clarendon[7], b Sept 3, 1840, d May 1, 1858
51. Charles Henry[7], b Oct 8, 1841, m. Helen P Kinnedy
52   Ann Eliza[7], b July 19, 1845, d Sept 21, 1845

SEVENTH GENERATION.

28. ANDREW LOVELL[7] FULLER, (*Ephraim*[6], *Ebenezer W*[5], *Ephraim*[4], *Caleb*[3], *John*[2], *John*[1]), b June 6, 1824, in Lancaster, d Sept 10, 1867, at Clinton, m May 19, 1845, Olive Howard

He resided in Clinton

Children

53   Emma Susan[8], b Apr 25, 1848
54   Francis H[8], b Apr 8, 1850
55   **Albert S.**[8], b Feb 25, 1852, m Ella Elizabeth Burritt
56   Andrew Clifford[8], b Aug 25, 1853; m Nov 10, 1882, Katherine Seger

39. GEORGE[7] FULLER, (*Nathaniel*[6], *Nathaniel*[5], *William*[4], *Caleb*[3], *John*[2], *John*[1]), b Oct 22, 1812 in Newton, d there June 14, 1887, aged 77 y, 7 m, 23 d, m Mary Jackson Call, b in Charlestown, d June 2, 1888, in Newton, aged 75 y, 0 m, 23 d, widow of George Fuller and dau of John Call, who was b in Boston

Children

57   George Edwin[8], b ——, in Charlestown, d Aug 23, 1861, in Newton, aged 16 y, 1 m, 14 d

41. GILMAN[7] FULLER, (*Nathaniel*[6], *Nathaniel*[5], *William*[4], *Caleb*[3], *John*[2], *John*[1]), b Oct 7, 1818, in South Framingham; d ——, m 1, Jan 23, 1850, Mary E Bowers, who d May 25, 1854, m 2, May 15, 1856, Susan A Bowers, who d Apr 3, 1859; m 3, ——, Harriet M Harriman, of Waldoboro, Me

Children

58. George T[8], b Feb 3, 1864

EIGHTH GENERATION.

55. ALBERT S[8] FULLER, (*Andrew L.*[7], *Ephraim*[6] *Ebenezer W*[5], *Ephraim*[4], *Caleb*[3], *John*[2], *John*[1]), b Feb 25, 1852, m Jan 16, 1877, Ella Elizabeth Burritt

Children

59   May Olive[9], b May 27, 1879
60   Burns Burritt[9] b Oct. 9, 1882
61   Howard A[9], b Mar 18, 1889

SIXTH GROUP

THIRD GENERATION.

JOHN³ FULLER, AND SOME OF HIS DESCENDANTS

19 John³ Fuller, (*Joseph , John¹*), b. Dec 15, 1680, in Newton; d 1718, aged 38 y 10 m ; m Feb. 25, 1816, Hannah (Jackson) Trowbridge, who d before 1740. She was the widow of James Trowbridge. Children ·

1 Joseph⁴, } twins, b Sept 21, 1716 { d Oct 6, 1716
2 Lydia⁴, } { d. Oct 5, 1716
3 Lydia⁴, b Dec 8, 1717; m. Jan 31, 1750, Nathaniel Felch of Watertown

SEVENTH GROUP

THIRD GENERATION.

JOSEPH[3] FULLER, AND SOME OF HIS DESCENDANTS

20. JOSEPH[3] FULLER, (*Joseph[2], John[1]*), b July 4, 1685, in Newton, d Apr 23, 1766, m May 11, 1719, Sarah Jackson, who d Nov 21, 1764, dau of Abraham Jackson

Children

1   **Abraham[4]**, b Mar 23, 1720, m Sarah Dyer
2   Elizabeth[4], b Oct 28, 1722, m May 11, 1749, Rev Isaac Jones of Weston

FOURTH GENERATION

1 ABRAHAM[4] FULLER, (*Joseph[3], Joseph[2], John[1]*), b Mar 23, 1720, in Newton, d there Apr 20, 1794; m Apr 13, 1758, Sarah Dyer, of Weymouth, who d Apr 7, 1803

He was Selectman 4 years, Town Clerk and Treasurer 27 years, Representative 18 years, and Judge, Court Common Pleas

His children, born in Newton, were

1   Sarah[5], b Apr 27, 1759, m 1781, Gen William Hull, and had Sarah[6], b Jan 20, 1783, Elizabeth[6], June 22, 1784, Abraham[6], b Mar 8, 1786, Nancy Binney[6], b June 19, 1787, Maria[6], b June 7, 1788; Rebecca[6], Feb 7, 1790; Caroline[6], b Apr 30, 1793, and Julia Knox[6], bapt. Mar 17, 1799

EIGHTH GROUP

———

THIRD GENERATION.

JONATHAN[3] FULLER, AND SOME OF HIS DESCENDANTS

21. JONATHAN[3] FULLER, (*Joseph[2], John[1]*), b Jan. 7, 1686, in Newton; d there Dec 1, 1764, m Oct 3, 1717, Sarah Mirick, who d Sept 21, 1772, dau of John Mirick

Children:

1. Elisha[4], b Mar. 15, 1719, d. Mar. 24, 1723
2. Sarah[4], b Oct 20, 1720; m Abijah Larned
3. **Jonathan[4]**, b July 23, 1723; m Eleanor Hammond
4. **Elisha[4]**, b Oct 11, 1725; m Esther Richardson
5. Esther[4], b Sept 28, 1727; m. May 2, 1751, Elisha Parker, and had Ebenezer[5] b 1752, Betsey[5], Caleb[5], Elisha[5], Ephraim[5], Esther[5], Jonathan[5], Mindwell[5], Reuben[5], and Sarah[5]
6. **Amariah[4]**, b July 17, 1729, m. Anna Stone
7. **Edward[4]**, b Dec. 31, 1735; m. Ruth Jackson.

FOURTH GENERATION.

3. JONATHAN[4] FULLER, (*Jonathan[3], Joseph[2], John[1]*), b July 13, 1723, in Newton, d ——; m Jan 7, 1747-8, Eleanor Hammond

Children, recorded in Newton

8. Margaret[5], b Nov. 21, 1749.
9. Sarah[5], b Mar 26, 1752; d May 6, 1808; m Jan 23, 1777, Lieut Joseph Craft, and had Beulah[6], Margaret[6], Elias[6], Anna[6], Eleanor[6], Jonathan[6], Moses[6], Martha[6] and Mary[6], twins, and Nathan Fuller[5].
10. Beulah[5], b May 22, 1753; d Dec 9, 1804; m Int Pub Dec 24, 1780, with Samuel Murdock Their children were Margaret[6], Beulah[6], Anna[6], Esther[6], Beulah[6] 2d, Sophia[6], and Peggy[6]
11. **Enoch[5]**, b Oct 6, 1754; m. Lydia Webb.
12. Elias[5], b Oct 26, 1756, perhaps the Elias that d Mar 19, 1799.
13. Edmund[5], b Feb 3, 1758.
14. Olive[5], b Dec 1, 1759.
15. Eleanor[5], b Sept 12, 1761.
16. Lucy[5], b Mar. 5, 1763.

9

4. ELISHA[4] FULLER, (*Jonathan*[3], *Joseph*[2], *John*[1]), b Oct. 11, 1725, in Newton, d. 1794, m. Nov 15, 1750, Esther Richardson, b 1725 in Newton

Resided in Newton

Children

17   Esther[5], b Sept 2, 1751; m July 16, 1772, Edward Hall, Jr, and had Polly[6], Esther[6], Lucy[6], Jesse[6] George[6], Elisha[6], Catherine[6], and Caroline[6]

18   **Elisha**[5], b Aug 10, 1753, m Sarah Bartlett

19   **Aaron**[6], b Feb 26, 1756, m Hannah Pond

20   Hannah[5], b. Feb 28, 1759

21   Rhoda[5], b June 19, 1761; d Sept 3, 1778

22   Patty[5], b. Aug 12, 1763, m Jan 10, 1791, Sylvanus Lowell and had Katy[6]

23   **Silas**[5], b Dec 21, 1765, m Ruth Hooge

24   Caty[5], b. Sept 10, 1768, d Mar 23, 1769

25   Caty[5], b Nov 25, 1770

26   Nabby[5], b May 5, 1773

6. AMARIAH[4] FULLER, (*Jonathan*[3], *Joseph*[2], *John*[1]), b July 17, 1729, in Newton, d there Feb 2, 1802; m Jan 20, 1757, Anna Stone, who d Jan 18, 1813

He was Selectman 2 years, was Captain of Militia, and with his Company of 105 men was in the battles of Lexington, Concord, and Dorchester Heights

Children

27   Catherine[5], b Sept 14, 1759, d Dec 29, 1828, m May 24, 1781 in Weston, Dea Ebenezer Woodward, and had Anna[6], Hannah[6], and Elijah[6]

28   Elijah[5], b June 12, 1762, d Sept 10, 1775

29   Meriel[6], b Apr 17, 1764, m Dec 29, 1795, George Ellis, of Medfield

30.   Anna[5], b Jan 29, 1770, m Jan 19, 1797, Henry Craft, and had Meriel[6], Polly[6], Myra[6], Anna[6], Henry[6], Nathan[6], and Martha[6].

7. EDWARD[4] FULLER, (*Jonathan*[3] *Joseph*[2], *John*[1]), b Dec 31, 1735, in Newton, d there Dec 12, 1810, m 1, Aug 23, 1759, Ruth Jackson, who d Aug 7, 1784, m 2, June 11, 1789, Abigail (Hammond) Marean, who d May 9, 1826

He was Selectman seven years and Representative one year, was Lieutenant at battles of Lexington and Concord, and Captain at the capture of Burgoyne's army

Children, born in Newton

31   Ruth[5], b July 19, 1762, m Jan. 11, 1800, Capt Edmund Trowbridge, and had Ruth[6], Stephen W[6], and Elizabeth W[6]

32   **Oliver**[5], b Nov 12, 1764, m Polly Eustis

33   **Jonathan**[5], b Apr 23, 1767, m 1, Betsey Bisbee; m 2, Hannah Bradstreet, m 3, Jane Creighton

34 Ezra⁶, b Sept 10, 1769, d Apr 25, 1854; m Mary Emmons, Feb 16, 1797 (Boston Rec.), who d. Sept. 26, 1856, in Newton, aged 90

35 Dorcas⁵, b Oct 26. 1771; m Nov 29, 1792, Jackson Durant, and had Charles⁶, Dorcas⁶, Eliza⁶, Jackson⁶, Julia⁶, Maria⁶, Nancy⁶, Ruth⁶, and Wm A⁶.

36 Jerusha⁶, b Mar 9, 1774, d 1848, m Sept 29, 1799, Capt Daniel Cooledge, and had eleven children.

37 **Edward⁵**, b. Aug. 17, 1776, m. Patty Upham

38 **Simon⁵**, b Feb 9, 1779; m 1, Abigail Dunbar; m 2, Mary Davis

39 Charles⁵, b. Mar 5, 1781

FIFTH GENERATION

11. ENOCH⁵ FULLER, (*Jonathan⁴, Jonathan³, Joseph², John¹*), b Oct 6. 1754, in Newton; d Jan 29, 1842, in Winslow, Me , m Sept 18, 1792, Lydia Webb, b Jan 22, 1775

He enlisted in the Revolutionary Army in May, 1778, under Capt Whipple, in Col Rufus Putnam's Regt of the Mass line He became blind returning from the war, in traveling over snow for 4 days, and in 1818 had not fully recovered his eyesight.

He lived in Winslow, Me

Enoch and Lydia Fuller had 12 children, among whom were

40 Nancy⁶, b ——

41 **Enoch⁶**, b ——, 1803; m. Harriet Warren

42 Sophronia⁶, b ——; m George Haliburton

43 Tryphosia⁶, b Nov 28, 1806, m Samuel Sewell

44. Lucy⁶, b Apr 19, 1809, m. Rev William Stinson

45 Abner⁶, b. Dec 25, 1811

46. Olive⁶, b ——; d young

47 Lydia⁶, b ——; m John Weymouth

48 Robert Webb⁶, b Dec. 14, 1818, d aged 35—and others that d in infancy.

18. ELISHA⁵ FULLER, (*Elisha⁴, Jonathan³, Joseph², John¹*), b Aug 10. 1753, in Newton; d Dec. 17, 1833, aged 78 (?) in Phillipston; m June 14, 1795, Sarah Bartlett.

Children:

49. Sally⁶, b. Dec 8, 1796

50 Joseph⁶, b Feb 24, 1798; d Oct 19, 1803

51 Infant, b. ——; d. Mar. 31, 1800.

52. Druce⁶, b. ——, 1803; d. Oct. 23, 1803.

53 Joseph Druce⁶, b Dec 19, 1804

54 Elizabeth⁶, b Feb. 24, 1808

55 Anna Maria⁶, b. Feb. 21, 1811; m Sept 12, 1832, William Glover and had two children.

56 Laomi Baldwin⁶, b ——, 1814, d. Aug. 7, 1816

19. Aaron⁵ Fuller, (*Elisha⁴, Jonathan³, Joseph², John¹*), b Feb 26, 1756, in Newton; d Oct 18, 1841, at Otisfield, Me, m 1, Nov 20, 1783, Hannah Pond, b Sept 14, 1764, d Jan 7, 1836, at Paris, Me , m 2, Apr 17, 1838, Mary Virgin

He lived in Standish, Me , previous to settlement in Paris, Me , about 1788

Children, all but the first child born in Paris, Me

57. **Artemas⁶**, b Oct 16, 1784, m Urania Shaw
58   Polly⁶, b July 10, 1787, d Nov 1868, m Josiah Dudley
59. **Joel⁶**, b Feb 25, 1789, m. Hannah Perry
60   **Aaron⁶**, b Apr. 13, 1791, m Martha (Patty) Norton
61   **Freeman⁶**, b. Oct 21, 1794, in Hannah Wing
62. **Simeon⁶**, b Oct 3, 1799, m Mary Ann Rawson.
63   **Daniel⁶**, b Oct 4, 1804, m Olive Norton

23. Silas⁵ Fuller, (*Elisha⁴, Jonathan³, Joseph², John¹*), b Dec 21, 1765, in Newton, d Nov 3, 1843 (Town Rec), Nov 3, 1844 (G S Rec.) , m July 30, 1793, Ruth Hooge, who d Jan 20, 1837

He is called Capt Silas Fuller.

Children, recorded in Newton

64   Lucinda⁶, b Dec 22, 1793, d Sept 17, 1794
65. John Bently Hooge⁶, b Feb 2 1795; m Mary Murdock, who d Mar 7, 1867, aged 63 y 10 m 10 d
66   Henry⁶, b. Aug 16, 1796, d Oct 18. 1802
67   Lucinda Otis⁶, b Feb. 15, 1799, m Oct. 26, 1823, Joel C Adams, and had Helen Lucretia⁷, Joel William⁷, John Bently⁷, Lewis Henry⁷, Sarah Louisa⁷, Mary Lucretia⁷, Catherine R ⁷, and William⁷.
68   William⁶, b June 10, 1803; d May 5, 1822
69   Mary Wright⁶, b July 6, 1807, m Int Pub Sept 2, 1827, with William Smith, children (Smith) Francis Henry⁷ Eugene Gilbert⁷, George W ⁷, William F ⁷, Frederick⁷, and Harnden F ⁷.
70. **Henry⁶**, b Apr 11, 1812, m Int Pub with Hannah W Jackson
71   Sarah Wright⁶, b Sept 10, 1815; m Int Pub, Dec 13, 1835, with William F Harnden.

32. Oliver⁵ Fuller (*Edward⁴, Jonathan³, Joseph², John¹*), b Nov 12, 1764, in Newton, d June 3, 1848; m Oct 29, 1792, Polly Eustis, who d June 3, 1838

He resided in Jay, Me.

Children

72   **Oliver⁶**, b Dec 5, 1793, m Lyda Barton
73   **Jackson⁶** b ——; m Mary Phinney
74   Catherine⁶, b ——
75.   **Edward⁶**, b ——
76   Lucy⁶, b ——; m Elisha Keyes, of Jay, Me , and had eleven children, all dead

77. Hannah⁶, b ——, m. Winston Alden, had one son. both dead

33. JONATHAN⁵ FULLER. (*Edward⁴, Jonathan³, Joseph², John¹*), b
Apr 23 1767, in Newton, d Nov 2, 1841, in Warren, Me, m Int Pub,
Aug 10, 1792, with Betsey Bisbee, of Duxbury, m 2. Hannah Bradstreet, b at Rowley, Oct. 1, 1777 (?), m 3, Dec 9, 1813, Jane Creighton
  Children
78 Sarah⁶ (Sally), b. ——, in Boston, m Andrew Fitzgerald
79 **Edmund⁶**, b Oct 3, 1804, m Ann Sibley
80. Lucretia⁶, b ——, m Int Pub Dec. 2, 1843, with William Water-
      man

37. EDWARD⁵ FULLER, (*Edward⁴, Jonathan³, Joseph², John¹*), b Aug
17, 1776, in Newton, d ——; m. Int Pub Sept 22, 1892, with Patty
Upham, b Dec 9, 1780
  They removed to Pembroke, N H.
  Children
81. Thomas⁶, b ——
82   Ezra⁶, b ——
83   Martha⁶, b ——
  No Fuller living in Pembroke in 1910

38 SIMON⁵ FULLER, (*Edward⁴, Jonathan³, Joseph², John¹*), b Feb
9, 1779, in Newton, d Jan 22, 1844, in Union, Me, m. 1, Nov 25, 1802.
Abigail Dunbar, of Warren, Me, m 2, Feb 17, 1831, Mary Davis
  He was a Baptist minister
  Children, all born in Union, Me
84 **Daniel D.⁶**, b Dec 6, 1803, m 1, Mary Young; m 2, ——
85. Almira⁶, b May 4, 1805, m Mar 26, 1829, Church Fisk, and had
      John⁷, Margaret A⁷, Ellen S⁷, Mary A⁷, William J A⁷, Simon
      Abel⁷, Kingsbury P⁷, Laura E⁷. and Inez E⁷
86   Sophronia⁶, b Mar 25, 1807, m Feb 6, 1825, William Young
87   **Henry D.⁶**, b Apr 30, 1809; m Eliza Young.
88   Mary D⁶, b June 6, 1812; m. Nov 26, 1829, George Leach
89. Louisa⁶, b Nov 22, 1821, m 1, May 4, 1842, Calvin Hemingway;
      m 2, ——

SIXTH GENERATION.

41. ENOCH⁶ FULLER, (*Enoch⁵, Jonathan⁴, Jonathan³, Joseph², John¹*),
b ——, 1803, in Winslow, Me, d there(?) ——, 1862; m ——, Harriet
Warren
  Children
90 Emily⁷, b ——
91 **Albert⁷** b ——, 1839, m 1, Mary Wister; m 2, Mary Keith
92 Andrew W.⁷, b ——, d 1863, a soldier of the Civil war

93   Samuel W [7], b ——
94   **Sidney K.**[7], b ——, 1849, m 1 Carrie L Hatch; m 2, Amanda T
      B Warren, m 3, Susan Hodges
95   Melvin C [7], b ——

57. ARTEMAS[6] FULLER, (*Aaron*[5], *Elisha*[4], *Jonathan*[3], *Joseph*[2], *John*[1]),
b Oct 16, 1784 in Newton, d Apr 1, 1863, in Lowell, m 1, Dec 26
1810, at Paris, Me, Urania Shaw, b Oct 16, 1788, d Oct 29, 1848, at
Lowell, m 2, Apr 1851, Julia Chamberlain
      Children, all born in Sumner, Me
96   Elvira J [7], b Nov 21, 1811, d in Lynn; m Andrew Keene, of
      Sumner, and had a dau, Emma J [8] Keene
97   **Alonzo F.**[7], b June 14, 1814, m 1, Mary Lincoln, m 2 Ann Rol-
      lins
98   Olive F [7], b Nov 16, 1822, d Jan 26, 1844; m Feb 6, 1842, A B
      F. Hildreth, his second wife; removed to Vermont, no issue
99   **Samuel S.**[7], b Dec 17, 1824, m Elizabeth N Reed
100   Sabrina H [7] b June 25, 1826, d. May 18, 1899, at Lima, O , m
      Henry H Crocker, in Lowell, and removed to Lima
101   Malvina F [7], b Oct 4, 1829, d Mar 1876 at Lima, O , m Dec 31,
      1849, in Nashville, N H , Richard Chandler, and removed to
      Lima, O had a son Edward[8] who d young

59. JOEL[6] FULLER, (*Aaron*[5], *Elisha*[4], *Jonathan*[3], *Joseph*[2], *John*[1]), b
Feb 25, 1789, in Paris, Me , d Mar 24, 1876, at Livermore Falls, Me ;
m Mar 24, 1816, Hannah Perry, of Chesterville, Me , b Jan 4, 1791
      He was a Captain in the War of 1812, and a farmer by occupation
was for many years Selectman and for some 15 to 20 years Tax Collector
      Children
102   **Albion King Parris**[7], b Feb 12, 1817, m 1, Sarah Jane West, m
      2, Sarah Ann Palmer
103   John Wesley[7], b Nov 24, 1819; d Dec 24, 1839
104   Polly Dudley[7], b Sept 24 1822, at Paris Hill, Me , d Mar 4, 1885,
      m 1, Isaac Richardson, m 2, Frank Packard, of Stoughton, had
      two children
105   Mary Ann Rawson[7], b May 17, 1825, at Fayette, Me , d Mar 23,
      1890, in John Dunham, of Livermore Falls, Me, and had two
      children
106   Charles R [7], b Nov 30, 1828, at Livermore Falls, d Aug 9, 1833
107   Adelia Octavia[7], b Feb 15 1832, at L Falls, d in infancy
108   Adeline Ellen[7], b Dec 24, 1833, at L Falls, d Jan 11, 1911; m
      her cousin, Wilbur F [7] Fuller (Daniel[6]) No 125 this Group, re-
      sided at Stoughton
109. Edwin Vinton[7], b Oct 8, 1837, d May 11, 1905, m Jennie Bod-
      well Perry , no children

60. AARON[6] FULLER, (*Aaron*[5], *Elisha*[4] *Jonathan*[3], *Joseph*[2], *John*[1]), b
Apr. 13, 1791, in Paris, Me ; d Apr 25, 1859, at Nashua, N H , m Jan

1, 1818, Patty Norton, b Sept 22, 1793, at Livermore, Me , d Jan 5,
1873, at Mt Vernon, Me

He was a Methodist minister

Children, the first six born in Paris, Me

110   Emeline M [7], b Oct 14, 1818, d Apr 4, 1884, at Mt Vernon, Me
111. **Charles Wesley** [7], b Mar 7, 1821, m Emma Dunn
112   **James Norton** [7], b Jan 13, 1823, m Mary King Hathaway
113   Martha Jane [7], b Dec 11, 1824, d June 2, 1902, at Los Angeles,
      Cal , m May 12, 1853, James M Blunt, and had Clara Martha [8]
      and John Franklin [8]
114   Sophia Ann [7], b July 29, 1829; d Jan 8, 1907, at Turner, Me , m
      Daniel Kilbreth, and had Cleora Gertrude [8] and Percy Howard [8]
115   **John Nelson** [7], b Oct 22, 1831, m Elizabeth Vanarsdale
116   Olive Chase [7], b June 2, 1835, in Sharon, Me , m Oct 12, 1870,
      Rev Horace Miller, and had Frances Asbury [8], Edna Leonore [8],
      Julius Gilmore [8], and Howard Vinton [8]
117   Mary Ellen [7], b. Jan. 21, 1841, in Livermore, Me , d Apr 4, 1903,
      in Beatrice Neb , m July 9, 1867, John E Abell, and had Clif-
      ford R [8] and Walter B [8]

61. FREEMAN [6] FULLER, (*Aaron* [5], *Elisha* [4], *Jonathan* [3], *Joseph* [2], *John* [1]),
b Oct 21, 1794, in Paris, Me , d Ma. 17, 1875, m ——, Nancy Wing,
who d 1878, in Paris, Me , dau of Reuben Wing

He was a farmer in Harrison, Me

Children ·

118   Hannah [7], b June 1, 1822, d Apr 10, 1902, at Harrison, Me , m
      Morris Hicks, of Bolston Mills, Me , had a son Edwin [8].
119. George W [7], b May 23, 1824
120. Andrew J [7], b Aug 31, 1831, m May 9, 1855, Amanda Melvina
      Richardson—had a son—both removed to South America after
      the death of the mother.
121   Silas B [7], b May 2, 1834, m and had children Is living (1912)
      with his invalid wife in Auburn, Me

62. SIMEON [6] FULLER, (*Aaron* [5], *Elisha* [4], *Jonathan* [3], *Joseph* [2], *John* [1]),
Oct 3, 1799, in Paris, Me , d Nov 29, 1841, in Rumford, Me ; m
July 3, 1827, Mary Ann Rawson, who married again, in March, 1843, Dr.
James Bullock

Simeon Fuller was a physician

His children were

122   Samuel Rawson [7], b ——, m Frances Emma Bush
123   Mary Arabella [7], b. ——, m Jan 25, 1860, Charles S Walkins, a
      banker at Davenport, Ia , and had Mary Emma [8], Frances Raw-
      son [8], Frederick S [8], and Rawson S [8]

63. DANIEL [6] FULLER (*Aaron* [5], *Elisha* [4], *Jonathan* [3], *Joseph* [2], *John* [1]), b
Oct 4, 1804, in Paris, Me , d July 27, 1847, in Brunswick, Me , m Olive
Chase Norton.

He was a Methodist minister.
Children
124 John Summerfield[7], b ——1830; d ——1855, unmarried
125 Wilbur Fisk[7], b 1834, m 1, Anna M Wording, m 2, Adelia E.
      Fuller, No 107 this Group.
126 Roscoe Watson[7], b 1839, m 1, Melissa Hopkins, m 2, 1903,
      Charlotte B Foster   Resides in Melrose, Mass
127 **Daniel Edward[7]**, b 1846, m 1, 1877, Emma J Blaisdell, m 2, 1888,
      M Emma Crassmeer

70. HENRY[6] FULLER, (*Silas[5], Elisha[4], Jonathan[3], Joseph[2], John[1]*), b
Apr 11, 1812, in Newton, d July 4, 1898, in Int Pub Oct 4 1840, with
Hannah W Jackson
128 William Jackson[7], bapt Oct 9, 1842, d Feb 26, 1868, in New-
      ton; unmarried
129 Lucretia Jackson[7], bapt Dec 7, 1845
130 Ruth[7], b about 1850; m Oct 28, 1874, J Henry Bacon
131 Elijah Woodward[7], b Nov 26, 1848
132 Mary Wight[7], b Oct 6, 1856, m Nov 30, 1900, Francis Murdock

72. OLIVER[6] FULLER, (*Oliver[5], Edward[4], Jonathan[3], Joseph[2], John[1]*), b
Dec 5, 1793, in Jay, Me , d there Aug 27, 1849, m Lydia Barton
      Children—all born in Jay, Me
133 Albert[7] b Apr 3, 1830, d Dec 4, 1850
134 Marcia A[7], b Aug 12, 1831, d July 21, 1904, m 1, Dr C H Lake,
      of Wilton, Me , m 2, P F Pike, of Fayette, Me , and had
      Mary Leona[8].
135 Emerson[7] b Feb 18, 1833; d Nov 17, 1862
136 Caroline[7], b Mar 15, 1835, d June 13, 1893
137 **Rawson C.[7]**, b Dec 13, 1836, m 1, Emily J Green, m 2, Nancy
      H Frost
138 William F[7], b June 30, 1842, d July 21, 1884

73. JACKSON[6] FULLER, (*Oliver[5], Edward[4], Jonathan[3], Joseph[2], John[1]*),
b ——, d Sept 30, 1873, aged 78; m ——, Mary Phinney, of Jay, Me
      Children
139 Americus[7], b Nov 1, 1834, m Amelia D Gould, of Wilton, Me ,
      Aug 21, 1864   They have no children
            He was for many years a missionary to Turkey, and Presi-
      dent of Aintab College, but is living, retired, (in 1906) at
      Saratoga, Cal.
140 Fernando[7], b ——; d July 31, 1841
141 Augustus[7], b ——; d Oct 1, 1844, aged 3 y 8 m
142 Lois A[7], b ——; m F M Wright, of Wilton, Me and had
      Mary A[8], Callie[8], Helena[8], Howard[8] and Florence[8].

75. EDWARD[6] FULLER, (*Oliver*[5], *Edward*[4], *Jonathan*[3], *Joseph*[2], *John*[1]), b. ——, d Aug 10, 1848, aged 46 y 6 m , m ——
Children

143   Emeline[7], b Oct 10, 1839, at Jay, Me , d Sept 15, 1903, at Malden, Mass , m Feb 1, 1860, at Chesterville, Me , Noah Greeley Cofren, of North Vienna, Me , and had George Albert[8], Lizzie[8] Sarah Gertrude[8] and Mildred Florence[8], b at Livermore Falls, Me , and Frank Edward[8], b at Farmington, Me

144   Florilla[7], b ——, d Sept 7, 1897, m Nov 8, 1863, Howard Sewall and had one child, Willis Fuller[8] Sewall, now (1907) a librarian in Toledo, O

79. EDMUND[6] FULLER, (*Jonathan*[5], *Edward*[4], *Jonathan*[3], *Joseph*[2], *John*[1],) b Oct 3, 1804, m Albion, Me , d ——, m Jan 20, 1829, Ann Sibley, b Jan 20 1806

145   Christopher Columbus[7], b Nov 28, 1829
146   William Sibley[7], b Dec 17, 1832
147   Judith[7], b Apr 28, 1837
148   Edmund Allen[7] b Nov 21, 1839
149   Selden Kimball[7], b Jan 14, 1842

84. DANIEL D[6] FULLER, (*Simon*[5], *Edward*[4], *Jonathan*[3], *Joseph*[2], John[1]), b Dec 6, 1803, m Union Me , d July 22, 1882, in Auburn, Me ; m 1, Feb 3, 1829 Mary Young, m 2, ——
Children

150   Simon A[7], b Apr 29 1829, m Union d Jan 25, 1844
151   Samantha O[7], b Apr 20, 1831, m Union; m Mar 27, 1853, Gilbert Taintor, and had two sons
152   Alden M.[7] b Jan 26, 1833 m Ellen Coburn
153   Hosea Y.[7], b June 5, 1834, m Lucy J Holmes
154   Elisha D[7], b Sept 7, 1835, m Mary L Brock, no children
155   Virgil E.[7], b Apr 10, 1837, m Clara Adams
156   Mary A[7], b Sept 4, 1838, m Carthage Me , d Apr 16, 1879, m Mar 31, 1855, Otis Wyman one son living (1911)
157   Betsey S[7], b May 25, 1840, m Carthage, d Nov 5, 1899, m June 13, 1856, Melvin L Winter, and had two sons living (1911)
158   Elmira J[7], b Mar 20, 1842, m Carthage d July 16 1899, m Dec 30, 1856 Daniel E Holt, and had 4 sons and 6 daugnters
159   Fidelia A[7], b Aug 22, 1845, d Jan 16, 1864
160   Julia Etta M[7], b Jan 21, 1842, m Carthage, m Dec 24, 1874, James C Drew, has one son; resides in Auburn, Me
Children by second wife
161   Simon A[7] b ——
162   George[7], b ——.

87. HENRY D[6] FULLER, (*Simon*[5], *Edward*[4], *Jonathan*[3], *Joseph*[2], *John*[1]), b Apr 30, 1809, m Union, Me , d there June 13, 1863, m Sept

14, 1834, Eliza Young, b May 26 1815, in Warren, Me.; d Nov 2, 1881, in Union

He was a farmer

Children, all born in Union

163   **Charles Y.**[7], b Jan 17, 1835, m Susannah W Gilchrist

164   Oliver K[7] b July 13, 1837, d June 1, 1863, a soldier of the Civil war

165   Nelson C[7], b Aug 31, 1839, d 1871 unmarried

166   Henry E[7], b Feb 14, 1842, d June 8, 1863 at New Orleans, on Steamer Antonia

167   Antoinette[7], b Aug 25, 1845, d Nov 15, 1853

168   Edgar[7], b May 29, 1851, d Apr 14, 1854

169   Rosetta[7], b Dec 20, 1854, d Nov 7, 1856

170   Ida F[7], b Apr 28, 1859, m 1, Sept 14, 1878, Wilbert George Payson, of Union, who d Oct 22, 1883, in Union, m 2, Jan 1, 1900, Samuel Evander Wentworth, children (Payson), Clarence Merton[8], and Wilbert George[8]

SEVENTH GENERATION.

91. ALBERT[7] FULLER, (*Enoch*[6], *Enoch*[5], *Jonathan*[4], *Jonathan*[3], *Joseph*[2], *John*[1]), b 1839, in Winslow, Me , m 1, Mary Wister; m 2, Mary Keith

Children by first wife

171   Andrew L[8], b ——.

By second wife

172   Norman K[8], b ——

173   George R[8], b ——

94. SIDNEY K[7] FULLER, (*Enoch*[6], *Enoch*[5], *Jonathan*[4], *Jonathan*[3], *Joseph*[2], *John*[1]), b 1849, in Winslow Me , m 1, Carrie L Hatch, m 2, Amanda T B Warren; m 3, Oct 6, 1887, in Lowell, Susan Hodges b June 8, 1869, in Winslow, Me

Children

174   S Warren[8], b ——

175   Carrie E[8], b ——

176   Edith A[8], b ——

177   Russell J[8], b ——

178   Eleanor[8], b ——

179   Merton[8], b Aug 4, 1892, in Winslow

97. ALONZO F[7] FULLER, (*Artemas*[6], *Aaron*[5], *Elisha*[4], *Jonathan*[3], *Joseph*[2], *John*[1]), b June 14, 1814, in Sumner, Me , d Dec, 1850, m 1, Mary Lincoln, of Easton, who d in Lowell, m 2, July 20, 1850, Ann Rollins

Children

180   A daughter, b ——; d ——, m ——

99. SAMUEL S[7] FULLER, (*Artemas[6]*, *Aaron[5]*, *Elisha[4]*, *Jonathan[3]*, *Joseph[2]*, *John[1]*), b Dec 17, 1824, in Sumner, Me , in July 20, 1850, Eliza-beth N Reed, who d May 7, 1895

He resides in Bridgton, Me. (1912) , a retired mill man—at one time designer for the Forest and Pondicherry Mills, and sometime Superintendent of the Washington Mills, at Lawrence

Children

181   Mary E[8], b May 16, 1853 , d July 17, 1875, in Lowell

102. ALBION KING PARRIS[7] FULLER, (*Joel[6]*, *Aaron[5]*, *Elisha[4]*, *Jonathan[3]*, *Joseph[2]*, *John[1]*), b Feb 12, 1817, at Paris Hill Me , d Nov 19, 1910, at East Livermore, Me , m 1, July, 1843, Hannah Jane West, of Jay, Me , who d Dec , 1862, m 2, 1865, Sarah Ann Palmer, of Lewiston, Me , who survived him

He resided on the farm purchased by him about 1862 in East Livermore   He served a year and nine months with the 22d Maine Regt in the Civil war

A newspaper obituary mentions as survivors of his 14 children

182   Irving[8], b —— resides in Jay, Me
183   Ambrose M[8], b about 1850, m Sept 6, 1873, at Newton, Mass, Eudora E Jones, b Needham, Mass , resides at Newton Upper Falls, Mass , and states there were seven other sons, and one daughter by first wife
184   Charles B[8], b ——, resides at Livermore Falls, Me
185   Elizabeth B[8], b ——, resides at Beverly, Mass , and two other children, now dead, by second wife

111. CHARLES WESLEY[7] FULLER, (*Aaron[6]*, *Aaron[5]*, *Elisha[4]*, *Jonathan[3]*, *Joseph[2]* *John[1]*), b Mar 7, 1821, in Paris, Me ; d Nov 15, 1902, at North Livermore, Me , m ——, Emma Dunn

He lived at North Livermore, Me

Children

186   Alice B[8], b June, 1869 , resides at North Weymouth, Mass (1910)

112. JAMES NORTON[7] FULLER, (*Aaron[6]*, *Aaron[5]*, *Elisha[4]*, *Jonathan[3]*, *Joseph[2]*, *John[1]*), b Jan 13, 1823, in Paris, Me , d May 23, 1901, at Wareham, in Mar 28, 1847, Mary King Hathaway

Children

187   Mary Fayette[8], b Mar 10, 1849, at Wareham, m Mar 18, 1905 Zenas A Tillson
188   **James Frederick[8]**, b ——, m 1, Sarah J Dyer, m 2, Lucy J Rogers, m 3, Nettie Staples
189   Eldorus Francis[8], b ——, d ——, m Hattie M Hathaway
190   Etta[8], b ——
191   George[8], b Feb 6, 1853, at Wareham, resides at Winthrop, Mass (1910)

192   Flora⁸, b ——, m David Donald, Winthrop
193   Charles N⁸, b Sept 16, 1856, d Jan 26, 1857, at Wareham

115. JOHN NELSON⁷ FULLER, (*Aaron⁶, Aaron⁵, Elisha⁴, Jonathan³, Joseph², John¹*), b Feb 22, 1831, in Paris, Me, d Nov 10, 1905, in Beatrice Neb, m ——, Elizabeth Van Arsdale, b Apr 14, 1848, in Illinois
  He was a member of the Nebraska Legislature in 1888
  Children, all born in Beatrice, Neb
194   Lulu⁸, b June 2 1869, d July, 1879
195   Julia⁸, b ——, resides (1910) at Beatrice
196   Mary⁸, b ——

127. DANIEL EDWARD⁷ FULLER, (*Daniel⁶, Aaron⁵, Elisha⁴, Jonathan³ Joseph², John¹*), b —— 1846, d ——, m 1, ——, 1877, Emma I Blaisdell, m 2 1883, M Emma Crassmeer
  Children
197.   Bertha Olive⁸, b —— 1881, in Brunswick, Me
198   Edward Simpson⁸, b ——, 1884, in Brunswick

137. RAWSON C⁷ FULLER, (*Oliver⁶ Oliver⁵, Edward⁴, Jonathan³, Joseph², John¹*), b Dec 13, 1836, in Jay, Me, m 1, Emily J Green, of Wilton, Me, who d Oct 1, 1871, m 2, Nancy H Frost, of Wayne, Me He resides in Wilton.
  Children·
199   A son, b Dec 6, 1865 d Jan 8, 1866
200   Vesta E⁸, b Feb 11, 1867, d Sept 27 1895
201   Lillian G⁸, b Feb 10, 1870, m S G Mandalain, and resides in North Attleboro

152. ALDEN M⁷ FULLER, (*Daniel D⁶, Simon⁵, Edward⁴, Jonathan³, Joseph², John¹*), b Jan 26, 1833, in Union, Me, d——, m July 27, 1856, Ellen Coburn
  Children
202   A dau b ——
203   A dau b ——
204   A dau b ——

153. HOSEA YOUNG⁷ FULLER, (*Daniel D⁶, Simon⁵, Edward⁴, Jonathan³, Joseph², John¹*), b June 5, 1834, in Union, Me, m Aug 11, 1864, Lucy J Holmes, of Stoughton
  They reside in Somerville
  Children
205   Lawrence Percival⁸, b May 23, 1866, d Sept 20, 1866
206   Henry Maynard⁸, b Feb 19, 1872, unmarried (1911)

155. VIRGIL F[7] FULLER, (*Daniel D[6], Simon[5], Edward[4], Jonathan[3], Joseph[2], John[1]*), b Apr 10, 1837, d ——, m. Jan. 19, 1871, Clara Frances Adams, b July 7, 1851, in Rumford, Me

Children

207 Della Frances[8], b Sept 2, 1871; d Jan 6, 1876
208 Hattie E[8], b Dec 28, 1873, } twins, { d, Mar 12, 1893
209 Nettie P[8], b Dec 28, 1873. } { m Jan 7, 1892, Wm H Freeman, reside at Rumford, Me
210 Herbert E[8] b Jan 31, 1876, d June 18, 1894
211 Mary A[8], b Nov 2, 1884

163. CHARLES Y[7] FULLER, (*Henry D[6], Simon[5], Edward[4], Jonathan[3], Joseph[2], John[1]*) b Jan 17. 1835, in Union, Me , m Aug 27, 1862, Susannah W Gilchrist, of Washington, Me

Children

212 Oliver Henry[8], b May 28, 1863, d Sept 11, 1891, in Union, m Apr 29, 1888. Adell C Manning, in Willimantic, Ct
213 Clara Etta[8], b Nov. 19, 1864, in Washington, Me
214 Charles Frank[8], b Jan. 27. 1867, d May 27, 1894, in Union
215 Alice May[8], b Apr 4, 1872; d May 27, 1855, in Union
216 **Wilbert Tilden[8]**, b Sept 16, 1876, m Rida R Robinson
217 Gladys Mildred[8], b Oct 28, 1889 in Union

EIGHTH GENERATION.

188. JAMES FREDERIC[8] FULLER, (*James N[7] Aaron[6], Aaron[5], Elisha[4], Jonathan[3], Joseph[2], John[1]*) b ——, m 1, —— Sarah J Dyer, m 2, Dec 25, 1880, Lucy J Rogers, of Orleans, who d Mar 15, 1885, at Wareham, m 3, May 2, 1886, Nettie L Staples

Children recorded at Wareham

218 Charles Frederic[9], b Dec 1, 1876
219 Frederic Lester[9], b Feb 14, 1887, d Sept 22, 1887
220 Percy Clifton[9], b Nov 26, 1888
221 Fayette Ellsworth[9], b Mar 13, 1892
222 Ernest Layton[9], } twins, b Feb 13, 1895
223 Edgar Clayton[9], }

216. WILBERT TILDEN[8] FULLER, (*Charles Y[7], Henry D[6], Simon[5], Edward[4], Jonathan[3], Joseph[2], John[1]*), b Sept 16, 1876, in Union, Me ; m Dec 20, 1899, in Warren, Me , Rida R Robinson

Children

224 Frank Bardeen[9], b Dec 14, 1900, in Union, Me

NINTH GROUP

THIRD GENERATION.

EDWARD³ FULLER, AND ONE OF HIS DESCENDANTS

23. EDWARD³ FULLER, (*Joseph²*, *John¹*), b. Mar 7, 1694, in Newton,
d there Nov 23, 1732, m Sept 21, 1726, Esther Bowen
Children
1   Lucy⁴, b. May 13, 1729

Melicent Rawson Fuller

TENTH GROUP

THIRD GENERATION.

IS.AAC³ FULLER, AND SOME OF HIS DESCENDANTS

24. Isaac³ Fuller, (*Joseph², John¹*), b. Mar 16, 1698. in Newton; d there June 10, 1745, m Sept 17, 1722, Hannah Greenwood, b Mar 4, 1699, d Mai 22, 1769, dau of John and Hannah (Trowbridge) Greenwood

His children were

1   Susanna⁴, b July 13, 1725, d Mar 12, 1748
2   **Joseph⁴**, b Aug 15, 1727, m 1, Mindwell Stone; m 2, Mehitable Craft.
3   Ruth⁴, b Sept 18, 1729, m Jan 1, 1752, Peter Durell, and had Susanna⁵, Hannah⁵, Peter⁵, John,⁵, and Isaac⁵
4   Lois⁴ b Dec 12, 1732, d Sept 3, 1749
5   Tabitha⁴, b Sept 7, 1734
6   Hannah⁴, b Nov 11, 1735, d Oct 15, 1797; m Sept 4, 1755, Daniel Stearns
7   Lydia⁴, b Oct 23, 1737, m June 30, 1756 Daniel⁴ Fuller, No 5 of the 4th Group
8   Abigail⁴, b ——, d 1753

FOURTH GENERATION.

2. Joseph⁴ Fuller, (*Isaac³, Joseph², John¹*), b. Aug 15, 1727, in Newton, d 1807, aged 80 (Hist of Newton); d Mai. 3 ——, aged 82 (Newton V R), m. 1, May 4 1756, Mindwell Stone, who d Feb 10, 1777, aged 46, m 2, Int Pub Apr 19, 1781, Mehitable Craft

Capt Joseph Fuller raised a company of 96 men foi Col Bullard's Regiment, maiched to Bennington, Skeensboro, and Lake George, and thence to Cambridge to guard the captured tioops of Burgoyne.

Children

9   Asa⁵, b June 17, 1757, m Betsey Winchester, Oct 5, 1786
10 Lois⁵, b 1758, m Mar 18, 1784, Joshua Park, and had Charles⁶, Joseph⁶, Joshua⁶, Asa⁶, Sukey⁶, Salome⁶, Daniel Harrington⁶, and William Aspinwall⁶.

11. Susanna[6], b Oct 9, 1760, m Int Pub Aug 5, 1781, with John
     Cook, of Watertown
12   Nabby[6], b July 14, 1765, m July 8, 1790, Edward Durant, and had
     Polly[6], Eliza[6], Edward[6], Samuel[6], and Thomas[6]
13   Mindwell[5], b July 14, 1765 (?), d Aug 3 1823, aged 60, m May 8,
     1793, Ebenezer White, and had Sarah Davis[6] Joseph[6], Lucinda[6],
     Ebenezer Davis[6], Mary Ann[6] Mindwell[6], William[6], Asa[6], and
     Asa[6] 2d

FIFTH GENERATION.

9. Asa[5] Fuller (*Joseph[4], Isaac[3], Joseph[2] John[1]*), b June 17, 1757,
in Newton, d —— at St Albans, Vt ; m Oct 5, 1786, Betsey Winchester

Children
14   John[6], b. 1794, m Mary Smith, no issue.
15   Eliza[6], b 1796, m. —— Seymour and had 7 children
16   Fanny[6], b 1799, went to Kentucky
17   **Joseph[6]**, b 1804, m Jane Hennessey
18   Mariett[6], b 1805, went to Ohio
19   Mary Ann[6], b 1810, m —— Booth, and removed to the West

SIXTH GENERATION.

17. Joseph[6] Fuller, (*Asa[5], Joseph[4], Isaac[3], Joseph[2], John[1]*), b. 1804,
d ——, m Jane Hennessey

Children
20   Edmund[7], b ——
21   Asa[7], b ——
22   Elizabeth[7], b ——.
23   Mary Jane[7], b ——

ELEVENTH GROUP

THIRD GENERATION.

THOMAS³ FULLER, AND SOME OF HIS DESCENDANTS

35. THOMAS³ FULLER, (*Jeremiah², John¹*), b Sept 12, 1701, ın Newton, d Nov 2, 1748, m. Apr 2, 1748, Elızabeth Ball, of Watertown

Children

1   Thankful⁴, b July 26, 1730
2   Rachel⁴, b July 12, 1734; d young
3   **Jeremiah⁴**, b May 14, 1736; m Sarah Robinson.
4   **Thomas⁴**, b Sept 25, 1738, m Hannah Kingsbury.
5   Nathan¹, b June 3, 1741; d Sept 21, 1822, m. July 4, 1764, Beulah
     Craft, who d Nov 16, 1818, aged 73.

He is called Col Nathan Fuller; was a soldıer of the Revolution
He was Representative in 1795 They had no chıldren Jackson's
Hıstory of Newton says, Col Nathan Fuller "wıll made ın 1817 gave
his estate to his nephew, Benjamın Fuller, after payıng small legacıes."
The legatees named ın the wıll were "Beulah, wıfe, Nıece Beulah Bacon.
Benjamın Fuller, Leonard Fuller, Nathan Fuller, nephews "

6. **Benjamın⁴**, b. Nov. 15, 1743, m Hannah Chıld

FOURTH GENERATION.

3. JEREMIAH⁴ FULLER, (*Thomas³, Jeremıah², John¹*), b. May 14, 1736,
in Newton; d ——, m. Feb 8, 1759, Sarah Robınson

He is probably the Jeremiah Fuller wıth wıfe Sarah, whose children
are recorded in Holden, Mass, as follows:

7. Elızabeth⁵, b. May 20, 1759
8   Sarah⁵, b Oct 12, 1760.
9   Hannah⁶, b Dec 3, 1762
10 Thomas S⁶, b July 23, 1764
11 Isaac⁵, b. Apr. 27, 1766.
12 Beulah⁶, b. Feb 3, 1768; probably d young.
13 Rachel⁵, b. Mar. 3, 1770.
14 Nathan⁶, b Dec 17, 1771
15 Jeremiah⁵, b Mar. 26, 1774

10

16   Beulah[5], b Oct. 9, 1779

4. THOMAS[4] FULLER, (*Thomas[3], Jeremiah[2], John[1]*), b Sept 25, 1738,
in Newton; d ——, m June 23, 1763, Hannah Kingsbury, of Needham
    Bond's Watertown Genealogy states that he is supposed to be the
father of Thomas[5] Fuller
17   **Thomas[5]**, b about 1764· m 1, Elizabeth Bond, m 2, Martha
        Stearns.

6. BENJAMIN[4] FULLER, (*Thomas[3], Jeremiah[2], John[1]*) b Nov 15, 1743,
in Newton, d ——; m May 12, 1768, Hannah Child, in Newton, Mass ;
he said to be of Waltham   Jackson's Hist of Newton, says "Benjamin
Fuller m Hannah Childs and settled in —— "
    Children mentioned by Jackson·
18   **Benjamin[5]**, b ——, m Susan Jackson
19   **Leonard[5]**, b ——, m Abigail Brigham
20   **Nathan[5]**, b ——; m Rebecca Brown
21   Beulah[5], b ——, m Nov 13, 1805, Joseph Bacon, and had Martha[6],
        Elizabeth Fuller[6], Joseph Newman[6], Beulah Craft[6], James Mon-
        roe[6], George Washington[6] John Adams[6], Thomas Jefferson[6] and
        Benjamin Franklin[6]

FIFTH GENERATION.

17. THOMAS[5] FULLER, (*Thomas[4], Thomas[3], Jeremiah[2], John[1]*), b
about 1764, d June 26, 1844 aged 80, in Jay, Me , m 1, Apr 28, 1789, in
Watertown, Elizabeth Bond, m 2, Aug , 1799, Martha Stearns, who was
bapt Sept 16, 1770
    Children by first wife
22   Thomas[6], b ——
23   **Nathan[6]**, b ——, m Minerva Eustis Cutler
24   Charles[6], b ——
25   Henry[6], b ——
26   Elizabeth[6], b Feb 20, 1792, d May 20, 1851; m May 22, 1819,
        Charles Stearns.
27   Salome[6], b ——
    Children by second wife
29   John[6], b ——, d 1831, unmarried
30   George Washington[6], b——, m Martha Noyes of Jay, Me , and
        lived there
31   Isaac[6], b ——; m —— lived in Dixfield, Me
32   Salome[6], b ——, 1800; m —— Carlton
33   Myra[6], b ——; d 1842, unmarried
34   Martha[6], b ——, m Joseph Webster, of Wilton Me
35   Maria[6], b ——, d June, 1846, unmarried
36   Catherine[6], b ——, d 1816.

18. BENJAMIN⁵ FULLER, (*Benjamin⁴, Thomas³, Jeremiah², John¹*), b. —— , d ——; m Dec 6, 1804, Susan Jackson, of Needham.
Children, recorded in Newton

37 Emeline⁶, bapt Feb 17, 1805, d Oct 11, 1805
38 Edwin⁶ ⎫
39 Enoch⁶, ⎰ twins, b Mar 16, 1808
40 Abraham⁶, b Apr 20, 1810, d Mar 20, 1883, in Somerville, m June 22, 1835, in Waltham, Lydia Bryant Craftes; resided in Worcester, Framingham, Waltham, and Somerville
41 Caleb Strong⁶ b. Apr 7, 1812; m Int Pub Sept 20, 1835, with Abigail H Cheney
42 Susanna Smith⁶, b Sept 15, 1814
43 Mary Jackson⁶, b Apr 23, 1817
44 Ann Eliza⁶, b. Aug 19, 1820
45 **Benjamin Franklin⁶**, bapt May 26, 1824, m Clara Dow

19. LEONARD⁵ FULLER, (*Benjamin⁴, Thomas³, Jeremiah², John¹*), b —— , d ——, m Int Pub Mar 1, 1817, with Abigail Brigham, "both of Watertown," m Mar. 23, 1817, in Marlboro
Children recorded in Newton

46 Marshall L⁶, bapt Sept 6, 1818
47 Harriet Newell⁶, bapt May 23, 1819
48 George Washington⁶, bapt June 3, 1821
49 Martha Ann⁶, bapt 1823
50 William Henry⁶, bapt. Apr 18, 1824
51 John Francis⁶, bapt Mar 12, 1826

20. NATHAN⁵ FULLER, (*Benjamin⁴, Thomas³, Jeremiah², John¹*), b —— , d ——; m Int Pub Mar 21, 1818, of Nathan Fuller of Watertown, and Rebecca Brown, of Newton, m Apr 7, 1819, in Newton
Children recorded in Newton

52 Nathan⁶, bapt June 3, 1827
53 Emeline Rebecca⁶, bapt June 3, 1827
54 Martha Elizabeth⁶, bapt. June 3, 1827
55 Mary Submit⁶, bapt June 3, 1827
56 Darius Smith⁶, bapt July 6, 1828

SIXTH GENERATION.

23. NATHAN⁶ FULLER, (*Thomas⁵, Thomas⁴, Thomas³, Jeremiah², John¹*), b Dec 19, 1790, in Jay, Me , d Dec 9, 1875, in East Dixfield, Me , m Feb, 1828, Minerva Eustis Cutler, b Oct 5, 1800, in Charlestown, Mass ; d Apr 19, 1876, in North Jay, Me.
Children, first four b in Jay, the others in E Dixfield.

57 Cyrus⁷, b Dec 14, 1830; d Nov 23. 1862, at Sly Park, Cal

58   Elizabeth B', b July 31, 1833, d Aug 24. 1888, at North Jay, Me
59   John', b Dec. 4, 1834, d May 16, 1862, at Sly Park, Cal.
60   **Charles H.'**, b Apr 30, 1836, m Mary A Stone
61   Nathan A ', b Aug 17, 1839, d June 4, 1865, at E Dixfield
62   William H ', b May 2, 1841, resides at La Cygne, Kan.
63   Darius E ', b Mar 23, 1843, resides at Norway, Me
64   Roslin A ', b Nov 18, 1844, d Oct 28, 1853, at E Dixfield

45. BENJAMIN FRANKLIN[6] FULLER, (*Benjamin[5], Benjamin[4], Thomas[3], Jeremiah[2], John[1]*), bapt May 26, 1824, in Newton. d Sept. 5, 1900 in Northampton, aged 76 y. 5 m 6d ; m ——, Clara Dow, b at Lyman, Me , d 1893, aged 66

Children.
65   Adele J.', b about 1853, in New Haven, Ct , m Jan 6, 1885, Alfred G Fearing, b Wareham, Ct

SEVENTH GENERATION.

60. CHARLES H ' FULLER, (*Nathan[6], Thomas[5], Thomas[4], Thomas[3], Jeremiah[2], John[1]*), b Apr. 30, 1836, in Jay, Me , d June 25, 1888, at East Dixfield, Me , m ——, Mary A Stone, of Dixfield, Me.

Children
66   Maurice A [8], b Dec 18, 1867, in Wilton, Me., m Sept 30, 1891, Jeanette M. Ellis

TWELFTH GROUP

THIRD GENERATION.

JOSHUA³ FULLER, AND SOME OF HIS DESCENDANTS

36. JOSHUA³ FULLER, (*Jeremiah²*, *John¹*), b. Apr 12, 1703; d Aug 23, 1777, aged 75, m ——, who d Nov 28, 1739, m 2, May 26, 1746, Anna Stearns, of Waltham, b Aug 2, 1718, d 1778, aged 61

He is called Captain Joshua

Children by second wife
1   **Joshua⁴**, b. Mar. 2, 1747, m. 1, Catherine Jackson, m. 2, Mary (Brewer) White
2   Ann⁴, b June 18, 1749, m May 13, 1774, Ephraim Whitney
3   **David⁴**, b Apr 18, 1751, m Sarah Williams
4   Moses⁴, b Apr 1, 1753
5   Eunice⁴, b Feb 15, 1756, d. 1778, m Col Josiah Fuller, as 2d w.
6   Rachel⁴, b Apr 29, 1760
7   Nathaniel⁴, bapt Feb 27, 1763, in Waltham.

FOURTH GENERATION.

1. JOSHUA⁴ FULLER, (*Joshua³*, *Jeremiah²*, *John¹*), b Mar. 2, 1747, in Newton; d there Nov 8, 1817, m. 1, Jan 21, 1773, Catherine Jackson who d June 3, 1777, aged 30 y., m 2, Apr 23, 1778, Mary (Brewer) White, who d Sept, 1808

He is called Lieut Joshua Fuller.

Children, reorded in Newton
8.   Henry⁵, b. June 21, 1773; d June 24, 1777.
9   **Joshua⁵**, b Sept 16, 1774; m Hannah Greenwood
10   Jacob⁵, b Mar 30, 1776, d Oct 18, 1778.
11   Catherine⁵, b ——; m. Aug 25, 1806, Charles Jackson.
12   Elijah⁵, b ——, d Oct, 1835, m and lived in South Boston
13   **James⁵**, b. ——.
14   Rebecca⁵, bapt Dec 2, 1781.

3. DAVID⁴ FULLER, (*Joshua³*, *Jeremiah²*, *John¹*), b Apr 18, 1751, in Newton, d ——; m —— 1779, Sarah Williams, who d Aug 1, 1812

Children, recorded in Newton

15   Eunice⁵, b 1779, d Oct 8, 1799, aged 20
16   David⁵, b ——; d Jan 12, 1826, aged 41, unmarried
17   Sarah⁵, b. May 1, 1787, d Sept 13, 1867, m Nov 15, 1815, Joel⁵ Fuller, No 18, 13th Group
18   Martha⁵, b. ——, d June 10, 1821, aged 28, unmarried
19   Hannah⁵, b. ——, m Apr 7, 1808, Joshua Goodrich

FIFTH GENERATION.

9. Joshua⁵ Fuller, (*Joshue⁴ Joshua³, Jeremiah², John¹*), b Sept 16, 1774, in Newton; d July 12, 1805, (Jackson) aged 31 m Mar 20, 1800, Hannah Greenwood, who m 2, Daniel Sauger of Watertown, and d. Sept, 1808, aged 29.

Children

20.   Henry⁶, b 1801, d. ——
21   **Stephen⁶**, b 1803; m Dorcas Howe
22   Catherine⁶, b 1805, m Apr 5, 1825, Charles Capen, and removed to Framingham.

13. James⁵ Fuller, (*Joshua⁴, Joshua³, Jeremiah², John¹*), b —— in Newton,, d Aug 6, 1850, aged 66, m ——, Beulah Greenwood.

He was Representative 3 years, and Senator 1 year

Children:

23   **James G.⁶**, b. ——, m
24.   Mary B⁶, b ——; m Int Pub Apr 28, 1839, with Samuel F Dix
        Children, James Fuller⁷ Dix, and Henry Samuel⁷ Dix

SIXTH GENERATION.

21. Stephen⁶ Fuller, (*Joshua⁵, Joshua⁴, Joshua³, Jeremiah², John¹*), b. ——, 1803, in Newton; d ——; m ——Dorcas Howe, b in England.

Children

25   Henry⁷, b ——
26   Joshua⁷, b ——
27   Joseph⁷, b ——
28   Harriet⁷, b ——
29   **Stephen Winchester⁷**, b Jan 1, 1836, m Lavinia Phebe Turner
30   Hannah⁷, b about 1853, m Sept 18, 1878, Charles Cole, b in Middleboro

23. James Greenwood⁶ Fuller, (*James⁵, Joshua⁴, Joshua³, Jeremiah², John¹*), b ——; d ——, m ——.

Children

31   **Arthur G.⁷**, b ——; m Sarah L Whitney
32   Alfred W⁷, b ——

SEVENTH GENERATION.

29. STEPHEN WINCHESTER[7] FULLER, (*Stephen[6], Joshua[5] Joshua[4], Joshua[3], Jeremiah[2], John[1]*), b Jan 1, 1836, in Charlestown; d Apr 28, 1905, in Somerville, m Feb 14, 1860, Lavinia Phebe Turner

He lived in Somerville

Children ·

33   Beulah E[8], b Nov 18, 1864, d Jan 1, 1865.

An adopted daughter, Grace M. Fuller, m Charles Pritchard

31. ARTHUR G[7] FULLER, (*James G[6], James[5], Joshua[4], Joshua[3], Jeremiah[2], John[1]*), b ——; m Sarah L Whitney

Children

34   Percy Whitney[8], b about 1878, m Sept 22, 1910, in Salem, Bertha Donaldson Barton, b. in Salem

THIRTEENTH GROUP

————

THIRD GENERATION.

JOSIAH³ FULLER, AND SOME OF HIS DESCENDANTS

40. Josiah³ Fuller, (*Jeremiah²*, *John¹*), b Dec 2, 1710, in Newton, d there 1793, aged 83, m Jan 14, 1738-9, Abigail Williams, who d Sept. 30, 1796, aged 84, dau of Isaac, Jr, and Martha (Whitman) Williams.

He is called Ensign Josiah Fuller

1 **Josiah⁴**, b Oct 24, 1739, m. 1, Anna Priest m 2, Eunice Fuller, m 3, Mary Dana, m. 4, Mary Woodward; m 5, Mary Perry

2 David⁴, b Oct 13, 1741; d Jan 13, 1741-2.

3 Phebe⁴, b Jan 29, 1744; m Feb 28, 1765, William Clark, Jr, and had Jonathan⁵

4 Abigail⁴, b Oct 24, 1745, m Feb 14, 1765, John Barber; m 2, Aug 18, 1785, Samuel Jenks. Children (Barber) John⁵, Samuel⁵, and Abigail⁵, twins, Elizabeth⁵ and Oliver⁵

5 Anna⁴, b June 4, 1746, m Benjamin Richards, of Roxbury

6 Mary⁴, b Oct 30, 1747, m Feb 22, 1770, Thomas Miller, Jr., and had Joseph⁵, Mary⁵, and Sarah⁵

7 Thankful⁴, b Feb 21, 1750

8 **Joseph⁴**, b July 29, 1751; m 1, Joanna Spring, m 2, Elizabeth Bacon

9 Susanna⁴, b. June 2, 1753, m Aug 24, 1771, Stephen Hastings, and had Josiah⁵ and Susanna⁵

10 Martha⁴, b Aug 21, 1755, m. Oct. 2, 1775, Daniel Stratton, of Weston

FOURTH GENERATION.

1. Josiah⁴ Fuller, (*Josiah³ Jeremiah², John¹*), b Oct. 24, 1739, in Newton, d there Mar. 22, 1825, m 1, Jan 15, 1761, Anna Priest, m 2, ——— 18, 1778, Eunice⁴ Fuller (Joshua³, Jeremiah², John¹), who d Sept 28, 1778; m 3, May 25, 1779 Mary Dana, m 4, Mary Woodward, m 5, Mary Perry He was Selectman 3 years, and Colonel of Militia

Children b in Newton

11. Eunice[5], }
12   Rachel[5] } twins, b Sept 13, 1778; d 1778
13   Sally[5], b Mar 9, 1781; m May 7, 1800, Amasa Winchester, of Boston
14   Anna[5], b Jan. 12, 1783, m Nov. 27, 1800, William Winchester, of Roxbury
15   Josiah[5], b Sept 18, 1785, m Sarah Greenough

8. JOSEPH[4] FULLER, (*Josiah[3], Jeremiah[2], John[1]*), b July 24, 1751, in Newton, d there Feb 23, 1813, m 1, —— 1777, Joanna Spring, who d July 25, 1784, m. 2, Mar, 1785, Elizabeth Bacon, who d —— 1819
He was Selectman for 3 years, and a deacon in the church.
Children recorded in Newton·
16   **Joseph[5]**, b —— 1777, m Lucena Loring.
17   Betsey[5], b Aug 15, 1782, d 1807
18   **Joel[5]**, b Aug 10, 1786; m Sarah Fuller, No 17, 12th Group
19   George[5], bapt June 1, 1788; probably d young
20   Nabby[5], b Sept 14, 1791
21   George[5], b Aug 21 1793; d July 21, 1802
22   Edmund[5], b Nov 23, 1790; m Apr 5, 1818, Mary Ann Howard
23   Mindwell[5], b June 19, 1796
24   Jeremiah[5], b Sept 9, 1797, d Jan 27, 1828
25   Sumner[5], b June 3, 1799
26   Maria[5], b Dec 12, 1800.
27   Jane[5], b Feb 1, 1803; d Sept 14, 1874, unmarried, resided at West Roxbury.
28   Mary Ann[5], b June 26, 1805
29   Seth[5], b July 16, 1807

FIFTH GENERATION.

15. JOSIAH[5] FULLER, (*Josiah[4], Josiah[3], Jeremiah[2], John[1]*), b Sept 18, 1785, in Newton, date of death not found; m. Apr 27, 1809, Sarah Greenough, who d Dec 30, 1815, aged 28
Children
30   **William Griffin[6]**, b. May 2, 1810, m. 1, Mary Richardson, m 2, Apphia E Burpee
31   Sarah[6], b Nov 30, 1811, m Silas Dean, and had dau Ellen Elizabeth[7], who resides at Stoneham
32   May[6], b Nov 19, 1813· d —— unmarried
33   **Josiah[6]**, b Dec. 25, 1815; m Cordelia M Stevens (?)

16. JOSEPH[5] FULLER, (*Joseph[4], Josiah[3], Jeremiah[2], John[1]*) b Apr 25 1777, d Apr 5, 1811; m Feb 26, 1805, Lucena Loring, of Barre
Lived at Union, Ct
Children.

34   Joanna L⁶, b Feb 11, 1807, d Nov 4, 1876, m Dec. 3, 1827, Wil-
       liam J Sherman
35   Adelphia⁶, b ——, m May 15, 1834, William C Janes of New
       Haven, Ct

18. JOEL⁵ FULLER, (*Joseph⁴, Josiah³, Jeremiah², John¹*), b Aug 10,
1786, in Newton, d there Dec 18, 1848, m. Nov 15, 1815, Sarah⁵ Fuller,
No 17, 12th Group
   Joel Fuller was Deacon, Selectman, and for four years Representative
   Children ·
36   Winslow⁶, b Oct 29, 1816, d Aug 4, 1828
37   **Henry⁶**, b May 30, 1818, m Eliza J Pike
38   David⁶, b June 28, 1822, d Sept 5, 1853, in Newton, m Roxey A.
       Flagg, Apr 10, 1845
39   Martha⁶, b July 3, 1825; d Sept 3, 1841

SIXTH GENERATION.

30. WILLIAM GRIFFIN⁶ FULLER, (*Josiah⁵, Josiah⁴, Josiah³, Jeremiah²,
John¹*) b May 2, 1810, in Newton, d——, m 1, May 10, 1835, Mary
Richardson; m 2, Nov 12, 1840, in New London, N H, Apphia E
Burpee
   Children by first wife
40.   Mary Francis⁷, b —— 1826; d —— 1856
41   Cornelia Ellen⁷, b —— 1839, d —— 1839
   By second wife.
42   William Almeron⁷, b June 2, 1842, d Sept 19, 1843
43   Georgianna Eva⁷, b July 14, 1845, resides in Stoneham
44   Wilhemina Cordelia⁷, b Apr 5, 1858, resides in Stoneham.

33. JOSIAH⁶ FULLER, (*Josiah⁵, Josiah⁴, Josiah³, Jeremiah², John¹*), b
Dec 25, 1815, in Newton, d there Oct 7, 1849, in Int Pub Mar 20,
1836, with Cordelia M. Stevens
   Children ·
45   John Stevens⁷, b Nov 18, 1838, m Mar 19, 1863, Mary A
       Wetherbee, of Newton, resides at Wellesley, no children
46   **William Ezra⁷**, b May 18, 1841, m Lucy J Wetherbee.
47   **George Greenough⁷**, b May 6, 1845, m Abby Susan York.

37. HENRY⁶ FULLER, (*Joel⁵, Joseph⁴, Josiah³, Jeremiah², John¹*), b
May 30, 1818, in Newton, d there Jan. 19, 1845; m Mar 29, 1842, Eliza
J. Pike, b Feb 11, 1819, in Jay, Me
   Children:
48   **Winslow⁷**, b Jan 8, 1843, m 1, Jeanette Fuller, m 2, Mrs Hattie
       E Gould

49   **Joel Henry**¹, b Aug 17, 1844, m 1, ——, m 2, ——

SEVENTH GENERATION.

46. WILLIAM EZRA⁷ FULLER, (*Josiah⁶, Josiah⁵, Josiah⁴, Josiah³, Jeremiah² John¹*), b May 8, 1841, in Newton, d Aug 27, 1890, m Feb 27, 1863, Lucy J Wetherbee, b July 16, 1846, d Dec 19, 1899, she m 2d. Dec 14, 1893, Stephen Francis Cate, his 2d w
   Children
50   Marian E⁸, b June 27, 1863, m Aug 17, 1887, Richard A Oldreive
51   **Walter C.⁸**, b Mar 28, 1865; m Mary A Marston
52   William Ezra⁸, b Nov 16, 1867; m June 18, 1893, Delia Anastasia Foy, who d May 3, 1906
53   **Arthur S.⁸**, b ——, m Eva M Wight
54   **Alfred S.⁸**, b Dec 30, 1875, m June 23, 1897, Amy Rose Sauer
55   Grace E⁸, b Mar 11, 1881
56   **Chester B.⁸**, b Mar 25, 1885, m July 1, 1906, Ellen Veronica Cashman

47. GEORGE GREENOUGH⁷ FULLER (*Josiah⁶, Josiah⁵, Josiah⁴, Josiah³, Jeremiah², John¹*), b May 6, 1845, in Newton, m Nov 12, 1869, Abby Susan York of Portland, Me
   Children
57   **Herman Dean⁸**, b Apr 4, 1879, m Aurelia W Fuller

48. WINSLOW⁷ FULLER, (*Henry⁶, Joel⁵, Joseph⁴, Josiah³, Jeremiah² John¹*), b Jan 18, 1843, in Newton· m 1, Feb 15, 1866, in Medina, N Y, Jeannette Fuller, dau of Edmund Fuller of Medina, she was b Sept 13 1839, and d. without issue, Apr 9, 1871, in Holt Co, Mo, m 2, in Holt Co, Mo, Jan 13, 1872, Mrs Hattie E Gould, b Apr 28 1838, in Waltham, d Dec 16, 1883, in Smith Co, Kan, m 3, Nov. 27, 1884, in Jay, Me, Ida Maria Pike, b Feb 24 1854, in Jay
   They resided in Dighton, Lane Co, Kan (1893), Crafts Gene
   Children
58   Henry Winslow⁸, b Oct 30, 1872
59   Henrietta Elizabeth⁸, b Jan 14, 1874
60   Joseph Warren⁸, b June 17, 1875
61   Hattie Jeanette⁸, b Apr 3, 1877
62   Ida Marie⁸, b Oct 23, 1887
63   Nelson Edward⁸, b Oct 24, 1890
64   Winslow Rae⁸, b Feb 3, 1893

49. JOEL HENRY⁷ FULLER, (*Henry⁶, Joel⁵ Joseph⁴, Josiah³, Jeremiah⁴, John¹*), b Aug 17, 1844, in West Newton, m 1, —— who d without issue, Mar, 1883, m 2, ——, Sept, 1883

Resided in Durango, Mexico
Children
65   Marie[8], b Aug 28, 1884

EIGHTH GENERATION.

51. WALTER C[8] FULLER, (*William E[7], Josiah[6], Josiah[5], Josiah[4], Josiah[3], Jeremiah[2], John[1]*), b Mar 28, 1865, in Newtonville; m Sept 1, 1886, May M Marston
   They reside at West Newton
66   Marion Gertrude[9], b Dec 20, 1888; m. Sept 14, 1911, Clarence R Howes
67   Gladys Mildred[9], b Dec 20, 1891, d Aug 4, 1892

53. ARTHUR S[8] FULLER, (*William E[7]. Josiah[6], Josiah[5], Josiah[4] Josiah[3], Jeremiah[2], John[1]*), b ——; m ——, Eva M Wight
   Resides in Newtonville
   Children
68   Marion[9], b ——
69   William[9], b ——

54. ALFRED S[8] FULLER, (*William E[7], Josiah[6], Josiah[5], Josiah[4], Josiah[3] Jeremiah[2], John[1]*), b Dec 30, 1875, in Newtonville, m June 23, 1897, Amy Rose Sauer, b Apr 21, 1876, at Newton Center
   They reside in Waltham
   Children
70   Dorothy Sampson[9], b Apr 17, 1898, in West Newton

56. CHESTER B[8] FULLER, (*William E[7], Josiah[6], Josiah[5], Josiah[4]. Josiah[3], Jeremiah[2], John[1]*), b ——, m ——. Helen Cashman
   Resides Waltham
   Children
71   Muriel[9], b ——

57. HERMAN DEAN[8] FULLER, (*George G[7], Josiah[6], Josiah[5], Josiah[4], Josiah[3], Jeremiah[2], John[1]*), b Apr 4 1879, in Lexington, m Sept 21, 1904, Aurelia W[4], Fuller, No 101 10th Group John of Ipswich line
   Resides at Waltham
   Children
72   Doris Madeline[9], b July 3, 1905
73   Richard Irving[9], b Nov 7, 1908

SOME DESCENDANTS

OF

JOHN FULLER of LYNN

AMERICAN FULLER GENEALOGY.

SOME DESCENDANTS OF JOHN FULLER OF LYNN.

"John Fuller of Lynn came to Boston in 1630." (H. W. Brainard's Mss.) Pope in his "Pioneers of Massachusetts" says John Fuller, joiner, Boston, bought land in Lynn, 9 (6) 1639, to be paid for by Edward Fuller of Olney, Bucks, England, and refers to will of Edward Fuller, probated Sept. 20, 1656. Pope also states that John testified in a case in Salem, 25 (2) 1651, aged 30 years. Brainard's Mss. states that John Fuller was Representative from Lynn in 1655, and again in 1674-1678; was Lieutenant in King Phillip's war, and refers to the Essex Historical Collections, Vol. 6, and the New England Historical and Genealogical Register, Vol. 50, as his authorities.

The published Vital Records of Lynn give date of his death Apr. 6, 1695, and his marriage in 1646 to Elizabeth Farrington, b. 1627, dau. of Edward Farrington, b. 1588, in Olney, England.

Children, born in Lynn.

1. John[2], Jan. 3, 1647; d. June 29, 1666.
2. Thomas[2], b. Jan. 15, 1649; d. about Aug. 14, 1666.
3. Elizabeth[2], b. "the last of May," 1652; m. Apr. 10, 1683, John Severus, and had John[3], Edward[3], William[3], Elizabeth[3], and Joseph[3].
4. **Edward[2]**, b. Jan. 12, 1654; m. Hannah Lewis.
5. **Elisha[2]**, b. Feb. 5, 1657; m. Elizabeth Walden.
6. **Joseph[2]**, b. Nov. 1, 1661; m. Rebecca Belcher.
7. **Benjamin[2]**, b. Dec., 1665; m. Susannah Ballard.

In the following arrangement, the four sons of John[1] Fuller, of Lynn, who married, are made heads of four Groups.

Each Group contains descendants of one of the sons, arranged by generations, and each descendant has an individual number, relative to the Group.

FIRST GROUP

SECOND GENERATION

4. EDWARD[2] FULLER (*John[1]*) b Jan 12, 1654, in Lynn, d there Mar 30, 1743, m May 12, 1686, Hannah Lewis

Children, recorded in Lynn

1   **John[3]**, b Jan 26, 1686-7, m. 1, Sarah Newhall, m 2, Hepzibah Hathorn; m 3, Hannah Prince
2   Mary[3], b Sept 18, 1689
3   Rebecca[3], b Dec 13, 1692
4   Edward[3], b May 29, 1695, d Mar 8, 1720-21
5   Hannah[3], b June 24, 1698
6   **Nathaniel[3]**, b Jan 5, 1700-1; m Anna Burrill
7   Abigail[3], b Apr 6, 1703
8   **Joseph[3]**, b Sept. 24, 1707, m Eunice Potter

THIRD GENERATION.

1. JOHN[3] FULLER, (*Edward[2], John[1]*), b. Jan 26, 1686-7, in Lynn; d there June 16, 1754, aged 67 y 4 m. 20 d ; m 1, Apr 17, 1712, Sarah Newhall, who d Dec 14, 1734; m 2, Jan 31, 1739-40, Hepzibah Hathorn, m 3, Sept. 15, 1746, Hannah Prince

He is called Capt John Fuller in records of 2d and 3d marriages

Children, as recorded in Lynn

John and Sarah had

9   Jonathan[4], b Dec 7, 1713, m 1, Sarah Lewis, Mar 2, 1748-9, who d July 1, 1751, m 2, Apr 15, 1755, Mary Wyman
10 Mary[4], b Aug 4, 1716
11 **Ignatius[4]**, b May 30, 1718, m Esther Newhall
12 **Edward[4]**, b Feb 4, 1721-2; m. Ruth Shepard.
13 Solomon[4], b July 10, 1724, d Nov 11, 1724
14 James[4], b Aug 9, 1726, probably d. young

Capt John and Hannah had

15 Melicent[4], b Sept 7, 1748
16 **James[4]**, b June 7, 1752

6. NATHANIEL[3] FULLER, (*Edward[2], John[1]*), b Jan 5, 1700, in Lynn, d June 26, 1730, in Boston, m May 9, 1723, Anna Burrill
　Children, as recorded in Lynn
17　Margaret[4], b Feb 5, 1724-5
18　**Nathaniel[4]**, b Mar. 12, 1726-7, m Hannah Mansfield
19　Samuel[4], b Jan 21, 1729-30; d Sept 5, 1743, in Chelsea

8. JOSEPH[3] FULLER. (*Edward[2], John[1]*), b Sept 24, 1707, in Lynn, d there May 29, 1766, m Dec 23, 1735, Eunice Potter
　He is called Capt Joseph His will mentions wife, son Joseph and daus Sarah and Lydia
　Children, as recorded in Lynn
20　Sarah[4], b July 27, 1737, m Apr 10, 1755, Col Ezra Newhall of Saugus
21.　Lydia[4] b Apr 8, 1740
22　**Joseph[4]**, b Mar 30, 1748, m Sarah Laith

FOURTH GENERATION.

11. IGNATIUS[4] FULLER, (*John[3], Edward[2], John[1]*), b May 30, 1718, in Lynn, d ——; m Dec 1, 1741, Esther Newhall, he dying: she m 2, Nov 18, 1758, Edward Brock
　Children, recorded in Lynn
23　**Jonathan[5]**, b June 9, 1742; m Mrs Hannah Fuller.
24　Sarah[5], b Feb 23, 1747-8, d Jan 17, 1754
25　Ignatius[5], b Aug 11, 1753

12. EDWARD[4] FULLER, (*John[3], Edward[2], John[1]*), b Feb 4, 1721-2(?), in Lynn, d Dec 12, 1802(?), in Lancaster, m Oct 24. 1745, Ruth Shepard
　Edward Fuller of Lynn bought of Daniel Houghton of Lancaster, 50 acres of land with buildings, in the southerly part of Lancaster, Apr 3, 1771, and also a tract containing 27 acres, both in that part of Lancaster now forming the town of Clinton
　In his will, made July 18, 1795, no mention is made of his wife, and the legatees are sons James, John, Edward, Solomon, and Ignatius, heirs of daughter Hannah Wallis, daughters Alice Warner, Sarah Taylor, and Sally Fuller
　Children, as recorded in Lynn
26　Hannah[5], b Mar 15, 1746-7, d before 1795, m May 10, 1769, Robert Wallis
27　Alice[5], b Aug 22, 1748, m ——, —— Warner.
28　**James[5]**, b Jan 3, 1750, m Sarah ——.
29　Sarah[5], b. Feb 17, 1755, m ——, —— Taylor
11

30 **Edward**[5], b ——, m Susannah Maynard   These mentioned in his will, succession not known
31 Solomon[5], b ——
32 John[5], b ——
33 **Ignatius**[5], b Oct 29, 1763, m Anna Reed
34 Sally[5], b ——, unmarried 1795

16. JAMES[4] FULLER, (*John*[3], *Edward*[2], *John*[1]), b June 7, 1752, in Lynn; d Jan 26, 1825, in Lynn, m Dec 11, 1774, Mary Martin
   Children·
35 James Prince[5], b Aug 5, 1775, bapt Aug 20, 1775, d Mar 26, 1787, in Marblehead
36 John[5], b Nov 1777; d Dec 26, 1777
37 Mary[5], b June 21, 1783; d Sept 6, 1784
38 James Prince[5], 2d, bapt. Mar 9, 1788
39 Sarah[5], bapt July 11, 1790

18. NATHANIEL[4] FULLER, (*Nathaniel*[3], *Edward*[2], *John*[1]), b Mar 12, 1726-7, in Lynn, d there May 22, 1799, aged 73, m Dec. 13, 1753, Hannah Mansfield
   Children, as recorded to Nathaniel and Hannah
40 Anna[5], b Oct 1, 1754
41 Samuel[5], b Sept 25, 1756
42 Mary[5], b Dec 3, 1758
43 **Nathaniel**[5], b Jan 29, 1762, m Abigail Lindsay
44 Abigail[5], bapt Sept 22, 1771
45 Hannah[5], bapt Sept 22, 1771
46 **Jonathan**[5], bapt Sept 22, 1771
47 William[5], bapt Sept 22, 1771
48 **Joseph**[5], bapt Sept 13, 1772, m Deborah Whipple
49 Daniel[5], bapt May 15, 1774
50 Peggy[5], bapt July 28, 1776
51 Rebecca[5], bapt May 24, 1778

22. JOSEPH[4] FULLER, (*Joseph*[3], *Edward*[2] *John*[1]), b Nov 30, 1748, in Lynn, d Nov 19, 1829, aged 81, m Oct 31, 1771, Sarah Laith, who d Sept 19, 1819
   Children, recorded at Lynn, to Joseph and Sarah
52 **Joseph**[5] b Mar 29, 1772, m Eunice Breed
53 **Oliver**[5], b Aug 21 1776, m Rebecca Chase
54 Sarah[5] b Aug 25, 1779
55 Lydia[5], b Dec 22, 1782
56 Betsey[5], b ——, 1787, d Aug 3, 1787, aged 4 mos
57 Betsey[5], 2d, b May 12, 1788, d Nov 23, 1794

FIFTH GENERATION.

23. JONATHAN⁵ FULLER, (*Ignatius⁴, John³, Edward², John¹*), b June 9, 1742, in Lynn, d ——, m Int Oct 13, 1765, with Mrs Hannah Fuller
Children
58 Sally⁶, bapt Apr 19, 1772
59 Esther⁶, bapt Nov 14, 1773
60 Ignatius⁶, bapt Dec 31, 1775
61 Susanna⁶, bapt Sept 13, 1778

28. JAMES⁵ FULLER, (*Edward⁴, John³, Edward², John¹*), b June 3, 1750, in Lynn; d July 23, 1831, in Lancaster, aged 81 years, m ——, Sarah ——, who d Nov 21, 1824
James Fuller was a soldier in the Revolutionary War
In his will made Apr 15, 1831, no mention of wife is made The legatees are daughters Sally and Esther, who are given the farm he lives on, in the southerly part of Lancaster (now Clinton) Legacies also to granddaughter Emeline Smith, dau Nancy, wife of Amos Sawyer, dau Mary Whitcomb, wife of John Goss, and to grandson Joseph Fuller.
James Fuller's first purchase of land in Lancaster (now Clinton) was 24 acres and 120 rods on the north end of "Clamshell Pond," in 1786
Children, from his will and records, succession not known
62 Nancy⁶, bapt. Nov. 9, 1777, m. Amos Sawyer
63 Sally⁶, b ——
64 Esther⁶, bapt May 20, 1781
65 Betsey⁶, bapt Apr 9, 1786, d. Nov 27, 1789
66 A dau ——, b ——, m —— Smith, and had dau Emeline
67 **James⁶**, b ——; m Sally ——
68 Mary Whitcomb⁶, b ——, m John Goss, 8 children

30. EDWARD⁵ FULLER, (*Edward⁴, John³, Edward², John¹*), b ——, d ——, m Oct 13, 1803, Susannah Maynard, of Berlin
Edward and Susannah Fuller were admitted to the Lancaster church from Berlin, Nov 11, 1804
These children as recorded were.
69 Caroline⁶, b Aug 1, 1804, bapt Nov 11, 1804
70. Joseph Shepard⁶, b Oct 4, 1805, bapt Nov 3, 1805; d Oct 28, 1806.
71 Mary Ann⁶, b. July 2, 1807, bapt Aug 30, 1807
72 Elsie⁶, b May 24, 1809, bapt July 9, 1809
73 James⁶, b May 28, 1811
74 Abner⁶, b Sept 19, 1813

33. IGNATIUS⁵ FULLER, (*Edward⁴, John³, Edward², John¹*), b , according to his own statement in application for pension, Oct. 29, 1763, d

Dec 15, 1856, aged 94, according to statements of descendants, in Peru, N Y , m Int Pub Mar. 3, 1787, with Anna Reed of Sterling, who d May 13, 1834, aged 65 y 1 m 13 d   In his statement for application for a pension he refers to 'one of his brothers, Edward Fuller "

Ignatius enlisted twice from Lancaster for service in the Revolutionary War   After the war he removed to Fitzwilliam, N H , thence after 4 years to Barre, Vt , thence after 14 years to Burlington, thence to Williston, thence to Milton, Vt , where he lived 4 years, and finally to Peru, N Y , where, in Jan , 1842, he had lived 23 years

Children ·

75.   Betsey[6], b July 27, 1788, in Sterling
76   Emery[6], b July 11, 1790, in Lancaster, m Hannah Town
77   Ann[6], b Sept 9, 1792, in Lancaster, d there Nov 9, 1794
78   Rebecca B [6], b Aug 7, 1795. in Fitzwilliam, N H
79   Sally[6], b Jan 11, 1797, in Fitzwilliam
80   Elsie[6], b July 11, 1799, d Mar 11, 1852; m ——, —— Wells
81   James[6], b Aug. 22, 1801 ; m 1, ——, m 2, Almira Mills
82   Hosea[6], b Feb 5, 1804, m Desire Church
83   Clara Reed, b Apr 5, 1806, in Barre, Vt , m. James Warford
84   Mary[6], b Apr 1, 1808
85   Lucius[6], b Oct 7, 1811 , m ——
86   Amanda[6], b June 30, 1813, d Nov 4, 1842
87   William[6], b May 9, 1815

43. NATHANIEL[5] FULLER, (*Nathaniel[4]*, *Nathaniel[3]*, *Edward[2]*, *John[1]*), b. Jan 29, 1762, in Lynn, d June 25, 1800 , m Feb 1, 1787, Abigail Lindsay, who d Oct 15, 1823

Children

88   Joseph[6], b Apr 4, 1788, d Sept 15, 1793
89   Nathaniel[6], b Sept 26, 1789, d May 26, 1807
90   Abigail[6], b May 27, 1791
91   Joseph[6], 2d, b Aug 1, 1794 , d Dec 2, 1877, aged 83 y 4 m 3 d
92   Huldah[6], b Mar 12 1798
93   Hannah[6], b Sept. 8, 1800

46. JONATHAN[5] FULLER, (*Nathaniel[4]*, *Nathaniel[3]*, *Edward[2]*, *John[1]*), bapt Sept 22, 1771, in Lynn , d ——, m Int Pub Dec 15, 1793, with Anna Johns, of Salem

Children, recorded in Lynn

94   Polly[6], b Apr 15, 1795
95   Nathaniel[6], b Mar 25, 1803 , m Sarah Bartlett
96   Jonathan[6], b Mar. 15, 1804

48. JOSEPH[5] FULLER (*Nathaniel[4]*, *Nathaniel[3]*, *Edward[2]*, *John[1]*), bapt Sept 13, 1772, d ——, m Sept 25, 1802, Deborah Whipple

Children, recorded to Joseph and Deborah in Lynn
97   Nathaniel[6], b Mar 25, 1803(?)
98   **William**[6], b Apr 28, 1807
99   Hannah Felt[6], b Jan 5, 1810
100. Daniel[6], b Mar 8, 1814

52. JOSEPH[5] FULLER, (*Joseph*[4], *Joseph*[3], *Edward*[2], *John*[1]), b Mar 29, 1772, in Lynn, d there Sept 11, 1815, aged 43 y 5 m 13 d, m Mar 18, 1795, Eunice Breed, who d. June 7, 1834, aged 60 years
  Children recorded to Joseph 3d and Eunice
101 **James**[6] b Sept 11, 1797, m Betsey Rich
102 **Joseph Madison**[6], b Dec. 20, 1801, m 1, Sally G Lye, m 2 Mary C Buffum
103 Maria[3], b Aug 5, 1803, d Feb 19, 1804
104 Maria Augusta[3], b Dec 9, 1806, d Jan 19, 1831

53. OLIVER[5] FULLER, (*Joseph*[4], *Joseph*[3], *Edward*[2], *John*[1]), b Aug 21, 1776, in Lynn, d there Feb 24, 1848, aged 72, m Aug 20, 1801, Rebecca Chase who d May 9 1827
  Children, recorded in Lynn
105 Oliver[6], b May 21 or 31(?), 1802, d June 13 1803
106 Rebecca[6], b Mar 18, 1804, d Oct 18, 1804
107 Rebecca Chase[6], b Dec 21, 1805
108 Oliver[6], 2d, b Aug 20, 1807
109 Sally[6], b Feb 2, 1813, d Oct 20, 1813

SIXTH GENERATION.

67. JAMES[6] FULLER, (*James*[5], *Edward*[4], *John*[3], *Edward*[2], *John*[1]), b ——, probably in Lancaster (part now called Clinton), d ——, m —— Sally ——
110 Joseph[7], b July 5, 1809, "son of Sally" (Lancaster V R), probably d young
111 Joseph[7], 2d(?), b about 1811 "Mar 11, 1861, Joseph Fuller, aged 50, b in Lancaster, to James and Sally, m Susan Peabody Cunningham" (Clinton Records)

76. EMERY[6] FULLER, (*Ignatius*[5], *Edward*[4], *John*[3], *Edward*[2], *John*[1]), b July 11, 1790, in Lancaster, d ——, 1840, in Barre, Vt, m ——, Hannah Town
  He was a freighter between Boston, Barre, and Montpelier, Vt
  Children, probably all born in Barre, Vt
112 Danforth Reed[7], b May 20, 1813
113 Clara[7], b May 12, 1815
114 **Enos T.**[7], b Oct 20, 1816; m Marietta Walker

115   Mark[7], b Dec 20, 1818
116   **David L.[7]**, b Jan 28, 1821; m Mrs Selma Ellis (Stevens) Stickney.
117.   Martha[7], b Aug 14, 1823; d ——, 1846, in Chicago
118.   Hosea Randall[7], b Mar 12, 1825
119   Rebecca Augusta[7], b Sept 24, 1827; d ——, 1853, in Barre, Vt
120.   Loomis Palmer[7], b. Nov. 23, 1829.
121   William Danforth[7], b Dec 24, 1834
122   Ellen Jane[7], b Dec 18, 1836, d 1890, in Barre, Vt

81. JAMES[6] FULLER, (*Ignatius[5], Edward[4], John[3], Edward[2], John[1]*), b Aug 22, 1801, in Barre, Vt, d ——, 1862, m 1, ——, m 2, Almira Mills

Children
123   Louise[7], b ——, m —— Stafford, and had Bertrand[8], Galen[8], James[8], and Leon[8]
124   **James W.[7]**, b ——, m ——
Children by second wife
125   **Edward[7]**, b Aug, 1838, m Elizabeth Bissell
126   Royal[7], b ——, d young
127   **Henry[7]**,   ⎫ twins, b ——, ⎰ m Helen Day
128   Henrietta[7], ⎭   ⎱ m 1, Isaac Allen, m 2, Nathan Weaver, lives in Peru, N Y Children Seth S[8], Almira[8], George[8], and Benjamin[8]

82. HOSEA[6] FULLER, (*Ignatius[5], Edward[4], John[3], Edward[2], John[1]*), b Feb 5, 1804, in Barre, Vt, d Mar 23, 1869, aged 63, m Desire Church.
Children
129   **Hosea B.[7]**, b Oct 4, 1852, m Kate M Ferris
130   John C[7], b Nov 30, 1854
131   Byron W[7], b Apr 16, 1858, resides in Peru, N Y
132   Anna L[7], b July 8, 1860
133   Ignatius I[7], b Aug 11, 1862

85. LUCIUS[6] FULLER, (*Ignatius[5], Edward[4], John[3], Edward[2], John[1]*), b. Oct 7, 1810, d Aug 29, 1877, m ——
Children.
134   Mary Daggett[7], b Mar 5, 1839, m. ——, —— Ayres
135   Jane[7], b. Apr. 8, 1842.

95. NATHANIEL[6] FULLER, (*Jonathan[5], Nathaniel[4], Nathaniel[3], Edward[2] John[1]*), b Mar 25 1803, in Lynn, d ——, m Apr 8, 1827 Sarah Bartlett
Children, recorded in Lynn

136   George[7], b June 2, 1831, d Jan 7, 1855, in Lynn; m Dec 31, 1852, Sarah Burgess

98. WILLIAM[6] FULLER, (*Joseph[5], Nathaniel[4], Nathaniel[3], Edward[2], John[1]*), b Apr 28, 1807, in Lynn, d ——, m Dec 14, 1828, Miriam Proctor Story
   Children, recorded in Lynn
137   Elvira Frances[7], b Sept. 9, 1832
138   Daniel William[7], b May 25, 1838

101. JAMES[6] FULLER, (*Joseph[5], Joseph[4], Joseph[3], Edward[2], John[1]*), b Sept 11, 1797, in Lynn; d Jan 26, 1825, m Nov 18, 1818, Betsey Rich who d Aug 15, 1835
   Children ·
139   Adaline Elizabeth[7], b Sept 12, 1819, m Int. Pub Nov. 24, 1842, with Amos P Tapley of Boston
140   Mary Ellen[7], b Sept 1, 1821; m Int. Pub June 12, 1842, with John C Abbott, of St Louis, Mo

102. JOSEPH MADISON[6] FULLER, (*Joseph[5], Joseph[4], Joseph[3], Edward[2], John[1]*), b Dec 20, 1801, in Lynn, d there Aug 10, 1871, aged 69 y 7 m 2 d ; m 1, Sept 11, 1828, Sally G Lye; m 2, Int Pub Feb 16, 1842 Mary C Buffum, who d Oct 20, 1865
   Children, recorded at Lynn
141   Charles[7], b July 21, 1843
142. Mary A [7], b. ——, d Dec 2, 1846, aged 1 y 7 m
143   Mary Ellen[7], b Sept 11, 1848, m June 25, 1874, James T Boyd
144   Ada Tapley[7], b ——, m June 25, 1874, George L Stowell

SEVENTH GENERATION.

114. ENOS T[7] FULLER, (*Emery[6], Ignatius[5], Edward[4], John[3], Edward[2], John[1]*), b Oct 20, 1816, in Barre, Vt., d ——, 1898. in Mechanicsville, N Y ; m Jan, 1848, Marietta Walker, b Barre Vt., Sept 20. 1820
   He was superintendent of the iron foundry at Mechanicsville
   Children .
145   John W [8], b Nov 4, 1846
146. Martha[8], b July 27, 1848, m A Patterson
147   Aurora W [8], b May 2, 1850; m N S Robinson
148   Ida Elnora[8], b Aug 7, 1852, d Jan 15, 1853

116. DAVID L[7] FULLER, (*Emery[6], Ignatius[5], Edward[4], John[3], Edward[2], John[1]*), b Jan 28 1821, in Barre, Vt ; d Dec 4, 1912, at Montpelier Vt , m Oct 31, 1847, Mrs. Selina Ellis (Stevens) Stickney, b Jan 6. 1823, at Montpelier, d. there June 6, 1897.
   He was a merchant

Children

149 **Charles H.**[8], b May 27, 1852, m Laura Brackett Hibbard
150 Eva Julia[8], b Aug 14, 1853, d May 10, 1872; unmarried.

124. JAMES W[7] FULLER, (*James*[6], *Ignatius*[5], *Edward*[4], *John*[3], *Edward*[2], *John*[1]), b ——, d Aug 1908, in Los Angeles, Cal , m ——
Children
151. Henry[8] b ——
152 Cora Vashti[8], b ——, resided in Sharpsville, Pa (1907)

125. EDWARD[7] FULLER (*James*[6], *Ignatius*[5], *Edward*[4], *John*[3], *Edward*[2], *John*[1]), b Aug —, 1838, m ——; d Oct. —, 1896 in ——, m ——, 1862, Elizabeth Bissell, who d Aug , 1908
Children
153 **Hobart T.**[8], b Apr , 1868
154 Nellie[8], b ——, m Ezra Day and resides at Valcour, N. Y

127. HENRY[7] FULLER, (*James*[6] *Ignatius*[5], *Edward*[4], *John*[3], *Edward*[2], *John*[1]), b ——, d ——, m ——, Helen Day
Resides at Redlands, California
Children
155 Percy[8], b ——, m ——
156 Harry[8], b ——, m ——
157 Leslie[8], b ——, m ——
158 Charles[8], b ——, m ——

129. HOSEA B[7]. FULLER. (*Hosea*[6], *Ignatius*[5], *Edward*[4], *John*[3], *Edward*[2], *John*[1]), b Oct 4, 1852, in Peru, N Y , d June 29, 1911, in Holyoke; m May 24, 1893, Kate M Ferris, who survived him
Children.
159 Raymond S[8], b Sept 9, 1895
160 Laura E[8], b Feb 15 1898, in Chicopee
161 Herbert H[8], b June 4, 1907

EIGHTH GENERATION.

149. CHARLES H[8] FULLER, (*David L*[7], *Emery*[6], *Ignatius*[5], *Edward*[4], *John*[3], *Edward*[2], *John*[1]), b May 27, 1852, m Dec 23, 1875, at Brooklyn, N Y, Laura Brackett Hibbard
He resides in Baltimore, Md
Children
162 Eva Laura[9], b June 2, 1877.
163 Kate Hibbard[9], b Nov. 15, 1880, m June 30, 1902, Isaac D Taylor, of Guthrie, Okla , and had Russell[10], b Sept 16, 1903, and Charles[10], b Dec 25, 1904

153. HOBART T[8]. FULLER, (*Edward[7], James[6], Ignatius[5], Edward[4], John[3], Edward[2], John[1]*), b Apr 1868, m ——, Libbie ——.

He is the proprietor of the Prospect Hill Stock Farm at Peru, N Y
Children

164   Ruth Helen[9], b ——, 1895
165   Florence E.[9], b ——, 1897
166   George D[9], b ——, 1902

SECOND GROUP

SECOND GENERATION.

ELISHA[2] FULLER, AND SOME OF HIS DESCENDANTS

5. ELISHA[2] FULLER, (*John[1]*), b Feb 5, 1657. in Lynn, d ——, m Sept 10, 1690, Elizabeth Walden

Children, recorded in Lynn, to Elisha and Elizabeth

1　Thomas[3], b July 4, 1691, m Abigail Gustin.

2　Sarah[3], b Oct 9, 1692

I have found no further records of this family

THIRD GROUP

SECOND GENERATION.

JOSEPH⁴ FULLER, AND SOME OF HIS DESCENDANTS

6. JOSEPH² FULLER, (*John¹*), b Nov 1, 1661, in Lynn, d ——, m Nov 30, 1687, Rebecca Belcher

Children, recorded in Lynn, to Joseph and Rebecca

1   Joseph³, b Aug 14, 1688

The Lynn Vital Records give the m of "Jesper" Fuller, Nov 3, 1687, to Rebecca Belcher, and the birth to Joseph and Rebecca —— There is no other mention of "Jesper" Fuller

The New England Register says "Joseph Fuller, shipwright, m Rebecca Belcher in Lynn, Nov 30, 1687 He settled in Boston " I find no mention of them in the Boston Vital Records

H W Brainard suggests that the Joseph Fuller of Fairfield, Ct, Public Records, Vol 1738, p 458, may be Joseph² Fuller His will, dated Oct 3, 1738 presented Feb 2, 1738-9, mentions sons Thomas, Edward, and daughters Mary, Catherine, and Ruth, who is deceased He was of Norwalk, Ct Mr Brainard also suggests comparison with record of Joseph Fuller of Chilmark, Mass, who may be Joseph² Joseph Fuller of Chilmark m June 13, 1719, Martha Hathaway of Falmouth   There are no family records of them either at Falmouth or in the Chilmark Vital Records

FOURTH GROUP

SECOND GENERATION.

BENJAMIN[2] FULLER, AND SOME OF HIS DESCENDANTS

7. BENJAMIN[2] FULLER, (*John*[1]), b Dec 16, 1665, in Lynn, d there
Aug 3, 1750, m Nov 5, 1690, Susanna Ballard
Children, recorded in Lynn, to Benjamin and Susanna
1 Abigail[3], b Jan 14, 1692-3
2 Susanna[3], b July 29, 1695
3 Mary[3], b Aug 11, 1698
4 Ruth[3], b Mar 21, 1700-1
5 John[3], b Aug 21, 1703
6 Elizabeth[3], b Feb 28, 1705-6
7 Benjamin[3], b Sept 11, 1708
8 Samuel[3], b Nov 24, 1711
I have found no further records of this family

JOHN FULLER of IPSWICH,

AND SOME OF HIS DESCENDANTS.

AMERICAN FULLER GENEALOGY.

JOHN FULLER OF IPSWICH AND SOME OF HIS DESCENDANTS

JOHN[1] FULLER, aged about 15 years, came to America on the ship Abigail, May 4, 1635, from England, with his brother William, aged about 25 years

William Fuller, according to Pope's "Pioneers of Massachusetts,' settled in Ipswich, proprietor in 1635, appointed gunsmith by the General Court in 1637, married 1639, sold house and land 1639, removed to Concord; from June 2, 1641, kept the mill, child Hannah b 8 (6) 1641, wife Elizabeth d 24 (5) 1642 Perhaps he is the William Fuller, locksmith, who bought land at Hampton 9 (12) 1647"

Other authorities call him 'William of Hampton" and state that he died childless

John settled in Ipswich and married Elizabeth Emerson, daughter of Thomas Emerson, who came to America in 1638, settled in Ipswich, and died there May 1, 1681, aged 81

John[1] Fuller removed to Salisbury about 1639, but returned to Ipswich before 1648, and was town surveyor in 1663, commissioner in 1664, and owned land near Rocky Hill. He died June 4, 1666, at Ipswich, and his widow married. between 1666 and 1672, Thomas Perrin His will was proved Sept 25 1666, and names sons John and William, "who have been sufficiently supplied by their uncle." daughters Susannah and Elizabeth,—"their grandfather hath early given them a portion"; names wife, sons James, Thomas, Nathaniel, Joseph, daughter Sarah, and a child unborn to have one seventh each, with wife and son James as executors

  2 **John[2]**, b about 1643, m Rachel Brabrick
  3 **William[2]**, b after 1645, m Susannah (Perkins) Boswell

Both the above were living in Hampton in 1689, when the estate of their brother Thomas was settled

4   **James²**, b about 1647, m Mary Ring
5   Thomas² b ——; d unmarried 1689 estate settled Sept 24, 1689
6   Susannah², b Aug 4. 1650 m Oct 26, 1671, William Story
7   Elizabeth², b May 31 1652, d June 30, 1715, m Mar 23, 1672 James King, b in England
8   **Joseph²** b ——, 1658, m Mary Wood
9   Sarah², b ——, m Nov, 1679, Nathaniel Hovey
10   **Nathaniel²**, b Jan. 1663, m Mary Jackson

SECOND GENERATION.

JOHN² FULLER, (*John¹*), b about 1643, in Ipswich, d about 1719, m Rachel Brabrick, probably daughter of John Brabrick

He probably settled in Hampton, N H

Vol 1, p 415, "Provincial Papers of N H." mentions John Fuller of Hampton, bound in the sum of £100, that Rachel, his wife, appear on account of witchcraft, 1680

Children

11   John³, b Jan 12, 1678(?), d Jan 19, 1715
12   Benoni², b Jan 12, 1678, d Feb 25, 1761, aged 83   He lived near Joseph L Marston, in North Hampton, N H
13   **James³**, b Mar 27, 1679, m Mary ——
14   Elizabeth³, b ——
15   Rachel³, b ——.
16   **Thomas³**, b Aug 27, 1695, m Hannah Chase

WILLIAM² FULLER, (*John¹*) b after 1645 in Ipswich, d ——; m ——, Widow Susannah (Perkins) Boswell, dau of Isaac Perkins

He is supposed to have settled in Hampton, N H

Children:

17   Abigail³, b Mar 10, 1690 in Ipswich

JAMES² FULLER. (*John¹*), b about 1647, d June 21, 1725, at Ipswich, m Oct 20, 1672, in Ipswich, Mary Ring. who d Oct 16, 1732, at Ipswich, aged 85 years

His will, dated Dec 19, 1723, was proved July 5, 1725

Children, born in Ipswich

18   **James³**, b Dec 2, 1673, m Phebe ——
19   Mary³, b May 30, 1675
20   John³, b Feb 20, 1676; probably d before 1723, not mentioned in his father's will
21   Elizabeth³, b Feb 25, 1678, published to Nathaniel Smith, Feb 20, 1702

22 Daniel[1], b Feb 24, 1680, living in 1700 in Ipswich, probably d before 1723, not mentioned in his father's will

23 **Nathaniel[1]**, b Feb 18, 1682, m 1 Mary Potter, m 2, Widow Elizabeth Perkins

24 Dorothy[1], b Dec 18, 1684, probably published July 21, 1715, to Josiah Stone

25 Susannah[1] b ——, published Sept 24, 1709, to Stephen Bennett

26 Hannah[1], b ——

The last two children not given in Ipswich Records—mentioned in New England Register, Vol 53

JOSEPH[1] FULLER, (*John[1]*), b ——, 1658, in Ipswich, d there Aug 22 1731, m Oct 1686, Mary Wood, b Oct 31, 1653, dau of Isaiah and Mercy (Thompson) Wood She died before her husband

Apr 1, 1680, Joseph Fuller lived with Simon Wood, brother of his wife Was sergeant of militia in Capt Turner's Co in the Falls fight in 1676

In Mar, 1692-3, the selectmen of Ipswich set off a lot to Joseph Fuller which he sold to his brother Nathaniel He was a carpenter by trade

In 1696 he bought of Samuel Bush his Suffield Proprietor's grant Nov 1, 1731, William Fuller was appointed administrator of the estate of Joseph Fuller, deceased No widow mentioned The administrator reported that "Joseph the eldest son hath acquitted ye estate by an instrument upon record at Springfield, to my satisfaction " The property was divided equally between William, John, Ebenezer Jacob, and Daniel Feb 26, 1742, Ebenezer and Jacob signed receipts for personal property

Children, born at Ipswich

27 **Joseph[1]**, b Aug 13, 1690, m 1, Bathsheba Hanchett, m 2, Elizabeth Hutchins

28 Thomas[1], b Apr 6, 1692, d young

29 **William[1]**, b Mar 7, 1694, m Sarah Waite

30 John[1], b May 16, 1698, d Sept 29, 1699

31 **John[1]**, } twins, b Apr { m 1, Mary Howard ; m 2, Hannah Lord
32 Benjamin[1], } 22, 1701, { d June, 1703

33 **Daniel[1]**, b Jan 30, 1702, m Anna Doliver

34 Benjamin[1], b Aug 20, 1705; d July 22, 1722

35 **Ebenezer[1]**, b Jan 10, 1707, m Mary Gritsman

36 **Jacob[1]**, b Mar 22, 1712, m Ann Harris

NATHANIEL[1] FULLER, (*John[1]*), b Jan 1663, in Ipswich, d there 1719, m Int Pub Oct 14, 1708, with Mary Jackson of Rowley She was published to her second husband, Samuel Ayres, June 23, 1721 Mary Fuller appointed administratrix, Nov 5, 1719

Children, born at Ipswich

12

37 Nathaniel³, b Nov 28, 1709, probably d young
38 Mary³, b —— Dec 28, 1724, "being above 15 years of age, she chose her step-father, Samuel Ayres, and mother, Mary Ayres, as her guardians."
39 Elizabeth³, bapt Dec 22, 1713, probably d young
40 Thomas³, bapt May 29, 1715, probably d young
41 **Nathaniel⁴**, bapt Jan 7, 1717 (Samuel and Mary Ayres appointed his guardians), m 1, Elizabeth Ireland, m 2, Deliverance Burke, m 3, Deborah Millet

GROUP ARRANGEMENT

In the group arrangement for descendants of John[1] Fuller of Ipswich, the eleven sons of the third generation who married and had children are made heads of eleven groups

Each group contains descendants of one of these eleven sons, arranged by generations

Each descendant has an individual number relative to the group

Individual No	Group No	LINEAGE OF HEAD OF GROUP		Date of Birth
13	1	James[3] *John*[2], *John*[1]		Mar. 22, 1679
16	2	Thomas[3], *John*[2], *John*[1]		Aug 27, 1695
18	3	James[3], *James*[2], *John*[1]		Dec 2, 1673
23	4	Nathaniel[3], *James*[2], *John*[1].		Feb 18, 1682
41	5	Nathaniel[3], *Nathaniel*[2], *John*[1]	bapt	Jan 7, 1717
27	6	Joseph[3], *Joseph*[2], *John*[1]		Aug 13, 1690
29	7	William[3], *Joseph*[2], *John*[1]		Mar. 7, 1694
31	8	John[3], *Joseph*[2], *John*[1]		Apr 22, 1701
33	9	Daniel[3], *Joseph*[2], *John*[1]		Jan 30, 1702
35	10	Ebenezer[3], *Joseph*[2], *John*[1]		Jan 10, 1707
36	11	Jacob[3], *Joseph*[2], *John*[1]		Mar 28, 1712

FIRST GROUP

THIRD GENERATION.

JAMES[3] FULLER, JOHN[2] and some of his descendants

13. JAMES[3] FULLER, (John[2], John[1]), b. Mar 27, 1679, in Hampton, N H, d ——, m ——, Mary ——

Children

1 James[4], b Dec 2, 1704, in Hampton
2 **Joseph[4]**, b. ——, in Hampton, m Joanna Seavey.
3 John[4], b Mar 4, 1711, in Hampton
4 Mary[4], b Aug 17, 1713 in Hampton, m Ithamar Seavey, and resided in Rochester, N H, in 1747
5 Elizabeth[4], b June 28, 1715, in Rye, N H, m Henry Seavey and had Joseph[5] bapt 1744 Joseph[5], 2d, b 1746, Catherine[5], b ——, and Olive[5], b 1748
6 **Jeremiah[4]**, b Sept 25, 1717, in Rye, N H., m Mary Scadgel
7 Lovey[4], b May 14, 1721, in Rye, m Oct 26 1747, William Wormwood

NOTE—That portion of Hampton in which James[3] Fuller settled was later annexed to Rye

FOURTH GENERATION

2. JOSEPH[4] FULLER (James[3], John[2], John[1]), b ——, in Hampton, N H, d ——, m Mar 8 1733, Joanna Seavey

Children, born in Rye, N H.

8. Elizabeth[5], b Sept 14, 1733, d young.
9 Joanna[5], b Dec 6, 1734, d young
10 Mary[5], b Aug 5, 1736
11 Joanna[5], b ——, 1737
12 Joseph[5], b Nov. 4, 1738
13 Elizabeth[5], b Sept 25, 1740
14 James[5], b ——, 1743
15 Hannah[5], b ——, 1747
16 Rachel[5], b ——, 1749
17 David[5], b ——, 1751
18. Sarah[5], b ——, 1753

19   Olly⁵, b ——, 1755

6. Jeremiah⁴ Fuller (*James³, John², John¹*), b Sept 25, 1717, in
Rye N H , d ——, m July 26, 1745, Mary Scadgel
  Children, born in Rye, N H
20   **George⁵**, b May 24, 1746
21   Richard⁵, b July 21, 1747
22   Sarah⁵, b ——, 1749
23   Margaret⁵, b ——, 1751, m Nov 23, 1769, Joseph Wallis
24   Christopher⁵, b ——, 1752
25   Mary⁵, b ——, 1754
26   Deborah⁵, b ——, 1756, m Mar 18 1780, Benjamin Wallis, both
     of Greenland, N H
27   Jane⁵, b ——, 1757
28   Jeremiah⁵, b ——, 1760
29   **Theodore A.⁵**, b ——, 1762 m Sarah Abbott

FIFTH GENERATION

20. George⁵ Fuller (*Jeremiah⁴, James³, John², John¹*) b May 24,
1746, in Hampton, N H , d Oct 10, 1825, in Hartland, Me , m ——,
Mary, who d Dec 23, 1818
  Children
30   **William⁶**, b ——
31   **David⁶**, b ——
32   **Warren⁶**, b —— , m Elizabeth Clark
33   **James⁶**, b Feb 1, 1773, m. 1, Rebecca Lancey, m 2, Betsey
     Lancey
34   George⁶, b ——, m Apr 26, 1797, Nancy York, of Brentwood,
     N H
  The above children probably not placed in order of birth The U S
Census of 1790 gives George Fuller in Exeter, N H , with 7 sons and
2 daughters

29. Theodore Atkinson⁵ Fuller, (*Jeremiah⁴, James³, John², John¹*),
b ——, 1762, in Rye, N. H ; d. ——, m. 1, Nov., 1780, Sarah Abbott,
who d ——, m 2, Oct , 1799, Hannah Jenness
  Children, by first wife
35   ——⁶, b ——, m ——, —— Hartshorn
  By second wife
36   Nancy⁶, b ——, m Joshua Stackford
37   Joseph⁶, b ——, m June 1, 1828, Mary F Gale

SIXTH GENERATION.

30. William⁶ Fuller (*George⁵, Jeremiah⁴, James³, John², John¹*), b
——, in Exeter, N H , d ——, m * ——.

He removed to Brentwood, N H

Children

38 A daughter, b ——, m —— York *

39 A daughter, b ——, m —— York †

*The history of Exeter, N H, mentions a William Fuller, who m Mar 31, 1806, Sukey Sleeper, and the Vital Records of New Hampshire mentions a William Fuller, b in Rye, N H, who m Margaret Crane, b in Brentwood, N H

†The Thurston Gene mentions Susan Ann York, dau of Jonathan and Phebe (Fuller) York

31. DAVID⁶ FULLER, (*George⁵, Jeremiah⁴, James³, John², John¹*), b ——, m Exeter, N H , d ——, m * ——

Removed to Concord, N H.

Children

40 A son, b ——

*The History of Exeter N H, mentions a David Fuller, who m Nov 13, 1800, Widow Anne Watson

32. WARREN⁶ FULLER, (*George⁵, Jeremiah⁴, James³, John², John¹*), b ——, d ——, m ——, Elizabeth Clark

Resided in Exeter, N H

Children

41 Margaret(?) b ——, m ——, —— Lord, and had son John

No replies to inquiries for information

33. JAMES⁶ FULLER, (*George⁵, Jeremiah⁴, James³, John², John¹*), b. Feb 1, 1773, in Exeter N H ; d Nov 2, 1845, in Hartland, Me , m 1, 1813, in Palmyra, Me, Rebecca Lancey, b Nov 16, 1793 in Chelmsford, d Apr 12, 1829, in Hartland, Me , m 2, ——, Betscy Lancey, b Jan 17, 1801, at Westford; d Jan , 1892 at Hartland, Me

He removed in 1802 to Warrenstown No 3, now Hartland, Me where he was the first settler

Children, by first wife

42 **John Warren⁷**, b Jan 16 1815, m Esther Butterfield

43 **Thomas⁷**, b Nov 17, 1816, m Laura Butterfield

44 **James⁷**, b Jan 10, 1819, m Sarah Ann Underwood

45 Elizabeth Ann⁷, b Apr 8, 1821, probably m Apr 1 1842, Josiah L Brown, and had William H ⁸, and Abby J ⁸

46 George⁷, b Apr 28, 1826; d Oct 10, 1828

Children by second wife

47. George L ⁷, b Apr. 11, 1831, d 1883, at Hartland , m Julia Graves · no issue

48 **Samuel L.⁷**, b Jan 15, 1833, m Mary ——

49 **Josiah L.⁷**, b May 1, 1835, m Sara Prince

50 **Edward K.⁷**, b Aug 23, 1837, m Angeline Stevens

51 Rebecca[7], b ——, m ——, John Larabie, and had Lizzie M[8], who m E Clark

SEVENTH GENERATION.

42. JOHN WARREN[7] FULLER, (*James[6]*, *George[5]*, *Jeremiah[4]*, *James[3]*, *John[2]*, *John[1]*), b Jan 16, 1815, in Hartland, Me , d Dec 1, 1887, in Lewiston, Me , m Mar 24, 1842, Esther Butterfield, b June 18, 1813, in Goffstown, N H , d Aug 3, 1883, in Lewiston, Me

Children

52 Mary[8], b Mar 1, 1843, in Hartland, Me , d 1892 on a steamer out of Bath, Me , m May 6, 1864, in Waterville, Me , Scott Wright b Sept 17, 1841, in Lewiston, Me , d there Dec 3, 1875   Children   Gertrude[9], b Aug 21 1869, in Pittsfield, Me , m Arthur P Irving, and had Francis [10] and Esther [10]

53 Lucy[8], b June 3, 1847, in Hartland , d there Jan 2, 1866

43. THOMAS[7] FULLER, (*James[6]*, *George[5]*, *Jeremiah[4]*, *James[3]*, *John[2]*, *John[1]*), b Nov 17, 1816, in Hartland, Me · d there May 19, 1904 , m 1845, Laura Butterfield, b Jan 8, 1816; d Apr 17, 1904, in Hartland

Children ·

54 Ellen[8], b ——; m Dec 25 1867, in Newport, Me , Harrison Rand-lett, and had Carl[9], Thomas[9], Belle[9], Minnie[9], Harry[9], and Laura E[9]

55 Laura[8], b ——, d. young

56 Elizabeth[8], b ——; d 1893, in Hartland , m E Jackson

44. JAMES[7] FULLER, (*James[6]*, *George[5]*, *Jeremiah[4]*, *James[3]* *John[2]*, *John[1]*), b Jan 10, 1819, in Hartland, Me , d there Dec 21, 1895 , m Sept 24, 1844, at Fayette, Me , Sarah Ann Underwood, b July 17, 1822 , d May 9, 1891

Children .

57 Elizabeth[8] b Dec 26, 1845 , d Oct 20, 1850 in Hartland

58 Joseph Hall Underwood[8], b Sept 15, 1847; d Nov 17, 1865

59 **James Lancey[8]**, b May 20, 1851 , m Katherine Taylor

60 Jennie[8], b Sept. 15, 1852

61 **Henry C.[8]**, b Feb 12, 1854: m Mary A Linn

62 Arthur W [8], b May 26, 1856, died young

63 Charles L[8], b May 14, 1859, d July 5, 1872, at Hartland

64 Harriet Underwood[8], b July 18, 1861, m W S Baker, of Bangor, Me , who d Sept , 1903

48. SAMUEL L[7] FULLER, (*James[6]*, *George[5]*, *Jeremiah[4]*, *James[3]*, *John[2]* *John[1]*), b Jan 15, 1833, in Hartland, Me , m ——, Mary ——.

Children, all b in Austin, Nevada

65 Omar[8] b ——

66   Lizzie⁸, b ——
67   Laura⁸, b ——
68   Ida⁸, b ——
69   Valeria⁸, b ——
70   Agnes⁸, b ——

49. JOSIAH L⁷ FULLER, (*James⁶, George⁵, Jeremiah⁴, James³, John², John¹*), b May 1, 1835 in Hartland Me   m ——, Sara Prince.
Children
71   Walter⁸, b ——, m Grace Rowell, res Worcester, Mass
72.   Ethel⁸, b ——, m E Clark, and had Sara Louise⁹, resides in
     Weymouth   (Letter unclaimed Feb, 1913)

50. EDWARD K⁷ FULLER (*James⁶, George⁵, Jeremiah⁴ James³, John¹ John¹*), b Aug 23 1837, in Hartland, Me , m ——. Angeline Stevens
Children
73   **Hudson⁸**, b ——, m M I French
74   Anne Lee⁸, b ——, m B Prescott, and had Frederick⁹
75   Odd⁸, b ——, m I. H Matthews, m 2, Sara Stevens

EIGHTH GENERATION.

59. JAMES LANCEY⁸ FULLER (*James⁷ James⁶, George⁵, Jeremiah⁴ James³, John², John¹*), b May 20, 1851, in Hartland, Me , d July 19, 1882, at Heppner Oregon, m Aug 11 1879, Katherine Taylor of Portland, Oregon, b Apr 28, 1856
    Children, born at Heppner, Ore
76   **Charles⁹**, b Sept 13 1880, m Lois Cochon
76a   Hubert⁹ b July 18 1882, d Sept 1882
77   Arthur T ⁹, b July 10, 1884
78   James L ⁹, b Nov 8, 1886, m Christina Linn

61. HENRY C ⁸ FULLER, (*James⁷ James⁶, George⁵, Jeremiah⁴, James³ John², John¹*), b Feb 12, 1854, at Hartland, Me ; d Apr. 10, 1903 in Boston Mass, m Dec 25, 1874, Mary I Linn, of Hartland, Me b Nov 18, 1856
    Children:
79   Grace Wilson⁹, b June 8, 1875, d Pittsfield, Me, Mar 31, 1901;
     m Dec 1, 1896, Geo Osborn, of Peabody, Mass
80   **James Elmo⁹**, b May 9, 1877, m Bertha Cherrington.
81   **Guy Goss⁹**, b July 25, 1880, m Edith Fuller
82   Carrol⁹, b Jan 27, 1884; d Aug 1886
83   Elmer Linn⁹, b July 12, 1886
84   Ralph Linn⁹, b Jan 2, 1889, d Sept 10, 1890

73. HUDSON⁸ FULLFR, (*Edward K⁷, James⁶ George⁵, Jeremiah⁴, James³, John², John¹*), b ——, m ——, M I French

Children ·

85 Claude⁹, b ——.

86 Annie⁹, b ——

NINTH GENERATION.

76. CHARLES⁹ FULLER, (*James Lancey⁸, James⁷, James⁶ George⁵, Jeremiah⁴, James³, John², John¹*), b Sept 13, 1880, in Heppner, Ore , m —— Lois Cochon, of Salem, Oregon

Children

87 Francis¹⁰, b ——.

88 Harriet¹⁰, b ——.

80. JAMES ELMO⁹ FULLER, (*Henry C⁸, James⁷, James⁶, George⁵, Jeremiah⁴, James³, John², John¹*), b May 9, 1877, in Hartland, Me , m June 10, 1903 Bertha Cherrington

Children ·

89 Linn¹⁰, b ——

81. GUY GOSS⁹ FULLER, (*Henry C⁸, James⁷, James⁶, George⁵ Jeremiah⁴, James³, John², John¹*), b. July 25, 1880, in Hartland, Me , m Dec 17, 1903, Edith¹⁰ Fuller (Spencer H⁹, Arminitus⁸, Fred F⁷, Esbon⁶, Abraham⁵, Joseph⁴, John³, Samuel², Edward¹) of the Mayflower Arminitus No 48 of 26th Group, p 235, Vol I and p 252, Vol II

Children

90 Grace¹⁰, b ——

91 Isabel¹⁰, b ——.

SECOND GROUP

THIRD GENERATION.

THOMAS[2] FULLER, AND SOME OF HIS DESCENDANTS

16. THOMAS[3] FULLER, (*John*[2], *John*[1]), b Aug 27, 1695, in Hampton, N H , d ——, 1766, in Sandown, N. H ; m at Hampton Falls, N H Oct 31, 1730, Hannah Chase, b May 10, 1711, dau of John Chase of Hampton

Children, born at Hampton Falls, N H

1   Rachel[4], b June 21, 1731 , m Abraham Welch
2   John[4], b May 9, 1733; probably d young
3   Benjamin[4], b Feb 14, 1735
4   Abigail[4] b Oct 10, 1737 , m Moses Hare
5   Elizabeth[4], b July 5, 1739 , m Jonathan Gooding
6   Elijah[4], b June 1, 1741 probably d young , not mentioned in will
7   Thomas[4], b June 21, 1745 , Revolutionary soldier , d Nov 25, 1819, a 73, in Bristol, N H , m ——, Sarah ——, who d Dec 13, 1824, in Bristol, a 102, no ch mentioned
8   **Chase**[4], b Apr 1, 1752; m ——, Lura ——
9   Anna[4], b Aug 17, 1754 , m Ebenezer Gove
10 **John**[4], b ——, 1756 , m Betsey Clough

Thomas[3] Fuller's will, made June 15, 1765, proved Oct 29, 1766, mentions sons Benjamin, Thomas (sole executor), Chase, and John, daughters Rachel Welch, Abigail Hare, Elizabeth Gooding, Anna Gove

The N E Register, Vol. 51, gives marriage of a Benjamin Fuller in Hampton, N H., Nov 5, 1766, to Sarah Jones Almsbury The History of Chester, N H mentions a Benjamin Fuller as a soldier in 1757 and 1777 and his widow living in 1822, aged 80

FOURTH GENERATION.

8. CHASE[4] FULLER, (*Thomas*[3], *John*[2], *John*[1]), b Apr 1, 1752, at Hampton Falls, N H , d ——, m ——, Lura ——

He settled in New Chester, N H , now Bristol, before Aug , 1774
Children

11 Hannah[6], b ——, 1774, in Bristol, m ——, —— Shute, and removed to Littleton, N H

12 Mary Connor[5], b July 3, 1776, at Pembroke N H, d May 17, 1845, at Bridgewater, N H, m Samuel Clifford, who d Sept 24, 1841, at New Hampton, N H, they had 4 children

13 Anna[5], b Jan 13, 1778, at Bristol, d at Littleton, N H, unmarried

14 Joseph[5] b June 14, 1779, at Bristol

15 Peter[5], b Oct. 18, 1782, at Bristol, rem to Littleton, N H 1805 9 children

16 **Thomas**[5], b May 13, 1787, at Bristol, m 1, Mary Clay, m 2, Lydia Clay

17 Dolly[5], b July 14, 1789, at Bristol

· 18 **Chase**[5], b Oct 15, 1792, at Bristol, m Hannah Worthen

19 Reuben[5], b Mar 9, 1795, d young

20 Huldah[5], b ——, m ——, —— Heath, rem to Littleton, N H

10. JOHN[4] FULLER (*Thomas*[3], *John*[2], *John*[1]), b ——, 1756, in Hampton Falls, N H, d ——, 1835, in Holland, Erie Co, N Y, m ——, at Sandown, N H, Betsey Clough

He enlisted during the Revolutionary War from Sandown, later, he removed to Piermont, N H and thence to Holland, N Y

Children, recorded in Piermont

21 Betsey[5], b Feb 28, 1773; probably d young

22 Joseph[5], b Jan 21, 1775

23 Timothy[5], b Sept 30, 1777

24 Anna[5], b Mar 4, 1779

25 **John**[5], b July 25, 1782, m Rachel Auld

26 Betsey[5], 2d, b July 15, 1783, m Micajah Emerson

27 David[5], b June 19, 1785

28 Miriam[5], b Nov 9, 1787

29 Sally[5], b June 20, 1790

30 Moses[5], b May 19, 1795

31 **Chase**[5], b Apr 22, 1797, m Nancy Kenyon

FIFTH GENERATION.

16. THOMAS[5] FULLER, (*Chase*[4], *Thomas*[3], *John*[2], *John*[1]), b May 13 1787, in Bristol, N H, d Mar 11, 1878, in Littleton, N H; m 1, Jan 15, 1809, Mary Clay, who d Jan 19, 1829, m 2, Sept 10, 1829, Lydia Clay, b July 15, 1793, d Apr 10, 1881, at Dalton, N H

He removed to Littleton in 1812

Children

32 Luther W[6], b Oct 14, 1810, in Lancaster, N H, d Dec 15, 1840

33 Edward R[6], b Aug 7, 1812

34 Chase C[6], b Nov 2, 1814

35 Robie C[6], b Jan 2, 1817, d May 15, 1847

36 Lydia Jane⁶, b Mar 20, 1820, d Aug 26, 1827
37 Lovina G⁶, b May 22, 1823, d Jan 31, 1855
38 Mary Jane⁶, b May, 1830; d May, 1830
39 **George Washington⁶**, b Oct 22, 1832, m Lucy Ann Fiske
40 Anne Jane⁶, b Sept 26, 1838

18. CHASE⁵ FULLER, (*Chase⁴, Thomas³, John², John¹*), b Oct 15, 1792, in Bristol, N H, d ——, m 1 ——, Hannah Worthen, who d in Bridgewater, N H, m 2, ——, —— Bartlett

He removed first to Bridgewater, and, after death of first wife, to Danville, N H

Children
41 Eliza⁶, b ——, m David Sargent, 5 children
42 Worthen⁶, b ——, m 1, Mary Sawyer, m 2, —— Sanborn
43 Harriet⁶, b ——, m ——, —— Meservy

25. JOHN⁵ FULLER, (*John⁴, Thomas³, John², John¹*), b July 25, 1782, in Piermont, N H, d Apr 20, 1868, at Boothbay, Me, m ——, Rachel Auld, who d Sept 20, 1849

He was a shoemaker, and it is said each of his 8 sons learned the trade

Children.
44 **Jason⁶**, b Oct 2, 1803, m Jane McClintock
45 **James⁶**, b Dec 19, 1804, m Eliza Hopper
46 Sarah Auld⁶, b Sept 24, 1806, m, 1825, William Adams, and settled in Thomaston Me, had Eliza Jane⁷, Olive Frances⁷, and William James⁷
47 Fanny⁶, b Dec 6, 1807, m Charles Spear of Lynn
48 Adeline⁶, b Oct 30, 1810, lived in Sumner, Me
49 **John⁶**, b Sept 18, 1813, m Martha Cromwell
50 Elizabeth⁶, b Jan 17, 1815, d Feb 7, 1897, at Portland, Me, unmarried
51 Mary A.⁶, b Dec 15, 1816, m, 1836, Capt David Robinson of Thomaston, Me.
52 **Samuel⁶**, b Feb 6, 1819, m Arletta Lewis
53 Jane⁶, b Apr 20, 1821; d 1891 in Portland, Me, m William G Chase
54 Franklin H⁶, b Nov 19, 1823; d Apr 8, 1851, unmarried
55 Harriet⁶, b Jan 4, 1825, resided in Portland, Me
56 **Manson Chase⁶**, b Feb 11 1827, m Sarah W L Richmond
57 Thomas S⁶, b Apr 24, 1830, resided in Gloucester
58 **Charles W.⁶**, b Nov 30, 1834, m Lucena W Davis

31. CHASE⁵ FULLER, (*John⁴, Thomas³, John², John¹*), b Apr 22, 1797, in Piermont, N H, d ——, 1879, m ——, Nancy Kenyon

Children
59 Philetus⁶, b ——

60   **La Fayette⁶**, b ——
61   Molly⁶, b ——
62   Polly⁶, b ——
63   Romanzo⁶, b ——.
64   Elizabeth⁶, b ——
65. Velona⁶, b ——
66   Zoroaster⁶, b ——
67   Oliva⁶, b ——
68   Millard⁶, b ——

SIXTH GENERATION.

39. GEORGE WASHINGTON⁶ FULLER, (*Thomas⁵*, *Chase⁴*, *Thomas³* *John² John¹*), b Oct 23 1832, in Littleton, N H , m Sept 19, 1852, Lucy Ann Fisk

He is a farmer, member G A R , was in Co I, 1st N H Heavy Artillery in the Civil War

69   **Charles Edward⁷**, b Aug 2, 1853, m Minnie Fuller

44. JASON⁶ FULLER, (*John⁵*, *John⁴*, *Thomas³*, *John²*, *John¹*), b Oct 2, 1803, in Boothbay, Me , d ——, ——, m May 16, 1826, Jane McClintock

He removed to Portland, Me

Children

70   Susan C⁷, b Nov 23, 1826, m Charles F Bryant
71   Mary Frances⁷, b Oct 7, 1827, m —— 1849, Nathaniel B Green-
       leaf
72   Rachel A⁷, b Sept 29, 1828, d young
73   Rachel J⁷, b June 20 1830, d Feb 23, m 1854 Wm H Johnson
74   Sarah E⁷, b Oct 5, 1831, resides at Woodford, Me
75   James⁷, b Feb 10, 1833, d at sea Oct , 1851
76   Martha W⁷, b Nov 21, 1834, m 1856 Robert Gould, res Port-
       land, Me
77   Waterman⁷, b Jan 12, 1831 d 1841

45. JAMES⁶ FULLER, (*John⁵*, *John⁴*, *Thomas³*, *John²*, *John¹*), b Dec 19 1804, in Boothbay, Me , d ——, —— in Ossawatomie, Kan ; m ——, —— Eliza Hopper

78   Ellen⁷, b ——, m —— Bruce res Teneva, Johnson Co , Kan
79   Mary⁷, b ——, d about 1880
80   James⁷, b ——, d in the Civil War
81   William⁷, b ——; resides at Fall River, Greenwood Co , Kan
82   Adelbert, b ——, a physician at Lane, Franklin Co , Kan

49. JOHN⁶ FULLER, (*John⁵*, *John⁴*, *Thomas³*, *John²*, *John¹*), b Sept 18, 1813, in Boothbay, Me , d Oct 8, 1903, in Norridgewock Me , m ——, ——, Martha Cromwell

He went to sea in early life, and was a sea captain for many years

Children

83   **Frederick Chase**[7], b June 2, 1844, m 1, Emma J Law, m 2, Alice T Sleeper

84   Mary Amanda[7], b Sept 24, 1846, in Rockland, Me , d Sept , 1880, in Norridgewock, Me , m June, 1869, Norman J Austin of Lowell, and had Martha Izetta[8], b Apr 17, 1870, and Charles O [8], b Mar 19, 1875, in Norridgewock

85   Vesta Arlena[7], b Oct 10, 1851, in Norridgewock, res Lewiston, Me (1909)

86   Fanny Olive[7], b Sept 7, 1855, in Norridgewock, res Lewiston Me (1909)

87   **Frank Adams**[7], b May 15, 1858, m Elizabeth Cole

52.   SAMUEL[6] FULLER, (*John[5] John[4], Thomas[3], John[2], John[1]*), b Feb 6 1819, at Boothbay, Me ; d there Jan 24, 1901, m Nov 6, 1848, Arletta Lewis

He resided at Boothbay

Children

88   Emma J [7], b July 11, 1849, d Mar 25, 1909; m Nov 7, 1875, Horace W Pinkham, no issue

89   Frank[7], b Sept 14, 1853, m Dec 4, 1883, Nettie E Adams

90   Martha[7], b Dec 25, 1860, d 1861

91   Abby F [7] b Dec 30, 1861, d 1863

92   Ralph H [7], b Sept 1, 1864, m Mar 7, 1887, Eva Gove, res Newport, R I

93   **John E.**[7], b Jan 15 1867, m Mary Hilton

56.   MANSON CHASE[6] FULLER, (*John[5], John[4], Thomas[3], John[2], John[1]*), b Feb 11, 1827, at Boothbay, Me , m 1857, Sarah W Lawson

He was living (1909) in Somerville, Mass

Children

94   Henry M [7], b ——.

95   Arabella[7], b ——

96   Anna M [7], b ——

97   Rachel[7], b. ——

98   Alice M [7], b ——

99   Harriet D [7], b ——

58.   CHARLES W.[6] FULLER, (*John[5], John[4], Thomas[3], John[2], John[1]*), b Mar 30, 1834, in Boothbay, Me , d about 1875, in Portland, Me ; m ——, ——, Lucena W Davis

He lived in Portland

Children

100   Augusta[7], b ——; m 1, Robert Weeks, m 2, ——, Ellery Anderson and resides at Mt Pleasant, S C.

101   **Charles W.**[7], b ——, m, Lynda Frances Blake.

60. LA FAYETTE[6] FULLER, (*Chase[5], John[4], Thomas[3], John[2], John[1]*), b
——, 1825, in ——, m ——, ——, Olivia Kellogg
Resided at Bowling Green, Caroline Co , Va
Children :
102 George[7], b ——
103 Arvilla Statira[7], b Apr 3 1853, in Carrolton, N Y , m in Peabody, Kan , Dec 14, 1872, Joseph W Whitney
104 Lavello[7], b. ——
105 Irene[7], b ——
106 William[7], b ——
107 Orpha[7], b ——
108 Lenora[7], b ——
109 Rupert C[7], b ——, m Irene Andrews

SEVENTH GENERATION.

69. CHARLES EDWARD[7] FULLER, (*George IV[6], Thomas[5], Chase[4], Thomas[3], John[2], John[1]*), b Aug 2, 1853, at Dalton, N H , m Mar 15, 1879, Minnie Fuller, b Apr 12, 1864, in Fairlee Vt , dau of Edward Fuller
Children ·
110 Jessie Mabel[8], b Aug 27, 1880

83. FREDERICK CHASE[7] FULLER, (*John[6], John[5], John[4], Thomas[3], John[2] John[1]*), b June 2, 1844, in Rockland, Me , m 1, Oct 13, 1866, Emma J Law of Lowell, m 2, Sept 5, 1900, Alice Thorndike Sleeper of Somerville
Resides in Somerville (1909)
Children
111 George Frederick[8], b July 26, 1868, m Sept 26, 1898, Lenora Burke , resides in Boston (1909)
112 **G. Albert[8]**, b Apr 10, 1870, m Ida E H Steinkrauss

87. FRANK ADAMS[7] FULLER, (*John[6], John[5], John[4], Thomas[3], John[2], John[1]*), b May 16, 1858, in Norridgewock, Me , m ——, ——, Elizabeth Cole of Smithfield, Me
He resides in Norridgewock (1909).
Children
113 Beryl Cole[8], b ——

93. JOHN E[7] FULLER, (*Samuel[6], John[5], John[4], Thomas[3], John[2], John[1]*), b Jan 15, 1867, in Boothbay, Me , m. Apr 30 1893, Mary Hilton
He resides at Boothbay Harbor, Me
Children

114   Emma Arletta[8], b Feb 27, 1894
115   Mildred Sarah[8], b May 2, 1896
116   Vira May[8], b Dec 25, 1898
117   Lewis Westman[8], b Feb 25 1901

101. CHARLES W[7] FULLER, (*Charles W*[6], *John*[5], *John*[4], *Thomas*[3], *John*[2] *John*[1]), b ——, m Dec 18 1887. Lynda Frances Blake
He resides in Claremont, N H
Children
118   Rufus[8], b ——, 1888
119   Ellery A[8], b ——, 1894
120   Kathleen[8], b ——, 1903

EIGHTH GENERATION.

112. G ALBERT[8] FULLER, (*Frederick C*[7], *John*[6], *John*[5], *John*[4], *Thomas*[3], *John*[2], *John*[1]), b Apr 10, 1870, m Oct 14, 1891 Ida E H Steinkrauss
Resides (1909) in Everett, Mass
Children
121   Albert[9], b ——
122   Frederick[9], b ——

THIRD GROUP

--- -- ---

JAMES[3] FULLER, AND SOME OF HIS DECENDANTS

THIRD GENERATION.

18. JAMES[3] FULLER, (*James[2]*, *John[1]*), b Dec 2, 1673, in Ipswich, d there Apr 9, 1753; m ——, ——, Phebe ——, who d June 20, 1746
Children
1 Phebe[4], b Sept 29, 1700, d Aug 15, 1739, published Mar. 3 1721-2, to Abraham Fitts, childreen b to them, Abraham[5], Daniel[5], Phebe[5], Mary[5], Abraham[5], 2d, James[5], and Sarah[5]
2 Daniel[4], b —— ——, only son, d. Nov. 19, 1724
3 Sarah[4], bapt Nov 8, 1713, m Jan 5, 1731-2, Samuel Fellows, and had Sarah[5].
4 Elizabeth[4], bapt Mar. 8, 1719, d Nov 19, 1783, probably m Jonathan Marshall, m. Int Pub Jan 15, 1742, children Elizabeth[5], Hannah[5], Daniel[5], and Rachel[5]
5 Hannah[4], bapt June 17, 1722, probably m May 22, 1746, Samuel Lakeman; children (Lakeman)[5], Phebe[5], Samuel[5], James Fuller[5], Nathaniel[5], and Elizabeth[5]

FOURTH GROUP

THIRD GENERATION.

NATHANIEL[3] FULLER, AND SOME OF HIS DESCENDANTS

23. NATHANIEL[3] FULLER, (*James*[2], *John*[1]), b Feb 18, 1683 in Ip-swich, d there Dec, 1752, m 1, published 24-6-1717, with Mary Potter dau of Thomas and Mary (Kimball) Potter, b Apr 3, 1697, d July 22, 1731, at Ipswich, m 2, Jan 14, 1733-4, Widow Elizabeth Perkins, who d July, 1770, at Ipswich His will is dated Nov 4, 1752, and proved Dec 25, 1752

Children b at Ipswich

  1   Mary[4] bapt 22-12-1718, d Nov 17, 1725
  2   James[4], bapt Dec 18, 1720; d Nov 19, 1725
  3   Nathaniel[4], bapt Sept 9, 1722, d Nov 15, 1725
  4   **Daniel[4]**, bapt Jan 17, 1724-5, m Katherine Pindar
  5   **Nathaniel[4]**, bapt Dec 25, 1726, m 1, Sarah Leatherland, m 2, Mary Holland
  6   James[4], bapt Feb 9, 1728, probably d before 1757
  7   Mary[4], bapt Mar 29, 1731, d Nov 14, 1731
  8   William[4], bapt Dec 1 1734, d 1757, m Int Pub Sept 19, 1755, with Anna Wainwright of Ipswich.
  9   Mary[4], bapt Apr 3, 1737, d Mar 12, 1798, m Feb 1, 1759, Ben-jamin Glazier, Jr, and had son Benjamin[5]
  10   Sarah[4], bapt Jan 14, 1738-9, m Int Pub Jan 26, 1760, with John Glazier

FOURTH GENERATION.

4. DANIEL[4] FULLER, (*Nathaniel*[3], *James*[2], *John*[1]), bapt Jan 17, 1724-5 in Ipswich; d there May 9, 1806, m Int Pub June 8, 1754, with Kath-erine Pindar, both of Ipswich, she d there July 5, 1812

Children

  11   Katherine[5], bapt Dec 14, 1755
  12   James[5], bapt Oct 30, 1758, d Sept 6, 1842, unmarried, he was a soldier of the Revolution.
  13   **William[5]**, bapt Mar. 22, 1761, m Lucy Hodgkins

14   Lucy⁴, bapt Feb 12, 1764

5. Nathaniel⁴ Fuller, (*Nathaniel³, James², John¹*), bapt Dec 25
1726, in Ipswich, d about 1778, m 1, Nov 28, 1759, Sarah Leatherland,
m 2, Int Pub Mar 5, 1768, Mary Holland, both of Ipswich, she d 1829
aged 88, at Elba, N Y

He is called Captain, and is said to have been commander of the
privateer "General Stark," and to have died of wounds received in an
engagement

Children

15   **Nathaniel⁵**, b Sept 4, 1760, m Hannah Hovey
16   Sarah⁵, bapt Nov 6, 1763
17   Susanna⁵, bapt Nov 27, 1768
18   **James⁵**, bapt Sept 16, 1770, m Hannah Kidder
19   **William⁵**, bapt Feb 12, 1775, m Rachel Cram
20   Mary⁵, bapt Oct 9, 1776

FIFTH GENERATION.

13. William⁵ Fuller, (*Daniel⁴, Nathaniel³, James², John¹*), b Mar
10, 1761, in Ipswich, d Sept ——, 1842, in West Gardiner, Me, m
Jan 14, 1787, Lucy Hodgkins, b June 10, 1764, in Ipswich, d May 3,
1846 (?), in Gardiner; date also given Sept 2, 1842(?)

He enlisted 4 times during the Revolutionary War, was a Sergeant
when discharged, was one of the guard which conducted André to
execution

Children—all but the last born in Ipswich

21   Hannah⁶, b Sept 17, 1787
22   Lucy⁶, b Dec 14, 1788, d ——, m Int Pub Sept 4, 1807, with
      Jesse Richards
23   Catherine⁶, b Feb 3, 1791
24   **William⁶**, b Feb 1, 1793, m 1, Phebe Chamberlain, m 2, Hannah
      Davis Brock
25   **David⁶**, b Jan 19, 1795, m Mary Drew
26   **James⁶**, b Jan 12, 1797, m Susan Brown
27   Abigail⁶, b Dec. 12, 1798, m Noah Pinkham
28. **Daniel⁶**, b Feb 1, 1801, m Anna Lord
29   Joseph⁶, b Feb 17 1803; nothing further learned
30   **George⁶**, b July 13, 1807, m. Hannah Stanwood Lord
31   Mary⁶, b Aug 20, 1810, m Capt Thad Spear

15. Nathaniel⁵ Fuller, (*Nathaniel⁴, Nathaniel³, James², John¹*), b
Sept 4, 1760, in Ipswich, d Dec 29, 1842, m May —, 1781, Hannah
Hovey, b Oct 15, 1762, d Jan 17, 1861, in Ipswich, dau of John and
Elizabeth (Huse) Hovey

He inherited from his father one share in the privateer 'General Stark", served in the war of 1812, and was taken prisoner and confined at Dartmoor

Children, said to have been 4 sons and 8 daughters

32
33
34
35.
36 **Nathaniel**[6], b Mar 23, 1791, m Elizabeth Harris
37
38
39
40
41
42
43 Charlotte[6], b June 21, 1807; m Aug 4, 1831, Abraham Burnham of Ipswich, and had Charlotte[7], b June 12, 1833, Abraham Perkins[7], b Sept 25, 1835, Daniel Spiller[7], b May 9, 1838, and Nathaniel[7], b Oct 22, 1840

Succession of Nathaniel[5] Fuller's children not known

18. JAMES[5] FULLER, (*Nathaniel[4], Nathaniel[3], James[2], John[1]*), bapt Sept 16, 1770, in Ipswich—date of birth given Aug — 1770, d Nov, 1863, in Elba, Genessee Co, N Y, m ——, 1795, in Bristol, N H, Hannah Kidder

He removed with his mother to Bristol, N H, and about 1815 to Elba, N Y

Children, said to have been 8 in number, 6 sons and 2 daughters, all but 2 lived and died in Western N Y

44
45 **Holland**[6], b ——, m May 28, 1820, Betsey Driggs
46
47
48
49
50 **James**[6], b Oct 8, 1809, m Mary Page.
51.
Two numbers dropped by error

Succession not known

19. WILLIAM[5] FULLER, (*Nathaniel[4], Nathaniel[3], James[2], John[1]*), bapt Feb 12, 1775, d at Lake City, Minn, aged about 87 years, m Mar 20, 1797, in Lyndboro, N H, Rachel Cram, b in Lyndboro, d in Irasburg, Vt They lived in Litchfield, Me, until 1816, when they removed to Irasburg

Children, four sons and four daughters

54 Mary⁶, b ——, m Justus Stevens Smith, Lyndboro, N H, and lived in Cambridge, Mass

55
56
57
58
59
60
61

Succession not known

The Ward family genealogy mentions m William Fuller to Sarah Ward, Mar 30 1836, and res Irasburg, had Charles, b Jan 20, 1837, Milo Joseph, b July 1, 1841, relation to William⁵ of Nathaniel⁴ not known, if any

Town clerk Irasburg, has no early records of Fullers in that town in his office

SIXTH GENERATION.

24. WILLIAM⁶ FULLER, (*William⁵, Daniel⁴, Nathaniel³, James², John¹*), b Feb 1, 1893, in Ipswich, d Jan 6, 1869, m 1, ——, 1816, Phebe Chamberlain, m 2, June 12, 1836, Hannah Davis Brock, who d Dec. 30, 1838
Children by first wife, all b in Gardiner, Me

62 John M ⁷, b July 27, 1817; d in Illinois; m ——, in Oquaka, Ill
63 Leonard⁷, b Feb 1, 1820, d in Illinois, m Matilda Murch
64 Sewall⁷, b Apr 18, 1822, d in Manchester, Me , m 1, Hannah Huntington, m 2, Margaret Leavitt, no children
65 William C ⁷, b ——; d in Gardiner, Me , m 1, Abbie Smith, m. 2, Hannah E Wharf(?), he had 2 children
66 Moses⁷, b Sept 27, 1826, d young in Gardiner, Me
67 Sanford⁷, b Sept 12, 1829, d in the army, m ——, Jane ——, 2 children
68 Charles E ⁷, b Nov. 6, 1831, m ——, lived in Santa Cruz, Cal , one child
69 A daughter, b ——
70 George W ⁷, b Mar 13 1834; d in Illinois about 1883, m Philena Bryant

Children by second wife
71 **Melvin Evander⁷**, b May 27, 1837, m Mary A. Stanchcliffe
72 Coris Ann Victoria⁷, b July 22, 1838, d Jan 20, 1895, at East Winthrop, Me , m July 1, 1855, Nahum M Stone, and had Lillie Ann⁸, Walter Nahum⁸, Albert Fuller⁸, and Emma Josephine⁸; Mr Stone b Oct. 14, 1833, d Feb 14, 1899
73 **Albert Warren⁷**, b Feb 6, 1840, m. 1, Lucy Pease; m 2, Lucy Davis

74   Ellen Hannah[7], b Apr 18, 1845, m Dec 24, 1861, Benjamin
     Franklin Peacock their children were Arthur Frank[8], b Sept
     13, 1865, m 1, Dec 24, 1889, Mary E. Witham, m 2, June 15
     1904, Ethel B Doucalt, no children, Elmer Ellsworth[8], b July
     25, 1873, m Dec 24, 1898 Mary Ardelia Curtis, and has 3
     children

25. DAVID[6] FULLER (*William[5]*, *Daniel[4]*, *Nathaniel[3]*, *James[2]*, *John[1]*), b.
Jan 19, 1795, in Ipswich, d Feb 16, 1869, in West Gardiner, Me, m
May 2, 1819, Mary Drew, lived in West Gardiner
     Children
75   Elizabeth E[7], b Aug 16, 1821, d Nov 5, 1888, in St Paul, Minn;
     m Feb 1, 1842, Richard B Getchell
76   **Elisha D.[7]**, b Sept 16, 1822, m Emeline Brock
77   **David H.[7]**, b Jan 2 1824, m Esther A Hildreth
78   Mary C[7], b Apr 10, 1826, d June 25, 1897, at Buffalo Prairie, Ill.,
     m June 10, 1849, Simon E Fox, lived in Illinois
79   Ursula G[7], b Feb 10, 1828, d in infancy
80   Erastus[7], b May 3, 1830, m 1, Dec 9, 1851, Lizzie Nerry, m 2,
     Amelia Stanchliffe; resides in Galesburg, Ill
81   Sarah H[7], b Nov 19, 1833, d May 5, 1889, in Leeds, Me, m Mar
     9, 1854, John Dillingham.
82   Rebecca Adeline[7], b Apr 3, 1838, m Dec 25, 1862, David Cram
     resides in Litchfield, Me

26. JAMES[6] FULLER (*William[5]* *Daniel[4]*, *Nathaniel[3]*, *James[2]*, *John[1]*), b
Jan 12, 1797, in Ipswich; d Mar. 3, 1871, in St Albans Me, m July 24,
1824, Susan Brown
     When 10 years of age he removed with his father to Gardiner, Me,
where he lived until 1841, then removed, with his family to St Albans
     Children, born in Gardiner
83   Lucy A[7], b July 6, 1825, m Dec 5, 1841, Asa Getchell, and had
     Rebecca J[8], b Sept 20, 1842, Clarence E[8], b Jan 18, 1854, and
     Luttie E[8], b Oct 3, 1860
84   Juliette[7], b Mar 17, 1827, d May 7, 1903, in St Albans, m Jan
     6, 1846, Rufus Robertson, and had Abby[8], b Feb 26, 1847 Ar-
     thur[8], Sept 27, 1848, Rufus Albert[8], Oct 27, 1850, Parker Dow[8]
     July 26, 1854, Isaac Osgood[8], Mar 11, 1856, Rosabel[8], Aug 24
     1858 Emma Foster[8], Aug 23, 1860, Winnifred[8], July 26 1862
     Juliette[8], Mar 18, 1864, Jennie[8], Aug 9 1867, Bertha[8], Nov 7,
     1868, and Ernest Walter[8], Aug 15, 1871
85. Hannah Neal[7], b Mar 18, 1829, d Apr 11, 1889, m Sept 20, 1846,
     Daniel Goodwin and had Frederick O[8], b July 29, 1847, James
     Fuller[8], June 28, 1849, Helen E[8], Oct. 4, 1851; Fanny[8], Jan,
     1855, Daniel[8], Oct 12, 1856, Walter W[8], Oct 21, 1858 George
     B[8], May 18, 1864, and Ira H.[8], Apr 2, 1866, lived in Stetson, Me
86   **Henry William[7]**, b Jan 19, 1831, m Caroline Tenney
87   Nancy L[7], b Jan 19 1833, m Jan 2, 1860, Charles H. Goodwin,
     and had J Woodbury[8], b Apr 12, 1861; Minnie Deveraux[8], July
     10, 1862, Charles Mower[8], Oct 30, 1863, Herman Griffin[8], Nov
     25, 1869, lived in Stetson Me

88   Joseph B.[7] b Dec. 13, 1834 d Dec , 1841
89   Alonzo E.[7] b Dec 11, 1836, m Mary E Tenney
90   Susan[7], b Mar 30, 1840, resides in Lewiston, Me
91   James[7], b Mar 27, 1842, in St Albans, Me, d Mar. 1, 1863, of fever in the army.
92   Sylvia[7], b Dec. 18, 1846, m 1, William Horn of West Gardiner, m 2, William M. Stanley, resides in Minneapolis, Minn

28. DANIEL[6] FULLER (*William[5], Daniel[4], Nathaniel[3], James[2], John[1]*), b Feb 1, 1801, in Ipswich, d Dec 8, 1886 in West Gardiner, Me , m. Jan 19, 1825. Anna Lord, b Aug 10, 1804, in Litchfield, Me , d Mar 23, 1876

He came with his parents to West Gardiner and lived with them until their death

Children, all born in West Gardiner

93   Abigail W.[7], b June 16, 1825, d Sept 5, 1861, m May 9, 1847, Daniel Tucker, and had Adelia[8], Angeline[8], and Edgar[8]
94   Augustin[7], b Feb 4, 1827; d ——, in California, unmarried
95   **George A.[7]**, b Apr 18, 1828, m Charlotte Swift
96   **Daniel F.[7]**, b. Sept. 12, 1829, m 1, Sarah A Swift; m 2, Clara A Jack.
97   Sarah A.[7], b May 19, 1831, d Oct 7, 1863, m Dec 29, 1848, Samuel Merrill, and had Frank[8], Carrie[8], Anne[8], and Arthur[8]
98   Martha C.[7], b Mar 9, 1833, d Oct 15, 1896, m May 3, 1854. Henry Roberts, and had Alphonso[8] and Hattie[8]
99   Andrew[7], b Apr 20, 1834, , d June 15, 1834
100 Harriet E.[7], b May 3, 1835, d Oct 15, 1884; m Nov 9, 1854, Asa W Plimpton, and had W Oscar[8] and Anne[8]
101 Lucy H.[7], } twins, b Sept 14, 1836 { d Sept 27 1836
102 Mary O.[7], } { d July 4, 1910, m Nov 13 1859, Dawson S Reed, and had Harry[8] and Edgar[8]
103 **Calvin R.[7]**, b Apr 16, 1838; m Catherine Milliken
104 **Jesse A.[7]**, b. May 1, 1840, m Lydia E Sherburn.
105 **Francis E.[7]**, b Dec 29, 1842, m Helen Herrick
106 Hiram O.[7], b Oct 14, 1844, d July 4 1845
107 **Horace A.[7]**, b Mar 26, 1849, m Mary C. Rogers.

30. GEORGE[6] FULLER (*William[5], Daniel[4], Nathaniel[3], James[2], John[1]*), b July 13, 1807, in Ipswich, d. June 1, 1878, m Mar 27, 1834, Hannah Stanwood Lord, b Jan 24, 1809, d Mar 25, 1901

Children,

108 Clementine[7], b Oct 30, 1834
109 **George Stanwood[7]**, b Nov 5, 1835, m Helen Maria Wiley
110 Philip Albion[7], b Apr 20, 1838, d Nov 15, 1840
111 William Henry Harrison[7], b. May 26, 1840, m 1, Emma Hatch, b 1842, d Nov 18, 1871, m 2, Jan 1, 1874, Martha Jane Fowler. b Feb 8, 1850, d Mar 30, 1892, no children
112 Joseph Warren[7], b Mar 8 1844; m Elvina Atkins
113 **Benjamin Franklin[7]**, b May 15, 1846 m Amanda Lyford Snow

114   **Charles Theodore**[7], b Mar 31, 1852, m 1, Laura E Laird, m 2,
        Annie Clement.

36. NATHANIEL[6] FULLER, (*Nathaniel*[5], *Nathaniel*[4], *Nathaniel*[3], *James*[2]
John[1]), b Mar 23, 1791, in Ipswich, d June 22, 1825, m Oct 2, 1820,
Elizabeth Harris
    Children
115   Mary E[7], b ——, 1821, m Dec 31, 1843, Reuben Daniels
116   Lydia L[7], b June 18, 1825

45. HOLLAND[6] FULLER, (*James*[5], *Nathaniel*[4] *Nathaniel*[3], *James*[2], *John*[1]),
b —— in Oakfield, Genessee Co, N Y , d ——, in May 28, 1820, Betsey
Driggs, b Athens, N Y, May 3, 1801
    Children
117.   Sarah Cleaveland[7], b Sept 22, 1824
118   George Driggs[7], b ——
119   James Franklin[7] b Sept 6 1827
120   Charles Hibbard[7], b Oct 24, 1842
        No replies to requests for information

50. JAMES[6] FULLER, (*James*[5], *Nathaniel*[4], *Nathaniel*[3], *James*[2], *John*[1]),
b Oct 8, 1809, in Bristol. N H , d May 24, 1884, at Vevay, Ingham Co ,
Mich , m ——, 1834, in Elba, N Y , Mary Page
    He removed with his father to Elba about 1815, and to Ingham Co
Mich , about 1856   He was a farmer, and one of the directors of the
First National Bank of Mason, Mich
    Children—succession not obtained
121   Emma J[7], b ——, d July 2, 1907
122   Haven S[7], b ——, resides in Portland, Ore
123   Otis[7], b ——, resides in Iona. Mich
124   Abbie B[7], b May 16, 1843, at Elba, N Y, m June 15, 1863, at
        Vevay, Mich , Gilbert Eli Corbin, and had Arthur[8] and Hollis[8],
        res St John, Mich
125   Alice[7], b ——, m ——, Frank Seeley   res Mason. Mich

SEVENTH GENERATION.

71. MELVIN EVANDER[7] FULLER, (*William*[6], *William*[5], *Daniel*[4], *Nathaniel*[3], *James*[2]. *John*[1]), b May 27, 1837, in Gardiner, Me , d Dec 18, 1912
in Peoria, Ill , m Nov 18, 1863, at Galesburg. Ill , Mary A Stanchcliffe
b Jan 24, 1842, at Edenborough, Pa   She resides at Peoria, Ill
    Children
126   **Howard M.**[8], b Apr 3, 1866, m Mary Norstead
127   Sarah Belding[8], b Aug 23, 1867, at Galesburg, m Sept 16 1896,
        at Peoria, Thomas J Simpson , resides at Peoria   Children
        Merle T[9], b Sept 16, 1897, Percy J[9], Dec 23, 1898, and Thomas
        J[9], July 27, 1909

128 Mary Olive[8], b Nov 15, 1870, at Galesburg, m Nov 15, 1894, at Peoria, George C Powers, resides at Peoria, has son Robert I[9], b Dec 12, 1899

129 Irwin L[8], b Sept 19, 1878, at Galesburg, m Apr 28, 1909, at Chicago, Ella Tenney, he is an attorney at Peoria

130 **George C.**[8], b Feb 12, 1884, at Peoria, m Reynold Johnson

73. ALBERT WARREN[7] FULLER,(*William*[6], *William*[5], *Daniel*[4], *Nathaniel*[3], *James*[2], *John*[1]), b Feb 6, 1840, in what is now West Gardiner, Me , known then as Gardiner City, m 1, ——, 1861, Lucy Pease of Monmouth, Me , who d Oct 20, 1874, m 2, July 16, 1879, Mary Davis of Hallowell, Me

He resides in Gardiner, Me

Children

131 A son, b ——; d in infancy

132 Bertha[8], b —— d Mar ——, 1900, m Sept —, 1888, William Goodrich of West Gardiner Me, who d 1910, they had one child, Ina[9], b Oct 1893, m Ray Richardson

133 Ethel Mae[8] b July 21, 1884, m July 2, 1904, Alfred Wessman of Hallowell, Me, and had Phyllis Fuller[8], b Dec. 16, 1905

76. ELISHA D[7] FULLER, (*David*[6], *William*[5], *Daniel*[4], *Nathaniel*[3], *James*[2], *John*[1]), b Sept 16, 1822, in West Gardiner, Me ; d there Apr 16, 1891, in Oct 4, 1847, Emeline Brock

Children

134 **Walter E.**[8], b May 22, 1852, m Sarah R Leach

77. DAVID H[7] FULLER, (*David*[6], *William*[5], *Daniel*[4], *Nathaniel*[3], *James*[2], *John*[1]), b Jan 2, 1824, in West Gardiner, Me , d Mar 17, 1854, in San Francisco, Cal , m Mar 15, 1848, Esther A Hildreth

Resided in West Gardiner

Children

135 **David F.**[8], b May 16, 1851, m Malvina Beach

86. HENRY WILLIAM[7] FULLER, (*James*[6], *William*[5], *Daniel*[4], *Nathaniel*[3], *James*[2] *John*[1]), b Jan 19, 1831, in Gardiner, Me , d Dec 17, 1901, in Wadena, Minn , m Jan 15, 1857, Caroline Tenney, b Aug 11, 1836, at St Albans Me

He lived in Minnesota, enlisted in the 8th Minn Regt and served until the close of the Civil War

Children

136 Maria Louise[8], b Sept. 15, 1858 m Nov 18, 1852 David E Jones, who d Sept 30, 1913 Children Evan Fuller[9], b Feb 13 1884· Byron Tenney[9], Feb 9, 1886, Asher[9], Feb 13 1895 and Paul[9], Dec 31, 1897

137 **James Tenney**[8], b Nov 22, 1871; m Sarah Pearl Clark

89. Alonzo E[7] Fuller (*James[6], William[5], Daniel[4], Nathaniel[3] James[2], John[1]*), b Dec 11, 1836 in Gardiner, Me , d Mar 12, 1904, in Dover, Me , m Feb 8, 1863, Mary E Tenney of St Albans, Me

He removed in 1840 to St Albans Me , and thence in 1890 to Dover, Me

Children

138   Anne L[8], b Sept 21, 1867, in St Albans m Apr 9, 1892, Charles H Rollins of China, Me no children, resides at Dover

139   Elizabeth M[8], b May 24, 1870, at St Albans , resides at Dover

95. George A[7] Fuller, (*Daniel[6], William[5], Daniel[4], Nathaniel[3], James[2], John[1]*) b Apr 18, 1828 in West Gardiner, Me , d Apr 5, 1908, m Nov 4 1860, Charlotte A Swift

He lived and died in West Gardiner, Me

Children

140   Eva[8], b ——

141   Edith H[8], b Apr 6, 1872, d Mar 23, 1906

'142   **Alberton George**[8] b Sept 18, 1864, m Ida Isabel Brown

96. Daniel F[7] Fuller, (*Daniel[6], William[5], Daniel[4], Nathaniel[3], James[2], John[1]*), b Sept 12, 1829, in West Gardiner, Me , d Apr 27, 1876. in Gardiner, Me ; m 1, Apr 20, 1857, Sarah A Swift, m 2, ——, Clara A Jack

Children

143   Jessie May[8], b ——

103. Calvin R[7] Fuller, (*Daniel[6], William[5], Daniel[4], Nathaniel[3], James[2], John[1]*), b Apr 16, 1838, in West Gardiner, Me , d Aug 4, 1910 in Naugatuck, Ct , m Dec 15, 1861, Catherine Milliken

Children:

144   Jennie[8], b ——

145   Harry[8], b ——

146   Mabel[8], b ——

147   Frank[8], b ——.

104. Jesse A[7] Fuller, (*Daniel[6], William[5], Daniel[4], Nathaniel[3], James[2], John[1]*), b May 1, 1840, in West Gardiner, Me ; d June 11, 1906, in Westbrook, Me , m Feb 1, 1865, Lydia E Sherburn.

Children

148   Elmer[8], b ——

149   Ida[8], b ——

105. Francis E[7] Fuller, (*Daniel[6], William[5], Daniel[4], Nathaniel[3], James[2], John[1]*), b Dec 29, 1842, in West Gardner, Me , m Nov 17 1874, Helen Herrick

They live on the Herrick place in West Gardiner, Me
Children
150   Blanche⁸, b ——

107. HORACE A⁷ FULLER, (*Daniel⁶*, *William⁵*, *Daniel⁴*, *Nathaniel³*, *James²*, *John¹*), b Mar 26, 1849, in West Gardiner, Me , m Feb 1, 1873, Mary C Rogers
They live on the place in West Gardiner, Me settled by his father and grandfather in 1806
Children
151   **Lewis W.⁸**, b Sept 5, 1874, m Neva Goodwin
152   Marion J⁸, b Nov 6, 1883, m Oct 2 1907, Harry F May, and has Bernice W⁹, b Feb 16, 1910, and Horace A⁹, June 23, 1911, both born at Asbury Park, N J

109. GEORGE STANWOOD⁷ FULLER, (*George⁶* *William⁵*, *Daniel⁴*, *Nathaniel³*, *James²*, *John¹*), b Nov 5, 1835, d Aug 29 1913; m Sept 27, 1864, Helen Maria Wiley, b Jan 12, 1837, d July 19, 1913
Children:
153   Florence Stanwood⁸, b Sept 29, 1865
154   **Frederic Howard⁸**, b Oct 30, 1868
155   Mary Cass⁸, b Dec 28, 1870, d Sept, 1871
156   Robinson Cram⁸, b May 16, 1877; d Mar, 1893

113. BENJAMIN FRANKLIN⁷ FULLER, (*George⁶*, *William⁵*, *Daniel⁴*, *Nathaniel³*, *James²*, *John¹*), b May 18, 1846, d. Feb. 12, 1912, m June 26, 1872, Amanda Lyford Snow, b Dec 24, 1846
Children
157   **Charles Benjamin⁸**, b Feb 13, 1875, m. Alice Elliot Lawrence
158   **George⁸**, b Apr 24, 1878, m Charlotte Frances Coombs

114. CHARLES THEODORE⁷ FULLER, (*George⁶*, *William⁵*, *Daniel⁴*, *Nathaniel³*, *James²*, *John¹*), b. Mar 31, 1852, m 1, Nov 11, 1874 Laura E Laird, b Sept , 1852, d Dec 15, 1876, m 2, Oct 11, 1881, Anne Clement, b Mar. 24, 1853, d June 2, 1890
Children
159   **Ernest⁸**, b Nov 25, 1876, m ——, Viva ——, b July 4, 1878
160   Emily C⁸ b July 30, 1884
161   Ray⁸, b May 18, 1887
162   Harry⁸, b May 26, 1890

EIGHTH GENERATION.

126. HOWARD M⁸ FULLER, (*Melvin E⁷*, *William⁶*, *William⁵*, *Daniel⁴*, *Nathaniel³*, *James²*, *John¹*), b Apr 3, 1866, at Galesburg, Ill , m 1887 at Bishops Hill, Ill , Mary Norstead

They reside at Peoria, Ill

Children

163   Earl H⁹, b Nov 21, 1888; m Aug 14, 1912, at Peoria, Edna
        Gardner; they reside at Jackson, Mich

164   Glen M⁹, b Jan 23, 1890, resides at Peoria

130. GEORGE C⁸ FULLER, (*Melvin E⁷, William⁶, William⁵, Daniel⁴
Nathaniel³, James², John¹*), b Feb 12, 1884, in Peoria, Ill , m Jan 22.
1907 at Minneapolis, Minn, Reynold Johnson

Reside at North Battleford, Sask, Canada

Children

165   Margaret L⁹, b Apr 16 1908, at Peoria, Ill

166   Irwin L⁹, b May 3, 1911, at Peoria

134. WALTER E⁸ FULLER, (*Elisha D⁷, David⁶, William⁵, Daniel⁴
Nathaniel³, James² John¹*), b May 22, 1852, in Hallowell, Me , m Dec
24 1875, Sarah R Leach

He resides in West Gardiner, Me, where he has been chairman of
the Board of Selectmen for many years

Children

167   Lena Estelle⁹ b Dec 21, 1879, m July 27, 1905, George Gross, and
        resides in Gardiner City

168   Laura Belle⁹, b Dec 21, 1882, m Sept 1, 1905, Frederic Johnson,
        and resides in Portland, Me

169   Henrietta G⁹, b Nov 26, 1889, m June 23, 1909, Ray Burns, and
        resides in Augusta, Me

135. DAVID F⁸ FULLER, (*David H⁷, David⁶, William⁶, Daniel⁴, Nathaniel³, James², John¹*), b May 16, 1851, in West Gardiner, Me , m
——, Malvina Bean

Resides in Hallowell, Me

Children

170   Pearle E⁹, b Apr. 2, 1875, m Aug 25, 1902, Maude Peacock,
        and resides in Augusta, Me

171   Lenora E.⁹, b Oct 7, 1880

137. JAMES TENNEY⁸ FULLER, (*Henry W⁷, James⁶, William⁵, Daniel⁴,
Nathaniel³, James², John¹*), b Nov 22, 1871, in Monticello, Minn , m
Aug 21, 1902, Sarah Pearl Clark, at Verdun, Neb

He resides at New Rockford, North Dakota

Children

172   Lois Lavina⁹, b Feb 2, 1904, at Le Roy, Minn

173   Henry Clark⁹, b Mar 9, 1905, at Le Roy

174   Ruth⁹, b Sept 10, 1906, at Zumbrota, Minn

142. ALBERTON GEORGE[8] FULLER, (*George A[7], Daniel[6], William[5], Daniel[4], Nathaniel[3], James[2], John[1]*), b Sept 18, 1864, in West Gardiner, Me , d there Apr' 4, 1913; m ——, 1892, Ida Isabel Brown, who survives him and resides with her children in Gardiner, Me (1914)

Children

175 Mildred Augusta[9], b Mar. 8, 1895, in West Gardiner, Me
176 Verne Alvin[9], b Mar 21, 1897, in Bangor, Me
177 Edith Annabell[9], b Nov 1, 1899, in Farmingdale, Me
178 Earl Burton[9], b Sept 15, 1902, in West Gardiner

151. LEWIS W[8] FULLER, (*Horace A[7], Daniel[6], William[5], Daniel[4], Nathaniel[3], James[2], John[1]*), b Sept 5, 1874, in West Gardiner, Me , m Sept 15, 1896, Neva Goodwin

They reside in West Gardiner

Children

179 Merle R[9], b Jan 4, 1898
180 Maurice A[9], b Feb 22, 1900
181 Esther L[9], b Apr 15, 1902
182 Adria R[9], b Aug 24, 1903
183 James H[9], b Nov 25, 1910
184 Lewis S[9], b Apr 4, 1912

154. FREDERIC HOWARD[8] FULLER, (*George S[7], George[6], William[5], Daniel[4], Nathaniel[3], James[2], John[1]*), b Oct 30, 1868 , m Feb 4, 1896, Eva Dale, b Dec 8, 1878

Children

185 Helen Bernice[9], b Feb 13, 1897; d Oct 6, 1909
186 Marion Buckley[9], b Sept 29 1899
187 Clifton Dale[9], b Sept 10, 1903.
188 Hester[9], b Sept 29, 1905
189 Walter Howard[9], b Jan 9, 1912

157. CHARLES BENJAMIN[8] FULLER, (*Benjamin F[7], George[6], William[5], Daniel[4], Nathaniel[3] James[2], John[1]*), b Feb 13, 1875, m June 27, 1906, Alice Elliot Lawrence b Jan 2, 1877.

He is a physician, residing in Waltham.

Children

190 Rosamond[9], b May 21, 1910
191 Charles Benjamin[9], b May 19, 1912

158. GEORGE[8] FULLER, (*Benjamin F[7], George[6], William[5], Daniel[4], Nathaniel[3], James[2], John[1]*), b Apr 24 1878 , m Aug 15, 1905, Charlotte Frances Coombs, b Apr 12, 1880

Children
192   Frances Snow[9], b July 13, 1907
193   Charlotte Coombs[9], b July 8, 1913

159. ERNEST[8] FULLER, (*Charles T[7], George[6], William[5], Daniel[4], Nathaniel[3], James[2], John[1]*), b Nov. 25, 1876, m. Aug 22, 1896, Viva ——,
b July 4, 1878
Children:
194   Beatrice Irene[9] b Apr 14, 1897.

FIFTH GROUP

THIRD GENERATION.

NATHANIEL³ FULLER, AND SOME OF HIS DESCENDANTS

41. NATHANIEL⁴ FULLER, (*Nathaniel²*, *John¹*), bapt Jan 7, 1717, in Ipswich, d ——; m 1, Nov 23, 1738, Elizabeth Ireland, who d Nov, 1739, m 2 Feb 6, 1740-1, Deliverance Burke "both of Ipswich," m 3, Jan 29 1749-50, Deborah Millet, of Beverly, who d Dec 14, 1758

He was a tailor by trade

Children

Nathaniel⁴, b Feb, 1741, probably the Nathaniel who d Jan, 1753
Deborah⁴, bapt Sept 24, 1752
Mary⁴, bapt Jan 4, 1756
Mary⁴, bapt Nov 5, 1758

SIXTH GROUP

THIRD GENERATION.

JOSEPH³ FULLER, AND SOME OF HIS DESCENDANTS

27. JOSEPH³ FULLER, (*Joseph²*, *John¹*) b Aug 13, 1690, at Ipswich, d Mar 7, 1763-4, (Suffield, Ct Record), m 1, Sept 8, 1715, Bathsheba, dau of John Hanchett, m 2, at Ipswich, Apr 29, 1729, Elizabeth Hutchins

Joseph³ Fuller received his portion of the estate of Joseph², his father, by deed, Nov 12, 1714, recorded in Springfield   The inventory of estate of Joseph³ Fuller, Apr 8 1745, shows "2 notes of Jacob Fuller of Norwich," his brother   Joseph³ Fuller's will was made Oct 10, 1743, probated Apr 10, 1744, at Northampton (Vol 6, p 212)

Children.
1   Mary⁴, ⎫ twins, b June 11, 1716; ⎰ d Apr 17, 1717.
2   Bathsheba⁴, ⎭   ⎱ Nothing further found
3   Mary⁴, b Feb 8, 1717-18
4   Sarah⁴, b May 31, 1720 d July 13, 1744; m Dec 28, 1743, William King, b Aug 10, 1741, in Suffield, Ct
5   Hannah⁴, b Oct 3, 1721, d Jan 2, 1722
6   Hannah⁴, b Sept 1, 1722, m Oct 25, 1748, Timothy Mather
7   **Joseph⁴**, b Aug 25, 1726; m Rebecca Norton

FOURTH GENERATION.

7. JOSEPH⁴ FULLER (*Joseph²*, *Joseph³*, *John¹*), b Aug 25, 1726, in Suffield, Ct , d there Mar 25, 1807, m Mar. 11, 1762, Rebecca Norton

Children, born in Suffield
8   Rebecca⁵, b Apr 7, 1764
9   **Joseph⁵**, b Nov 11, 1765, m Mary King
10 Apollos⁵, b Dec 21, 1767; d Aug 18, 1770
11 **John⁵**, b May 7, 1770, m. Mary Remington
12 **Apollos⁵**, b May 29, 1772, m Rebecca Smith

FIFTH GENERATION.

9. JOSEPH⁵ FULLER, (*Joseph⁴, Joseph³, Joseph², John¹*), b. Nov 11, 1765, in Suffield, Ct , d there Dec 17, 1843, m June 30, 1796, Mary King, who d June 30, 1835, aged 71.

Children recorded in Suffield

13 **George⁶**, b June 24, 1798, m Eliza Fuller
14 Mary⁶, b Sept 11, 1800; d June 28, 1806
15. **Joseph⁶**, b July 13, 1803, m Cordelia Smith
16 **William Franklin⁶**, b Apr 8, 1806; m 1, Harriet Jewett, m. 2, Mary Fowler

11. JOHN⁵ FULLER, (*Joseph⁴, Joseph³, Joseph², John¹*), b May 7, 1770, in Suffield, Ct , d there Aug 21, 1834, m Jan. 25, 1798, Mary Remington

Children.

17 John⁶, b May 5, 1800; d July 8, 1864; m May 5, 1829, Sybil Remington Nothing further found
18 Eliza⁶, b July 29, 1802; m Nov 24, 1824, George Fuller.
19 Mary⁶, b Sept 1, 1807, m Aug 16, 1840, Thomas Remington

12. APOLLOS⁵ FULLER, (*Joseph⁴, Joseph³, Joseph², John¹*), b May 29, 1772, in Suffield, Ct , d Oct 6, 1847; m Dec 5, 1793, Rebecca Smith, who d Jan 25, 1862, aged 89

Children recorded in Suffield

20 **Gamaliel⁶**, b Apr 16, 1795, m Maria Hathaway.
21 **William⁶**, b Nov 1, 1796, m 1, Emily Granger, m. 2, Maria Fuller
22 Apollos⁶, b Apr 21, 1803; d Sept 13, 1827.
23 Harriet⁶, b Nov —, 1805, d ——, m Mar. 30, 1830, Hiram K Granger
24 **Henry⁶**, b. Apr. 20, 1808, m Jane Button.

SIXTH GENERATION.

13. GEORGE⁶ FULLER, (*Joseph⁵, Joseph⁴, Joseph³, Joseph², John¹*), b June 24, 1798, in Suffield, Ct ; d Nov 8, 1873, m Nov 24, 1824, Eliza Fuller, b July 29 1802, No 18 of this Group She d Jan 25, 1865

Children.

25 Child, b Nov 14, 1826; d Nov 14, 1826
26 Mary Elizabeth⁷, b May 22, 1828, d Apr 27, 1906.
27. Eliza A.⁷, b June 25, 1830; d Nov 26, 1912, m May 30, 1849, George Remington, who d Jan 31, 1902
28 Jane M⁷, b Aug 16. 1835, d July 2, 1836
29 **George H.⁷**, b June 17, 1837; m Sarah F Hathaway

14

15. Joseph[6] Fuller, (*Joseph[5], Joseph[4], Joseph[3], Joseph[2], John[1]*), b July 13, 1803 in Suffield, Ct , d ——, m May 25, 1830, Cordelia Smith, b Aug 15, 1808, in Chester; d Feb 15, 1896

Children

30 Reuben T[7] b July 20, 1831, d Sept 8, 1831
31 Caroline R[7], b Sept 14, 1832, m May 16, 1873 or 4, Ashbel C Harmon
32 Horace S[7], b Apr 10, 1835, d Dec 30, 1910, in Hartford, Ct
33 Dwight S[7], b Oct 5, 1837, m Sarah J Fowler They reside in Suffield, Ct, where he is a director in the National and Savings Banks He was Representative in 1895 and 1896 No children
34 Sarah J[7], b Feb 17, 1841, d Dec 1, 1871, m Oct 7, 1868, Ashbel C Harmon
35 Frank[7], b May 15, 1844, d July 7, 1847
36 Mary[7], b Apr. 16, 1849, m Sept 22, 1870, Joseph B Fairfield, and had Julia Louise[5], b Jan 24, 1878

16. William Franklin[6] Fuller, (*Joseph[5], Joseph[4], Joseph[3], Joseph[2]. John[1]*), b Apr 8, 1806, in Suffield, Ct ; d Dec 22, 1893, m 1, Nov 12, 1828, Harriet Jewett, b in Middletown, Ct, June 2, 1860, d Mar 14, 1872, in Lafayette, Ind , m 2, Aug 27, 1874, Mary Fowler, who d Dec. 30, 1897, aged 90, in Suffield

Children

37 Harriet Louisa[7], b Sept 28, 1829, in Suffield, m May, 1847, Lucius Duel Hart, and had Charles Franklin[8], b 1855, in Oregon, Frank Edward[8], and Frederick Edwin[8], twins, b 1857, in Oregon, Harriet Lydia[8], b Sept 25, 1859, in Oregon, Nellie Adelaide[8], b Aug 15, 1868, in Jefferson, Mich , and Augustus DeWitt[8], b Nov 5, 1875, in Eugene City, Oregon
38 Lucy King[7], b June 26, 1831, d July 6, 1831, in Suffield
39 Mary Elizabeth[7], b Aug 16, 1834, d Oct 18, 1840, in Jefferson, Mich
40 Julia Maria[7], b Jan 21, 1837, in Jefferson, Mich , d July 16, 1857, in Lafayette, Ind
41 Mary Frances[7], b Aug 9, 1840, in Jefferson, Mich
42 Joseph Augustus[7], b June 2, 1843, in Jefferson, m Jan 16, 1870, in Indianapolis, Ind , Martha Olive Edwards No issue
43 Adelaide Jewett[7], b May 29, 1846, in Jefferson, m Dec 26, 1867, in Lafayette, Ind , Nathaniel A Chamberlain, and had Mary Frances[8], b Jan 31, 1868, in Lafayette, Augustus Claire[8], b Oct 25, 1875, in Montmorenci, Ind ; Raymond Gregory[8], b July 13, 1877, at Shawnee Mound, d 1896, in Denver, Colo , Orlo Jewett[8] twin, b July 13, 1877, d 1877; Lynn Closser[8], b Jan 24, 1881, at La Porte, Ind , and O Louise[8], b Dec 22, 1882, at Canyon City, Colo , d Feb 19, 1886, in Denver, Colo

20. Gamaliel[6] Fuller, (*Apollos[5], Joseph[4], Joseph[3], Joseph[2], John[1]*), b Apr 16, 1795, in Suffield, Ct ; d Jan. 24, 1852, in Springfield, m May 1, 1822, Maria Hathaway, who m 2d, Gamaliel Fuller's brother William

Children of Gamaliel and Maria (Hathaway) Fuller, all born in Suffield, Ct., were

44 **Hiram Gamaliel⁷**, b Oct 23, 1823, m ——
45 **Luther H.⁷**, b Sept 7, 1830, m Nancy C Bugbey
46 **Maria Jane⁷**, b Mar 16, 1834, d Nov 22, 1900, m Oct 29, 1855, Carnot O Spencer, of Essex, Ct
47 **Apollos Sanford⁷**, b Oct 18, 1829 or 30, m 1, Hannah Johnson, m 2, Mrs Minerva Lorane Taylor
48. **James Hazard⁷**, b Mar 22, 1837, m Ruth Ann Raymond

21. WILLIAM⁶ FULLER, (*Apollos⁵, Joseph⁴, Joseph³, Joseph², John¹*), b Nov. 1, 1796, in Suffield, Ct , d there Nov 17, 1874, m 1, Nov 25, 1823, Emily Granger, who d Dec 26, 1856, aged 59; m 2, Nov 5, 1861, Maria Fuller, widow of his brother Gamaliel

Children, all born in Suffield

49 **William Henry⁷**, b Nov 19, 1825, m, Sarah Adaline Hare
50. Catherine⁷, b June ——, 1833, d Nov 20, 1840
51. Edward A.⁷, b Aug 22, 1842, m Sept 23, 1862, Sarah Leonard Pease b Feb 1, 1844, in Suffield, dau of Don and Susan (Alden) Pease They have no children He has been first Selectman of Suffield since 1904; represeented Suffield in the General Assembly of Connecticut from 1904 to 1911, is a member of the Second Baptist Church; director of the Conn State Prison, director National Exchange Bank of Hartford, member of several fraternal associations, and a soldier of the Civil War

24. HENRY⁶ FULLER, (*Apollos⁵, Joseph⁴, Joseph³, Joseph², John¹*), b Apr 20, 1808, in Suffield, Ct ; d Apr 3, 1881, m Sept 20, 1832, Jane Button, who d Sept 13, 1891, aged 78

Children recorded in Suffield

52 Charles⁷, b May 5, 1834; d June 5, 1835.
53. **Cecil H.⁷**, b May 19, 1836, m Emma J. Kendall
54 Harriet⁷, b. May 10, 1840; d May 23, 1840
55 Charles D⁷, b Jan 17, 1847, d Jan 21, 1865

SEVENTH GENERATION.

29. GEORGE H⁷ FULLER, (*George⁶, Joseph⁵, Joseph⁴, Joseph³, Joseph², John¹*), b. June 17, 1837, in Suffield, Ct , m. Nov. 19, 1862, Sarah T. Hathaway, at Washington, Mass She d Oct 17, 1890

He resides in Suffield

Children.

56 Emma E⁸, b Nov 3, 1863, m Aug 22, 1888, Arthur B Call, and had Frances M⁹, b June 6, 1889, and Raymond F.⁹, Nov 29, 1881. Frances M Call m. Oct 17, 1911, at Pasadena, Cal, Arthur T Gaylord, and had Stanley W¹⁰, b Apr 10, 1913
57 Frances M⁸, b Aug 23, 1865, m June 6, 1894, E E Clark, and had Ernest M.⁹, b. May 3, 1895

58   Martha A[8], b Sept 21, 1868, m Feb 10, 1892, Egerton Hemen-
way, and had Marjorie F[9], b Oct. 6, 1894

44. HIRAM GAMALIEL[7] FULLER, (*Gamaliel[6]*, *Apollos[5]*, *Joseph[4]*, *Joseph[3]*, *Joseph[2]*, *John[1]*), b Oct 23, 1823, in Suffield, Ct ; d Aug 2, 1897, at Akron, O , m ——
Children:
59   Mary Maria[8], b Feb 18, 1859, in Akron, O where she now (1914) resides

45. LUTHER HATHAWAY[7] FULLER, (*Gamaliel[6]*, *Apollos[5]*, *Joseph[4]*, *Joseph[3]*, *Joseph[2]*, *John[1]*), b Sept 7, 1830, in Suffield, Ct , d Feb 28, 1894, in Vernon, Ct , m Dec. 1, 1855, Nancy C Bugbey
Children
60   Clara Maria[8], b Jan 23, 1862, in Suffield, m Oct 20, 1887, Rev Edward Wright Potter, and had Clara May[9], b May 2, 1889, and Edward Keeney[9], b May 2, 1891

47. APOLLOS SAFFORD[7] FULLER, (*Gamaliel[6]*, *Apollos[5]*, *Joseph[4]*, *Joseph[3]*, *Joseph[2]*, *John[1]*), b Oct 18, 1829 or 1830, in Suffield, Ct , d Oct 13, 1893, in Cedar Falls, Ia , m. 1, ——, Hannah Johnson, m 2, ——, Mrs Minerva Lorane Taylor
Children by first wife .
61   Clara[8], b ——, d young
62   Frank G[8], b ——, was living, some years ago, in Kentucky
By second wife
63   Hal Carnot[8], b Mar 10, 1875, m June 12, 1907, Ann Hamilton, and resides (1914) in Lehigh, Iowa
64   Marie L[8], b Aug 1, 1879, resides in Mason City, Iowa

48. JAMES HAZARD[7] FULLER, (*Gamaliel[6]*, *Apollos[5]*, *Joseph[4]*, *Joseph[3]*, *Joseph[2]*, *John[1]*), b Mar 22, 1837, in Suffield, Ct ; d Oct 21, 1874, in Springfield, m Oct 22, 1861, Ruth Ann Raymond, who m 2d, Henry J Granger, of Suffield
Children ·
65.   Alice Spencer[8], b Jan 25, 1866, in Suffield, now (1914) and for 32 years, a resident of Hartford, Ct
66   Anna Raymond[8], b June 28, 1875, in Agawam, m June 12, 1900, in Hartford, Ct , William Edwin Stanton, b July 17, 1873, in Sterling, Ct   Three sons have been born to them , Edward Fuller[9], b Mar 21, 1904, in Sterling, Raymond Hayes[9], b Mar 11, 1910, in Hartford, d Mar 23, 1910, and Harwood Raymond[9], b Oct 28, 1913

49. WILLIAM HENRY[7] FULLER, (*William[6]*, *Apollos[5]*, *Joseph[4]*, *Joseph[3]*, *Joseph[2]*, *John[1]*), b Nov 19, 1825, in Suffield, Ct ; d Dec 28, 1890, at

Dansville, N Y; m Sept 16, 1851, Sarah Adaline Hare, of East Brookfield

Children, all born in Suffield

67   William Francis, b June 14, 1852, m 1, Harriet Arabella Spencer, m 2, Isabella Thompson
68   Charles Sumner, b Oct 10, 1855, m Emma F Dudin
69   Emily Adaline[8], b Oct 9, 1857, m June 7, 1876, 1 Luther Spencer, resides in Suffield

53. CECIL HENRY[7] FULLER, (*Henry*[6], *Apollos*[5], *Joseph*[4], *Joseph*[3], *Joseph*[2], *John*[1]), b. May 19, 1836, in Suffield. Ct , m 1, Nov 17, 1859, Emma Jane Kendall, who d Feb 21, 1899, m 2, May 2, 1900, Mrs Helen M. King

He resides in Suffield

Children

70   Apollos[8], b Nov 24, 1860; m May 10, 1883, Nellie M Haskins
71   Addie Jane[8], b. May 4, 1863, d Jan 7, 1865   .
72   Harriet Maria[8], b Dec 1, 1865, m Oct 6, 1887, Howard A Henshaw, and has Edith F[9], b July 29, 1889, Mary E[9], Nov 20, 1892, Walter R[9], Nov 16, 1899, and Wallace H[9], Mar 15, 1902   Edith F m Feb 8, 1913, Burt K Spencer, and has W Howard Spencer[10], b Nov 29, 1913
73   Lizzie Kendall[8], b June 8, 1870, m Oct 2, 1890, Charles E Haskins, and has Edward N[9], b June 10, 1895, J Harold[9], Apr 25, 1902, and Howard F[9], Apr. 5, 1906
74   Jennie Louise[8], b Dec 5, 1871, m Feb 12, 1900, Zenas H Sikes, and has Marion E[9], b Mar 6, 1904, and Ralph F[9], b June 11, 1908
75.   **Henry**[8], b Dec 6, 1877, m Hattie S Johnson
76   Anne Gertrude[8], b. Mar 2, 1882, m Mar 29, 1913, Frang G Pomeroy, of Windsor Locks, Ct

EIGHTH GENERATION.

67. WILLIAM FRANCIS[8] FULLER, (*William H*[7], *William*[6], *Apollos*[5], *Joseph*[4], *Joseph*[3], *Joseph*[2], *John*[1]), b June 14, 1852, in Suffield, Ct d Nov 29, 1909, in Hartford, Ct ; m 1, Apr 25, 1877, Harriet Arabella Spencer, m 2, ——, Isabelle Thompson

Children, of first wife

77   Bessie Young[9], b Feb 24, 1881; resides in Suffield
78   William Spencer[9], b Oct 28, 1885, m Nov 22, 1910, Amy B Street, b in Lebanon, Ct   They reside in Suffield

68. CHARLES SUMNER[8] FULLER, (*William H*[7], *William*[6], *Apollos*[5], *Joseph*[4], *Joseph*[3], *Joseph*[2], *John*[1]), b Oct. 10, 1855, in Suffield, Ct ; m ——, Emma F. Judin

He resides in Suffield, where he is cashier of the First National Bank

Children, all born in Suffield

79   Lawrence Ives[9], b Nov 18, 1889
80   Sumner Francis[9], b Oct 25, 1892
81   Dorothy Adaline[9], b Dec 12, 1898

75. HENRY[8] FULLER, (*Cecil H*[7], *Henry*[6], *Apollos*[5], *Joseph*[4], *Joseph*[3], *Joseph*[2], *John*[1]), b Dec 6 1877, in Suffield, Ct ; m Apr 12 1900, Harriet S Johnson, b in Southwick

Children

82   Cecil H[9], b May 5, 1903, d Sept 30, 1904
83   Maria Kendall[9], b Jan 9, 1906
84   Nellie E[9], b May 11, 1908
85   Allan H[9], b June 25, 1913

SEVENTH GROUP

THIRD GENERATION.

WILLIAM² FULLER, AND SOME OF HIS DESCENDANTS

29. WILLIAM³ FULLER, (*Joseph²*, *John¹*), b Mar 7, 1694, in Ipswich, d there May 27, 1754, m Int Pub 27-8-1716, with Sarah Waite Children, born in Ipswich

1. Sarah⁴, bapt Aug 13, 1721, d May 8, 1736
2. William⁴, bapt Mar 29, 1724, d Sept. 3, 1736
3. Lucy⁴, bapt Aug 28, 1726; d Mar 19, 1767, m Int. Pub May 4, 1745, with David Andrews· had children (Andrews) Lucy⁵, Mary⁵, Hannah⁵ and William⁵
4. Thomas⁴, bapt May 11, 1729, d. Sept 17, 1736.
5. Benjamin⁴, bapt Aug 1, 1731; d Sept 11, 1736
6. Joseph⁴, bapt Feb 10, 1733-4, d. Sept 11, 1736
7. Sarah⁴, bapt. Oct 24, 1736

EIGHTH GROUP

THIRD GENERATION.

JOHN³ FULLER, AND SOME OF HIS DESCENDANTS

31. JOHN³ FULLER, (*Joseph²*, *John¹*), b Apr 22, 1701, at Ipswich, d. ——, m Int Pub Dec 10, 1726, with Mary Howard, who d Nov 28, 1728; m 2, July 29, 1731, at Ipswich, Hannah Lord   Between 1740 and 1745 he removed to Hampton, Ct

Children by second wife b at Ipswich

1   **John⁴**, bapt May 7, 1732, m Hannah Kimball
2   Samuel⁴, bapt Jan 20, 1733-34, m Sarah Reed
3   Daniel⁴, bapt June 13, 1736, m Patiena Steadman   No children, adopted a daughter
4   **Joseph⁴**, not in Ipswich V R but given by Newton Fuller as b Nov 28, 1738, m Mary Holt
5   William⁴, b Jan 25, 1740, m Lucy Hodgkins
6   Hannah⁴, b June 12, 1743, m Apr 17, 1766, Rev Elijah Fitch and had one child—a son, Elijah Lord Fitch, b Dec 12, 1766

FOURTH GENERATION.

1. JOHN⁴ FULLER (*John³*, *Joseph²*, *John¹*), bapt May 7, 1732, in Ipswich, d ——, m ——, Hannah Kimball, and resided in that part of Mansfield, Ct. now called Hampton

Children, succession not known

7   William⁵, b ——
8   **Benjamin⁵**, b June 6, 1758, m 1, Joanna Trowbridge, m 2, Clarissa Utley
9   John⁵, b ——, d about 1807
10   Jesse⁵, b ——
     and perhaps others

4. JOSEPH⁴ FULLER, (*John³*, *Joseph²*, *John¹*), b Nov 28, 1738, in Ipswich, d Jan 29, 1805, in Hampton, Ct; m Nov 7, 1771, Mary Holt, who d Oct 23, 1824, aged 72

He lived in Hampton, Ct

Children

11 Mary⁶, b Oct 13, 1772, m ——, 1793, D⁻ Thomas⁵ Fuller (6th
    Group, Thomas of Woburn line), and had Emma⁶, b ——, 1794,
    d 1874, unm , Mary⁶, b ——, 1796, d 1824, m 1815, Dr
    Theodore Pomery, Elizabeth⁶, b 1798, d 1870, m 1828, Judge
    Eben Morehouse, Catherine⁶, b 1801, d 1838, m 1822, Rev
    E S Barrows

12 Chloe⁵, b Dec 11, 1774, m Nov 21, 1803, Dr Trumble Dorrance

13 **Elijah⁶**, b Apr 21, 1777, m Dec 5, 1803, Ruth Robinson

14 Joseph⁶ b Jan 6, 1779, m ——, 1809, Elizabeth Fish.

15 Elisha⁶, b Jan 30, 1782, m Oct 29, 1805, Phebe Burnham

16 Harvey⁶, b Sept 13, 1784, m Dec 16, 1810, Lydia Denison

17 Daniel⁵, b Feb 14, 1789, m ——, 1821, Mary Bird

NOTE—The genealogy of Joseph⁴ Fuller, (John³, Joseph², John¹),
and his descendants, here given, came from correspondents of the late
Newton Fuller, genealogist, of New London, Ct I find no such
Joseph Fuller mentioned in the Vital Records of Ipswich. W. H F

FIFTH GENERATION.

8. BENJAMIN⁵ FULLER, (*John⁴, John³, Joseph², John¹*), b June 16
1758, in Hampton, Ct (formerly a part of Pomfret, Ct), d Mar 26
1840, at Hampton, m 1, Sept 28, 1780 Joanna Trowbridge who d
Aug 19, 1822, "both of Pomfret;" m 2 Apr 16, 1823, Clarissa Utley,
who survived him, and was pensioned in 1853, aged 73 years, and had
Warrant, No 26626 for 160 acres of bounty land issued to her, May
20, 1856, on account of her husband s services in the Revolutionary
War

The pension papers mention Benjamin's brothers John and Jesse
Fuller

Children

18 Benjamin⁶, b May 1, 1781, m 1, Lucy Hodgkins, m 2, Sarah
    Goddard

19 **Elisha⁶**, b Jan 26, 1783, m 1, Polly Spencer, m. 2, Irene Francis

20 **Daniel⁶**, b Oct 7, 1785, m 1, Zernah Hall, m 2, Betsy Neff, m
    3, Lydia Jones

21 **James⁶**, b Jan 29, 1788, m Pamelia Warren

22 Thomas⁶, b Aug 16, 1790, d Nov 3, 1841; m Mar 14, 1827,
    Margaret S Preston, who d. July 1, 1853 No record of
    children

23. Lester⁶, b. Sept 29, 1794, d Oct 8, 1818, aged 24, in Vernon, Ct
     He was a physician

24 **Lewis⁶**, b Oct 20, 1797, m Eliza Holt

13. ELIJAH⁵ FULLER, (*Joseph⁴, John³, Joseph², John¹*), b Apr 21,
1777, in Hampton, Ct , d Apr 30, 1864, m Dec 5, 1803, Ruth Robinson
Children

25   Laura P⁶, b Apr 14, 1809; d Nov 14, 1871, m ——, 1833, Rev Sidney Mills

26   **Thomas A.⁶**, b Sept 8, 1812, m Harriet DeForest

27   Marcia E⁶, b Jan 1, 1815, m ——, 1842, Dr Erastus King

28   Fitch E⁶, b July 12, 1820, m 1. ——, 1846, Harriet McCall; m. 2, ——, 1851, Adelia M McFarland

SIXTH GENERATION.

19. ELISHA⁶ FULLER, (*Benjamin⁵, John⁴, John³, Joseph², John¹*), b Jan 26, 1783, in Hampton, Ct , d ——, m 1, ——, Polly Spencer; m 2, ——, Irene Francis

     Children

29   Francis D ⁷, b about 1823, m Feb 26, 1846, Fanny M Clark

30   Joseph Henry⁷, b. Feb 23, 1827, in Ashford, Ct ; m. Nov 23, 1852, Mary Juliette Adams, b May 28, 1828, dau of Moses Adams of Canterbury, Ct
     Perhaps there were other children

20. DANIEL⁶ FULLER, (*Benjamin⁵, John⁴, John³, Joseph², John¹*), b Oct 7, 1785, in Hampton, Ct ; d Jan 6, 1882, m. 1, Jan. 1, 1809, Zernah Hall, who d Feb 24, 1820; m 2, Sept 26, 1820, Elizabeth Neff, who d Nov 29, 1850; m 3, ——, Lydia T. Jones.

     Children.

31   Delia Amanda⁷, b Dec 10, 1809, m June 16, 1840, Nathan Coleman, of Coventry, Ct , and had Orton E ⁸, Henry D ⁸, Stewart⁸, Mary F ⁸, Alice⁸, and Laura W ⁸ Coleman

32   **Andrew Hall⁷**, b Oct 19, 1811, m 1, Harriet Preston, m 2, Cornelia Tillinghast

33   **Samuel Stearns⁷**, b. Nov 20, 1813; m Olive Hibbard

34   Aden⁷, b Mar 5, 1816, d Dec 28, 1816

35   Ruth Hall⁷, b Feb 28, 1818, d Mar 29, 1906, m Nov 27, 1838, Charles H Butters.

36   Lucinda⁷, b Oct 20, 1822, d Nov 3, 1830

37   Clarissa Utley⁷, b May 8, 1826, d. Apr 30, 1908, m Sept 8, 1847, Ethan A Barrows.

38   Ann Eliza⁷, b Jan 28, 1830; d Feb 5, 1833

39   **Daniel Ellison⁷**, b June 11, 1831, m Mary Ann Cleveland

21. JAMES⁶ FULLER, (*Benjamin⁵, John⁴, John³, Joseph², John¹*), b Jan 29, 1778, in Hampton, Ct , d Apr 29, 1884, in Hampton, m Dec. 17, 1808, Pamelia Warner, who d May 5, 1866.

     Children:

40   Mary J ⁷, b June 11, 1810

41   James W ⁷, b Jan 23, 1813

42   Laura J ⁷, b May 19, 1815

43   Albert⁷, b May 27, 1817

44 Josiah W⁷, b May 14, 1820
45 Dorianna⁷, b Oct 18, 1823
46 John B⁷, b June 10, 1826; m Mar 30, 1858, in Pittsfield, Mass,
   Fanny E Root
47 George⁷, b Aug 10, 1829
48 Dwight⁷, b Aug 24, 1833
49 **George W.⁷**, b May 29, 1836, m Eunice Hammond

24. Lewis⁶ Fuller, (*Benjamin⁵, John⁴, John², Joseph², John¹*), b
Oct 20, 1797, in Hampton, Ct, d ——, m ——, Eliza Holt, b in
Hampton, Sept 18, 1800, d May 26, 1860
 Children
50 Jacob H⁷, b about 1821, m Dec 24, 1874, in Paxton, Mass, Sarah
   C (Harrington) Pickett b in Phillipston, Mass, dau of David
   and Olive G Harrington
51.
52
53
54
55

26. Thomas A⁶ Fuller, (*Elijah⁵, Joseph⁴, John³, Joseph², John¹*), b
Sept 6, 1812, d ——, m ——1840, Harriet DeForest.
 Children
56 **Charles A.⁷**, b Aug. 17, 1841
57 Antoinette DeForest⁷, b Aug 3, 1840, d June, 1862
   No information as to places" of birth, marriage, death or
   residence furnished

SEVENTH GENERATION.

32. Andrew Hall⁷ Fuller, (*Daniel⁶, Benjamin⁵, John⁴, John³, Joseph², John¹*), b Oct 19, 1811, in ——, d Apr 27, 1891, in ——, m 1,
——, Harriet Preston; m 2, ——, Cornelia Tillinghast
 Children
58 Harriet P⁸, b Apr. 8, 1839, m June 21, 1865, Lucian Fuller

33. Samuel Stearns⁷ Fuller, (*Daniel⁶, Benjamin⁵, John⁴, John³,
Joseph², John¹*), b Nov. 20, 1813, at Mansfield Center, Ct ; d June 30.
1905, at Mansfield Four Corners, Ct, m Mar. 4, 1841, Olive Hibbard,
who d Mar 2, 1902, dau of Gen Daniel Hibbard
 Mr Fuller was postmaster at Mansfield, Ct nearly 50 years
 Children
59 Louisa M⁸, b Nov 27, 1842
60 Mary Elizabeth⁸, b Sept, 1844, m Oct 15, 1872, Orrin C West
   and had Ernest⁹, Mabel⁹, and Grace⁹

61   Samuel H.[8], b Mar 1, 1846, m Mary A Ledoit
62   Ninetta A[8], b Feb 4, 1850; d Nov 2, 1885
63   Charlotte A[8], b Sept. 3, 1852; d May 2, 1871

39. DANIEL ELLISON[7] FULLER, (*Daniel[6]*, *Benjamin[5]*, *John[4]*, *John[3]*, *Joseph[2]*, *John[1]*), b June 11, 1831, in Mansfield, Ct , m in Mansfield, Ct , June 30, 1853, Mary Ann Bussel Cleaveland. b Sept 1, 1835, in Ware
  He is a carpenter and stone mason at Mansfield, Ct
  Children
64   Joseph Cleaveland[8], b Nov 22, 1853; m Mary Jane Hubbard
65   Andrew Eugene[8], b Jan 11, 1859
66   Lydia Climena[8], b Mar 6, 1861, d 1904, m Nov 24, 1886, George
       P Edwards

49. GEORGE W[7] FULLER, (*James[6]*, *Benajmin[5]*, *John[4]*, *John[3]*, *Joseph[2]*, *John[1]*), b May 29, 1836, in Hampton, Ct , d there Mar 30, 1910; m May 31, 1870, Eunice Hammond, b Oct 25, 1848, in Hampton, where she now (1914) resides
  Children
67   Henry H[8], b Apr 10, 1871, m Apr 20, 1904, Florence Morse.
       No children   Resides Middleboro, Mass
68   James M[8], b Apr 6, 1873, m Nov. 20, 1907, Mae Beymer   No
       children   Live in Weehawken, N J
69   Blanche[8], b Aug 6, 1875; m Sept 3, 1908, George L Ingalls, and
       had George W[9], b Oct 13, 1909, d Oct 14, 1909, William Sher-
       wood[9], b Feb 26, 1912   Reside in Norwich, Ct
70   Helen[8], b Apr 10, 1879, m Sept 2, 1909, Dr Dwight Milton
       Lewis, and had Richard Fuller[9], b May 4, 1910, d Mar 27, 1914,
       Dwight Milton[9], b Feb 5, 1914   Resides in New Haven, Ct
71   Alfred H[8], b Mar 12, 1882, m Mar 30, 1909, Edith B. Rice   Re-
       sides in Hampton, Ct
72   George L[8] b June 16 1884; m Oct 17, 1908, Eva Church   Re-
       side in Norwich, Ct
73   Priscilla Alden[8], b Apr 30, 1886, a teacher in N Y City.
74   Millie Bowen[8], b Sept 6, 1887, a teacher in N Y City
75   Ray Palmer[8], b June 18, 1890, m Nov 29, 1911 Helen H.
       Spalding

56. CHARLES A[7], FULLER, (*Thomas A[6]*, *Elijah[5]*, *Joseph[4]*, *John*, *Joseph[2]*, *John[1]*), b Aug 17, 1841, m June 23, 1869, Mary F Mathewson
  He resides in Sherburne N. Y
  Children
76   Louise[8], b Sept 9, 1870, m Mar , 1894, Charles L Carrier, and
       had Harriet D[9], b. Sept 1896, and Rush F[9], Mar , 1898
77   Marion D[8], b May 8, 1884, m Sept , 1906, Ward N Truesdell

EIGHTH GENERATION.

61 Samuel H[8] Fuller, (*Samuel S[7], Daniel[6], Benjamin[5], John[4], John[3], Joseph[2], John[1]*), b Mar 1, 1846, in Mansfield, Ct , m June, 1872, Mary A Ledoit.

Children ·

78 Alice A[9], b July 26, 1876, m Aug , 1891, Judson L Kilbourne, and had Grace M[10], b Jan 9, 1894, Howard[10], July 19, 1895, Florence H[10], Mai , 1897, John E[10], May, 1899, Ruth A[10], Mar 1, 1901, and Bernice[10], Oct 4, 1902

79 **Arthur S.[9]**, b Mar 3, 1878, m Marian Louise Warren

80 Eva M[9], b July 31, 1887

64. Joseph Cleaveland[8] Fuller, (*Daniel E[7], Daniel[6], Benjamin[5], John[4], John[3], Joseph[2], John[1]*), b Nov 22, 1853, in Mansfield, Ct , m Feb 4, 1873, Mary Jane Hubbard

Lives at Mansfield Four Corners, Ct

Children

81 **Charles Jefferson[9]**, b July 6, 1873, m Cora M Kenyon

82 **Harvey Eugene[9]**, b Apr 17, 1876, m Helen M Fisher

83 Maud Lillian[9], { twins b   } m Mar 28,1899, Israel D Phelps

84 Minnie Lavinia[9], } Sept 7, 1879, { lives in Mansfield, Ct

85 Aileen Medora[9], b Dec 30, 1881, lives in Hartford, Ct

86 Irving Washington[9], b Nov 24, 1886, lives in West Upton

75. Ray Palmer[8] Fuller, (*George W.[7], James[6], Benjamin[5], John[4] John[3], Joseph[2], John[1]*), b June 18, 1890, in Hampton, Ct , m Nov 25, 1911, Helen H Spaulding

He resides in Hampton

Children

87 Alden Holt[9], b Dec 3, 1913

NINTH GENERATION.

79. Arthur S[9] Fuller, (*Samuel H[8], Samuel S[7], Daniel[6], Benjamin[5], John[4], John[3], Joseph[2], John[1]*), b Mar 3, 1878, in ——, m Nov 10, 1908, Marian Louise Warren

Children

88 Mildred[10], b Apr 20, 1913

81. Charles Jefferson[9] Fuller, (*Joseph C[8], Daniel E[7], Daniel[6], Benjamin[5], John[4], John[3], Joseph[2], John[1]*), b July 6, 1873, in Mansfield, Ct ?, m Dec 18, 1901, Cora M. Kenyon.

Resides in Mansfield (Hanks Hill), Ct

Children

89   Bertha[10], b Sept 12, 1903

    82. HARVEY EUGENE[9] FULLER, (*Joseph C*[8], *Daniel E*[7], *Daniel*[6], *Ben-jamin*[5], *John*[4], *John*[3], *Joseph*[2], *John*[1]), b Apr 17, 1876, in Mansfield, Ct ,
d Aug 17, 1911 , m Dec 22, 1902, Helen M Fisher.
    He lived in Mansfield, Ct
    Children
90   Sidney C[10], b Jan 30, 1905 , d Apr 6, 1905.
91.   Viola M[10], b Jan. 10, 1906
92   Beatrice H[10], b Apr 2, 1908.
93   Nettie E.[10], b. Nov 10, 1909

NINTH GROUP

THIRD GENERATION.

DANIEL³ FULLER AND SOME OF HIS DESCENDANTS

DANIEL³ FULLER, (*Joseph²*, *John¹*), b Jan 30, 1702, in Ipswich; d before Aug. 22, 1731, in Gloucester, m Oct. 17, 1726, in Gloucester, Anna Doliver of that place

He lived in the West Parish of Gloucester

Children

1   Ann⁴, b Oct 26, 1727
2   **Daniel⁴**, b Dec 5, 1730, m Keturah Rust

FOURTH GENERATION.

DANIEL⁴ FULLER, (*Daniel³*, *Joseph²*, *John¹*), b Dec 5, 1730, in Gloucester, lost at sea about Nov 22, 1755; master of Capt Bennett's schooner", m Nov 5, 1751, Keturah Rust of Gloucester

Children ·

3   Keturah⁵, b Nov. 3, 1754, m Oct 9, 1772, Francis Bennett, b in Gloucester, July 12, 1749

TENTH GROUP

THIRD GENERATION.

EBENEZER[2] FULLER AND SOME OF HIS DESCENDANTS

35. EBENEZER[3] FULLER, (*Joseph[2], John[1]*), b Jan 10, 1707, in Ipswich, d ——, m Aug 31, 1731, Mary Gritsman (Gretman in Intentions)

He removed from Ipswich about 1750, lived for a time at Plympton, Mass, and settled in Lisbon, Ct

Children, bapt at Ipswich

1 Joseph[4], bapt Mar 25, 1733, d May 17, 1736
2 Mary[4], bapt Feb 2, 1734-5, d Jan 11, 1755
3 Ebenezer[4], bapt Feb 20, 1736, d May 3, 1738
4 **Ebenezer[4]**, bapt Oct 7, 1739
5 Elizabeth[4], bapt Mar 30, 1746
6 **Nathaniel[4]**, bapt Feb 24, 1750, m Lydia Holmes

FOURTH GENERATION.

4. EBENEZER[4] FULLER, (*Ebenezer[3], Joseph[2], John[1]*), bapt Oct 7, 1739, in Ipswich; d ——, m Int Pub Mar 11, 1758, with Elizabeth Williams, both of Ipswich

Children.

7 Ebenezer[5], b ——

6. NATHANIEL[4] FULLER, (*Ebenezer[3], Joseph[2], John[1]*), bapt Feb 24, 1750, in Ipswich, d ——, m 1, Mar. 29, 1770, at Plympton, Lydia Holmes, m 2, 1797, Anna Bartlett

Children, born in Oxford, Me

8 **Caleb[5]**, b Feb 10, 1771, m. Hannah Perkins
9. **Nathaniel[5]**, b Dec 27, 1772; m Anna Noble
10 Abigail[5], b Feb 3, 1775, m. Abner Rawson of Paris, Me, and had Evander Fuller[6], b Feb 6, 1794, Orissa[6], b Aug 6, 1795, Sabra[6], b Apr 28, 1797, Lyman[6], b May 6, 1799, Louisa Abigail Fuller[6], b Feb 5, 1807, Diantha Jane Angeline[6], b Nov 11, 1808, and George Burrill[6], b July 21, 1815
11. Sophia[5], b Feb 24, 1777, m Mar 3, 1799, William Clark Whitney of Hebron, Me

12   Lydia[5], b May 7, 1780, m Apr 3, 1800, Bartholemew Cushman, of Hebron Me, and had a dau Lydia[6], m Joseph Hammond, and dau Jeannette[6] m John R Hammond

13   Lucy[5], b May 12, 1783, m Stephen Pratt

14   **Ira[5]**, b Sept 24, 1786, m Sally Merrill

15   Parmelia[5], b Jan 4 1794, m 1 May 6, 1825, Samuel Merrill, m 2 John Bessey

FIFTH GENERATION

8. CALEB[5] FULLER (*Nathaniel[4]*, *Ebenezer[3]*, *Joseph[2]*, *John[1]*) b Feb 10, 1771, m Oxford, Me d ——, m ——. Hannah Perkins, dau of Gideon Perkins of Plymouth

    Caleb Fuller was one of the early settlers of the town of Paris, Me
Children, all born in Paris

16   Harvey[6], b Apr 21 1795, m Temperance Howard

17   **Lewis[6]**, b Jan 31, 1797, m Betsey Dunham

18   **Alden[6]**, b Mar 4, 1799, m Sally Cushman

19   Amos[6], b June —, 1801, m Miranda Perry

20   Nathaniel[6], b Sept 12, 1803, m Elmira Pike

21   **Caleb[6]** b Nov 12, 1805, m 1, Luda Monroe; m 2 Elizabeth B Swift

22   Charles[6], b Mar 4, 1808, d 1811

23   Drusilla[6], b Jan 31, 1810, m Daniel Perkins and settled in Woodstock, Me

24   Cornelius[6], b ——, d young

25   **Andrew J.[6]**, b Sept 15, 1822, m Harriet Marston

9. NATHANIEL[5] FULLER, (*Nathaniel[4]*, *Ebenezer[3]*, *Joseph[2]*, *John[1]*), b Dec 27, 1772, m Hebron Me, d ——, m Apr 11 1797, Anna Noble b July 9, 1769 in Gray, Me, d Aug 24 1861, in Oxford, Me
Children—born in Oxford

26   **Ava Stuart[6]**, b Oct 20, 1798, m 1, Charlotte Merrill, m 2, Jerusha (Cushman) Marston

27   Orrin Noble[6], b Jan 10, 1800

28   Mary[6], b Oct 22, 1801, d Dec 3, 1859, m Dec 3, 1827, Bartlett Cushman Holmes

29   A son, b Aug 1803, d Aug, 1803

30   **Ezra Goold[6]**, b July 12, 1804, m Maria Cushman

31   **Sullivan[6]**, b June 12, 1806, m Abigail Trott

32   **Benjamin Goold[6]**, b May 5, 1808, m Myra Cushman

33   **Elbridge Gerry[6]** b May 12, 1811, m Sarah Bennett

14. IRA[5] FULLER, (*Nathaniel[4]*, *Ebenezer[3]*, *Joseph[2]*, *John[1]*), b Sept 24, 1786, m East Oxford, Me, d ——, m May 2, 1816, Sally Merrill of Hebron Me, and lived in Oxford, Me

Children

34   Merrill W[6], b ——, d Jan 13, 1818
35   James Osgood[6] b Feb 11, 1818
36   **Charles P.**[6] b Apr 2, 1820
37   Prescott H[6], b Feb 28, 1822
38   Harriett N[6], b June 6, 1824
39   George C[6], b Feb 15, 1826
40   Augustus Ira[6], b Apr 17, 1828
41   Sarah Jane[6], b May 13, 1830
42   Jabez Henry[6], b Sept. 17, 1832, d May, 1833
43   Janette H[6], b Apr 8, 1835
44   Edward H[6], b Aug 1, 1838

SIXTH GENERATION.

17. LEWIS[6] FULLER (*Caleb[5]*, *Nathaniel[4]*, *Ebenezer[3]*, *Joseph[2]*, *John[1]*), b Jan 31, 1797, m Paris, Me, d ——, m Nov 25, 1820, Betsey Dunham, dau of Asa and Lydia Dunham

Children

45   Elizabeth[7], b Sept 21, 1822, m Oliver Pratt
46   Lewis[7] b Oct 22, 1825 d young
47   George G[7], b May 2, 1828, m Losina F Chandler, May 8, 1852
48   **Caleb[7]**, b Aug 16, 1830, m 1, Martha B Curtis, m 2 Marietta A Curtis
49   Cornelius P[7], b Nov 24, 1832, m Mary Burr
50   Angeline R[7], b Apr 1, 1834 m 1, Robert O Hayes m 2, Jacob Annas
51   Mary P[7], b Mar 22, 1837, m James H Barrows
52   Nathaniel[7] b July 30 1838, d July 30 1864, soldier of the civil war
53   Oliver L[7], b Apr 2, 1842, m 1, Jeannette Foss, m 2, Florence Whitcomb

18. AIDIN[6] FULLER (*Caleb[5]*, *Nathaniel[4]*, *Ebenezer[3]*, *Joseph[2]*, *John[1]*) b Mar 4, 1799, m Paris Me, d. ——, m July 1823, Sally Cushman, b May 20, 1799, d Aug, 1840

Children

54   Aiden[7] b Jan 19, 1824
55   Sarah J[7] b Jan 6, 1831
56   William[7], b Feb 10 1832
57   Albert C[7], b June 20, 1836

21. CALEB[6] FULLER, (*Caleb[5]*, *Nathaniel[4]*, *Ebenezer[3]*, *Joseph[2]*, *John[1]*), b Nov 12, 1805, in Paris, Me, d May 8, 1890, m 1, June 16 1831 Luda Monroe, b July 9, 1800, d July 23, 1845, m 2, Dec 28, 1846, Elizabeth B Swift, b Jan 27, 1828, d Dec 31, 1892

He was a M E clergyman and ministered in Bath Augusta, Hallowell, Farmington Belfast, Rockland, Gardiner, and Portland, Me

Children by first wife

58 Mary Monroe[r] b Apr 18. 1835, d 1835

59 Anne Augusta[r], b Sept 15, 1837, m Nov 15, 1859, E K Boyle b Feb 14 1835 in Palmyra, Me , d Apr 24, 1874 Children Edwin F[s], b May 24, 1861

By second wife

60 Ella Elizabeth[r] b Nov 3, 1847, m Sept 17, 1873 Albert Hassam Davis, b Nov 1, 1846 Children   Carle F[s], b Sept 5, 1875 and Albert Hassam[s], b Aug 16, 1882

61 Abbie C[s], b Oct 13, 1851; d Aug 7, 1854

25. ANDREW J[6] FULLER, (*Caleb[5], Nathaniel[4], Ebenezer[3], Joseph[2], John[1]*) b Sept 15 1822, in Paris, Me , d —, in July, 1843, Harriet Marston

He was a physician in Bath, Me

Children

62 —, b —, d —

63 —, b —, d —

64 A daughter, b —, m Samuel C Barker

26. ASA STUART[8] FULLER (*Nathaniel[5], Nathaniel[4], Ebenezer[3], Joseph[2] John[1]*), b Oct 20, 1798, in Oxford, Me , d Aug 7, 1876, in Hebron, Me , m 1, Jan 6, 1822, Charlotte Merrill of Hebron, Me , m 2 Apr 18, 1841, Jerusha (Cushman) Marston, who d. Apr , 1884, in Hebron

Children

65 **Leonard C.[r]**, b Dec 27, 1828, m Emily White

66 Louisa[r], b Mar 29, 1831

67 Emily[`], b — d aged 9 years

68 A child that d young

30. EZRA GOOLD[6] FULLER, (*Nathaniel[5], Nathaniel[4], Ebenezer[3], Joseph[2], John[1]*), b July 12, 1804, in Oxford, Me . d —, in Mar 20, 1828. Maria Cushman

In 1877 he was a farmer in South Abington, Mass

Children

69 Orrin Augustus[r], b Jan 20, 1830

70 Cordelia[r], b Apr 28, 1831

71 Helen A[r], b. —, d Aug 30, 1848

31. SULLIVAN[6] FULLER, (*Nathaniel[5], Nathaniel[4], Ebenezer[3], Joseph[2], John[1]*), b June 12, 1806, in Oxford, Me , d there Dec 24, 1892, m Dec 23 1838, Abigail Trott of Windham, Me , who d Nov , 1881.

He was a farmer in Oxford

Children,

72   Emily I T⁷, b 1840
73   **Julius T.⁷**, b Nov 22, 1842
74   Alphonso S⁷, b 1844
75   Eugene T⁷, b 1848.

32. BENJAMIN GOOLD⁶ FULLER, (*Nathaniel⁵, Nathaniel⁴, Ebenezer³, Joseph² John¹*) b May 5, 1808, in Oxford, Me , d Aug 17, 1884 m. Jan 10 1834, Myra Cushman, b June 21, 1805 , d Sept 6, 1889
     He lived in Poland and Andover, Me
     Children

76   Sarah A⁷, b June 1, 1835, in Poland, d Oct 20, 1897
77   Lydia A⁷, b May 23 1837, in Poland
78   **Harvey C.⁷**, b Dec 26, 1839 m 1, Adelia Cummings , m 2, Caroline M Martell
79   **Morrill M.⁷**, b Aug 24, 1842 , m Hattie Pike

33. ELBRIDGE GERRY⁶ FULLER, (*Nathaniel⁵, Nathaniel⁴, Ebenezer³, Joseph², John¹*), b May 12, 1811 in Oxford, Me , d 1884, in Oxford , m. Oct 29, 1849, Sarah Bennett, who d about 1875, at Page s Mills, Me
     He lived in Oxford
     Children

80   **Francis Edgar⁷**, b Aug 24 1852 , m Fanny Lewis Marston
81   Etta⁷ b ——, in Roxbury, Mass , d ——
82   George Washington⁷, b —— in Roxbury

36. CHARLES PORTER⁶ FULLER, (*Ira⁵, Nathaniel⁴, Ebenezer³, Joseph², John¹*), b Apr 2, 1820, at East Oxford, Me , m May 8, 1842, Abbie A Swift b June 3, 1820
     Children, born in Paris, Me

83   Charles P⁷, b Dec 30, 1844
84   Augusta S⁷, b Dec 16, 1846 , m Eugene E Read

SEVENTH GENERATION.

48. CALEB⁷ FULLER, (*Lewis⁶, Caleb⁵, Nathaniel⁴, Ebenezer³, Joseph², John¹*), b Aug 16, 1830, d Apr 27, 1906 m 1 Martha B Curtis, m 2, Marietta A Curtis
     Children

85   **Herman A.⁸**, b Nov 11, 1854, m Ida W Andrews
     By second wife
86   Lulu⁸, b Dec 13, 1862, d June 20, 1867
87   Winnie S⁸ b Apr 22, 1869 , m ——, George W Ridlon, and had
        Bertha A⁹, b Feb 6, 1895 They reside at West Paris, Me

65. Leonard C[7] Fuller (*Iva Stuart[6], Nathaniel[5], Nathaniel[4], Ebenezer[3], Joseph[2] John[1]*), b Dec 27, 1828, in Oxford Me , d about 1888 in Hebron, Me , m ——, Mrs Emily White of Boston

Children

88 Amelia[8], b ——, d aged 12 years

73. Julius T[7] Fuller, (*Sullivan[6], Nathaniel[5] Nathaniel[4], Ebenezer[3], Joseph[2], John[1]*), b Nov 22, 1842, in Oxford, Me., m May 13, 1874 Anne Clark Holmes

Children

89 Edward F[8], b Apr 27, 1875
90 Agnes H[8], b June 19, 1882

78. Harvey Chandler[7] Fuller, (*Benjamin G[6] Nathaniel[5], Nathaniel[4] Ebenezer[3], Joseph[2], John[1]*), b Dec 26, 1839, in Poland, Me , m 1, Adelia Cummings, b Mar. 1, 1840, d Aug 18 1869, m 2, Mar 4, 1877 in Minneapolis Minn , Caroline Maria Martell, b June 20, 1848, in Nova Scotia

Resides in Seattle, Wash

Children

91 Rollingston[8], b Aug 15, 1869, d Aug 22, 1871
92 Rollingston[8], b Jan 30 1878, at Minneapolis m Oct 10 1905 Maude Baker b Oct 21 1881 in Lincoln, Neb
93 Louis C[8] b Sept 21, 1879, d June 16, 1882
94 **Wallace Joseph**[8] b June 1, 1881 , m Georgiana Moore
95 Louis[8], b ——, 1882, d ——, 1884, at Rush City, Minn
96 Harriet Spencer[8], b Jan 18, 1884, at Rush City, Minn , d Jan 1, 1905 , m June 17 1904 George H Moorehead
97 Jennie Cushman[8], b June 19, 1887 at Seattle. Wash ; d Nov 29, 1898.
98 Clarence Benjamin[8], b May 2, 1891, at Seattle

79. Morrill M[7] Fuller, (*Benjamin G[6], Nathaniel[5], Nathaniel[4], Ebenezer[3], Joseph[2], John[1]*), b Aug 24, 1842, in Andover, Me , m Dec 25 1870, Hattie Pike, b Sept 2, 1845 in Norway, Me

He resides in Norway, Me

Children

99 Nettie M[8], b Aug 27, 1872
100 Lizzie M[8], b May 28, 1876, m June 22, 1898, Louis M Brooks, and has Doris Louisa[9], b May 11, 1901

80. Francis Edgar[7] Fuller, (*Elbridge G[6], Nathaniel[5], Nathaniel[4], Ebenezer[3], Joseph[2], John[1]*), b Aug 24 1852, in Oxford, Me , m Oct 13 1880, Fanny Lewis Marston, at and of Jamaica Plain

They reside in Watertown

Children

101. Amelia Wynkoop[9], b Aug 28, 1881, m Somerville Mass   m Sept 21, 1904, at Watertown, Herman Deane[6] Fuller (George G[7], Josiah[6], Josiah[5], Josiah[4], Josiah[3], Jeremiah[2], John[1] or Newton), Group No 13 b Apr 4, 1879, m Lexington   resides in Waltham   Children   Doris Madeline[9], b July 3, 1905, and Richard Irving[9], b Nov 7, 1908

102   Anne Lewis[9], b June 20 1883, m Somerville, d there Dec 26, 1883

103   Edith Marston[8], b Sept 6 1884, m Roxbury

104   Ellen Richardson[9], b June 24, 1889, m Allston

105   John Morrill[8], b June 21, 1894, m Lexington

EIGHTH GENERATION.

85. HERMAN A[8] FULLER, (*Caleb[7], Lewis[6], Caleb[5], Nahtamiel[4], Ebenezer[3], Joseph[2], John[1]*), b Nov 11, 1854, d June 5, 1891, m ——, Ida W Andrews

Children

106   Ralph A[9], b Sept 19, 1881

107   Olive M[9], b Mar 10, 1883

94. WALLACE JOSEPH[8] FULLER (*Harvey C[7] Benjamin G[6], Nathaniel[5], Nathaniel[4], Ebenezer[3], Joseph[2], John[1]*), b June 1, 1881, m Pine City Minn, m Sept 24, 1903 at Minneapolis, Minn, Georgiana Moore, b 1880 at Santa Barbara, Cal

Resides Los Angeles California

Children

108   Francis Joseph[9], b Feb 21, 1904

109   Cecil Michael[9], b Aug 1, 1906

ELEVENTH GROUP

THIRD GENERATION.

JACOB² FULLER AND SOME OF HIS DESCENDANTS

36. JACOB³ FULLER, (*Joseph²*, *John¹*), b Jan 25, 1711, in Ipswich, d Dec 23, 1798 in Hanover, Ct , m 1 (Int Pub Oct 12, 1734), Ann Harris, who d Apr 25, 1773, in Hanover, m 2, Nov 29, ~~1744~~; in Han-*1774* over Mehitable Robertson, b about 1738, d Oct 19, 1784

Jacob Fuller of Windham. Ct, bought land in Norwich. Ct, from Isaac Woodward of Canterbury, Ct, on Mar 14, 1743,—100 acres lying in Newent, in said Norwich (Norwich land records) He removed to Lisbon, Ct, about 1743

The will of Jacob Fuller of Lisbon 'being advanced in years, is dated Jan 6, 1795 He left to sons Jacob, Josiah, and Joseph Fuller. 40 shillings

To sons John and Ebenezer Fuller "my farm I now live on"

To son Benjamin Fuller, land in Canterbury, Ct

To daughter Anna Wentworth, £100

To sons Daniel and David Fuller, land in the 'nue state "

In the division of property, Daniel, 7th son, has land in Chelsea, Vt

Children, the first four recorded in Ipswich

1   Jacob⁴, b Nov. 13, 1735, d May 10, 1736
2   Jacob⁴, 2d, b Sept 7, 1737
3   Josiah⁴ b July 17, 1739
4   Ann⁴, b Oct 17 1740, d July 2, 1745
5   Joseph⁴ b Jan 2, 1743, d Aug 4, 1745
6   **Joseph⁴** 2d, b May 3, 1746, m 1, Priscilla ——, m 2, Mrs Ann Walker
7   William⁴, b Oct 29, 1748, d Feb 7, 1750
8   **John⁴**, b June 28, 1751, m Wealthy Kazer
9   Ann⁴, 2d, b Apr 3, 1754, m May 21, 1775, Sylvanus Wentworth lived and died in Windsor, Mass Children   Nijah⁵, b Apr 20, 1777 , Anna⁵. Jan 7, 1779, Hannah⁵, Feb 4. 1781 , Sylvanus⁵. Oct 29, 1782, William⁵ Feb 6 1785, Nijah⁵, 2d, May 12, 1788, William⁵, 2d, Dec 8, 1790, Joseph⁵, Nov 24, 1792 (lived at Rome, N Y), and Almira⁵, Nov 11, 1797

10   Benjamin⁴ b June 27, 1756
11   **Ebenezer⁴**, b July 3, 1760, m Juan Fernandez Elderkin.
12   **Daniel⁴** b Sept 6, 1775, m Delight Smith
13   **David⁴**, b Oct 5, 1777, m Sally Childs

FOURTH GENERATION.

6.   JOSEPH⁴ FULLER, (*Jacob³, Joseph², John¹*) b May 3, 1746, in Lisbon, Ct according to family history removed to Providence, R I, and I suppose that the Deacon Joseph Fuller who died there May 3, 1822, aged 76, is identical with the Joseph⁴ Fuller above mentioned

The R I Vital Records mention that "Mrs Priscilla Fuller, wife of Dea Joseph Fuller died in Providence, Apr 7, 1815, aged 71," and also mention the marriage of Dea Joseph Fuller and Mrs Ann Walker, in Providence June 19, 1817, by Rev Mr Osborne

Dea Joseph Fuller was a Trustee of the Chestnut St M E Church from Jan 2, 1819, to May 3, 1822, date of his decease

Vol 18 of Arnold s V R of R I states that Dea Joseph Fuller was second in command in the battle of Rhode Island

'The Gazettee" of Providence, Saturday morning, May 4, 1822, gives an obituary notice as follows   "Died, in this town, yesterday morning, *the day that ended his 76th year*, Mr Joseph Fuller, who, for more than 60 years has been a follower of the meek and lowly Jesus, and for many years deacon and father of a church in this town

'He bore a long and distressing sickness with Christian patience, and died in the assurance of entering into that rest which remains for the children of God

The friends of the deceased are requested to meet at his late residence in Westminster St. at half past two o'clock tomorrow, from whence his remains will be carried to the Methodist Chapel, where a discourse will be delivered on the occasion '

The Gazette" of May 18, 1822, contains an auctioneer's notice of sale the same day, at the late residence of Mr Joseph Fuller in Westminster St of furniture, tools, and stock of a tool maker's shop

Children   I find no mention of children born to Dea Joseph Fuller, but a letter to P of H W Brainard of Hartford from a N Y genealogical correspondent, dated Mar 22, 1904, says   "A brother of my grandfather was adopted by Dea Joseph Fuller of Providence, R I, and changed his name from Joseph Field to Joseph Fuller '

It seems quite probable that the Joseph Fuller, Jr, who was married Sept 30, 1794, in Providence, by Elder James Wilson of the Beneficent Congregational Church to Lucy Potter was this adopted son, and also that the Abby P Fuller, "only daughter of Joseph Fuller," who was married Aug 22, 1816, by the same Elder, in the same place to Anthony B Arnold, was the granddaughter of Dea Joseph⁴ Fuller by his adopted son

House Built by Ebenezer Fuller, Probably About 1780, in Hanover, Conn. (Part Now Called Spreague.)

8. John[4] Fuller, (*Jacob*[3], *Joseph*[2], *John*[1]), b June 28, 1751, at Lisbon, Ct , d June 21, 1813, m May 21, 1778, Wealthy Kazer, who d Oct 29, 1843, aged 85

He resided at Hanover, Ct He served 3 years, 11 mos , 11 days in the Revolutionary War and his widow received a pension

Children

14 Abijah[5], b Oct 18, 1779, m Sarah Starr
15 Anna Nancy[5] b Sept 29, 1781, d June 4, 1833, m Jan 27, 1803, William Tracy, lived in Hanover , had three children
16 **Jacob[5]**, b June 17, 1783, m Abigail Paine
17 Hannah[5], b Jan 24, 1785, d Aug 25 1856, m John Murray lived in Norwich, Ct Children Abby[6], b —— Amanda[6] m Elisha Beckwith, of Norwich, Ct , Mary Ann[6], m —— Smith of Springfield, Mass, Sarah[6], m —— Allen of Worcester Juliette[6] m 1, ——, m 2, —— Johhnson, of Norwich, Ct John[6], and Dr Frank[6], of New Haven, Ct
18 John[5], b Nov 17, 1787, m Juliana M Hastings
19 **Alanson[5]**, b Jan 26, 1789, m Anna K Farnham
20 Lucy L[5], b Mar 22, 1791, d Feb 26, 1875, in Canterbury, Ct , m John L Spencer, and had John L[6], b ——, d Sept, 1851, in Amherst, Mass
21 William[5] b Mar 20, 1794, d Oct 27, 1797
22 Sally Eliza[5], b Apr 15, 1796, d Oct 6 1846, m Jan 15, 1818 Lavius Farnham, and had Lavius Fuller[6], b Dec 22, 1819 Erastus[6] b Oct 7, 1821, and Mary[6], b ——
23 Wealthy Maria[5], b Feb 21, 1799, d Mar 9, 1878, m Dec 15, 1830, Solomon Whipple Bushnell, b June 15, 1804, d Feb 16, 1884 Children were John Fuller[6], b Mar 20, 1831, d May 11, 1891, m Ann McGrannell, Juliana Maria[6], b Sept 6, 1832, lives in Brooklyn, N Y, 439 E 4th St m Nov 13, 1854 James Price, b Apr 10, 1814, in Waterford, Ireland, d Aug 14, 1891, Eliza Sisson[6], b Mar 20, 1834, m June 18, 1852 Stephen E Wilcox, Dwight Brown[6], b Aug 21, 1837, d Jan 5 1900, in Canterbury, Ct , m Jan 22, 1876, Emily F Trowbridge, Henry Martyn[6], b May 26, 1840, m Jan 25, 1877, Hannah Adelaide Hyde, and resides in Canterbury, Ct , Sarah Jane[6] b Apr 17, 1843, in Scotland, Ct , d Jan 20, 1900, m Oct 13, 1881, Albert Easton, of South Killingly, Ct

11. Ebenezer[4] Fuller, (*Jacob*[3], *Joseph*[2], *John*[1]), b July 3, 1760, in Lisbon, Ct , d Sept 16, 1840, in Hanover, Ct , m Nov 12, 1782, Juan Fernandez Elderkin, b July 21, 1765, d May 24, 1844, in Hampton, Ct buried in Hanover, Ct , where she had lived

He was a soldier of the Revolutionary War, and a pensioner, served in General Waterbury's Brigade, and in Col Oliver Smith's Regt Gen John Tyler's Brigade

Children—all born in Hanover, Ct

24 **Luther Elderkin[5]**, ⎱   ⎰ m Polly Witter
25 Ebenezer[5],   ⎰ twins, b Dec 23, 1783 ⎱ d ——, 1783
26 Avander[5], b Apr 4, 1786, m 1, Joanna Witter, m 2, Desire Allen
27 Charlotte[5], b Dec 31, 1788, d Jan 3, 1875 m Jan 15, 1807

Erastus Allen, b Nov 6 1783, d Aug 28, 1856, lived in Scotland, Ct, and had there Nelson[6], b Feb 1, 1808, d Dec 24, 1884, m 1, Dec 2, 1834 Miranda A Foster, of Hampton, Ct, who d May 24, 1844, m 2, ——,1846, Sarah Denison, m 3, Nov 17 1870 Mary Stears, Lyman[6], b Nov 22, 1809, d May 15 1891, went to Chicago, Ills, m Dec 1, 1836, Charlotte Lilley, who d Dec 17, 1887. Milton[6], b June 2, 1812, d Aug 6, 1895, lived in Westminster, Ct, was blind in last years, m Feb 3, 1833, Lucretia Meach, who d Oct 18, 1870, Lucretia[6], b Mar 28 1814, d Apr 15, 1881, m Nov 1, 1841, Lemuel A Charter, Eliza[6], b May 18 1817, d Dec 8, 1901, m Walter Beach, who d Sept 25, 1889 Fidelia[6], b Nov 28, 1820, d Nov 19, 1912, m Dec 22 1853, L Fuller Farnham, b Dec 22, 1819, d May —, 1893, Lora Fuller[6], b May 16, 1823, d Nov 6, 1905, m Oct 21 1850, Geo W Stark, who d Jan 28, 1854, Denison Elderkin[6] b Jan 29, 1826, d Aug 7, 1909, m Oct 18, 1852, Julia Elizabeth Smith b May 3, 1832, living in Scotland, Ct. (1913), Emma Jane[6], b Jan 20, 1828, d Feb 20, 1828

28 Lora Elderkin[5] b Jan 28, 1793, d Oct 20, 1822
29 **Jesse Stoneman**[5], b Sept 1, 1795, m Hannah Congdon
30 **Chester Lyon**[5], b Sept 5, 1800, m Mary Bottum
31 Nelson Lyon[5], b July 14, 1803 d July 14, 1803
32 **George Denison**[5], b Sept 8, 1804, m Susan Sophia Cleveland
33 Emeline Fernandez[5], b Oct 4 1808, d Mar 14, 1887, m Mar 17, 1834, Marcus Lyon of Canterbury, Ct b June 1806, d May 9, 1880, lived in Danielson, Ct, and had Rockwell Fuller[6], b Jan 31, 1835, d Sept 13, 1901, m Aug 12, 1859, Jennie Elizabeth Canney, b June 24, 1842, Frances Mary[6], b Oct 10, 1839; lives in Howard, R I, m Feb 26, 1881, Varnum Bicknell who d Mar 9 1887, Abbie Fernandez[6], b Mar 24, 1843, lives in Centreville, R I, m 1 Jan 25, 1876, Samuel L Tillinghast, who d Aug 14 1896, m 2, Feb 19, 1899, Dr Moses Fifield who d Apr 9, 1900

12. Danifl[4] FULLER, (*Jacob[3], Joseph[2], John[1]*) b Sept 6, 1775, in Hanover, Ct, d Nov 13, 1847, m Nov 28, 1799, Delight Smith, b June 17, 1781, d Jan 29, 1849

He removed to Chelsea, Vt, about 1800

Children, born in Chelsea, Vt

34 Nelson[5], b Oct 22, 1800, d ——
35 Amanda[5], b May 11, 1802
36 Caroline[5], b Oct 29, 1803, d Aug 20 1828
37 Samuel S[5], b May 5, 1806
38 Sally[5], b Jan 7, 1808, m —— Hall
39 Mary[5] b Feb 4, 1810, d Mar 28 1857, m Feb 21, 1833, Lewis S Skinner
40 Daniel[5], b Dec 16, 1811 d May 29, 1860, m Augusta Ann Hoyt
41 John D[5], b Aug 30 1813, m Prudence Ann Bliss
42 Catherine[5], b Aug 15, 1815, m June 12, 1836, Hiram Capron
43 William R[5] b May 14 1817
44 Frederick P[5], b Feb 14, 1819

MR. AND MRS. LUTHER E. FULLER—24.

EMELINE (FULLER) LYON—33.   GEORGE D. FULLER—32.

LUTHER E. FULLER—24.

AVANDER FULLER—26.   CHARLOTTE (FULLER) ALLEN—27.

MARCUS LYON—33.

45   Fanny M[5], b July 30, 1821, d Oct 15, 1841
46   George A[5], b Dec 25, 1823, d Jan 29, 1851
47   Ann Eliza[5], b Apr 11, 1827, m Benjamin Coleman

13. DAVID[4] FULLER, (*Jacob*[3], *Joseph*[2], *John*[1]), b Oct 5 1777, m Hanover, Ct, d Apr 13, 1854, m Jan 23, 1800, Sally Childs, b Mar 12, 1780, d Sept 29, 1866
  Probably lived in Chelsea, Vt
  Children·
48   Ebenezer C[5], b Aug 30, 1801; d Sept 13, 1806
49   Diantha[5] b May 23, 1803, d Jan 20, 1826, m —— Sanborn, and left one dau Diantha[6], b Mar , 1825, d Sept 29, 1860
50   Fernandez[5], b Apr 24, 1805, d Mar —, 1890
51   Edwin[5], b Apr 13, 1807, d Aug —, 1890
52   Polly F[5], b July 27, 1809, d Feb 1, 1827
53   **David Robertson**[5], b Aug 27, 1811, m 1, Mary J Eastman m 2, Mary J Hoit, m 3, Cordelia Wood
54   Sally R[5], b Oct 13, 1813, d Jan 11, 1882, m Jan 4 1842 John P Bliss of Chelsea, Vt, and had 3 children
55   Cordelia[5], b Nov 13, 1815, d May 18, 1883
56   Infant, b Jan, 1817, d Jan, 1817
57   Orissa[5], b Sept 21, 1818, d Apr 21, 1838
58   **Fordyce**[5], b Dec 5, 1821, m Aurelia Hayes
59   Joseph O[5], b Jan 25, 1824, d Apr 23, 1835

FIFTH GENERATION.

14. ABIJAH[5] FULLER, (*John*[4], *Jacob*[3], *Joseph*[2], *John*[1]), b Oct 18, 1779, in Hanover, Ct, d there Sept 23, 1816, m Feb 17, 1805, Sarah Starr of Thompson, Ct, b Sept 25, 1782, d Feb 28, 1857, in Charlton, Mass
  He resided in Hanover, Ct   His widow removed to Charlton and in 2, David Lamb, a widower with two sons, who married her two daughters
  Children, born in Hanover, Ct
60   Ebenezer Starr[6], b June 1, 1806, d June 15, 1841
61   Wealthy Eliza[6], b Feb 4, 1808, d May 8, 1808
62   Sarah Adaline[6], b June 30, 1811, d Oct 22, 1874, m May 3, 1840, Ziba, son of David Lamb, b July 24, 1814, d Oct 22, 1874   Children, all born in Charlton   Charles Edwin[7], b Mar 16, 1841, d Dec 3, 1912, in W Pownal, Me, Charles Darwin[7], b June 30, 1843, d July 3, 1887   Ebenezer Theodore[7], b Sept 9, 1845, d Aug 15, 1846, Marilla Adaline[7], b June 28, 1849, m Oct 2, 1878, William A Hersey, and resides in W Pownal, Me, Frances Clawson[7], b July 16, 1850, d Mar 15, 1851
63   Friendship Field[6], b Aug 4, 1813, d Oct 22, 1882, m Nov 22, 1838, Ebenezer, son of David Lamb, and had Sarah Ellen[7], b Nov 25, 1839.
64   John Abijah[6], b July 21, 1815, d Dec 29, 1815

16. JACOB⁵ FULLER, (*John⁴, Jacob³, Joseph² John¹*), b June 17 1783, in Hanover, Ct , d Apr 5 1839, in Providence, R I , m Jan 27, 1811, Abigail Paine, b Apr 6, 1792, in Seekonk, Mass , d Apr 1, 1856, in Providence

He was a physician

Children

65   **Joseph Benjamin Franklin⁶**, b Dec 3, 1811, m Mary Ann Davis
66   John P⁶, b Apr 2, 1815, d May 15, 1861 unmarried, lived in Norwich, Ct —a distinguished surgeon
67   Abigail Paine⁶ b June 20, 1823, d July 22, 1829, in Seekonk
68   Abigail Frances⁶, b May 8, 1831, d Apr 19, 1888, m ——, 1863 George Edwin Heywood, and had George F ⁷, b Apr 4, 1864 in Providence, R I , who m in Malden, Mass , Emma F Hadley, b Dec 1, 1862
69   Henry Jacob⁶, b Nov 4, 1832, d Sept 17, 1866 He was a physician

19. ALANSON⁵ FULLER, (*John⁴, Jacob³, Joseph², John¹*), b Jan 26, 1789, in Hanover, Ct , d there Nov 28, 1859, m Feb 23 1818, Anna K Farnham, who d Mar 14, 1863

He lived awhile in Windham, Ct, where the last 4 children were born, but returned to Hanover

Children, the first 5 b in Hanover, Ct

70   Mary Ann Zerviah⁶, b Aug 30, 1819, d Apr 18 1859
71   Henry Alanson⁶, b Mar 9, 1821, d Nov 9, 1860, m June 6, 1849, in Boston, Elizabeth L Smith Resided in Boston
72   Rodolphus Wolcott⁶, b May 22, 1822, d Mar 10, 1907, in Hanover, Ct , m Sept 27, 1865, Abby Sweet Lived in the West
73   Earl Knight⁶, b Aug 17 1824, d Mar 6, 1833, in Windham, Ct
74   Samuel Hamilton⁶, b Aug 5, 1826 d July 31, 1849
75   Lydia Wells⁶, b Apr 11, 1828, d Feb 7, 1890, m ——, 1852, Edwin A Hough
76   **John Murray⁶**, b Mar 12, 1830, m Hannah A Wilcox
77   Julia Ellen⁶, Apr 20, 1832, d Apr 27 1913 Lived in Hanover
78   Jane Rudd⁶, b Jan 1, 1834, d Aug 12, 1839

24. LUTHER ELDERKIN⁵ FULLER, (*Ebenezer⁴, Jacob³, Joseph², John¹*), b Dec 23, 1783, in Hanover, Ct , d there Sept 10, 1863, m Jan 1, 1807, Polly Witter, b May 9, 1788 in Canterbury Ct , d May 7, 1867

He was a soldier of the war of 1812, and a pensioner, and resided in Hanover, Ct

Children

79   **Pearley Brown⁶** b Oct 7, 1807 m 1, Sarah L Williams, m 2, Esther Palmer Smith
80   Mary Eliza⁶, b July 13, 1809, d Dec 26, 1833, in Hanover, Ct ; m Apr 23, 1832, Chauncey Knight Bushnell, b Feb 25, 1805, d Mar 2, 1895 Lived in Norwalk They had a dau , Mary Witter⁷ Bushnell, b July 23 1833, d Aug 30, 1854, in Hanover Ct

81   **Ebenezer⁶**, b Sept 16, 1813, m Harriet L Bolles

26. AVANDER⁵ FULLER, (*Ebenezer⁴, Jacob³, Joseph², John¹*), b Apr 4, 1786, in Hanover, Ct , d there Sept 17, 1873, m 1, Nov 2, 1811, Joanna Witter, b July 2, 1792, d May 19, 1826, m 2, Jan 1, 1828, Desire Allen, b Dec 26, 1795, d May 23, 1862

He lived in Hanover

Children ·

82   Abbie Priscilla⁶, b Sept 22, 1812, d Aug 4, 1832
83   Dolly Sharp⁶, b Jan 3, 1815, d Feb 21, 1891, m Jan 24, 1835, Amos Loomis, b Oct 12, 1812, d Jan 23, 1849   Lived in Lebanon, Ct   Children   Joanna Witter⁷, b Jan 10, 1836, living in Norwich, Ct ; m Oct 15, 1856, Lyman W Randall, b June 18, 1830, d Mar 16, 1878, m 2, Dec 16, 1883, Frederick L Gardner, b Mar 5, 1832, d Jan 31, 1905, Amos Witter⁷ b Feb 11, 1838 d at sea about Feb 12, 1865 Emma Sabina⁷, b Oct 4, 1843, d Dec 28, 1907, in Bristol, Ct , m in Norwich, Ct, Sept 1892, Watson Giddings b Apr 4, 1830, in Hartland, Ct , d Apr 1, 1905, in Bristol, Ct , Avander Fuller⁷, b Feb 1, 1845, d at sea, Elizabeth W ⁷, b Sept 15, 1849, d Dec 30, 1852
84   **Asa Witter⁶**, b July 31, 1817, m Nancy Woodworth Collins
85   Sarah Kinne⁶, b June 12, 1819, d Jan 29, 1875, m Mar 19, 1845, Jared B Fillmore, b Oct 24, 1822, d Oct, 1892   Children   Sarah Eliza⁷, b Apr 9, 1847, m Mar 20, 1867, Dr Charles N Palmer of Lockport, N Y, b May 25, 1841, Clarence Jared⁷, b Feb 6 1853, m Ora Maconda McGinnis in 1874

29. JESSE STONEMAN⁵ FULLER, (*Ebenezer⁴ Jacob³, Joseph², John¹*), b Sept 1, 1795, in Hanover, Ct , d July 27, 1851, m ——, Hannah Congdon

Lived in Norwich, Ct

Children

86   Samuel⁶, b Nov 29, 1821, d Sept 14, 1822
87   Sarah E ⁶, b Aug 4, 1826, d Aug 8, 1851, m William P Smith of New London, Ct
88   **David Congdon⁶**, b Jan 23, 1823, m 1, Fanny E Strickland, m 2, Jane Gardner
89   **George Denison⁶**, b Dec 27, 1828, m Josephine A Northrop

30. CHESTER LYON⁵ FULLER, (*Ebenezer⁴, Jacob³, Joseph², John¹*), b Sept 5, 1800, in Hanover, Ct , d Sept 11 1888, m Mar 1, 1826, Mary Bottum, b Dec 28, 1803, d Dec 31, 1893

He lived in Norwich, Ct

Children

90   Caroline⁶, b Dec 8, 1826, d Nov 2, 1845
91   Amelia⁶, b Aug 1, 1828, d May 4, 1850, m Dec 12, 1847, Wm H Mabrey, b Dec 27, 1823, d ——, in Philadelphia, Pa , had a son Stephen I ⁷ b Nov 2, 1849, d Apr 2, 1877, m July 20, 1871, Mary France

92   Delia[8], b Aug 1, 1828, d June 15, 1881, m Sept 9, 1848, Erastus
     O Andrews, and had Anne Andrews[7] b Mar 16, 1850, m
     Sept 18, 1872, Albert S Comstock
93   **Charles C.[8]**, b Sept 15, 1832, m Lucy M Stead

32. GEORGE DENISON[5] FULLER, (*Ebenezer[4], Jacob[3], Joseph[2], John[1]*), b
Sept 8, 1804, in Hanover, Ct , d Apr 11, 1883, in Norwich, Ct , m 1
Dec 7, 1834, Susan Sophia Cleveland, b in Norwich, May 7, 1809, d
there May 30, 1838, she was sister of President Cleveland's father, m
2 Mar 15, 1841, Hannah Maria Havens, b Feb 22, 1817, d Dec. 25
1853

He was a merchant in Norwich, Ct, for 40 years

Children, b in Norwich

94   Harriet Stuart[6], b Sept 13, 1835, d Jan 19, 1911, m Sept 26
     1865, Lewis A Hyde b Aug 8, 1826   Lived in Norwich   Chil-
     dren b there   Susan Cleveland[7], b Aug 30, 1866 (several
     years missionary in Turkey), Harriet Louisa[7], b Mar 26 1869
     George Fuller[7], b Mar 19, 1871; Gertrude Stuart[7] b Sept 12
     1873 (Instructor Mt Holyoke College), Jessie Elizabeth[7], b
     Feb, 27, 1877
95   **William Cleveland[6]**, b May 25, 1838, m Mary Jane Nowell
96   Anna Havens[6], b Dec 31, 1841, d July 21, 1842
97   **George Havens[6]**, b Sept 13, 1843, m Sarah Elizabeth Case
98   **Edward Denison[6]**, b Nov 13, 1845, m Angeline P Norton
99   Anna Maria[6], b Mar. 12, 1848, m Aug 27, 1872, Aaron W
     Dickey, b Jan 25, 1847, in Elba, N Y, d July 11, 1910   Chil-
     dren   George Havens[7], b Nov 6, 1874, d Aug 11, 1890, Alice
     Fuller[7], b Feb 3, 1876, m Oct 7, 1903, Charles Jared Abell, b
     Bozrah, Ct , Oct 8, 1869, d Sept 5, 1911
100 **Walter[6]**, b Nov 13 1850, m Nellie Elizabeth Deane
101 Daniel Havens[6], b Nov 13, 1853, d July 18, 1854

53. DAVID ROBERTSON[5] FULLER (*David[4], Jacob[3], Joseph[2], John[1]*), b
Aug 27, 1811, in Chelsea, Vt , d June 12, 1887, m 1, Mary J Eastman
of Tunbridge, Vt , who d June, 1838, aged 22 , m 2, ——, Mary J Hoit,
b July 7 1811: d Mar 22, 1858, m 3, ——Cordelia Wood, b Sept 29
1828, in Washington, Vt , d May 19, 1905

Children, all born in Chelsea, Vt, but two youngest born in Washington, Vt

102 Sarah Jane[6], b Aug 28, 1837; m ——, —— Prince, resides Wor-
     cester, Mass
103 John H[6], b Aug 10, 1842, d Feb 3, 1863
104 Joseph O[6], b Dec 1, 1844, d Oct 25, 1866
105 Alice A[6], b Mar 4, 1849
106 Luther L[6], b Mar —, 1854, d Feb 9, 1856
107 Jennie B[6], b Jan 20, 1857; d same day
108 Hattie[6], b Feb 29, 1858, d June 8, 1863
109 Herbert[6], b Mar —, 1859, d Dec 25, 1859
110 Bertha A[6], b Nov 2, 1860

111   Dora A⁶, b Aug 2, 1862
112   Albert P⁶, b Nov 6, 1864
113   Lewellyn N⁶, b Dec 5, 1866
114   Sally R⁶, b Apr. 6, 1870

58. FORDYCE⁵ FULLER, (*David⁴, Jacob³, Joseph², John¹*), b Dec 5, 1821, in Chelsea, Vt , d Apr 15, 1882, m July 4, 1847, in Lowell, Mass , Aurelia Hayes, b July 5, 1824, in Jackson, N H , d Apr 26, 1894
      Children, all but the first child, born in Chelsea, Vt
115   Fordyce Eugene⁶, b Mar 28, 1849, in Lowell
116   Francis Hayes⁶, b June 10, 1851, d Nov 16, 1852
117   George Wood⁶, b July 11, 1853
118   Fanny Elizabeth⁶, b Nov 3, 1856
119   **Edwin Daniel⁶,** b June 5, 1859, m Edith May Taplin Taplin.
120   Laura Rosamond⁶, b Aug 28, 1863

SIXTH GENERATION.

65. JOSEPH BENJAMIN FRANKLIN⁶ FULLER, (*Jacob⁵, John⁴, Jacob³ Joseph² John¹*), b Dec 3, 1811, d July 31, 1898. in Norwich, Ct , m Aug 20, 1853, Mary Ann Davis
      He was a physician in Norwich, Ct
      Children
121   Franklin Davis⁷, b Jan 11, 1857: d Feb 6. 1907. in Brooklyn N Y , m Feb 17, 1887, Clara Jones Hammett, b Oct 9, 1858 She resides in Norwich, Ct

76. JOHN MURRAY⁶ FULLER, (*Alanson⁵, John⁴, Jacob³, Joseph², John¹*), b Mar 12, 1830, in Windham, Ct , d Mar 26, 1905, m Jan 31, 1853, Hannah Ann Wilcox, b Aug 28, 1837; d Jan 7, 1883
      He lived in Hanover, Ct
      Children
122   Effie⁷, b ——— 1854, in Norwich, d ———, in Hanover
123   Anna E⁷, b Jan 1, 1857, lives in Hanover, Ct (1913)
124   **Alanson⁷,** b Dec 22, 1859, m Apr 1897, Flora Rist
125   Amy Jane⁷ b Sept 19, 1861, m Dec 3, 1890, Rev James W Abelard, b Mar 18, 1857 Children, Grace Hanna⁸ b Dec 29, 1891, Ruth Avery⁸, b Feb 13, 1893, Effie Elizabeth⁸, b July 25, 1894, Florence Catherine⁸, b Dec. 12, 1904
126   Henry Avander⁷, b. June 21, 1865
127   Julia Edith⁷, b June 8, 1869, m ———, Chester E Hough of Hartford, Ct
128   John Edwin⁷, b. Sept 15, 1873
129   Edna Brewer⁷ b Nov 2, 1876, m Sept 27, 1899, Edwin C James, living in Wickford, R I Children, Doris Louise⁸, b June 28, 1901, and Earle Fuller ⁸, b Sept 10, 1903

130   Grace Murray[r], b July 14, 1880, m ——. Edward Tucker, of
       Sprague, Ct

79. PEARLEY BROWN[6] FULLER, (*Luther E*[5], *Ebenezer*[4], *Jacob*[3], *Jo-
seph*[2] *John*[1]), b Oct 7, 1807, m Hanover, Ct, d Aug 27, 1877, in
Derby, Ct, m 1, May 1, 1833, Sarah Lyon Williams b Feb —, 1814, d
Apr 6 1834, aged 20, m 2, ——, Esther P Smith, b ——, 1811 in
Canterbury, Ct d ——, 1867, in Scotland Ct

   He removed to Scotland Ct, in 1843

   Children—the first three born in Hanover, the others in Scotland

131   **Robert Bruce**[r], b Apr 26, 1836, m Harriet A Prentice

132   Dwight[r]., b Nov 23, 1837, d Oct 15, 1857

133   Thomas Hart[r] b Feb 22, 1840, lives in Washington, D C,
       graduate of Yale, Class of 1863, employe U S P O, is not
       married

134   Susan Esther[r], b Oct 28, 1843, d Nov 11, 1873, in Scotland, Ct

135   Emma Alice[r], b Mar 4, 1845, d July 5 1886, in Washington,
       D C, m in New Haven, Ct, Dec — 1877, William Harrison
       Chadsey of Rushville, Ills, b May 15, 1840, d Apr 30, 1911,
       in St Louis, graduate Harvard, Class of 1864

136   Luther[r], b June 22 1847, lives in Washington, D C, graduate
       of Yale Class of 1871

81. EBENEZER[6] FULLER (*Luther E*[5], *Ebenezer*[4], *Jacob*[3], *Joseph*[2]
John[1]), Sept 16, 1813, in Hanover, Ct, d Nov 10, 1874 in Norwich,
Ct, m ——, 1837, Harriet L Bolles, b Feb 28, 1817

   He lived in Norwich, Ct

   Children

137   **James E.**[7] b Sept 2, 1838, m Rebecca Hope

138   Mary Louise[r], b Nov 21, 1841, d July 31, 1842

139   Mary Louise[r], 2d b Mar 22, 1844, m Jan 16, 1872, Gaybert
       Barnes, of Middletown, Ct, b Oct 10, 1848, d Oct 10, 1895
       Children, all but the youngest born in N Y City, Bessie[8], b
       Mar 15, 1873, m Aug 18, 1895, Franklin A Galloway, of Low-
       ville, N Y, Rachel[8], b Dec 21, 1874, m Aug 18 1895, Charles
       F Little, Jr, b Apr 7 1873, Sarah Bolles[8], b Feb 5 1876,
       Duane[8], b Oct 29, 1877, d Sept 13, 1899, at Camp Presidio,
       San Francisco, Cal, Ebenezer Fuller[8], b Oct 26, 1879, Anne
       Coit[8], b Aug 24 1882 in Brooklyn, N Y

140   **Alvan Bond**[r], b June 3, 1847, m 1, Sarah Ellen Treadway, m 2,
       Flora Arabella Tufts

141   Martha Evans[r], b Jan 13, 1850, d Dec 23, 1884, m Mar 30,
       1872, Reon Barnes, of Middletown, Ct, b Dec 9, 1845, brother
       of Gaybert Barnes Children Reon[8], b Aug 3 1873, m June
       2, 1910, Laura B Bowdoin Martha Cynthia[8], b Sept 11 1875,
       m Aug 14, 1895, Harold Barnes Roberts, b Aug 8, 1869, in
       Boston Alice Twombly[8] b Jan 9, 1882 m Aug 2 1900, Joseph
       D Lawrence, Jr

MR. AND MRS. PEARLEY B. FULLER—79.

MR AND MRS. EBENEZER FULLER—81, MARTHA E. FULLER—141.

SUSAN ESTHER FULLER—134.   DWIGHT FULLER—132.

ROBERT BRUCE FULLER—131.

WILLIAM H. CHADSEY—135.   EMMA A. (FULLER) CHADSEY—135

DR. ASA W. FULLER—84.

84. ASA WITTER⁶ FULLER, (*Avander⁵, Ebenezer⁴, Jacob³, Joseph²
John¹*), b July 31, 1817, m Hanover, Ct , d Jan 29, 1877, m June 30
1839, Nancy Woodworth Collins, b ——, 1812, d ——, 1833
　He removed to LeRoy, N Y about 1850, was a physician
　Children
142　Sarah Jane⁷ b May 16, 1840, d Feb 17, 1900
143　**Benjamin Asa⁷**, b Oct 17, 1846, d Aug 7, 1891, m Alice Cowan

88. DAVID CONGDON⁶ FULLER, (*Jesse S⁵, Ebenezer⁴, Jacob³, Joseph²,
John¹*), b Jan 3, 1823, probably in Norwich, Ct ; d 1870, m 1, Sept 2,
1850, Fanny E. Strickland, m 2, ——, Jane Gardner
　Children by first wife
144　A son, b ——
　By second wife
145　Eugene⁷, b ——.
146　Edward⁷, b ——

89. GEORGE DENISON⁶ FULLER, (*Jesse S⁵, Ebenezer⁴, Jacob³, Joseph²,
John¹*), b Dec 27, 1828, in Norwich, Ct , d Nov 1, 1911, in Hartford,
Ct m Mar 31, 1849, Josephine A Northrop, b Mar 17, 1833, d Sept
13, 1910
　Children
147　George A ⁷, b May 27, 1850, in Norwich, lives in Wethersfield, Ct
148　Sarah A ⁷, b May 14, 1856, in S Coventry, Ct , d Aug 22, 1886
149　Jessie C⁷, b June 17, 1861, in S Coventry, d Aug 17, 1862
150　Mabel J ⁷, b June 7, 1868, in Willimantic, Ct , d. Mar 11, 1878
151　Edna Edith⁷, b May 21, 1871, in Willimantic, m July 28, 1896,
　　　Burton B Holcomb, b July 28, 1870, in W Hartford, Ct , lives
　　　in Wethersfield, Ct

93. CHARLES C⁶ FULLER, (*Chester L⁵, Ebenezer⁴, Jacob³, Joseph²
John¹*), b Sept 15, 1832, in Norwich, Ct ; d Oct 15, 1880; m Sept 24,
1856, Lucy M Stead, b Nov 1, 1834, resides in Norwich, Ct (1913)
　Children, born in Norwich
152　Mary L⁷, b Sept 25 1857, d July 6, 1911, in Los Angeles, Cal ,
　　　m Nov 25, 1880, Oscar Gardner, b Feb 6, 1856, living in Los
　　　Angeles
153　**Frederick Lincoln⁷**, b Apr 11, 1861, m Apr 13, ——, Rebecca
　　　H Bell, b Nov 12, 1867　He lives in Dayton, O , an inventor
154　**Charles Owen⁷**, b Dec 24, 1867, m Oct 28, 1889, Ida M Ogden,
　　　b Apr 16, 1870, in Greenwich, Ct　He resides in Trenton,
　　　N J

95. WILLIAM CLEVELAND⁶ FULLER, (*George D⁵, Ebenezer⁴, Jacob³,
Joseph², John¹*), b May 25, 1838, in Norwich, Ct ; d Oct 17, 1908; m
Feb 11, 1865, in Williamsport, Md, Mary Jane Nowell, b there Apr

16

24, 1836 He was a machinist, residing after the Civil War, in
McKeesport, Pa
    Children:
155 George W S', b Jan 6, 1866, in Williamsport, Md , d July 30,
        1874, in McKeesport, Pa

97. GEORGE HAVENS⁶ FULLER, *(George D⁵, Ebenezer⁴, Jacob³ Joseph², John¹)*, b Sept 13, 1843, in Norwich, Ct , m July 20, 1876 Sarah
Elizabeth Case, b Dec 23, 1847
    He resides in Wichita Kan
    Children .
156 Elizabeth Havens', b May 3, 1877, in Springfield Mo

98. EDWARD DENISON⁶ FULLER, *(George D⁵ Ebenezer⁴ Jacob³, Joseph² John¹)*, b Nov 13, 1845, in Norwich, Ct , d Jan 9, 1909, m
Oct 5, 1876, Angelina P Norton, b Aug 30, 1853, in Branford, Ct
    Children
157 Mary Norton', b Dec 25, 1880, in Norwich, Ct , d in Branford
        Ct , Aug 15, 1881

100. WALTER⁶ FULLER, *(George D⁵, Ebenezer⁴, Jacob³, Joseph²
John¹)*, b Nov 13, 1850, in Norwich, Ct , d Feb 24, 1907, in Hartford,
Ct , m in Corning, Ia , Sept 14, 1880, Nellie Elizabeth Dean, b in N
Y State, Sept 10, 1855 , resides at Woodbury, N J
    Children
158 Walter Deane' b June 5, 1881, in Corning, Ia , m in Roxbury,
        Pa Sept 14, 1911 Sara Ella Kane, b in Pottsville, Pa , July
        4, 1888 They reside in Woodbury, N J

119. EDWIN DANIEL⁶ FULLER, *(Fordyce⁵, David⁴ Jacob³, Joseph²,
John¹)* b June 5, 1859, in Chelsea, Vt , m Feb 19, 1889, Edith May
Taplin, b, Feb 19, 1871
    He resides in Lowell, Mass
    Children
159 Earle Edwin', b July 22, 1892
160 Glenn Charles', b May 30, 1894

SEVENTH GENERATION

124. ALANSON⁷ FULLER, *(John M⁶, Alanson⁵ John⁴, Jacob³, Joseph²
John¹)*, b Dec 22, 1859, in Hanover, Ct , m Apr , 1897, Flora Rist
    Children
161 Howard⁸, b Apr —, 1898

MRS. JAMES E. FULLER—137.

MRS. ALVAN B. FULLER—140.   ALVAN B. FULLER—140.

JAMES E. FULLER—137.

131. ROBERT BRUCE[7] FULLER, (*Pearley B[6]*, *Luther E[5]*, *Ebenezer[4]*, *Jacob[3]*, *Joseph[2]*, *John[1]*), b Apr 2, 1836, in Hanover, Ct , d Apr 5, 1900, in Washington D C , m Aug 20, 1874, in Norwich, Ct , Harriet Augusta Prentice, b May 15, 1849, in Norwich

Children

162   Homer Gifford[8], b Jan 10, ,1879, in Derby, Ct , m in Cuba, N Y Feb 1, 1910 Meta Kramer, of San Francisco, Cal , b Sept 8, 1881 He is a physician, residing in Washington, D C (1913)

163   **Hubert Bruce**[8], b June 15 1880, m Florence Batty Dennis

164   Helen Celia[8], b Apr 10, 1888; resides in Washington, D C

137. JAMES E[7] FULLER, (*Ebenezer[6]*, *Luther E[5]*, *Ebenezer[4]*, *Jacob[3]*, *Joseph[2]*, *John[1]*) b Sept 2, 1838, in Norwich, Ct.; d July 11, 1912, m June 17, 1867, in South Carolina, Rebecca Hope, b Oct 23, 1844, in London, England

Children

165   Rebecca Hope[8], b Apr 10, 1868, in Brooklyn, N Y , m in Norwich, Ct , Apr 10 1888, Rev Francis Peck Bachelor, Yale graduate of 1885, b in Lebanon, Ct , Sept 25, 1862 , living in Talcottville, Ct Children, Frances Hope[9], b June 16, 1889, in Lebanon Ct , Muriel[9], b Sept 24, 1890, Norwich Ct , Wellesley graduate, 1912, post-graduate student Yale, Theodore[9], b Oct 18, 1893, in Hockanum, Ct , Robert[9], b July 17, 1896, in Hockanum, Isabel[9], b Dec 12, 1898, Christine[9], b Apr 24, 1902, Clementine[9], b Mar 20, 1907, in Hockanum

166   Margaret Witter[8], b Jan 23, 1872, in Brooklyn, N Y , lives in Norwich, Ct

167   Edward[8], b July 20, 1874

168   Charlotte[8], b Aug 20, 1878, m Dec 10, 1904, Guy Warner Eastman, b Oct 7, 1881 , d May 17, 1907 , graduate Boston Inst Tech

169   Harriet Louise[8], b May 1, 1882, lives in Norwich, Ct

140. ALVAN BOND[7] FULLER, (*Ebenezer[6]*, *Luther E[5]*, *Ebenezer[4]*, *Jacob[3]*, *Joseph[2]*, *John[1]*), b, June 3, 1847, in Norwich, Ct , d July 1, 1902, m 1, Jan 13, 1867 Sarah Ellen Treadway, b —, 1849, d Jan 27, 1867, m 2, Sept 24, 1875, Flora Arabella Tufts, b Mar 21, 1858, in Malden Mass

Children

170   Alvan Tufts[8] b Feb 27, 1878, at Charlestown, Mass , m in Paris, France, July 12, 1910, Viola Theresa Davenport b in Somerville, Mass , May 29, 1882

171   Martha Hope[8], b May 1, 1884 in Charlestown, m in Brookline, Mass , Oct 17 1911, Oscar Lawrence Halsey, b Sept 2, 1874, in Brooklyn, N Y

143. BENJAMIN ASA[7] FULLER, (*Asa W[6]*, *Avander[5]*, *Ebenezer[4]*, *Jacob[3]*, *Joseph[2]*, *John[1]*), b Oct 17, 1846, d Aug 7, 1891, in LeRoy, N Y m July 12, 1873, Alice Cowan, living (1914) in LeRoy

He was a physician

Children

172   Clara Louise[8], b Apr 21, 1876, m Sept 7, 1898, James Henry
      Barrows, b Oct 28, 1868, in Genesee, N Y , resides in LeRoy.
      No children

153.   FREDERICK LINCOLN[7] FULLER, (*Charles C[6]*, *~~Charles~~ Charles L[5]*, *Ebenezer[4]*, *Jacob[3]*, *Joseph[2]*, *John[1]*), b Apr 11, 1861, in Norwich, Ct , m Apr
13, 1883, Bebecca H Bell b Nov 12, 1867

He is an inventor, and resides in Dayton, O , where he is at the
head of the invention department of the National Cash Register Co

Children

173   Lucy May[8], b Sept 25, 1896

154.   CHARLES OWEN[7] FULLER, (*Charles C[6]*, *~~Charles~~ Charles L[5]*, *Ebenezer[4]*,
Jacob[3], *Joseph[2]* *John[1]*), b Dec 24, 1867, in Norwich, Ct , m Oct 28
1889, Ida M Ogden, b Apr 16, 1870, in Greenwich, Ct

He lives in Trenton, N J

Children

174   Frederick Ogden[8] b June 8, 1890 in Waterbury, Ct

175   Gertrude May[8], b Oct 5, 1892, in Trenton

176   William Gardner[8], b Feb 11, 1895, in Trenton

177   Mildred Stead[8], b Aug 4, 1897, in Trenton , d May 2, 1898

EIGHTH GENERATION.

163.   HUBERT BRUCE[8] FULLER, (*Robert B[7]*, *Pearley B[6]*, *Luther E[5]*,
Ebenezer[4], *Jacob[3]*, *Joseph[2]*, *John[1]*), b June 15, 1880, in Derby, Ct , m in
Chanute Kan , May 25, 1910, Florence Batty Dennis, b Jan 1, 1887

He graduated from Yale College, Class of 1901, and is a lawyer and
author, residing in Cleveland, Ohio

Children

178   Harriet Lois[9], b Aug 19, 1911, in Washington, D C.

HELEN CELIA FULLER,   HUBERT BRUCE FULLER,   MRS. HUBERT BRUCE FULLER,
164.   163   163.

MRS. HOMER GIFFORD FULLER,   HOMER GIFFORD FULLER.
162.   162

Sitting—LUTHER FULLER,   THOMAS HART FULLER.
136.   133.

ROBERT FULLER

OF

DORCHESTER AND DEDHAM,

AMERICAN FULLER GENEALOGY.

ROBERT FULLER OF DORCHESTER AND DEDHAM, AND SOME OF HIS DESCENDANTS

Not much information has been found concerning the early history of Robert Fuller of Dorchester

Pope in his "Pioneers of Massachusetts," says Robert Fuller was in 'Dorchester in 1640, removed to Dedham, he and his wife received to church from Dorchester 19 (11) 1648" (Second wife) "Wife's name Ann —— Wife d 4 (5), 1646?, m 2, Sarah ——, who d 2 (4), 1686 He d Dec 14 1688 Will probated Apr 28, 1690 Bequests to grand-children John and Prudence Ranger, to son Jonathan and daughter Mary Richards "

The History of Dorchester," says he probably came to America during the 'second emigration" so called, a passenger on one of the four vessels that came to America between 1635 and 1640

Children recorded in Dorchester and Dedham

1 **Jonathan²**, b June 15 1643, m ——, Mary ——
2 Benoni², b June 16, 1646?, d Sept 5, 1646
3 Sarah², b Sept 21, 1647
4 John², b Nov 26, 1649, probably d 1678, in Dedham
5 Patience², b Feb 22, 1651
6 Mary² b Mar 1, 1653

SECOND GENERATION.

1. JONATHAN² FULLER, (*Robert¹*), b June 15, 1643, in Dorchester, d —— 1720, in Dedham, m ——, Mary —— who d Mar 20, 1701 Children, all born in Dedham

7 Rachel¹ b Dec 3, 1673; m Oct 27, 1698, Joseph Bent, of Milton

and had Mary[4], Joseph[4], John[4], Rachel[4], Elizabeth[4], Sarah[4], Ebenezer[4], Experience[4], Thankful[4]

8 Sarah[3], b May 4, 1676
9 Mary[3], b Apr 20, 1679, d young
10 **Samuel[3]**, b. Feb 15, 1681, m 1, Sarah Fisher, m 2, Elizabeth Crane
11 **John[3]**, b Dec 3, 1684, m Mary Guild
12 Mary[3], 2d, b Feb 21, 1687
13 Joshua[3], b Nov 23, 1689, d young
14 Joshua[3], 2d, b Dec 15, 1691, probably the Joshua Fuller that d Feb 25, 1765
15 Jonathan[3], b Aug 19, 1694

THIRD GENERATION.

10. SAMUEL[3] FULLER, (*Jonathan[2]*, *Robert[1]*), b Feb 15, 1681, m Dedham, d Mar 28, 1765, m 1, Feb 10, 1705-6. Sarah Fisher, who d July 12, 1714, m 2, Jan 15, 1717-18, Elizabeth Crane, who d Aug 6, 1760

Children recorded in Dedham

16 Sarah[4], b Oct 17, 1706, d Feb 13, 1771, aged about 65
17 Samuel[4], b Aug 14, 1709, probably d May 12, 1752
18 Esther[4], b Mar 1, 1711, d July 29, 1714
19 Mary[4], b Aug 19, 1712, d Nov 20, 1712
20 **Benjamin[4]**, b Mar 9, 1720, m 1, Hannah Wadsworth; m **2**, Sarah Ballard
21 **Seth[4]**, b Sept 23, 1721, m Sarah Mackanah
22 Hannah[4] b Mar 1, 1722-3
23 Elizabeth[4], b Nov 28, 1724, d Mar 24, 1725
24 Mehitable[4], b. Feb 21, 1727-8

11. JOHN[3] FULLER, (*Jonathan[2]*, *Robert[1]*), b Dec 3, 1684, m Dedham, d ——, m 'May ye ——," Mary Guild

Children

25 John[4], b Mar 20, 1714, m Mrs Anna Fales
26 Mary[4], b Jan 17, 1715-6, m Dec 4, 1732, David Whiting

Group Arrangement.

Benjamin[3], Samuel[3], and John[3], sons of Jonathan[2] Fuller, are made heads of three Groups, arranged by generations, and each descendant given an individual number relative to his Group

FIRST GROUP

— - —

BENJAMIN⁴ FULLER, AND SOME OF HIS DESCENDANTS

FOURTH GENERATION.

20. BENJAMIN⁴ FULLER, (*Samuel³, Jonathan², Robert¹*), b Mar 9, 1720, in Dedham; d there Feb 9, 1762, m 1, Mar 20, 1740, Hannah Wadsworth, of Milton, who d Dec 15, 1746, m 2, Sept 15, 1748 Sarah Ballard

Children, all born in Dedham

1   A son, b Sept 10, 1742, d Sept. 12, 1742
2   Elizabeth⁵, bapt July 10, 1743, d July 10, 1743
3   **Benjamin⁵**, bapt Oct 20, 1745, m Mary Graves
4   Hannah⁵, bapt July 4, 1749
5   Samuel⁵, bapt Dec 2, 1750
6   Elizabeth⁵, 2d, bapt Oct 1, 1752
7   **Stephen⁵**, bapt Dec 22, 1754, m Hannah Felch
8   Lucy⁵, bapt Nov 14, 1756
9   **Thaddeus⁵**, bapt Oct 15, 1758; m Susannah Oliver
10 **Rufus⁵**, bapt Sept 7, 1760, m Hannah Billings.

FIFTH GENERATION.

3. BENJAMIN⁵ FULLER, (*Benjamin⁴, Samuel³, Jonathan², Robert¹*), bapt Oct. 20, 1745, in Dedham, d there May 4, 1785, Oct 29, 1767 Mary Graves, who d Jan 6, 1784, aged 37

Children

11 Mehitable⁶, b Nov 7, 1768
12 Lucy⁶, b Jan 23, 1771
13 ⎫
   ⎬ Two children that d Sept 21, 1775
14 ⎭
15 A child that d Dec. 24, 1783

7. STEPHEN⁵ FULLER, (*Benjamin⁴, Samuel³, Jonathan², Robert¹*), b Dec 18, 1754, in Dedham, d Feb 9 1839, in Francestown, N H , m

Sept 10, 1778, in Walpole, Hannah Felch b Feb 22, 1755, d May 16, 1833, in Francestown

He lived in Walpole when he enlisted, Sept , 1777, in the Massachusetts Militia, for service in the Revolutionary War   About 1781, he removed to Francestown, N H

Children

16   **Samuel**⁶, b Mar 21, 1780, m Abigail Terren
17   **Rufus**⁶, b Feb 12, 1782, m Martha Dow
18   **Jared**⁶, b Dec 28, 1783, m Thankful Story
19   Hannah⁶, b Dec 27, 1785, d Aug 5, 1822
20   Lucy⁶, b Dec 31, 1787, m 1, July 26, 1813, Uzziah Kemp of Francestown, N H , m 2, Ebenezer Talbot of Francestown, d Lowell Apr 12, 1862
21   Asenath⁶ b Mar 22 1791, d Feb 26, 1824
22   Sarah⁶, b Oct 6, 1793
23   Betsey⁶, b Dec 10, 1796, d Feb 11, 1827, in Francestown, N H

9. THADDEUS⁵ FULLER, (*Benjamin⁴, Samuel³, Jonathan², Robert¹*), b Oct 14, 1758, in Dedham; d ——; m Dec 11, 1793, Susannah Oliver(²)

He was a Revolutionary soldier, and a prisoner, who removed to Francestown, N H, and was on tax list there in 1793

In 1821 he was living in Athens, O, aged 62 years, and his wife was 57 years old in 1822

The only child I find mentioned is

24   A child that d in Francestown in 1792

10. RUFUS⁵ FULLER, (*Benjamin⁴, Samuel³ Jonathan² Robert¹*), b Aug 30, 1760, in Dedham, d Sept 6, 1840, at Bradford, N H , m Mar 3, 1785, Hannah Billings of Sharon, b Feb 12, 1762; d Oct 11, 1847, in Bradford, N H

He was a soldier of the Revolution, who enlisted 1st in 1778, 2d in 1779 and 3d in 1780

Children, all born in Francestown, N H

25   Richard⁶, b May 14, 1786, removed to and d in Bradford, N H
26   **Rufus**⁶, b Mar 24, 1790, m Sarah Aiken
27   Curtis⁶, b July 30, 1791, m Hannah Gobin
28   Hannah⁶, b Dec 8, 1802, d —— in the West, m Perley Martin of Sutton

SIXTH GENERATION.

16. SAMUEL⁶ FULLER (*Stephen⁵ Benjamin⁴, Samuel³, Jonathan², Robert¹*), b Mar 21, 1780, d Feb 25, 1874, in Deering, N H ; m ——, Abigail Terren of Francestown, N H , who d in Lowell, Mar 21, 1794

Children, all born in Francestown, N H , but the last mentioned

29 Ephraim⁷, b June 4, 1830; m Harriet A Newton, removed to Arizona
30 William T⁷, b Jan 5, 1832, m Janette Durgin, removed to Lowell and d there
31 Mary P⁷, b May 3, 1836; d ——, in Lowell, m Abraham Melvin
32 Daniel D⁷, b Dec 7, 1839, d Apr 28, 1843
33 Samuel D⁷, b Sept 24(?), removed to the Sandwich Islands

17. RUFUS⁶ FULLER, (*Stephen⁵, Benjamin⁴, Samuel³, Jonathan², Robert¹*), b Feb 12, 1782, in ——, d ——, m —— Martha Dow
Children, born in Francestown, N H
34 **Rodney G,**⁷, b ——, m Sarah A Haywood
35 Clarissa⁷ b ——
36 Sarah⁷, b ——
37 Martha⁷, b ——
38 Emeline⁷, b ——

18. JARED⁶ FULLER, (*Stephen⁵, Benjamin⁴ Samuel³ Jonathan², Robert¹*), b Dec 28 1783 in ——, d May 19, 1854, in Dunbarton, N H : m Nov 21 1811, Thankful Story, b June 15, 1791, in Dunbarton; d there Apr 15, 1863, dau of Daniel Story of Essex, Mass
Children, b in Dunbarton
39 Caroline⁷, b Aug 26, 1812
40 Henry Harrison⁷, b Jan 14 1815
41 Asenath⁷, b July 21, 1817
42 Mary Page⁷, b Feb 5, 1819, d July —— 1834
43 Stephen Nelson⁷, b Jan 10 1822; d Dec 17, 1825
44 Daniel Burnham⁷, b Sept 16, 1823
45 Elizabeth Maria⁷, b Feb 19, 1826, m Benjamin Greer and had Henry⁸ and Benjamin⁸
46 William Nelson⁷, b June 5, 1828, d Apr 21, 1899 in Dunbarton, m ——
47 Stephen Brainard⁷, b July 26, 1830
48 Harriet Davenport⁷, b Aug 8, 1833
49 Mary Story⁷, b Mar 12, 1837, m Aaron Smith and had Harriet D⁸ and Elizabeth M H⁸

26. RUFUS⁶ FULLER, (*Rufus⁵, Benjamin⁴, Samuel³ Jonathan², Robert¹*), b Mar 24, 1790, in Francestown, N H , d ——, m Nov 22, 1814, Sarah Aiken of Deering, N H b there Apr 14 1794, d July 25, 1876 at Concord, N H
Children, born in Francestown
50 Richard F⁷, b Nov 12, 1815, m Jan. 19, 1845, Ellen W Heath of Hopkinton, N H
51 Henry M⁷, b Aug 29, 1817, d Nov 14 1890, at Concord N H , m Nov 14, 1860, Jennie George

SEVENTH GENERATION.

34. RODNEY G⁷ FULLER, (*Rufus⁶, Stephen⁵, Benjamin⁴, Samuel³, Jonathan², Robert¹*), b ——, in Francestown, N H , d ——, in Dorchester, in Mar 31, 1836, Sarah A Haywood, b in St Albans, Vt.

He was a machinist by trade

Children recorded in Newton

52 Catherine W⁸, b June 20, 1837, in Newtonville; m Sept 9, 1855, Charles Fenner, b in Jewett, Ct

53 Emeline A⁸, b July 15, 1840, in Needham

54 Maria L⁸, b Aug 22, 1844, in Newtonville

55 Mary F⁸, b Nov 25, 1845, in Newtonville

56 Sarah J⁸, b Oct 22, 1848, at Newton Upper Falls.

57 Frederick Rodney⁸, b May 8, 1851, in Newton

SECOND GROUP ·

SETH¹ FULLER, AND SOME OF HIS DESCENDANTS

21. SETH⁴ FULLER, (*Samuel³ Jonathan² Robert¹*), b Sept 23, 1721, in Dedham, d there Oct 29, 1793, m Mar 19, 1752, Sarah Mackanah who d Oct 4, 1803, aged 81

Children, b in Dedham

1 **Seth⁵**, b Feb 8, 1752, m 1, Rebecca Moore, m 2, Abigail Fuller.
2 Eleanor⁵, b May 1, 1754; m Apr 21, 1785, Asa Everett
3 **Eliphalet⁵**, b Feb 26, 1756, m Eleanor Ellis
4 **Jason⁵**, b Nov 20, 1757, m Catherine Farrington
5 **Jonathan⁵**, bapt Jan 6, 1760, m Anna Guild
6 Mary⁵, bapt Apr 11, 1762

FIFTH GENERATION.

1. SETH⁵ FULLER, (*Seth⁴, Samuel³ Jonathan² Robert¹*), b Oct 8, 1752, in Dedham, d Sept 5, 1825, in Francestown, N H, m 1, June 5 1777, Rebecca Morse of Dedham, who d Apr 19, 1801, aged 47; m 2, Nov 4, 1802, Abigail⁵ Fuller (*David⁴, David³, Thomas², Thomas¹* of Dedham)

Rebecca Fuller, wife of Seth, was dismissed from Dedham church to Francestown church Feb 26, 1792

Seth Fuller settled in Francestown in 1777

Children, all born in Francestown

7 Cynthia⁶, b Mar 2, 1778, d Mar 25, 1780
8 Rebecca⁶, b Oct 19, 1780, m Daniel Page of Plainfield, Vt
9 **Ira⁶**, b Jan 15, 1783, m. Hannah Gould
10 Polly⁶, b. ——, m Int Pub Oct 14, 1809, with Joel Gay of Dedham
11 Azubah⁶ b ——, m Feb 2, 1817, Willard Fairbanks of Dedham
12 Seth⁶, b ——, d Nov. 20, 1878, in Northern Texas, m Olive Manning of Lyndboro, N H.
13 Clarissa⁶, b ——; d Aug 1, 1834, in Hancock, N H, m Arnold Hutchinson of Hancock

3. ELIPHALET⁵ FULLER (*Seth⁴, Samuel³, Jonathan², Robert¹*), b

Feb 26, 1756, in Dedham, d there Aug 15 1827, m 25, 1786, Eleanor Ellis who d Sept 23, 1844, aged 86

Children

14   **Ellis**[f], bapt Sept 17, 1792, m Lucy Gay

15   Ira[d], bapt Sept 17, 1792

16   Lucy[e] bapt Sept 17, 1792, d May 19, 1816, m Feb 25, 1816, —— Potter

17   Infant that d May 18, 1790

4. JASON[5] FULLER, (*Seth[4], Samuel[3], Jonathan[2], Robert[1]*), bapt Nov 20, 1757, in Dedham, d Mar 3 1840, aged 82, at Walden Vt , m June 8 1784 Catherine Farrington of Dedham who d July 29, 1843

He was a soldier in the Revolution and removed to Francestown, N H , in 1784, and in 1809 to Walden, Vt

Children, born in Francestown

18   Catherine[6], b May 31, 1786, m ——, —— Dean

19   Jason[6], b Dec 16, 1787

20   Roxana[6], b ——, m —— —— White

21   Irena[6], b ——, m ——, —— Dow

5. JONATHAN[5] FULLER, (*Seth[4], Samuel[3], Jonathan[2], Robert[1]*) b Dec 19 1759, in Dedham, d there Apr 8, 1834, m Mar 18, 1784, Anna Guild, who d Dec 28, 1843, aged 82

He served in the Revolutionary War and always lived in Dedham

Children:

22   Willard[6], bapt May 26, 1799

23   Sally[6], bapt May 26, 1799, m Feb 11 1812, Jabez Boyden

24   **Samuel Guild**[6], bapt May 26, 1799, m Peggy Gould

25   Roxy[6], bapt May 26, 1799, m Apr 8, 1817, John Morse

SIXTH GENERATION.

9. IRA[6] FULLER, (*Seth[5], Seth[4], Samuel[3], Jonathan[2], Robert[1]*), b Jan 15, 1783, m Francestown, N H , d Jan, 1864, in Princeton, Ills , m Dec 15, 1803, Hannah Gould, b Nov 8, 1787, d Feb 9, 1854

Children, all b in Francestown

26   Susan[7], b ——, 1804, d Feb , 1877, m July 1, 1823, Aaron Fisher of Francestown, and had Henry[8], Charles[8], Augustus[8], Maria[8], Joel[8]

27   Cynthia[7], b Nov 8, 1808; d Oct 1847, m ——, 1834, Seth Page of Plainfield, Vt , and had a dau Ellen[8], now dead

28   Mary[7], b Aug 22, 1810, d Jan 7, 1882, in Brooklyn, N Y ; m ——, 1833, Theodore L Hastings of Framingham, and had Mary Helen[8], b ——, d ——, in Brooklyn, N Y , Josephine[8] b 1842, d in Lowell, and Isabella[8], b July 31, 1846

29   **Ira Ellis**[7], b Feb 7, 1812, m Catherine Whittall

30 **Joel G,**[7] b Dec 12, 1816; m Elma M Clark
31 Hannah Frances[7], b Jan 22, 1826, m Sept 25, 1849, Joel Anson
Gay, and has two daughters, Clara Frances[8] and Hattie E
Chase[8] She is now (July 1914) living in Norwood, Mass
32 Emily A[7], b Mar 1, 1828, d Oct 26, 1911, m ——, 1855, Caleb
Ellis, no issue

14. ELLIS[6] FULLER (*Eliphalet[5], Seth[4], Samuel[3], Jonathan[2], Robert[1]*),
bapt Sept 17, 1792, at Dedham, d there Mar 23, 1857, m Aug 1, 1815,
Lucy Gay, who d June 18, 1868, aged 76 y 1 mo 18 d
  Children, recorded in Dedham
33 **Alvan[7]**, b about 1829, m Frances C Coville

24. SAMUEL GUILD[6] FULLER, (*Jonathan[5], Seth[4] Samuel[3], Jonathan[2],
Robert[1]*), bapt May 26, 1799, m Dedham d June 11, 1853, in Sharon,
m Apr 24, 1816, Peggy Gould of Sharon, who d May 13, 1844
  Children, recorded in Dedham
34 Hannah[7], bapt June 22, 1823, d July 22, 1836
35 **Samuel Gould[7]**, bapt June 22, 1823, m Elizabeth C Fenno

SEVENTH GENERATION.

29. IRA ELLIS[7] FULLER, (*Ira[6], Seth[5], Seth[4], Samuel[3], Jonathan[2] Robert[1]*), b Feb 7, 1812, in Francestown, N H, d Jan 4, 1886, in Rollo,
Ills m in New York City, Nov 22, 1851, Catherine Whittall
  Children, all b in New York but the youngest, b in Princeton, Ills
36 **Henry Harvey[8]**, b Dec 6, 1852, m Ella Gertrude Whitver
37 Kate Isabel[8], b Sept 18, 1854 m Mar 12, 1878 Charles W Whitman, and has 3 daughters, all living (1914)
38 Josephine Hannah[8], b Sept 20, 1856
39 Ira Edgar[8], b Mar 11, 1859, d Sept 1, 1910

30. JOEL G,[7] FULLER, (*Ira[6], Seth[5] Seth[4], Samuel[3], Jonathan[2], Robert[1]*)
b Dec 12, 1816 in Francestown, N H, d June 18, 1896, in Princeton,
Ills., m ——, Elma M Clark of Rumney, Vt, who also d in Princeton,
  Children
40 Charles C[8], b ——, said to reside in Chicago (1914)

33. ALVAN[7] FULLER, (*Ellis[6] Eliphalet[5] Seth[4] Samuel[3], Jonathan[2]
Robert[1]*), b about 1829 in Dedham, d ——, m Jan 5, 1869, Frances
C Coville
  Children, b in Dedham
41 Alvin E[8], b Mar 21, 1870, d Dec 3, 1871, aged 1 y 8 mos 12 d

35. SAMUEL GOULD[7] FULLER, (*Samuel Guild[6], Jonathan[5], Seth[4], Samuel[3], Jonathan[2], Robert[1]*). bapt June 23, 1823, in Dedham, d Feb 15 1898 in Sharon, m Int Pub Feb 18, 1842, with Elizabeth C Fenno of Braintree

Children, recorded in Sharon

42 **George Samuel[8]**, b Nov 5 1843, m Sarah J Weeman
43 **Edward Jarvis[8]**. b Jan 30, 1854, m Sarah V Willet

EIGHTH GENERATION.

36. HENRY HARVEY[8] FULLER, (*Ira E[7], Ira[6], Seth[5], Seth[4], Samuel[3], Jonathan[2], Robert[1]*), b Dec 6, 1852. in New York, m Jan 11, 1877 Ella Gertrude Whitver

Resides in Princeton, Ills., has been Circuit Clerk there for nearly 24 years (1914).

Children, all born in Walnut. Ills

44 Clarence Ellis[9], b Dec. 13, 1877, d Apr 17, 1892
45 **John Edgar[9]**, b Feb 3, 1881, m Della Earnest
46 Kate Darlene[9]. b Dec 6, 1884
47 Gertrude Bell[9], b Aug 21, 1892

42. GEORGE SAMUEL[8] FULLER, (*Samuel Gould[7], Samuel Guild[6], Jonathan[5], Seth[4], Samuel[3], Jonathan[2], Robert[1]*), b Nov 5, 1843 in Sharon, m June 20, 1866, Sarah J Weeman of Standish, Me.

Children

48 Ida Louisa[9], b Mar. 28, 1868

43. EDWARD JARVIS[8] FULLER, (*Samuel Gould[7] Samuel Guild[6], Jonathan[5], Seth[4], Samuel[3], Jonathan[2], Robert[1]*), b Jan 30, 1854, in Sharon; m ——, Sarah J Willet

Children, recorded in Sharon

49 Edith May[9], b Sept 26, 1883, d Mar 1, 1907
50 Samuel Edward[9], b Jan 27, 1887
51 Henry Jarvis[9], b Mar 18, 1892

NINTH GENERATION.

45. JOHN EDGAR[9] FULLER, (*Henry H[8], Ira E[7], Ira[6] Seth[5], Seth[4], Samuel[3], Jonathan[2], Robert[1]*), b Feb 3, 1881, in Walnut, Ills , m Dec 24, 1903, in Garrett, Kansas, Della Earnest

Resides in Princeton, Ills

Children, all born in Princeton

52 Earnest[10], b June 22, 1905
53 Harry[10], b Jan 6, 1908.
54 Donald Whittall[10].
55 Richard Kinnear[10].   } twins, b Jan 8 1910

THIRD GROUP

_____ _ _

JOHN[4] FULLER, AND SOME OF HIS DESCENDANTS

FOURTH GENERATION.

23. JOHN[4] FULLER, (*John[3] Jonathan[2], Robert[1]*), b Mar 20, 1714, in Dedham d ——, m Jan 3, 1739-40. Mrs Anna Fales

Children baptized in Dedham

1 John[5], bapt Jan 17, 1741-2

2 Anna[5], bapt Aug 29, 1742

3 Stephen[5], bapt Sept 16, 1744

4 Stephen[5], 2d, bapt Sept 9, 1750

5 Anna[5], 2d, bapt Jan 7, 1753

6 Molly[5], bapt May 13, 1759

No further mention of this family, or any member of it, in the Dedham town and church records

17

SUPPLEMENT

TO

VOLUMES ONE AND TWO

OF

FULLER GENEALOGY

FIRST GROUP

DESCENDANTS OF EDWARD FULLER OF THE

"MAYFLOWER"

Additions marked A—Corrections marked C

A No 8 Daniel[f] Fuller, b Aug 22, 1759 or 60, in Bolton, Ct ; m Oct
18 1785, Sarah McIntire, b Aug 22, 1768, in Vergennes, Vt He
d Aug 27 1836, in Alexander, Genessee Co , N Y , was a Revolutionary pensioner who lived in Salisbury, Ct , in 1776, and after
the war in Teignmouth, Vt , then 28 years in Essex Co , N Y ,
and then removed to Alexander His widow was living about
1840 in Pomfret Vt (?) They had David[5], b Feb 23, 1783,
Daniel[5] Mar 5 1787 and Polly[5], Dec 18, 1792

\ No 15 Joanna, m Justis Chapin

C No 16 David[f], d Apr 17, 1845 It was his wife Elsie who d May
20, 1790

A His granddaughter, Mrs George Engel, of Caledonia, Minn , in
letter of Mar 29 1914 states that her grandfather was Captain David Fuller, b in Keene, N H , served as Captain in 1812,
m Miss Orinda Bingham removed to Saranac, N Y , before
the war and lived there during the war , also till most all his
children were grown up, then moved to Keesville, N Y See
under No 40, Luman Fuller below

A No 40 Luman[8] Fuller, b Aug 25, 1798, in Keene, N H , d ——,
m Alba, Ia , m ——, Mariah Stiles at Keene (now North Elba)
Essex Co , N Y He removed with his parents when only 12
years old to Keene, thence to Wisconsin and later to Alba, Ia ,
where he died He had 11 children—dates of birth not known,
except for those below, whose data were found in the Groton
Avery Genealogy Marietta Augusta[9], b 1833, in Keene, N. Y ,
d Jan 6, 1897, at Saranac Lake, N Y ; m Feb 7, 1857, Simeon
Fayette Avery, b Nov 25, 1832, at North Elba, N Y , and had
Leslie Jason[10], Oct 10, 1858, Lillian F[10], Oct 28 1860, Jasper
A[10], Feb 21, 1863, Wilber F[10], June 27, 1865 Luman[8] Fuller's
daughter, Purlina Lunancy[9], b Apr 6, 1836, in Keene, N Y , now
called North Elba, m Sept 3 1854, Julius Augustus Avery, b
Apr. 8, 1830, at Keene, d Dec 15, 1854, at Rubicon, Wis , and she
removed to Caledonia, Minn , where she married George Engel

and now (1914) resides She had one child, Lorin Eleazer
Avery by first husband She has a younger sister living All of
the other children of Luman are dead No reply made to request
for further information

A No 62 John Harvey⁵, d Mar 15, 1881, in Southwick, m Mar 16,
1826, Elizabeth Hastings of Suffield, Ct

A No 92 Heman Hastings⁹, d May 6, 1898, his wife, Lucy J ——
b in Washington, Mass, d Sept 2, 1892, in Suffield, Ct

IN SUPPLEMENT VOL II.

A Page 236, Vol II Albert Chittenden⁹ Fuller (Daniel⁸, Samuel⁷,
Joshua⁶, Samuel⁵, Barnabas⁴, Samuel³, Samuel², Edward¹), b May
4, 1830, in Brant, N Y , d June 16, 1835, m 1, Dec 25, 1851,
Lucy Marsh, who d Aug 2, 1854, at Irving, N Y , m 2, Feb 16,
1856, Sophronia Marsh

He served in the 100th Regt N Y Vols as sergeant in the
Civil war, was in the battle of Fair Oaks, Va For 17 years he
was a locomotive engineer on the Lake Shore and Mich South-
ern Railway living at Irving and Silver Creek N Y
    Children

1 Juliette²⁰ b Nov 3, 1853 at Irving, N Y , m 1, Oct 1, 1874,
William A Watt, b Sept 9, 1848, at Sheridan, N Y., m 2, Oct
9 1901, Albert H Stebbins, and resides at Bradentown, Fla
Children (Watt) Lucy¹¹, b July 15, 1875, Susan Emelyn¹¹ b
Mar 26, 1877, and Juliette¹¹, b ——

Jennie Marsh¹⁰, b Sept 26 1860, m Oct 26, 1881, Alfred Star-
ling, and had Beulah Grace¹¹ Nov 30, 1882, Albert¹¹, July 23
1885, Gertrude¹¹ Jan 26, 1887, and Vera¹¹, Sept 14 1891

William Harrison¹⁰, b Sept 25, 1863, m 1891, Jean McAndrews
and had William Harrison¹¹, b Nov, 1900

George Harriott¹⁰, b Oct 14, 1871, m Dec, 1901, Ola McLean
and had Albert Chittenden¹¹, b 1902, d 1903 or 4, George Albert¹¹, b 1907, Herbert S ¹¹, b 1913

Dadora¹⁰, b Oct, 1875, d May 8, 1883

C Page 239 George Theodore¹⁰, b Dec 23, 1852, d Mar 21, 1899, and
George Theodore¹¹ resides at Laurium, Mich, not Lawrence
The 4th child was Russell, not Russell J, and the 5th child,
Helen Graham, was b Aug 3, 1892

SECOND GROUP, VOL I

A No 7 Isaac⁶, m Apr 18 1754, Susan Wadsworth of Pembroke
Mass, and it was probably his brother Seth who m Deborah
Ford of Pembroke Mar 8, 1764

A No 18 Tirzah⁸ (Fuller) Pinkham, d June 15, 1887 m Isaac
Myrick

A No 29 Mary Smith⁹, d May 9, 1887, m —— Hathaway

A No 30 Abbott, d Nov 27, 1855, son Edward b Mar 27, 1852, dau
    Mary b Feb 24 1855
A No 36 Herschel', d Nov 24, 1905

SIXTH GROUP

A No 8 Solomon Lathrop', was a private in Capt Paul Langdon's
    Co in 1775
A No 9 Ezekiel' m Jan 3 1782, Mary Bartlett
A No 40 Martha⁸, Springfield G S Records, Henry Starkie, d July
    25, 1841, aged 56   Children   Martha A⁹ d Sept 13, 1817, aged
    17 mos , Henry W⁹, d July 14 1821 aged 2 y 5 m , Henry F⁹,
    d Feb 4 1845 aged 23
C No 84 Catherine dau of Hon *Nathan* Weston
A No 120 Henry J¹⁰ McLean, d Nov 27, 1913
A No 142 William Hyslop⁹ Fuller   His daughter, Melicent Rawson¹⁰
    Fuller, was born Monday, Mar 27, 1911, at 2 45 P M
A No 174 John N⁹   His dau Ivah L¹⁰, b May 12, 1858, Springfield
    Rec   Newton V R give marriage of J H Fuller, aged 21, b
    Somers, Ct , son of Asa and Keziah, to Sarah B Fisk, born and
    of Newton aged 20, dau of Calvin and Martha Fisk
C No 221 Henry Weld⁹ was b in Augusta, not Bangor, Me , was in
    business in Bangor, not Boston
A and C No 222 Melville Weston⁹, m 1, Calista Ophelia Reynolds, b
    Oct 16, 1837 , d Nov 13, 1864 buried at Graceland, Chicago,
    Nov 16, 1864 aged 26 y 27 d   He m 2, May 30, 1866
A No 223 Frederick A⁹, m Sept 17, 1871, Ellen M Strong, and had
    Frederick¹⁰, b Apr , 1874, resides at Taunton
A No 225 Benjamin A G⁹, m Apr 11, 1874, Alice Bartlett, and had
    Margaret¹⁰, b Apr , 1875, and Ethel¹⁰, b, Dec , 1877
A No 227 Hiram E⁹, m June 17, 1872, Mary E Gordon, and had
    Mary¹⁰, b ——
A No 243 Norman W¹⁰.   Holyoke Rec give his marriage to Rebecca
    Shaw, and son Norman A¹¹, d Feb, 1863, aged 1 y 8 m
A No 270 Austin¹⁰, d in Rome, N Y
A No 293 Samuel E¹⁰, d Feb 25, 1910, in Hudson
A No 335 Lillian May¹⁰, d Oct 18, 1910, in Springfield
A No 354 David Lyon¹⁰, d Dec 2, 1913, in Thomaston, Me
A No 382. Frederick A¹⁰, b and d in Chicago
A No 383 Henry F¹⁰   His first w. d Feb 21, 1899, m 2, Dec 10,
    1901, Olive Lucy Miller of New London, Ct   Children   Dorothy
    Converse¹¹, b Nov. 19, 1894, Catherine Weston¹¹, Oct 20, 1896,
    Charles Hamblin¹¹, Feb 21, 1904 , d young; Henry Frederick¹¹,
    Mar 24, 1905, Nathan Rockwood¹¹, May 13, 1907; Olive Lucile
    Miller¹¹, b Dec 22, 1912
A No 384 Florence¹⁰   Children   Henry Fuller¹¹ Saunders, b Jan 1,
    1887, d Aug 24, 1905, Goddard Weld¹¹ Saunders, b Feb 13, 1900

A No 385 Nathan *Weston*

A No 386 Grace Weston[10], m 1891, d Mar 7, 1893, had one child, Melville Fuller[11], b Feb 18, 1893, d May 24, 1893

A No 388 Mary C[10], d Dec 21, 1910, m —— Manning, had child that d Nov 30, 1892

A No 389 Mildred[10]; m 1891

A and C No 390 Pauline Cony (not Corey), b May 1870, m 1, 1889, —— Aubrey, m 2, Samuel N Moore, M D

A No 390a Melville Weston [10], b Oct 12, 1871, d Jan 16, 1874

A No 391 Catherine Martin Weston[10]

A No 392 Jane Brown[11]

A No 394 Weston[10]   Living (1914)

A No 453 Frederick Myron[11], m Oct 15, 1910, Ethel Lenora Hollen, dau Lawrence B and Minnie B Hollen of Mt Vernon, N Y

A No 480 Warren Meacham[11], m Sept 27, 1910, Alice E Munsell, dau of No 290

NINTH GROUP

A No 37 Sarah S[9] Daughters Emma[10], b 1860, Harriet[11], b 1865

TENTH GROUP

A No 49 William Henry[9], d Nov 17 1911, at Claremont N H

A No 69 Eugene A[10], m Sept 10, 1902, Euger Lena Larson, dau b Sept 14, 1903

ELEVENTH GROUP

A No 93 Charles W[9], m 1 July 29, 1857, Maria Elizabeth Barker

A No 96 James M[9], b May 16, 1825, m Sara N Coe

TWELFTH GROUP

A No 53 Nathan[6], removed to Horton, Nova Scotia

SIXTEENTH GROUP

A No 15 Dolly[9], d in Erie Co, Pa 1848

A No 24 Luther Rice[9], d Aug 1, 1910 at Shelburne Falls

EIGHTEENTH GROUP

A No 28 Dr George Ephraim[8], d Dec 23, 1913, at Monson

C No 77 Emma Jane[9] m Adoniram J Ross

TWENTY-SECOND GROUP

A and C No 6 Obadiah[7] Fuller, (William W[6], William[5], John[4] John[3], Samuel[2], Edward[1]), b May 30, 1784, in East Haddam, Ct , d Sept 6, 1825, in Carlton, N Y , m Feb 12 1806, Achsah Gates

b June 15, 1784, d Oct 21, 1843, dau. of Ephraim Gates
Children Beulah, b in Paris, N Y, the other in Lyndonville,
N Y

Achsah⁷ b Nov 13, 1806, d June 16, 1849, unmarried

Beulah⁸, b Oct 23, 1808, m Oct 26, 1826, Sheldon Tomlin

Oria⁸, b Sept 30, 1810, d June 24, 1844, m May 9, 1831, Eben
Greeley of Attica, N Y

Obadiah Norman⁸, b Apr 26, 1813, m Mary Sophronia Buck

John⁸, b July 12, 1815, d Sept 9, 1854, m Sept 17, 1837, Betsey
Greenman No issue

Otis⁸, b Dec 31, 1817, m Lorinda Barry

Lydia Gates⁸ b Sept 22, 1820, d Apr 2, 1877, m June 29, 1856,
Isaac Van Fleet No children

William Ward⁸, b July 11, 1823, m 1, Emeline Skillinger, m 2,
Louisa Morris

Obadiah Norman⁸, b Apr 26, 1813, in Lyndonville, N Y, d Mar
6, 1872, in Waterman, Ills, m Oct 22, 1834, Mary Sophronia
Buck, and had

Harvey L.⁹, b Sept 22, 1835, m Sarah L Brady

Rosette⁹, b Apr 14, 1837, d Nov 23, 1908, m ——, Charles F
Mighells, and had two children

Antoinette⁹, b Apr 7, 1839, m Jan 17, 1866, William H Wilt-
berger, and had three children

Edwin A.⁹, b Oct 5, 1843, m 1, Lizzie Bateman, m 2, Mary Pate

Adelbert Udney⁸, b Sept 21, 1846, m Susan Curry

Otis⁸, b Dec 31, 1817, in Lyndonville, N Y; d Apr 2, 1877, in
Waterman, Ills, m Oct 9, 1845, Lorinda Barry, b Mar 30, 1820
d Sept 16, 1906
Children

Emorette Adel⁹, b July 31, 1846, m Oct 30, 1867, Charles L Wilt-
berger, b Nov 26, 1840, d Apr 18, 1901 Children Walter
Otis¹⁰, b Feb 12, 1869, Etta L¹⁰, b Sept 4, 1873; Frank¹⁰, b Apr
8 1875, Dora¹⁰ b Mar 2, 1882

Smith Ferguson⁹, b July 13, 1850, m Achsah Greeley

Harvey L⁹, b Sept 22, 1835, m Oct 15, 1863, Sarah L Brady, b
July 28 1836, and had

Carrie L¹⁰, b July 15, 1864

Lewis G¹⁰, b July 4, 1868, m Oct 6, 1892, Winnie Woods No
children

Dwight Adelbert¹⁰ b Apr 4, 1870, m Esther Walker

Mary¹⁰, b Apr 7, 1875, d Mar 29, 1912, m Richard Abrams

James G.¹⁰, b Sept 12, 1880, m Lulu Douglas

Edwin A[9], b Oct 5, 1843, m 1, Sept 25, 1870, Lizzie Bateman, who
    d ———, m 2, Nov 26, 1889, Mary Pate, who d ———
      Children
Laura[10], b May 15 1872
Harvey L[10], b Oct 5, 1890

  Adelbert Udney[9] b Sept 21, 1846, d June 30 1914 m Sept 26
    1867, Susan Curry, and had
Frank[10], b Dec 24 1868, d July 24, 1870
Charles[10], b May 15, 1870, m Eugenia Normandin
Lydia[10], b Apr 12, 1873, m ——— Gillett, 3 children, res Colorado
John[10], b Oct 16 1876, m Mary Marshall

  Smith Ferguson[9], b July 13 1850, m Lyndonville, N Y , m Mar 20,
    1872, Achsah Greeley, b Oct 30, 1856
  He resides in Waterman Ills
    Children, all born at Waterman, and now (1914) living there
Clyde[10], b Mar 1, 1875, m Dec 29, 1901, Euphemia Riggle, b Mar
    12, 1875, no children
Robert Otis[10], b Oct 27, 1879, m Essie Foote
Orra May[10], b July 21, 1882, m June 28 1905, Herman Beiler, b Oct
    29, 1878, has 2 daughters
Glen Smith[10], b June 12, 1893

  Dwight Adelbert[10], b Apr 4, 1870, m Mar 23 1898, Esther Walker
      Children
Ruth[11], b Apr 25, 1901

  James G[10], b Sept 12, 1880, m Apr 23, 1908, Lulu Douglas
  He is Professor in the Wisconsin State University, Madison, Wis
      Children
Harold D[11], b Sept 17, 1912

Charles[10], b May 15, 1870, m Dec 10, Eugenia Normandin
      Children
Irene[11], b Dec 7, 1891
Frances[11], b Oct 7, 1893
Everette[11], b June 25, 1895
Merle[11], b Nov. 2, 1897
Zilla[11], b Nov 2, 1901
Vodel[11], b May 20, 1904
Gennelle[11], b Dec 5, 1905
Charles[11], b July 6, 1911

  John[10], b Oct 16, 1876, m Nov 12, 1896, Mary Marshall
      Children

Marjorie[14], b Sept 10, 1901
Newman[14], b Mar 31, 1906

    Robert Otis[12] b Oct 27, 1879, m Waterman, Ills , m Mar 28, 1911,
    Essie Foote, b Dec 25, 1884
        Children all b in Waterman Ills
Miriam[14]. b Apr 26, 1912
Wallace F[14], b June 1, 1913

A and C No 9 William Ward[7] Fuller (William W[6], William[5], John[4],
    John[3] Samuel[2], Edward[1]) b Feb 2, 1788, bapt May 18, 1788, at
    East Haddam, Ct , d ——, 1847, at Oconomowac, Wis , m May
    26. 1811, Abigail Gates, who d ——, 1838, in Carlton, N Y , sister
    to Achsah, wife of Obadiah
        Children
  Linnau[8], b Jan 19, 1815, d July 6, 1904, at Eaton Rapids, Mich
    (See Vol 1)
Stephen[8], b Feb 16, 1817, m Rachel Taylor
Hiram[8], b Nov 2, 1818, m Charlotte ——
Lavinia[8] b Feb 1, 1820, d 1897 at Carlton, N Y , m Israel Ship-
    man and had Volney J[9] (resides Jacksonville, Fla) , Alice[9] (re-
    sides Albion, N Y) , Abbie[9], dead, Warren[9], b Jan 25, 1845, d
    1903 , Beulah[9] (Mrs Beulah Piatt, Albion N Y) , Ransom M[9],
    resides Emerson, Iowa.
Eliza[8], b Apr 2, 1822, d Aug 6, 1874, Carlton, N Y , m Matthew
    Godsey Only child Libbie[9] (Godsey) Selheimer, b Jan 30, 1851,
    Carlton, N Y , living at Point Breeze, N Y
Philo[8], b Jan 27, 1827 , d Nov 18, 1904, Sacramento, Cal m ——
    no children
Maria[8], b Dec 25, 1830 , d Apr 14. 1877, Sandwich, Ills , m Di
    M E Ballou no children
Julia Abigail[8], b Feb 4, 1835, d Mar 8, 1903, at State Center, Iowa ,
    m Sept 11, 1861, at Carlton, N Y, John W Dobbin Children
    Ward Fuller[9], b July 26 1862, at Sandwich, Ills ; resides at
    Bertrand, Neb , Frederick Lee[9], b June 29, 1866, Alice Eliza[9],
    b Feb 9, 1868, and Walter Ransom[9], b July 27, 1872, at State Cen-
    ter, Iowa Fred Lee and Alice E reside at State Center, Wal-
    ter R at Great Falls, Montana

    Stephen[8] b Feb 16 1817 , d Aug 26, 1886 at Sandwich, Ills , m
    ——, Rachel Taylor, b in Wayne Co , N Y , Apr 9, 1822 d
    1914, at Aurora, Ills
        Children
Delos[9], b ——; d ——
W G[9], b ——, resides Los Angeles, Cal
Stephen[9], b ——

E M⁹, b ——, resides Des Moines, Ia
Abbie⁹, b ——, resides Aurora, Ills
Hattie⁹, b ——, m W A Nelson, resides Aurora
Adelia⁹, b ——, d ——

Hiram⁸, b Nov 2, 1818, d 1846, at Little Rock Ills, m Char-
    lotte ——
He was buried at Plano, Ills
    Children
Amelia⁹, b ——
Adelaide⁹, b ——

TWENTY-THIRD GROUP

A No 59 Chauncey D⁹, b May 5, 1817, at Northumberland, Pa , d
    July 7, 1890, at Elodrado Springs, Mo , m Jan 7, 1841, at Frank-
    lin, Ills , Lydia Avery, b Mar 19, 1824, d July, 1849, at Modena,
    Ills   Children   Alice⁹, b Apr 3, 1842, m George Washington
    Gharratt, resides at Eldorado Springs   Orange⁹, b Apr 24,
    1845, resides at Wagoner, Kan   Zura⁹, b Dec 21, 1848, m
    Fanny Clark and resides at Hastings, Neb
A No 60 Miles Avery⁸, m 1 Jan 12, 1841, Anna Avery, b Jan 26,
    1822   Children, b at Modena Ills   Caroline Lucy⁹ b 1843 d
    young, Della Matilda⁹, b Aug 12, 1845, m William Isaac Cross,
    and resides at Guthrie, Okla

TWENTY-SIXTH GROUP

A No 12 Milton⁷, m Aug 28, 1808, Polly Ward, b Mar 2 1784 d
    July 22, 1826 He d Feb, 1849 They had a 4th child Lydia⁸, b
    ——, m George Bissell
A No 20 Isaac⁷ His wife Minerva d Aug 23, 1885, at Concord, N H
A No 37 Sarah Ana⁷, d Oct 26, 1911
A No 52 Esbon Gillette⁸ His 1st wife d Aug 11, 1853, m 2, Oct 5
    1865, she d Nov 20, 1878 His dau Amelia, b Nov 15 1836
    d May 7, 1863, m Major J W Church, who d 1905 Dau
    Alida Elizabeth Fuller, b Mar 30, 1845, d May 17, 1903
A No 53 Milton Hinckley⁸, d Feb 28, 1856 His son Adelbert⁹, d
    July, 1878, at Ovid, Mich Milton H had also a dau Althea⁹, b
    ——; d 1870
A No 54 Mary⁸, m Williston Sexton, and had dau Lydia⁹
A No 74 Gardner⁸, d Jan 1, 1914, at Williamsville, N Y
A No 76 Andrew Jackson⁸ The Colton Genealogy gives his birth-
    place as Ferrisburg, Vt He m 2, June 28, 1864, Susan Colton,
    b Oct 2, 1828, at Georgia, Vt , d Jan 1, 1887, at Swan Lake, Ia
    Children, all b at Paw Paw Grove, Ills   Martha⁹, b Apr. 22,
    1865, m George Clark Stevens Quintus Colton⁹, b July 29

1867, m Aug 28, 1899, Florence Laura Guthrie, and had Laura
L[10], b Apr 21, 1900, at Wilford, Ia   Laura[9], b Mar 24 1870,
d June 29, 1877

A No 122 Daniel Webster[9], d at Fullerville, N Y, Nov 8, 1905, m
June 22, 1861, Lucy Irene Woodcock

A No 142 Hiram Erwin[10], d Sept. 19, 1903, unmarried

A No 143 Ina May[10], b Jan 18, 1864, had also dau Lucy Irma, b
Sept 7, 1889

A No 144 Grant W[10], had a dau Louisa Towne[11], b Feb 1, 1902

C No 145 Martha Vauche[10], b Dec 20, 1872, m in the old Fuller
Home at Fullerville Iron Works, N Y, Mar 9, 1898, William
James Milligan, b Sept 18, 1860   Children   Margaret Irene[11]
b Apr 7, 1905, Martha Fuller[11], b May 28, 1909, both b at
Lowville, Lewis Co, N Y

A No 146 Sherman Daniel[10], m at Gouverneur, N Y. Della Margaret Harvey, b Aug 18, 1875   Children   Norman Webster[11],
b Apr 20, 1902, Dorothy Margaret[11], b June 22, 1905, both b
at Emeryville, N Y.

C No 147 Minnie Vauche[10], b June 2, 1869, m May 17, 1892, James
Edward Bishop, b Mar 8, 1869

TWENTY-SEVENTH GROUP

A No 3 Elizabeth[9], m Nov 13, 1785 John Arnold

TWENTY-EIGHTH GROUP

A No 105 Matthew[5] and Joanna   The U S Census, 1790(?) mentions Joanna Fuller family of three in Hillsdale N Y, one son
over 16 and a daughter

DESCENDANTS OF DR SAMUEL FULLER

FIRST GROUP

Additions-marked A—Corrections marked C

A No 29 Isaac[6] was b Apr 30, 1771, bapt June 23, 1771

A No 65 Darius Albert[8], b Apr 7, 1820, d Mar 8, 1849, aged 29 y 11 m 20 d , m Dec 20, 1844, Jane F Sampson

A No 170 William W[9] had dau. Blanch H , b June 7, 1886

A No 196 William John[9] had also Benjamin Butler[10], b Nov , 1905

A No 198 Samuel A[9], b in Dresden, Me , m July 1, 1895, at Somerville, Mass , Sadie Isabella Dean, and had Dorothy Isabella[10], b Mar 3, 1897, Susan Beatrice[10], b Sept 1, 1898, William D[10], b June 22, 1900 Samuel A[10], Oct 27, 1901, and Earl R[10], b Apr 20, 1908

A No 258 Orlistus Conant[9], m Aug 10, 1910, at Livermore Falls, Me , Edna F Howard

SECOND GROUP

A No 3 Seth[6] applied for pension from Hartford, Vt , Mar 6, 1820, age 66, was at battle of Trenton and Princeton, was discharged 1777 at Chatham, N J

A No 4 Samuel[6] m Sarah Freeman Feb 9, 1796

A No 30 Philo Francis[8] lived in Andover, Vt , d in Chester, Vt His dau Mary E[9], b June 30, 1858, m. Sept. 28, 1891, Volney J Wood, son Irving[9], b Aug 12, 1861, d Feb 1, 1881, son Ellsworth[9], b June 1, 1863, resides at Jackson, Mich , a son and dau , twins, b Feb 9, 1870, d Mar 23, 1870, and Mar. 8, 1871

A No 42 Charles Carrol[8], b Dec 24, 1913, in Pittsfield, Mass

A No 59 Jonathan Kingsley[8], d Jan. 23, 1913

A No 69 Frank[9], b Apr 12, 1856, resided in Hadley, Mass.

THIRD GROUP

A No 7 Eunice[5], m July 28, 1760, Ebenezer Robbins

A No 11 Zephaniah[6], b July 31,1750

A No 16 Ebenezer[4] and Joanna Gray m June 21, 1721

A No 26 Ephraim Holmes[7] m Apr. 12, 1812, Lydia Johnson

A No 29 George[7] is given also by Medford, Mass, Vital Records, Daniel S[8], b July 9, 1819, d July 8, 1846, Mary E[8], b June 6, 1825, Ellen M B[8], b Apr 25, 1827, Henry A[8], b Apr 25, 1831

A No 38 Deborah C[5], m May 28, 1837, Elbridge G Winsor

FOURTH GROUP

C No 3 Samuel[4] m Oct 22, 1747 His son Benjamin[5] probably m

Dec 15, 1774, Abigail King of Kingston The U. S Census,
1790, gives an Abigail Fuller with a son under 16 years of age
in Plympton, Mass

FIFTH GROUP

A No 5 Susannah[5] d Mar 17, 1782, ch (Dingley) Levi[6], b Oct 18
1756, Desire[6], b Feb 7, 1758; Susannah[6], b Apr 26, 1764 Jacob[6],
b Nov 1, 1767, Ezra[6], b Aug. 5, 1770, John[6], June 6, 1773

A No 7 Ezra[6] m Elizabeth Weston Nov 23, 1758

C No 19 John[4] m Mrs Mercy Cushman Nov 14. 1764

A No 25 Hannah[6] d Sept 16, 1835, ch (Shurtleff) Roswell[7], b July
7, 1816; Luther[7], Mar 19, 1818, George[7], Jan 21, 1820, Phebe[7]
Dec 24, 1821, Gideon[7], Mar. 1, 1824; Hannah F[7], Mar 22, 1826
Robert[7], May 29, 1827

A No 34 Consider[6] d in West Paris, Me, aged over 90 Of his
children, Christiana[7] m Charles B Brooks, Chloe[7] m Rufus
Farrar, Lucy B[7] m Eli H Cushman, Consider C[7] m Sally C
Greeley, Betsey[7] m Jonathan Fickett, Abigail[7] m Stephen
Davis, Lovica[7], m Stephen Davis, Lydia Jane[7], m Joseph H
Briggs

A No 61 Sylvanus[7] d Oct 22, 1891

C No 63 Benoni[7] m Mar 23, 1848

A No 79 Joseph[7] d Nov 16, 1885, in Conklin, N Y, m in Middle-
burg, N Y, Matilda Luce, who d Sept 23, 1879, at Marshalltown, Ia Of their children, James Summers[8], b Mar 31, 1838
Middleburg, N Y, m 1, May 22, 1861, Emily F Earle, who d
Sept 23, 1879, Marshalltown, Ia, m 2, Dec 31, 1891, Jennie
——, no issue Lucius Emery[8], b. Dec 25 1844, in Corbettsville
N Y, m. in Elmira, N Y, May 1, 1867, Salina Euphenia La
France, and had i Tessie Lillian[9], b June 12, 1869, in Liscomb Ia
ii Asa Glenwood, b Dec 24, 1874, in Corbettville, m in Marion
Kan, Aug 15, 1899, Nettie Jane White iii Alice Irene[9], b Apr 5
1876, Corbettsville, m Dec 24, 1895, in Agricola, Kan, Albert
T Tumbleson, and had Pearl Rhodes[10], b June 18 1900, in
Agricola Everett D[10], b. Nov 3 1902, in Waverley, Kan
iv. Clara May[9], b May 21, 1881, in Ellis, Kan v Charles Sumner[9],
b Sept 18, 1883, in Ellis vi. Nellie La France[9], b. May 23, 1885,
in Ellis, and Ada Le Mon[9], b Oct 8, 1887
Charles Edward[8], b Mar 10, 1847. in Binghampton, N Y, m in
Conklin, N. Y, Apr 5, 1870 Anne May Banta, b Nov 13, 1850,
and had Archie Edward[9], b Mar 5, 1872, d Apr 29, 1889 Grace
May[9], b June 20, 1874, m Sept 6 1898, Jared Nelson Meeker,
and had, b at Clifford, Pa, Merritt F[11], b June 19, 1900, at
Thomhurst, Pa, and Jaredine Gertrude[10], b Aug 29. 1901 Nettie
Alice[9], b Aug 7, 1882 Alice Emma[8], b Jan 16, 1852, at Bridge-
water, Pa, m 1, in Binghampton, N Y, Oct 2, 1875, Athens Wil-

ham Aylesworth, m 2, Apr 7, 1883, Levi Lewis Roe By 1st husb had George S Aylesworth[9], b Oct 11, 1876, by 2d husb Lida Lillian[9] Roe b Feb 12, 1884

A No 80 Stillman[7] d Nov 19 1864 at Hilton Head, S C , m 1, Apr, 1872, in Liberty, Pa, Henrietta Webster, b Dec 14, 1820, d Aug 21, 1849, in Liberty, m 2, Oct, 1850, Lydia Cogswell Smith, b July 19, 1819, in Roxbury, N Y , d Dec 20, 1891, Silvara Pa Children all by first wife Francis Stillman[8], b Oct 24, 1844 at Rhiney Creek Pa , m Jan 1, 1879, Demica Wilbur and had Jennie May[9], b May 6, 1880, Mary E[8], b Aug 8 1849, d Aug 10, 1849

A No 138 Maria A[8], m Nov 29, 1849, William H Crosby

C No 145 Irving H[8], m 1, Celia M Purmort, m 2, Nov 21, 1893, Emma L Packard

A No 160 John Nichols[8], d Sept 17, 1863

C No 178 Frederick[8], b March 13, 1837

C No 223 Nathaniel Thomas[8]

C No 224 Maria Thomas[8], b Sept 6, 1837

A No 286 Edwina Fay[9], had also Hans V Brieson b Feb 4, 1912, in New York Dau Gerrida shown in halftone opposite

C No 290 Mary Breese[9], was b Aug 30, 1871

C No 293 Walton B[9], not Walter B

C No 295 Charles T Staniels of Concord N H

C No 336 } It was Frederick Pardee[9] not Theodore S[9], who m Margaret Stevens Cissel
337

A No 396 Charles L[10], had also a son, Charles Alden[11], b Apr 18, 1910

SIXTH GROUP

A No 7 John[6] Elizabeth, wid John, Jr , d Dec 16, 1842 Sally, dau John and Hannah, d May 11, 1794, aged 1y, 1d

C No 15 Emily[7], m July 29, 1820, Capt Charles Robbins

A No 20 Jabez[4] His widow, Mercy (Gray) Fuller, d Aug 13 1782

A No 25 Hiram[7], d Sept 19, 1815

A No 26 Sara D[7], m Nov 24, 1844, Thomas F Staples

C No 36 Arabella Johnson[8], b Aug 21, 1848

A No 39 Emma Ann[8], b Sept 18, 1847, d Aug 17, 1848

EIGHTH GROUP

A No 3 John[5] His wid, Joanna, m 2, Jan 3, 1749, Joseph Waterman, of Middleboro, Mass

A No 22 Zerviah T[8] had also Laura Ann[8], b —

A No 24 Solomon[8], according to Wareham, Mass Rec, m Apr 15, 1851, Catherine Besse

A No 26 Ephraim[8] His 4th child was Harriet Nye[9], who m Alvah Bennett

A No 41 Josiah Kingman[8] His 6th child was Josiah F, b 1851, m Nov 29, 1899, Roxanna St Pierre

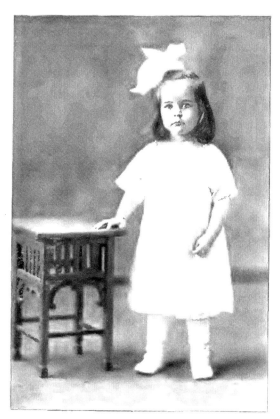

GERNDA V. BRIESEN.

A No 56 Henry Allen[9], m May 1, 1882, Sarah W. Sherman

C No 57 Ella F[9], was the 7th child, and Adelaide L b Nov. 1, 1860, the 6th

A No 59 Mary Ellen[9] (Humphrey) had Nellie Estelle[10], b Dec 27, 1874

A No 71 Thomas G m 3, Dec 7, 1908, Mary E. Wheeler

A No 100 George Edward[10], m. Oct 11, 1911, Helen Reed Inglis

A No 104 Herbert Thomas[10], had dau Lillian Alice, b July 10, 1911

TENTH GROUP

A No 10 Eunice[6], m Jan. 14, 1790

A No 33 Charlotte[9], m James W. Cooper

A No 34 Ebenezer Frank[9], b Feb 24, 1851, m Adelaide F Howe.

A No 35 Elbertice E[9], b May 20, 1855; m Olive Crowell

TWELFTH GROUP

A No 8 Benjamin[6], m Sept 8, 1777

A. No 9 Reliance[6], d June 26, 1817

A No. 13 Barzillai[6], had also Jarvis[7], b ——, d Nov, 1795, aged 6m, and Emma[7], b ——, d Sept 14, 1808, in 7th year His 2d w d Feb 13, 1828

A No 21 Jacob[6], d Mar 6, 1845, m 1, Feb 20, 1800 She d Feb. 22, 1805; 2 w d Feb 13, 1828

A No 41 James[7], had also a 4th child, Miles[8], b ——, m ——; children, Austin[9], b —— Minnie[9], b. —— Mary[9], b —— Hattie[9], b. June 5, 1870, m. Dec. 3, 1888, James Leslie Burgess Res, Hartford, Ct

A No 47 Barzillai[7], b Mar 15, 1783, in Easton, Mass.; d Oct 14, 1849, in Hanson, Mass ; m Dec 29, 1819, Patience Beals, and had Lucius T[8], b Oct 19, 1822; m Eliza B —— and Nancy D[8], b ——, 1833

A No 76 Betsy[7], m Sept 30, 1824

A No 77 Josiah[7], m June 16, 1825

A No 80 Mary Flagg[7], d Mar 9, 1822

A No 143 Harriet G[8], m Mar 16, 1841, Alexander Andres Boyden, who d in Sharon, Mass, Oct. 6, 1870 She had 3 sons, Henry Alexander[9], b. in Easton, Mass, Dec 24, 1841 Clarence Fuller[9], b Mar 5, 1846, in Attlebore, Mass, and Clinton Augustus[9], b Mar 15, 1853, in Worcester

A No 148 Henry J[8], m Nov 9, 1862

A No 235. Frederick A[9], m Sept. 25, 1878, Evelyn A. Francis.

A No 244 Alden[9], m June 30, 1903, Clementine Boyden

THIRTEENTH GROUP

A No. 4. Capt Lemuel[6] Fuller d May 11, 1842, aged 73, at Worthington, Mass. and Susanna, his 1st wife, d Sept 1, 1812, in 36th year He m 2, Apr 4, 1813

A No 13 Lemuel S⁶ had Henry M⁷, who d June 25, 1842, aged 6m, 11d

A No 19 Eliza⁶, m Mar 10, 1824

A No 21 Flavia⁶ A child of that name appears to have d Feb 10, 1807, aged 3 months, and also a Flavia, b ——, who m Eben Cudworth, Feb 2, 1832

A No 22 Nancy Haskell⁶, bapt Sept 2, 1812, m Feb 21, 1839, Alno Atwood, at Hinsdale, N. H.

A No 46 Mary Ellen⁷, b Jan. 7, 1848

A No 55 Nathaniel⁷, d May 13, 1902, aged 78-2-13 By a second wife he had Emma W⁸, b May 23, 1859, m May 23, 1876, Hiram E. Wright, and Lizzie P⁸, b Sept 8, 1869, at Weymouth, m Nov 17, 1886, Emery S Leonard.

A No 59 Eustis William⁷, had son Frederick W.⁸, b Mar 20, 1866

A No 61 Benjamin F.⁷, and Lucy had Mary⁸, b Sept 22, 1847

A No 74 Heman N⁸, m 2, June 22, 1882

A No 84 Nathan Henry⁸, had Albion E⁹, b Nov 9, 1874, and Louise C⁹, b Oct 4, 1878, at Raynham, Mass

FOURTEENTH GROUP.

A No 1 Jonathan⁶, m Aug 31, 1774

A No 15 Zachariah⁶, d June 26, 1830, aged 42, and w d May 29, 1828, aged 33, at Plainfield, Ct

A No 31 Sophia⁶, b Feb 2, 1798

A No 47 Judge William Eddy Fuller, d Nov 9, 1911, at Taunton, Mass

INDEX TO FULLERS

NOTE—The figures refer to the page on which the name is found
When the same name occurs more than once on same page, it will
appear but once in the index

Albert Edward, 110
Albert H , 107
Albert K , 108, 110
Albert M , 69
Albert Milton, 67, 69
Albert P , 239
Albert Warren, 197, 201
Albeiton George, 202, 205
Albion E , 274
Albion King Parris, 134, 139
Alden, 37, 41, 123, 225, 226, 273
Alden Holt, 221
Alden M , 137, 140
Alexander, 35, 37, 40, 67, 68
Alexander B , 67
Alfred H , 220
Alfred S., 155, 156
Alfred W , 150
Alice, 54, 56, 69, 85, 86, 161, 200, 268
Alice A , 221, 238
Alice B , 139
Alice Eliza 85
Alice Emma, 271
Alice F , 108
Alice Irene, 271
Alice M , 46, 190
Alice May, 141
Alice Spencer, 212
Alida Elizabeth, 268
Allan H , 214
Allen, 75, 78
Almira, 38, 133
Alonzo E , 199, 202
Alonzo F , 134, 138
Alpheus, 60
Alphonso S , 228
Althea, 268
Alvan, 255
Alvan Bond, 240, 243
Alvan E., 255
Alvan Tufts, 243
Alvin, 105, 106, 107, 108
Alvin Elbridge, 107
Alvin W , 110, 111
Amanda, 164, 234
Amariah, 129, 130

Amasa, 33, 34, 35, 36, 103, 105, 112, 113, 114, 115
Ambrose, 50, 52
Ambrose M , 139
Ambrose Snow, 43
Amelia, 229, 237, 268
Americus, 136
Amerillis, 104
Amos, 103, 118, 119, 225
Amos Jones, 51, 53
Amy Jane, 239
Andrew, 34, 35, 36, 38, 40, 44, 107, 109, 199
Andrew Clifford, 125
Andrew Eugene, 220
Andrew Hall, 218, 219
Andrew J., 116, 135, 225, 227
Andrew Jackson, 39, 43, 268
Andrew L , 115, 138
Andrew Lovell, 123, 125
Andrew W , 133
Angelina, 106
Angeline R , 226
Ann, 13, 17, 104, 122, 149, 164, 223, 231
Ann Eliza, 125, 147, 218, 235
Anna, 75, 90, 114, 122, 123, 130, 152, 153, 162, 186, 187, 257
Anna B , 38
Anna E , 239
Anna Electa, 54
Anna Havens, 238
Anna L , 166
Anna M , 190
Anna Maria, 131, 238
Anna Nancy, 233
Anna Raymond, 212
Annie, 12, 14, 48, 49, 64, 70, 77, 78, 84, 185
Anne Augusta, 227
Anne Gertrude, 213
Anne J , 105
Anne Jane, 188
Anne L , 202
Anne Lee, 184
Anne Lewis, 230
Ansel A., 24, 25

Clarissa, 61, 113, 251, 253
Clarissa Utley, 218
Clark, 106
Claude, 185
Clementine, 199
Clerisa, 61
Clifton Dale, 205
Clifton Merrill, 23, 24
Clyde, 266
Columbia Morrison, 83
Consider, 271
Cora A , 115
Cora Anstis 116
Cora Field, 92
Cora Vashti, 168
Cordelia, 78, 227, 235
Cordelia, II L , 81
Coris Ann Victoria, 197
Cornelia Ellen, 154
Cornelius, 225
Cornelius P , 226
Curtis, 250
Cynthia, 253, 254
Cyrus, 147
Dan Malta, 73
Danforth Reed, 165
Daniel, 48, 49, 50, 51, 53, 57, 118,
119, 132, 135, 162, 165, 177, 179,
193, 194, 195 199, 216, 217, 218
223, 231, 232, 234, 261
Daniel Burnham ,251
Daniel D , 137, 251
Daniel Dunbar, 40, 44
Daniel Edward, 136, 140
Daniel Ellison, 218, 220
Daniel F , 199, 202
Daniel Havens, 238
Daniel K , 56, 58
Daniel S 270
Daniel Webster, 269
Daniel William, 167
Darius Albert, 270
Darius E , 148
Darius Smith, 147
David. 21, 90, 149, 150, 152, 154,
180, 181, 182, 187, 195, 198, 231,
232, 235, 261

David Congdon, 237, 241
David Crocker, 76, 80
David F , 201, 204
David II , 198, 201
David L , 166, 167
David Lyon, 263
David Robertson, 235, 238
Davis C 67
Davis S , 65, 66
Deborah, 51, 106, 181, 207
Deborah C , 270
Deborah Salome, 51
Delia, 28, 238
Delia Amanda, 218
Delilah, 105
Della Frances, 141
Della Matilda, 268
Delos, 267
Desiah, 102
Desire, 74, 75
Desire F , 83
Dexter, 105, 108
Dexter N , 108, 110
Diantha, 235
Dilecta, 61
Dolly, 187
Dolly, 264
Dolly Sharp, 237
Donald Hills, 46
Donald Pinkerton 44
Donald Wellington, 93
Donald Whitall, 256
Dora A , 239
Dorcas, 60, 118, 131
Dorianna, 219
Dorilus Morrison, 83
Doris, 87
Doris Madeline, 156
Dorothy, 102, 114, 177
Dorothy Adahrie, 214
Dorothy Converse, 263
Dorothy Isabella, 270
Dorothy Margaret, 269
Dorothy Sampson, 156
Douglas Wardwell, 46
Druce, 131
Drusilla, 225

Elizabeth B, 139, 148
Elizabeth Charlotte, 116
Elizabeth E, 86, 198
Elizabeth Havens, 242
Elizabeth J, 33
Elizabeth Jones, 46
Elizabeth M, 202
Elizabeth Maria, 251
Elkanah, 18, 19, 71
Ella Elizabeth, 227
Ella Burnett, 25
Ellen 29, 183, 189
Ellen A, 41
Ellen F, 83, 273
Ellen H, 108
Ellen Hannah, 198
Ellen Jane, 166
Ellen M B, 270
Ellen Maria, 53
Ellen Richardson, 230
Ellen S., 107
Ellery, 28
Ellery A, 192
Ellery Briggs, 29
Ellis, 254, 255
Ellsworth, 270
Elmer, 202
Elmer A, 115
ElmerAmas, 116
Elmer B. H, 41
Elmer Linn, 184
Elmira, 105, 114
Elmira, J, 137
Elsie, 163, 164
Elvira, 114
Elvira Frances, 167
Elvira P, 134
Elwin, 115
Emeline, 65, 67, 137, 147, 251
Emeline A, 252
Emeline Fernandez, 234
Emeline M, 135
Emeline Rebecca, 147
Emery, 164, 165
Emerson, 136
Emily, 105, 133, 227, 272
Emily A, 255

Emily Adaline, 213
Emily Ann, 80
Emily C, 203
Emily E, 56
Emily Farrar, 116
Emily I T, 228
Emily J, 82
Emily S, 105
Emma, 42, 109, 217, 273
Emma Ann, 272
Emma Alice, 30, 240
Emma Arletta, 192
Emma Curtis, 67
Emma E, 24
Emma J, 190, 200
Emma Jane, 264
Emma Susan, 125
Emma W, 274
Emorette Adel, 265
Enoch, 129, 131, 133, 147
Enos T, 165, 167
Ephraim, 122, 123, 251, 272
Ephraim Hayward, 123
Ephraim Holmes, 270
Erastus, 198
Ernest, 203
Ernest Harrison, 93
Ernest Jackson, 115
Ernest Layton, 141
Ernest Lorin, 88
Erwin J, 144, 116
Esbon Gillette, 268
Esther, 65, 112, 122, 129, 130, 163
  248
Esther L, 205
Esther M, 209
Ethel, 121, 184, 263
Ethel E, 45
Ethel Mae, 201
Ethel Margaret, 121
Etta, 139, 228
Eudora Frances, 92
Eudotia, 104
Eugene, 241
Eugene A, 264
Eugene P., 228

Herschell, 263
Hester, 205
Hezekiah, 102, 103, 104, 105
Hinds, 83
Hiram, 67, 68, 80, 81, 85, 86, 267, 268, 272
Hiram E, 263
Hiram Erwin, 269
Hiram Gamaliel, 211, 212
Hiram J, 57
Hiram O, 199
Hobart T, 168, 169
Holland, 196, 200
Holly Granger, 44, 46
Homer Gifford, 243
Horace A, 199, 203
Horace S, 210
Horatio, 79
Hosea, 164, 166
Hosea B, 166
Hosea Randall, 166
Hosea Y, 137
Hosea Young, 140
Howard, 242
Howard A, 126
Howard Allen, 92
Howard M., 200, 203
Hubert, 184
Hubert Bruce, 243, 244
Hudson, 184, 185
Huldah, 50, 118, 164, 187
Ichabod, 64
Ida, 41 55, 184, 202
Ida Emily, 115
Ida Louisa, 256
Ida Louise, 58
Ida Elnora, 167
Ida F., 138
Ida Marie, 155
Ignatius, 160, 161, 162, 163
Ignatius L, 166
Ina May, 269
Ira, 225, 253
Ira Edgar, 255
Ira Ellis, 254, 255
Irene, 191, 266
Irena, 254

Irving, 121, 139, 270
Irving H, 272
Irwin L 201, 204
Irwin Pierce, 117
Isaac, 37, 42, 50, 74, 75, 77, 98, 102, 112, 113, 114, 115, 119, 143, 145 146, 262, 268, 270
Isaac Richardson, 113, 114, 115
Isabel, 185
Isabella, 56
Isabelle, 42
Isaiah Gifford, 91
Ithamar, 49
Ivah L, 263
J H, 263
Jabez, 13, 14, 16, 34, 35, 36, 272
Jabez Henry, 226
Jacob, 27, 149, 177, 179, 208, 231, 233, 236, 273
Jacob H, 219
Jackson, 132, 136
James, 80, 98, 101, 102, 103, 104, 106, 149, 150, 160, 161, 162, 163, 164, 165, 166, 167, 176, 179, 180, 181, 182, 183, 188, 189, 193, 194, 195, 196, 198 199, 200, 217, 218, 273
James Blossom, 76
James E, 240 243
James Edward, 29, 30
James Elmo, 184, 185
James Franklin, 200
James Frederick, 139, 141
James G, 150, 265, 266
James Greenwood 150
James H, 205
James Hazard, 211, 212
James Henry, 90
James L, 184
James Lancey, 183, 184
James M, 220, 264
James Martin, 30
James Norton, 135, 139
James Osgood, 226
James Prince, 162
James Summers, 271
James Tenney, 201, 204

19

48   OTHERS

INDEX TO PERSONS

OF NAMES OTHER THAN FULLER

— — ——

NOTE—The figures refer to the page on which the name is found
When the same name occurs more than once on same page, it will
appear but once in the index

McClintock, Jane, 188, 189
McFarland, Adelia M , 218
McFarlane, Robert. 66
    Thomas, 66
McGinnis, Ora Maconda, 237
McGrannell, Ann, 233
McGregor, Alice, 41, 44
McIntire, Mary, 36, 39
    Sarah, 261
McKinley, Abner, 83
    Helen, 83
McLean Henry J., 263
    Ola, 262
Meach, Lucretia, 234
Meader, Charles, 42
Meeker Jared N , 271
    Merritt F , 271
    Jardin G , 271
Mehuren, ———, 41
    Harold E , 41
    Herbert S , 41
    William E , 41
Meiggs, Calvin, 22
Melvin, Nancy, 76 80
Merriam, Abel, 37
    Ann E , 109
Merrill, Anne, 199
    Arthur, 199
    Carrie, 199
    Charlotte, 225, 227
    Frank, 199
    Sally, 225
    Samuel, 199, 225
    Oliver H , 81
Messenger, Louise S , 56, 58
Meservey, Arista, 37
    Edward, 37
    Margaret T., 37
    Theresa A , 37
Mighells, Charles P , 265
Milliken, Catherine, 199, 202
Milligan, Margaret Irene, 269
    Martha Fuller, 269
    William James, 269
Mills, Abby Ella, 120
    Almira, 164, 166
    Elizabeth, 80

    Sidney, 218
Miller Celinda, 51, 53
    Edna Leonore, 135
    Frances Asbury, 135
    Horace, 135
    Howard Vinton, 135
    Joseph, 152
    Julius Gillmore, 135
    Mary, 152
    Olive Lucy, 263
    Sarah, 152
    Thomas, Jr , 152
Millet, Deborah, 178, 207
Minard Ann, 51, 54
Minick, John, 129
    Sarah, 98, 129
Mitchell, ———, 24
Monroe, Luda, 225, 226
Moody Mahala P , 37 40
Moore Anna B , 39 43
    Georgiana, 229, 230
    Samuel H , 104
    Samuel N 264
Moorehead, George H , 229
Morgan, Jennie N , 53, 58
Morley Arthur W 53
    Charles Lyman, 53
    Fanny C , 53
    Frank N , 53
    Lillie A , 53
    Lucy M , 53
    Nelson W , 53
    Newton F , 53
    Thomas B . 53
Morris, Amy, 64, 65
    Amos, 64, 65
    Louisa, 265
Morrison, Anne E 107
    Betsey, 78, 83
    Cyrus, 78
Morse, Eunice, 123 124
    Florence, 220
Morton, Hannah, 12, 15
    Martha, 35
Mosher, Mary, ———
Mossman, Mary F , 42, 45
Moulton Olive A , 106

Spencer, Loley, 17
    Mary, 17, 49
    Olive, 17
    Phebe, 17
    Polly, 217, 218
    Thaddeus, 17
    W Howard, 213
Spring, Joanna, 152, 153
Springer, Samuel, 83
Stackford, Joshua, 181
Stafford, ———, 166
    Bertrand, 166
    Galen, 166
    James, 166
    Leon, 166
Stanchcliffe, Amelia, 198
    Mary A , 197, 200
Standish, Miles, 11
Staniel, Charles T , 272
Stanley, William N , 199
Stanton, Howard Raymond, 202
    Raymond Hayes, 212
    William Edwin, 212
Staples, Thomas F , 272
    Nettie L., 139, 141
Stark, George W , 234
Starkie, Henry, 263
    Henry F , 263
    Henry W , 263
    Martha A , 263
Starr, Sarah, 233, 235
Starring, Albert, 262
    Alfred, 262
    Beulah Grace, 262
    Gertrude, 262
    Vera, 262
Stead, Lucy M , 238
Steadman, Patrona, 216
Stearns, Anna, 19, 149
    Charles, 146
    Daniel, 143
    Emily, 23, 24
    Lydia, 112
    Martha, 146
    Silas, 113
Stears, Mary, 234
Stebbins, Albert H , 262

Stephens, Kathleen W , 43, 46
Stevens Abner 104
    Albert N , 77
    Amelia Emma, 67
    Angeline, 182, 184
    Breese J , 67
    Charles, 77
    Charles E , 77
    Cordelia M , 153 154
    Eddie, 104
    Elizabeth, 101
    George Clark 268
    Harriet, 77, 104
    Hiram, 77
    Horatio N , 77
    Isaac, 104
    James M , 106
    John, 104
    Juliette, 106
    Mahala, 104
    Marshall, 106
    Mehitable, 104
    Melissa, 104
    Minerva 106
    Ora, 106
    Roxana, 77
    Ruth 106
    Samantha, 104
    Sara, 184
    Selina Ellis, 166
    Walter, 104
    Warren, 104
Steward Charles E , 68
Stewart, Martha, 50 52
Stickney, Mrs S E , 166, 167
Stienkraus, Ida E H , 191, 192
Stiles, Mariah, 261
Stilphen, ———, 75
Stinson, William 131
Stockwell, Edwin F , 115
Stone, Anna 129, 130
    Albert Fuller, 197
    Emma Josephine, 197
    Josiah 177
    Levi, 81
    Lillie Ann, 197
    Mary A , 148

Stone, Mindwell, 143
    Nahum M., 197
      Walter Nahum, 197
Story, Miriam P., 167
    William, 176
Street, Amy B., 213
Strickland, Fanny E., 237
Strong, Ellen M., 263
Stover, Alexander A., 37
    Althea, 37
    Angie, 37
    Frederick, 37
    Jacob, 37
    Leander, 37
    Leantha, 37
    Lizzie, 37
    Lysander C., 37
    Martha A., 37
Stowell, George L., 167
Stretton, Ebenezer, 98
    Daniel, 152
Sturgis, William A., 23
Styles, George, 104
    Hannah, 104
    Roxy, 104
    William, 104
Sumner, Alice, 120
Sweet, ———, 76
    Abby, 236
Swift, Abbie A., 228
    Charlotte A., 202
    Charlotte, 199
    Elizabeth B., 225, 226
    Sarah A., 199, 202
Sylvester, Asa, 79
    Ernest E., 79
    Edwin, 79
    Frances, 79
    Henry, 79
    Pamelia, 79
    Pauline, 79
Taintor, Gilbert, 137
Talbot, Frances Delia, 91
Talcott, Judith P., 78, 84
Tapley, Amos P., 167
Taplin, Edith Mary, 239
Taylor, ———, 161

Charles, 168
Georgiana D., 114, 115
Isaac D., 168
Jasper, 13
Katherine, 183, 184
Mrs. Minerva Lorane, 211, 212
Rachel, 267
Russell, 168
Sarah, 161
Teeter, Charles H., 109
    Heber F., 109
    Jennie M., 109
    Roy O., 109
Tenney, Caroline, 198, 201
    Ella, 201
    Mary E., 199, 202
Thacher, Elizabeth, 15, 17
Thompson, Isabella, 213
    Mary, 104, 107
    Mercy, 177
Thurston, Kirk John, 57
Tiffany, Philemon, 49
Tilden, Calvin, 49
Tillinghast, Cornelia, 218, 219
    Samuel L., 234
Tillson, Zenas A., 139
Titcomb, Elizabeth, 81, 86
Tobey, ———, 28, 29
    Anna, 74, 75
Tomlin, Sheldon, 265
Town, Hannah, 164, 165
Tracy, William, 233
Trask, Rochel, 104, 105
Treadway, Sarah Ellen, 240
Trott, Abigail, 225, 227
Truesdell, Ward N., 220
Trowbridge, Edmund, 130
    Elizabeth W., 130
    Emily F., 233
    George, 124
    Hannah, 143
    Hannah (Jackson), 98, 127
    Harriet L., 124
    Joanna, 216
    Mindwell, 97
    Ruth, 130